Learning Life

The Path to Academic Success and Personal Happiness

FIRST EDITION

Dr. Adam Burke, PhD, MPH, LAc
San Francisco State University

Rainor Media / San Francisco

Learning Life
by Adam Burke

Copyright © 2015 Adam Burke. All rights reserved.

Except as permitted under the United States Copyright Act of 1976, no part of this publication may be reproduced or distributed in any form or by an means, or stored in a database or retrieval system, without the prior written permission of the publisher. Send all inquiries to info@learninglife.com.

ISBN 978-0-9633961-8-1

Published by Rainor Media

Cover/Book Design: Rose Paz Wierenga

Printed in the United States of America.

Library of Congress Cataloging-in-Publication Data
Burke, Adam
Learning Life / Adam Burke - 1st Edition
p. cm.
Includes index
ISBN 978-0-9633961-8-1
1. Academic Achievement 2. Success-Psychological Aspects   3. Career Development

http://www.learninglife.com

Table of Contents

Invitation — v

I. Foundations

1	A Learning Life	The Perspective	1
2	Setting Goals – Academic & Personal Vision	Goals	17
3	Imaging Success	Imagery	37
4	Mindful Learning – The Power of Self-Awareness	Mindfulness	55
5	Continual Improvement & Quality	Quality	75

II. Learning Stages And Strategies

6	Academic Skills – Acquisition	Stage I	99
7	Academic Skills – Integration	Stage II	119
8	Academic Skills – Display	Stage III	139

III. Life Skill Development

9	Managing Time & Change	Adaptability	159
10	Reducing Stress & Increasing Equanimity	Equilibrium	183
11	Cultivating Emotional Literacy	Compassion	205
12	Making Effective Decisions	Wisdom	225
13	Changing Habits	Self Organizing	245

IV. Applications

14	A Healthy Lifestyle	Health	271
15	Social Support – Friends, Family & the World	Relationships	293
16	Life Purpose & Career Clarity	Career	307
17	Personal Finances & Abundance	Sufficiency	327
18	You and the World	Service	345

Resources — 355

Subject Index — 368

Invitation

This is the beginning, the threshold of a path. You are looking down this path into the future. The image at the end of the path will vary from one person to the next. What one sees will depend on how each life was lived, and that is a function of what was learned along the way.

I think that many people who choose the path of a learning life never stop. Once they begin they just keep going. They find it compelling, experiencing in real ways how that path leads to greater success and deeper happiness for self and others. Indeed there are many paths we can choose. Some get us closer, some take us further away. One is not necessarily better than the other, we all make choices. If one decides to choose happiness, however, the path of a learning life can be a useful one. So this is an invitation to you. You are invited to take a journey down this path, to see for yourself if it can help you on your way.

What is a learning life? For the sake of explanation let us continue with the path metaphor for a moment (displayed in the figure below). Life is indeed like a journey down a path. We are endlessly moving through space, from here to there, and through time, from past into future. This is the field within which all things exist, the field of time and space. As we move through time and space we pass through many Environments.

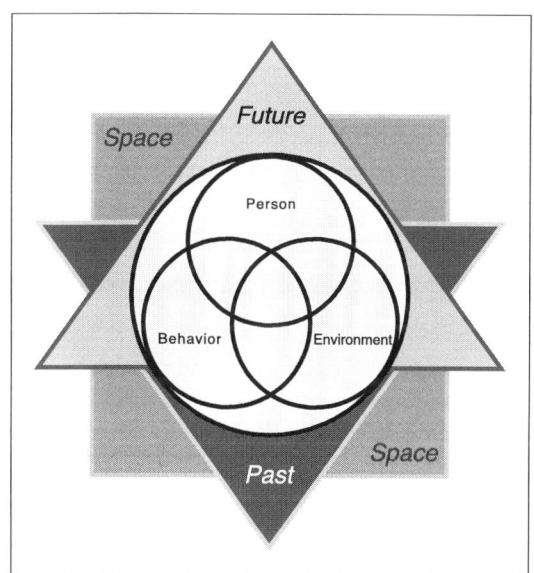

We hike through forests, stroll down city streets, meet people, hear the birds sing, feel the breeze on our face, watch the sun rise and the stars come out. There are buildings and traffic, meetings, phone calls, wars, births, deaths, disease, winter and spring. As we move through these environments we also have an inner experience and an outer expression. The Person represents our inner experience – thoughts of the past, worries about the future, dreams and plans, feelings of anger and joy, bodily states of stress and relaxation. These inner energies contribute to the outward expression of Behavior – walking in balance, cooking a healthy meal, negotiating a better contract, riding a horse, loving your parents, studying for the math quiz, playing an accordion, navigating by the stars, all the outflows of life. This interdependent wheel of life, this interplay of Person, Behavior and Environment, is the matrix within which learning occurs. As this wheel moves through time and space we have an endless opportunity to work with the inner experience of thoughts, feelings and bodily states, with our behaviors, and with our engagement of the environments of life. Doing this consciously, with the intention to learn and grow, and ideally using effective strategies, is what a learning life is all about.

Specifically, the purpose of this book is to support your success. *Learning Life* takes a holistic approach to the goal of academic and personal achievement, integrating cross-disciplinary understanding from the fields of neuroscience, psychology, philosophy, and ancient mind-body traditions for greater life mastery. Learning is a process of going from not knowing to knowing, from not being able to do to being able to do. In *Learning Life* we approach this process in an intentional fashion. This text/course provides a specific path, based on empirical evidence and best practices, an approach to make the process of learning and growth more efficient and more effective.

As with conventional student achievement texts, information on academic skills, time management, financial planning, and related topics is presented. More importantly, however, this work integrates several unique elements, rooted in evidence-based research, to enhance effectiveness and positive expectancy for academic and personal success.

The *Learning Life* text is comprised of four sections – Foundations, Learning Strategies, Life Skills, and Applications. The Foundations are a central aspect of this text, an approach to learning developed over many years of working with many students in diverse contexts. This section consists of three core elements. The first is training in mindful awareness to enhance self-understanding, memory, task focus, and learning. It is about being awake in order to learn. The second is about clear goals and goal-oriented mental imagery to reinforce goal-oriented action, positive expectancies, and improved self-efficacy, an "I can do that" attitude. The third core element integrated throughout the text is the concept of continual improvement/quality.

The second section, Learning Strategies, provides a model of learning and specific strategies for all aspects of academic success. Having the right strategy makes the world of difference, not having the right strategy makes learning harder, period. The third section focuses on specific Life Skills that are essential for success in human environments, from the home, to the office, to the planet. These include emotional literacy, time and stress management, decision-making, and habit change. The final section looks at Applications in the field of work, relationships, health, finances and civic engagement. The text/course emphasizes self-reflection, problem solving, use of data/feedback, and making constructive change in all areas of life. It is about building an effective life. Ultimately the information and skills are applied in an active research format, based on a learning-by-doing orientation, which focuses on a personal change process related to academic/life success.

Pre-emptive Apology for Imperfections
Things change. When you have been around for a few years you see ideas come and go. Understanding of how things work is endlessly changing. I have sought to integrate the best of what was accessible at the time of writing, and no doubt with the next edition there will be some changes based on new understandings. Until about 100 years ago well-educated people believed that our Milky Way Galaxy contained all of the stars in the universe. It is now estimated that there are hundreds of billions of galaxies. It goes on an on like that. So if you find some inconsistency with current understanding then please pass the information along (info@learninglife.com). Thank you!

Seek Care as Needed
This book provides many important and useful strategies for greater life success. If someone is dealing with more serious physical or emotional challenges that affect function and happiness, however, it is important to seek professional care or other suitable resources. It is hard to be one's own doctor. This book is not intended to provide medical or mental health information or advice. Self-care is an essential skill for an effective life, and a critical component of intelligent self-care is getting help when it is needed.

This is the Beginning
... and you are invited. See you down the road...   AB

SECTION I

FOUNDATIONS

1. A Learning Life
2. Setting Goals – Academic & Personal Vision
3. Imaging Success
4. Mindful Learning – The Power of Self-Awareness
5. Continual Improvement & Quality

A Learning Life

I don't know how to do that yet, but I will learn.

CHAPTER THEMES
- Introduction
- A Learning Emphasis
- Key Concepts

Starting Right Now

The place where it all starts is right here, right now, in this present moment. What holds many people back from greater happiness is that they are out of the moment, they live in a remembered past or an anticipated future. Consider this scenario – a person sees an interesting stranger and wants to start a conversation. A thought arises to walk over and say, "Hello!" Then suddenly there is a memory of a previous experience, one that did not go so well – yikes! The mind imagines the other person looking put-off, and the anticipation of possible rejection begins to grow. In a heartbeat, where there was enthusiasm and hope there is now doubt, the potential for failure and embarrassment. The remembered past and the anticipated future have influenced the present possibility, no action is taken, an opportunity is lost.

But the story does not have to end that way. We have the power to change our lives. Instead of just responding unconsciously we can learn to work with life more intentionally in the moment. With a bit of understanding and awareness we can start turning each experience into a foundation for greater accomplishment and satisfaction. It all begins in this very moment – starting right here, right now.

A Holistic Approach to Academic Success

In this book we will consider success from a holistic perspective. We all have our own ideas of what constitutes success, and by contrast, what represents a lack of success. In this material world people often confuse success with having a bunch of stuff. If you travel the globe and wander through the malls, markets, bazaars, emporiums, boutiques, thrift shops, and outlets you will see the mass of nameless humans acquiring this and that. We are acquisitive by nature, and reasonably so, as we actually do need things to survive and to be productive, we do need stuff. But how much stuff do we really need? Most of us probably know someone who is quite well off financially, has a lot of stuff, and who is still dissatisfied, incomplete. As the saying goes – money does not buy happiness.

In this book we will consider success more holistically. A holistic perspective recognizes that we need stuff, and the money or equivalent resources to acquire it. But it also recognizes that we need more than physical things if we are going to be truly happy. Why so? Because in the end, ultimately, nature triumphs, and takes back all our hard earned stuff, the same way nature reclaims the fallen tree, relentlessly breaking it down into its original elements. I remember visiting a favorite uncle of mine in Canada, he was not doing so well, he was dying. He had been a veteran, a prisoner of war, lost a son to mental illness, suffered a good number of hardships, but despite it all he maintained a solid attitude, a great laugh, and a love for life. When I saw him he was well aware of his impending demise. He said, "You can't win this race old boy. Life always wins in the end." He died several months later. When you ask elders, like my uncle Eric, what success looks like they often say the same things – success is good health, loving and being loved, doing something useful with your life, being connected to something bigger than yourself, and, yes, having enough money to take care of business, the more the merrier.

So if life is fleeting (and it is) then perhaps it makes sense to focus our energies on life's more enduring values – health, quality relationships, financial stability, using our skills productively and making a contribution to the world, and connecting to something bigger than ourselves. We all have different needs, but these bigger life goals of health, love, and meaning can be a place to start the conversation of what academic and life success can mean.

> **REFLECTION: WHAT DOES SUCCESS MEAN TO YOU?**
>
> Take a few moments to write down your thoughts about what success means to you. Think of success in the long term, what you want from your life, for yourself and others.
>
> I will know I am successful because…

A Learning Emphasis

In addition to a holistic perspective this book will also emphasize active learning as a foundation for life successful. A famous psychotherapist named Virginia Satir once wrote, "What I am today is a comment on what I have learned, not on my potential" (Englander-Golden & Satir, 1990). That is a humanist perspective. The implication is that we are learning organisms, learning beings. It implies that because we are learners we have the potential to correct mistakes, to reduce limitations in understanding or skill, and to succeed in life, to become a better self. In this book we will emphasize that idea, that learning is a fundamental human capacity, and that our capacity to learn is the foundation for a successful life, in the deepest and broadest sense of what that means.

Change

So why a learning emphasis? There are several reasons. The first has to do with the nature of life. We are residents of the time-space matrix. Change is a natural product of the interaction of time and space. In this realm everything is always changing. Relationships start and end, bodies get old, babies are born, spring flowers fill the meadows, droughts cause food riots, raccoons eat the dog food, there are two unopened containers of ice cream in the freezer. Epic, minor, brief, enduring, good, bad, it is all changing, all the time. There will never be an end to change, there will always be problems to solve. It is the nature of life. It is where we live. Understanding the principles and strategies of learning allows us to respond faster and more effectively to those inevitable changes. Many people fail to understand one of Darwin's main points. It was not about being the smartest, fastest, strongest. It was about being able to successfully adapt to changes in the environment. The one that adapted, fit the new puzzle the best, thrived and survived. Those who did not, did not. So in the change filled day-to-day world that we inhabit, one of the keys to successful adaptation to life's challenges is the ability to learn (Darwin, 1859).

Historic Moment

The second reason for a learning emphasis has to do with where we are right now, this historic moment. The world is changing today at a dramatically rapid pace. We are standing on the threshold of a monumental shift in human experience. When I moved back to San Francisco I was consulting and doing a bit of part-time teaching at the SFSU Multimedia Studies Program. One evening Doug Englebart, inventor of the mouse and GUI (graphical user interface, now common on all computers), came to give an informal talk to a small group of faculty members and students. He spoke of the inability of societies at the brink of radical change to sufficiently predict the size and impact of what was coming. He suggested that we were at such a point in human history, standing on the brink of a networked global information technologies phase change. He compared it to the changes that occurred when Johannes Gutenberg introduced moveable type printing in the 1400's. That technological innovation was influential in fundamentally creating the world we know today, from the birth of the Renaissance to the modern information age. Englebart suggested that we cannot predict the consequences of such singularly pivotal innovations because nothing like them previously existed. They have no precedent. They are radically new innovations and their ultimate impact will be difficult to anticipate. Indeed, it may even be reasonable to suggest that the change that is coming today will be bigger and come faster than during previous periods of change, given the catalyzing nature of global media and commerce, allowing the sharing of insights and ideas near the point of their conception with a mass audience. Learning is essential for continued success and productivity in this new age.

Who You Are

Most importantly, the third reason for a learning emphasis relates to our nature, to the nature of our existence. Joseph Campbell, a renowned scholar of world mythology, once wrote, "The privilege of a lifetime is being who you are" (Walter, 2011). The implication is that we have a potential that is dormant within, a birthright, a destiny. That potential, like a seed, will not germinate if it is not properly cultivated. Our personal potential grows when we step into the river of life and learn how to work with life skillfully, day by day, month by month, year by year. There is no one else like you on the planet. No one has your genes, your gifts, your potential. Only you can be you. The privilege of a lifetime, indeed, is being who YOU are, bringing out the best of the gifts that family, community and nature have endowed you with, and giving those gifts to the world. According to Campbell, that is our great adventure, the journey of becoming our fullest self.

There are many possibilities in life, many things we can do and become. Certainly not all of us will be concert pianists, major league football players, or Nobel laureates in chemistry or literature. There are literally millions of kids in the United States who play football in grade school, high school, and college, yet only a few thousand who play at the professional level. Most of the 7 billion humans on the planet will never reach the rarefied heights of historic fame. Yet everyone can accomplish the most important life mission, moving closer to who they were born to be. The venerated Chinese sage Confucius once stated that some are born with natural ability, some obtain success through study, and others acquire it only after significant trial and effort. In the end, however, the gift achieved by all of them is the same. Whether we are born with it, patiently work on it, or diligently strive to attain it, we all have the potential for remarkable lives. In the end the brass ring is the same for all.

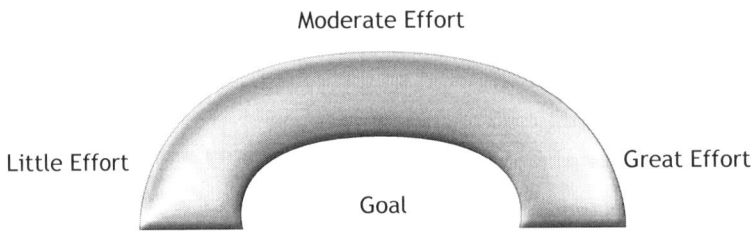

Our Journey Begins

So this book is about a learning life. It is about recognizing that we are learning organisms, and that through learning new things, mastering life at new levels, we become more of who we were born to be. In the moment a person commits to a learning life, their journey begins, the adventure of a lifetime truly begins. Certainly an obvious place for learning is in the classroom. The other essential venue for true learning is in our daily life, in the thick of it all, where we apply our knowledge to meet life's demands. By the end of this book, if you go through the chapters and complete the practices, you will have new understandings and skills that will help you to embrace life more fully, to get more done, to have more fun, to give more to the world, in other words, the keys to open the door to a most incredible life adventure.

So to get things started, it is time to memorize a key phrase. There will be additional phrases or axioms like this for every chapter of the book. These are the 18 Principles or foundations for an effective learning life (go to the Resources section at end of book for the full list). It might seem quaint at first, sloganish, but these phrases really are an essential part of our process. In time their value as practical resources will become more evident (so please do give it a try). The first line we need to memorize is the following:

"I don't know how to do that yet, but I will learn."

Why use that line for the opening quote of this book? Because, first and foremost, it captures the essential idea in this book – that we are learning organisms. Second, it implies that by doing, exploring, experimenting, getting information, getting feedback, trying and potentially failing, we can learn how to do something we could not do before, and then our life becomes fuller, we have more capacity, more agency. Finally, the phrase is optimistic, there is hope because we can learn. Indeed, one of the reasons that a person may resist doing something is because he or she does not possess the competence to do it yet. Research shows that if a person lacks a sense of self-efficacy (being effective) with a particular task, then often he or she will not make an effort to do the task for fear of failure and possible embarrassment. Our brain makes a calculation (usually an unconscious calculation), based on our previous life experiences, our holistic sense of self, that given a perceived lack of competence, it would not make sense to put in the effort. So instead of even trying one bit the individual lacking self-efficacy just sits on the couch and watches television, which requires very little energy and is a nice distraction. They sit there comfortably, distracted, as the adventure of life passes them by.

This is a ***very important point***. One of the big reasons people often resist trying things in life, is not that they ultimately lack the capacity to do it, NO, it is because ***they do not know how to do it YET***. Very different concepts - ***incapable of doing it*** versus ***don't know how to do it yet***. Why would we expect someone to do something well if they had never learned how to do it? Not reasonable. Like Confucius said, some people are born with a natural ability for music, math, gymnastics, cooking, interacting with others, but even they have to work at all the other things in life, like everyone else. How can someone expect to ride a horse, solve geometry problems, write a good paragraph, cook a healthy dinner, ask someone for a date, or balance a checkbook, if that person never learned how? Not being able to do those things is not evidence that a person is stupid. Nope, not at all. It is proof that ***he or she never learned how to do those things***, either at all, or not in the right way. **HOWEVER, we CAN learn how**. Not everything in life is amenable to a learning solution. We cannot learn to flap our arms and fly like a bird because we are not anatomically designed for flight. We can, however, learn to fly a hang glider, or a plane, or a wingsuit. For many, many, many things in life *learning is the path* from here to there. So let's repeat together 3 times please –

"I don't know how to do that yet, but I will learn."

"I don't know how to do that yet, but I will learn."

"I don't know how to do that yet, but I will learn."

Some Considerations

Whether you are using this book in a formal classroom setting, on your own at home, or with a work group, there are a few norms that you should please consider seriously. The first is to do the work. This book is about you. You may think some of the exercises are trivial and you may want to skip them, but you are encouraged to try. They are intended to illuminate and reinforce important concepts and skills. If you go to a weekend workshop, and come home with one or two good ideas or skills, that is not a bad investment (depending on the entrance fee of course). Sometimes all you need is one new idea to change your life. The ugly duckling got one idea – "Hey, I'm not a freaking duck!" – and its life was changed forever, in that instant, past, present and future. I remember a student reporting at the end of the semester that she had not taken the assignments very seriously and that she had wasted a huge opportunity (this was after she heard presentations by her classmates and recognized how much some of them had changed). To her credit she confided that she had a serious issue with alcohol and while listening to other students addressing their diverse learning/life challenges she found herself inspired and committed to finally start to do something about it. I truly hope she did, for everyone's sake. Sadly, it is a similar story every semester, some people just do not put in the effort, and like most things in life, what you get out depends on what you put in. The second norm is to cut yourself some slack. It takes time to get good at things. You get better at the piano by sitting and intentionally, consciously practicing. Things take time. Third, cut your classmates some slack and help them out. You learn by helping others learn. Finally, do not give up, just keep at it, everything changes, learning is a process, it takes time, just like life.

Key Concepts

At this point it would be useful to introduce some important concepts that we will be working with in the upcoming chapters.

Learning

One obvious sign of learning is that we remember something – a name or date, a dance step, an idea or belief passed on in your family. It is now in mind and body and can be displayed as needed. One way neuroscientists think of memory is as a neural path strengthened by repetition (Dubnau et al., 2003). We find a similar notion in the ancient Chinese classic, the *Tao Te Ching*, one of the worlds most widely translated literary works. The title word Tao is often interpreted to mean 'Way' or 'Path', and refers to a way of living that leads to greater freedom, happiness, virtue and power. The character Tao is actually composed of two radicals or elements, chuo 辶 'head' and shou 首 'go', which may express the idea of intelligent movement along a path. You see where you want to end up, and then you head in that direction taking the best possible route to get there. Over time that route becomes more familiar and the path more visible, the way a forest path becomes more obvious as animals consistently use the same route down to the pond day after day. The way of learning is like that. It involves the deepening of a path or pattern in the brain and mind, the path from here to there, from not being able to being able.

In this book we will also examine the psychological processes and neurological mechanisms underlying effective learning. If we understand how the mind/brain process information, and create memories and behaviors, we can more fully appreciate why some approaches to learning will be more productive than others, such as using repetition to enhance long-term memory and recall. We will also explore learning as a three phases process involving acquisition, integration and display. So throughout the book expect to see related information and insights from research studies in neurology, psychology, and the information sciences.

Mindful Awareness

Mindful awareness is one of the primary learning strategies we will employ in this book. The purpose of mindful awareness is to become more aware of our momentary experiences, both internal and external, to increase our presence in daily life. One of the main reasons for integrating the practice of mindful awareness into this book is that it is much harder to make changes in life, to learn, or to build capacity, if we are not aware of what we are doing, thinking, feeling, or saying. By becoming aware of our responses to life, in the moment, we begin to recognize our habitual patterns, our conditioned mind at work. This helps us notice which patterns serve our highest good and which do not, and that is the beginning of lasting change. In this book we will explore mindfulness as both a meditation practice (a specific mental training), and also as a self-monitoring, self-awareness technique that can be used at any point throughout the day. Both of these methods focus on being aware of experience in the moment, paying attention to what is happening right now, such as paying attention to whether we are off task or on task, goofing around or getting it done.

Mental Imagery/Priming and Goal Commitment

Mental imagery and goal setting is another key practice we will work with in this book. Mental imagery involves the internal production of experience so that it resembles the actual event. It can include rich sensory detail, emotions, and movement (Finke, 1989; Lang, 1979). Imagery is believed to play a role in a variety of human cognitive functions, such as encoding memory, navigating through the physical environment, and social interactions (Pearson et al., 2008). There is substantial evidence supporting the value of mental imagery for health and healing, sports, the performing arts, education, goal achievement, and many other applications (Barnes et al., 2004; Driskell et al., 1994; Galyean 1983; Martin & Hall, 1995). Imagery can be used to shape personal attitudes and beliefs, to improve performance, to increase motivation and persistence, and to sharpen goal focus. In this book we will work with mental imagery as a tool to help shape and enhance goal clarity, commitment and attainment. Specifically, we will work with the Priming method.

The Learning Life Problem Solving Model

The third main strategy we will work with is a problem solving orientation. One of the common elements of continual improvement, and a learning life, is solving problems. We will work with a specific approach to problem solving in this text, the *Learning Life Problem Solving Model.* The model uses ideas from continual improvement and cybernetics. From continual improvement we emphasize ongoing problem identification and solution. From cybernetics, which is the study of self-regulatory systems, we use feedback to correctly navigate the environment and reach goals (Wiener, 1948). The Learning Life Problem Solving Model provides a way to look at life challenges (in school, home, work, the world) in a simple and straightforward fashion. It can help us see where we are, where we want to be, the best path to get there, and whether we are making progress along the way. The basic model is presented here. It begins with a reflection on where we are and where we want to be. Solutions are researched and considered, and a decision is made. The solution is then tested and evaluated.

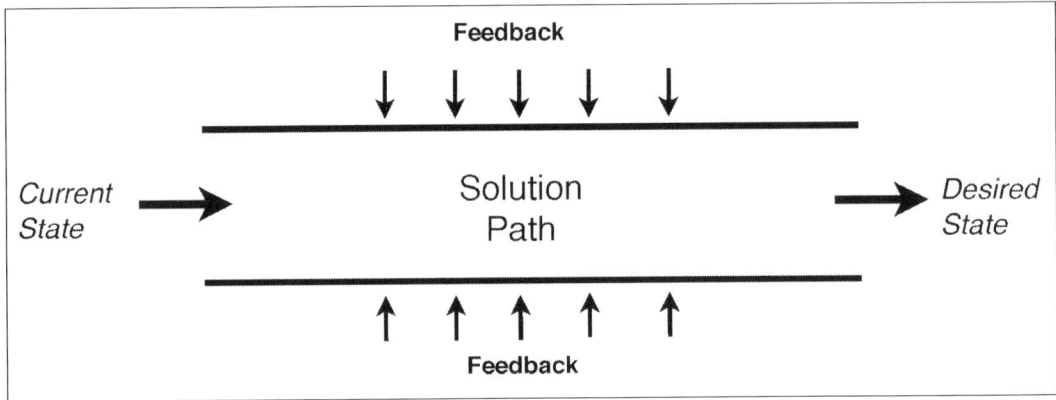

Continual Improvement — Kaizen

Continual improvement is a systems management philosophy and practice that emphasizes ongoing problem identification and solution. It is a cornerstone to a life characterized by growth and success. The specific continual improvement philosophy we will work with is called Kaizen 改善. The word 'kai' means change and 'zen' means good, so Kaizen refers to change for the good, or improvement. Brilliantly, Kaizen is not about working harder. I love that. On the contrary, it is about working smarter. A primary goal is to reduce all forms of waste, including wasting our own time and energy. One of the simple ways to cultivate this habit is to start bringing more quality into the things we do. A focus on quality will naturally lead to greater effectiveness.

The Learning Life Wheel Model - Interdependence and Interaction

The Learning Life Wheel Model represents the three primary spheres of our human experience – Person, Behavior, and Environment. It offers a systems view of our experience, a holistic view. It recognizes life's innate interdependencies. Something in the environment, like getting a low score on an evaluation, sets off thoughts and feelings (doubt and anxiety), which result in behaviors (getting angry with housemates), which have an affect on our environment (they feel upset and rejected) – an endless loop. The Person represents everything that is happening inside of us, our thoughts, emotions, physiological processes. The Environment is the world we live in. Behavior is what the world sees, how we are known. One of the keys to success in school and in life is self-management or self-direction. That requires being able to recognize these three interactive and interdependent elements and to work with them effectively, such as, reading the environment, recognizing how it affects our thoughts and feelings, regulating those thoughts and feelings, and making the most skillful behavioral responses.

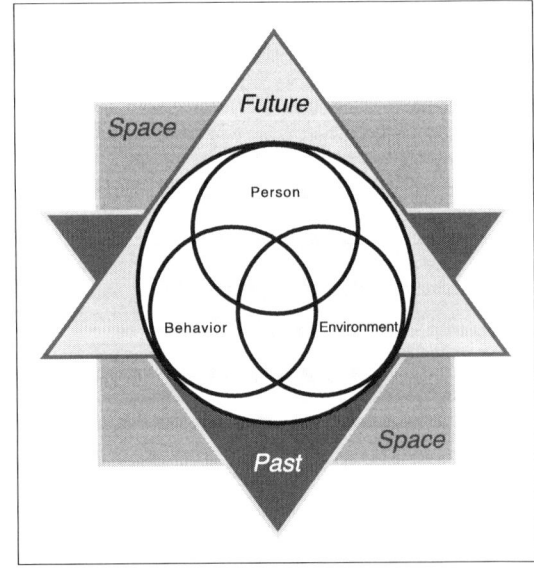

Learned Helplessness / Conditioned Mind and Body

Learned helpless is a theory of human behavior developed by psychologist, Martin Seligman, of the University of Pennsylvania. The original research studies showed that if an animal was chained and shocked (it could not avoid the shock) it learned that its situation was helpless, no escape from future shock. Once conditioned in this way the animal could be unchained, and if shocked again, it would just sit there and endure the pain (Seligman, 1975). It would not act to escape the shock. It had learned to be helpless, a passive recipient versus an active agent.

Although this research became the basis for an important theory of human depression, that is not the reason for our interest. Rather, we will use this concept to understand how individuals get unplugged. Through a variety of life experiences people learn that they are 'bad at math', 'not good in social situations', 'clumsy'. By virtue of such mental conditioning people do not even think to try, they just sit there letting life go by, believing they are still chained in the past. Many of our responses to life – avoiding studying, getting easily aggravated by housemates or a partner, self-criticism, eating foods that do not support well being, drinking too much – can be a function of reactive, highly conditioned, mind-body patterns. What we want is greater agency, an increased ability to make informed choices and to act on those choices. One of the main goals of the learning paradigm presented in this book is to recognize that *we can* develop a sense of what binds us, *we can* begin to envision more productive ways of living, *we can* learn new strategies to awaken that potential, and *we can* begin that journey right now to greater freedom, power and happiness, one step at a time, one breath at a time, one day at a time. Knowledge can set us free.

The Stress Response and the Emotional Brain

We will examine various ideas about stress and coping in upcoming chapters. One of the key lessons that we will focus on is that the stress response is a built-in program designed to protect us and support our survival. If there is a perceived threat in the environment a remarkable cascade of neurology, emotion, and physiological responses are set in motion so that we can stay live (and eat dinner again tonight). Although the stress response may not feel good, the racing heart and sweaty palms, it is an essential resource for survival and success. The potential problem with the stress responses, however, is that it can become overly engaged, once activated the stress response can persists longer than it actually needs to for the sake of survival. The system can get trigger-happy. We begin to anticipate problems, getting stuck in a worry loop, a fear loop. That is less constructive. Our goal will be to recognize when the response is engaged, learn to use it as a resource as much as possible, and ultimately to become more proficient at regulating our stress reactivity so that we can feel the stress response but not let it stop us from doing what we need to do. Learning more about the body's stress response process is a first step in understanding it and working with it. Adopting effective self-management skills will ultimately increase life choices, more room to play, unhindered by fear.

The Dopamine Reward Circuit

Our brains are structured to seek reward and avoid punishment. Sounds obvious, and it is, but it is also quite subtle. In this book we will examine how various structures in the brain, such as the dopamine reward circuit, affect our experience of the world by shaping our desires, decisions, behaviors and memories. Understanding some of the basics can help us learn why we do what we do and how we can shift out of less productive 'reward' patterns over time. If an unproductive behavior gets rewarded then that behavior becomes stronger. When we avoid a big pile of intimidating work and eat cookies instead, then our procrastination gets rewarded, strengthened. By understanding how our internal reward system works we can begin to shift into a new, more productive habits that carry us more quickly to our goals.

Self-Efficacy

Two important concepts related to human learning are self-efficacy and expectancy. Self-efficacy is essentially the belief that we have the ability to do a specific thing (Bandura, 1997). If you ask a group of twenty people, "Raise your hand if you feel comfortable writing a large research paper," you will probably get a fairly small response. The people who raise their hands and say they feel comfortable will most likely have a higher *sense of self-efficacy* about their writing skills. It is the same with music. "Who plays an instrument? Who plays it well?" The folks who say they play it well will most likely have a higher sense of self-efficacy about their musicianship, they are competent at playing music, they can do it effectively.

The CRITICALLY IMPORTANT point is that if someone has a limited or low sense of self-efficacy about something, like math, speaking in public, or hitting a baseball, then they might not even try to do the task, make no effort at all, or only a marginal effort. What happens when we do not try? NOTHING! Yup, nothing happens, no raise, no new boyfriend or girlfriend, no home run, no sense of accomplishment from taking on a challenge and meeting it and succeeding (or even failing, which is part of learning). Optimism, effort, and small successes lead to growing self-efficacy over time. It takes time to learn new things, "I don't know how to do that yet, but I will learn." As we learn something new and become more skilled at it our self-efficacy grows. We would probably not expect to have much self-efficacy for something we have never done, or 'failed' at it in the past. We would be less likely to have high self-efficacy for something if we were taught that people like us (age, gender, race, social status) were not good at it. Doing something, and succeeding (and failing too), bit by bit, over time, develops our sense of competence with new endeavors, our self-efficacy. Avoiding that task provides no opportunity for self-efficacy to grow.

Expectancy

Expectancy relates to our belief that something will or will not happen. It is what we expect from life. A person can have high self-efficacy, knowing that they play the piano quite well. That same person, however, could have a low sense of expectancy for getting into a particular music program, as the acceptance rate for the program is about 1 in 500, and those who get in often know someone on the faculty. Research has similarly found that low expectancy can also reduce a person's effort and persistence toward a goal (Eccles & Wigfield, 2002). Making estimations of expected success can be a smart idea. Why waste energy on options with a low probability of success. The challenge is that we may at times hold low expectations based on some self-limiting beliefs. We will explore this concept of limiting beliefs in more detail in upcoming chapters.

Attribution, Positive Self-Talk, and Self-Acceptance

Attribution is an important concept in the field of psychology. It looks at how we make meaning of our life experiences, how we explain to ourselves and others why something happened, the story we tell in order to make sense of things (Weiner, 1986). Attribution is part of our human need to understand why things happen. Why didn't she say hello? Why did that seagull take my chips and not his? Why did the boss send this email to me and no one else? Why are they imposing trade restrictions? Why did the Prime Minister not attend the banquet? We make attributions about our own behaviors, the behavior of others, and of life events. Attributions can be positive or negative, accurate or inaccurate (very), and they can seriously affect our willingness to persist with challenges. They are often based on limited information and are heavily influenced by our past experiences. If a student is not good at math and he gets an A on a math exam he might attribute that good score to luck, rather than to having studied. By contrast, someone who is pretty good at math might attribute her D to having a bad teacher, rather than to insufficient study time. Attribution is one of the strategies (typically unconscious) that we all use to make sense of life. Our attributions influence our choices. If we are not aware of our attributions, and if we do not work to reduce self-limiting attributions, then they can reinforce unproductive habits for a lifetime. In this text we will use mindful awareness, positive self-talk, and the cultivation of self-acceptance as important tools for working with attribution.

Resources and Resourcefulness – A Self-Assessment

When starting a new project it is useful to do an initial assessment. We want to see what we already have so we can determine what we still need. A person would not go shopping without assessing what they needed to buy, and making sure they put some silver in their pocket to purchase those goods. In that same vein, we want to do an initial assessment now to get a sense of what resources we currently possess, both internal and external, that can be used to support a successful life journey. Having resources is a key to coping with the challenges and stresses of life. If you had to go through school without books, a computer, teachers, lab equipment, and other essential resources there would be much less learning and a lot more stress. Resources can be family, institutions, personal qualities, money, time, productivity tools, almost anything that helps you reach your destination. Appropriate resources can significantly increase our sense of efficacy and positive expectancy, and ultimately our success.

Table 1 shows the relationship between resources, stress and coping. The four elements of the model are Demand (the potential sources of stress), Available Resources, Perceived Cost of failure, and resultant Levels of Stress. The Demand (stressor) is what is pulling on us in the moment, such as a challenging midterm exam on Monday morning. If a student has a challenging exam the Demand would be high. Let us also say the student finds out she does not have lecture notes for the material that will be covered on the exam. An important resource is missing (Available Resources - low). Also, the student has to pass the class to get out of academic probation (Perceived Cost - high). This configuration - of challenging exam (high demand), paired with no notes (low resources), and the potential to get kicked out of school (high cost), would result in a very high level of stress for most people. If we take that same scenario, but instead the student has good lecture notes available (Available Resources - high), then the stress level drops to moderate. That student still has the high demand of a challenging exam, but is now supported with productive resources to help her succeed (which probably increases her sense of positive expectancy for success).

TABLE 1: Resources and Coping

The Demand - Stressor	Available Resources	Perceived Cost	Level of Stress
High (big exam)	Low (no notes)	High (expulsion)	High (sweating)
High	High	High	Moderate
Low	Low	Low	Low
Low	High	Low	Very Low

So what makes a resource useful? Having it, and as needed, using it. We want to use the resources in our lives to succeed, to make a difference, to grow. That is being resourceful, being full of resources. I am always amazed when I go to the graduation ceremony each year and see the valedictorians. They took the same classes as other students, they are about the same age, many of them actually come from more challenging backgrounds and situations, and yet there they are. Are they that much smarter? Sure, some of them are pretty darn smart. Did they use their resources, such as classes, study sections, and office hours more effectively, probably yes. They took advantage of what was available and found creative ways to get things done. They were resourceful. Resourcefulness is the opposite of helplessness. It is the recognition that there are things around us and inside of us that we can use to get ahead, to solve problems, to make improvements day by day.

Dr. Milton H. Erickson, an important contributor to the evolution of contemporary psychotherapy, thought about this issue quite a bit. He recognized that each person, even if challenged by a life problem, had tremendous resources within, the potential to be resourceful. Part of his approach in working with people, and helping them move toward greater independence and self-respect, greater agency, was to have them recognize those resources, tap into them, and start using them. He once wrote, "It is important to have a sense of security, a sense of readiness, a full knowledge that come what may you can meet it and handle it and enjoy doing it. It's also a nice learning to come up against a situation that you cannot handle, and then later think it over and realize that too was a learning that's useful in many, many different ways. It allows you to assess your strength. It also allows you to discover the areas in which you need to use some more of your own security, which rests within yourself... Reacting to the good and the bad and dealing with it adequately, that's the real joy in life" (Bandler et al., 1996).

One thing that I find very helpful in his advice is the idea that being resourceful does not mean we have it all figured out. He wrote, "…reacting to the good and bad and dealing with it *adequately*."

He did not say you need to be perfect or that you always need to have the answer. Nope, he said if you respond, and even if you fail, there is learning there. It is adequate, a good start. You are showing agency. And when it is not perfect, "...you need to use some more of your own security, which rests within yourself." Tapping our own inner resources, our own inner security, trusting that we are learning beings. That is key to a successful life. Step by step, day by day, the journey unfolds.

Assessment of Resources

Most universities will provide an abundance of resources to help their students succeed. They will not always do the best job informing students of those resources, however. Use this Reflection activity to learn more about what your university has to offer. Is that important? Yes, there are probably a number of things you may not know about, offered by your university, or otherwise available to you, that could make your process more effective. When student first come to college it can be a big change. Maybe the first time seriously away from home, having to deal with laundry, being homesick, confusion about classes and majors, too much party time leading to low energy and mild depression. All of that is normal and usually passes in due time. Managing in the meantime, and thriving for the duration, is the goal. Getting a handle on resources, internal and external, is a key.

REFLECTION

So let's do a quick self-assessment of current resources. Having useful resources can make a big difference in coping, in our willingness and ability to move into the thick of things, where the rewards are. An assessment of resources can give us a sense of what we have and what we still need. The goal of this task is to create a list of resources that are available to you, useful to you, in your life right now.

1. Personal

List the qualities that you possess within yourself, essential resources that help you achieve your goals and cope with life's challenges.

_____
_____
_____
_____

2. Social

List the social resources that are available to you in your life.

_____
_____
_____
_____

3. Environmental

List community and institutional resources that are or could be useful.

Integrative Learning Project

The last thing to introduce in this chapter is the *Integrative Learning Project* (ILP). We mentioned earlier that different approaches to learning produce different results, and that some are better than others. That said, one of the best ways to learn anything is to use it, to work with it, to do it, in a meaningful way. The ILP will be our vehicle for learning about learning. It involves selecting some aspect of life you want to modify, develop, or improve, and applying the various strategies discussed in the next 17 chapters toward that successful transformation.

> **REFLECTION**
>
> Take a moment and think about what might be a good focus for your Integrative Learning Project. We are just starting, so it does not have to be a final decision, just the beginning, a contemplation. For this exercise make a list of things in your life where there is some room for improvement. Consider things that would help you move forward with important academic/life goals.

...And Now We Begin

I hope that you have a truly transformative experience as a result of working through this book. Good luck with this most important and incredible journey, the journey of a learning life. May it be epic.

SUMMARY

In this chapter we considered what it means to be successful, reflecting on success in the bigger sense of that word, beyond the accumulation of stuff. A key to success is recognizing and working with our innate capacity to learn. Incapacity does not reflect capacity, it reflects a lack of learning. The response, "I don't know how to do that yet, but I will learn." Why? Whether we like it or not, we have to learn. Everything keeps changing, and today the pace of change is coming even faster with the advent of new technologies and global expectations. More important than learning to adapt to a changing world, however, is to learning to understand who we are as individuals and a members of a global community. To catalyze our learning life we will work on a number of important concepts and skills in this book. Primary skills will include mindful awareness, mental imagery, goal setting, and problem solving. Essential concepts include continual improvement, understanding the nature of interdependence of environment, person and behavior, the roles of learned helplessness and resourcefulness in ehancing growth and capacity, the power of reward and coping, and the importance of self-efficacy, and expectancy. It all starts right here. It all starts right now.

REFERENCES

Bandler R, Grinder J, DeLozier J. *Patterns of the Hypnotic Techniques of Milton H. Erickson, M.D. Volume II*. Santa Cruz: Grinder & Associates; 1996.

Bandura A. *Self-Efficacy: The Exercise of Control*. New York: W.H. Freeman; 1997.

Barnes PM, Powell-Griner E., McFann K, Nahin RL. Complementary and alternative medicine use among adults: United States, 2002. Advance Data. 2004;27(343):1-19.

Eccles JS, Wigfield A. Motivational beliefs, values, and goals. *Annual Review of Psychology*. 2002;53(1):109-132.

Englander-Golden P, Satir V. *Say It Straight: From Compulsion to Choices*. Palo Alto: Science and Behavior Books; 1990.

Darwin Charles. *On the Origin of Species by Means of Natural Selection, or The Preservation of Favoured Races in the Struggle for Life*. London: John Murray; 1859

Driskell JE, Copper C, Moran A. Does mental practice enhance performance? *Journal of Applied Psychology*. 1994;79(4):481-492.

Dubnau J, Chiang AS, Tully T. Neural substrates of memory: from synapse to system. *Journal of Neurobiology*. 2003;54(1):238-53.

Finke RA. *Principles of Mental Imagery*. Cambridge: The MIT Press; 1989

Lang PJ. A bio-informational theory of emotional imagery. *Psychophysiology*. 1979;16(6):495-512.

Martin KA, Hall CR. Using mental imagery to enhance intrinsic motivation. *Journal of Sport & Exercise Psychology*. 1995;17(1);54-69.

Galyean B. The use of guided imagery in elementary and secondary schools. *Imagination, Cognition and Personality*. 1982-1983;2(2);145-151

Pearson J, Clifford CW, Tong F. The functional impact of mental imagery on conscious perception. *Current Biology*. 2008;18(13);982-986.

Seligman MEP. *Helplessness: On Depression, Development, and Death*. San Francisco: W.H. Freeman; 1975.

Walter R, editor. *A Joseph Campbell Companion: Reflections on the Art of Living*. San Anselmo: Joseph Campbell Foundation; 2011.

Weiner B. *An Attributional Theory of Motivation and Emotion*. New York: Springer-Verlag; 1986

Wiener Norbert. *Cybernetics, or Communication and Control in the Animal and the Machine*. Cambridge: MIT Press; 1948.

Setting Goals
Academic & Personal Vision

2

I know my goals.

CHAPTER THEMES
- Goals
  - Research, Benefits, Qualities
- Vision & Goal Clarification
- Problem Solving Model

There is a tremendous power that comes from having a clear vision, a sense of what you are supposed to do, of where you are supposed to go, your purpose, your destiny. Research shows that people with clear goals tend to have better outcomes, whether that is with relationships, finances, careers, health, all of it. In this chapter we will examine the power of goals – why they are important, how to create them, and the best ways to put them to work for a life of greater success and happiness.

The Benefits of Goals

Why work on goal clarification and goal setting? There are a number of benefits to be derived from clear goals. Here are some of the important ones.

1. Goals provide information on what you value

Clear goals provide insight into what we truly value in our lives, which of the millions of choices in life stand out above the rest. It can be very helpful to generate a list of top goals now and then to see what persists, to see which goals consistently show up again and again. The ones that do can tell you a lot about where your true passion lies. For many reasons we may not act on those persistent goals, or commit to them, but at least we can begin to recognize them. They show up over and over again, like a real friend. They will not go away, even if we ignore them for a time. That is useful information. The process of periodically contemplating big picture life goals can be illuminating, providing insight into what matters in life, what calls you, what will get you up and going each and every day, wanting to make a difference in the world.

2. Goals create focus

A second benefit of clear goals is that they help to create focus and focus has power. Consider laser light versus ordinary candescent light, like light from a flashlight. A flashlight projects a beam of light composed of all the wavelengths or colors of the spectrum, resulting in a white light. Also, the photons or light particles in that beam of light are moving in various directions and frequencies, resulting in light that is diffused and weak. Laser light, by contrast, is the result of all the photons being in the same wavelength. That singular wavelength of light is what produces the specific color beam, like a red or green laser (it is monochromatic). In addition to having the same wavelength the light particles in a laser become highly organized, the waves line up and move in phase with each other (they are said to be coherent). That produces the characteristic intense, narrow laser beam. When the light energy becomes organized in that fashion it can be very powerful. A CO_2 laser, for example, emits light in the infrared spectrum and can burn through metal, a beam of light burning through metal! Clear goals bring a coherence to our life, helping us to move forward with alignment of mind and body, focused, intense, powerful.

3. Goals lead to rewards and that can increase motivation

Accomplishing a goal often results in getting a reward, obtaining something desirable. The accomplishment of a particular goal may be associated with a higher salary, a better relationship, a sense of pride, or a longer and healthier life. Humans seek rewards, rewards are intrinsically motivating, our brains are hardwired to move toward reward and away from punishment (Ferari et al., 2008). If we have personally relevant, clear, rewarding goals, there will be an intrinsic urge to make them a reality. They will be motivating. Creating a select list of goals, that lead to desired rewards, will result in goals that are more likely to be acted on with enthusiasm, energy and persistence. Linking goals and rewards can be a very powerful strategy.

4. Goals increase action, persistence and coping

There is a great Indian saying, "If a person's hair is on fire, he will find water." There are many reasons people have goals they do not act on. If the goal is to get the next breath of air and stay alive, however, there will be a great urgency to attain that goal. That goal is no longer personal, in a psychological or social sense, it is biological, one's entire being recognizes the fundamental threat to survival. A goal of that magnitude will motivate high persistence for any sane person. The majority of our goals, however, lack that same level of gravity. They may be perceived of as important, but remain in limbo for years, perhaps for a lifetime, no action ever taken, no accomplishment ever enjoyed.

Research shows that mastery goals, goals where one pursues true growth in capacity, predict persistence (Elliot et al., 1999). If we can find our core goals, goals that we can be committed to and passionate about, then our goals will instill action and greater accomplishment. If a goal is important we will deal with the obstacles. When a goal is paramount the obstacles in the way become less relevant. You just do it. "If my hair is on fire, I will find water." When you get truly inspired by your goals the obstacles may even become part of the solution, using the boulders in the path as a way to climb higher and reach the intended destination. The obstacles become the stairway to the next level. With a clear and potent goal it is easier to stay on task, for longer periods of time, with more confidence, commitment, energy, enthusiasm, and inspiration. You are committed to get that next breath.

5. Goals engage strategic thinking

A potent goal can activate our strategic thinking and make us better problem solvers. If it is really important to get back into the house, really important, like the baby accidentally got locked inside, mom and dad will get in. When you have an important goal you work overtime, you use a wider range of resources, you get others involved, you find a way in. If the goal is compelling and the first attempt failed a second attempt is sure to follow, then another, then another. A hungry person will find something to eat. Our ancestors entered new worlds, migrating across vast stretches of the earth. They did not arrive with guidebooks about local flora and fauna. They could not email ahead to book a place to stay. They learned by trial and error – what tastes good, what is safe to eat, what is easy to catch. They were forced to be creative, eating all forms of crawling, flying, prickly, mushy things. Necessity is indeed the mother of invention, of strategic and creative thinking, of persistence. The biological goal of survival is a powerful driver – air, food, water, sleep, safety, kinship, reproduction. If we can harness that type of energy for other less primal life goals, recognizing the importance of those goals to our well-being, happiness, and ability to contribute meaningfully, then those goals can similarly help to awaken a most brilliant fire within.

6. Goals engage the lateral prefrontal cortex

The lateral prefrontal cortex is an essential part of our strategic planning and decision making process (Tanji & Hoshi, 2008). Should I have the candy bar or not? If we do not have a preset goal oriented toward healthy eating then the brain's quick acting pleasure center may prevail. The goal-free semiconscious person just grabs the candy bar and down it goes, nary a thought. When we strengthen goals and goal commitment, and develops plans to achieve those goal, the slower acting prefrontal cortex gets involved. As the goal strengthens it creates a feedback loop, there is a reduced tendency to just grab the candy bar and eat it. We become less habitual. We become more reflective in our decision making and life planning, which means more insight and control.

Research on Goals

Susan Kobasa was a research psychologist at the City University of New York. She was intrigued by the idea that individual personality characteristics might have some role in health outcomes. In one of her classic studies she interviewed a group of business executives. They all had fairly stressful jobs. She assessed each of them on a variety of personality characteristics, and then looked at common themes, comparing those who got sick and those who did not. She found a constellation of three common characteristics in the individuals who stayed well (Kobasa, 1979).

1. Commitment

The first thing she found was that the individuals who stayed healthy in the face of ongoing stress had a stronger commitment to a personal vision. They had a commitment to their goals. The individuals who had a clear purpose, a reason for going to work each day, a source of inspiration in their lives, were more resilient. This finding suggests that when we have an important goal, then our life has a purpose, we have meaning, and that meaning awakens the spirit and the spirit protects us. There are many reported cases of elders who lived to see a grandchild born, or made it to a landmark 100th birthday, and then expired shortly after the event. An important goal, a commitment to something personally meaningful, can be the flame that keeps the fire burning for another day. Finding something to commit to can be personally empowering, as it gives us meaning. That is probably one of the draws for terrorist groups. These organizations provide clear purpose and a sense of contributing to a personally important goal. It is a chance for a meaningful life for many individuals whose opportunities are otherwise often quite limited. Unfortunately many people find meaning this way, in someone else's war, and lose track of their own unique potential for good.

2. Challenge

The second characteristic of the resilient executives, despite their stressful jobs, was that they did not view their problems as hassles, obstacles, or reasons to give up. Rather, they saw problems as challenges, as opportunities, as the place of growth. Seeing problems as challenges can activate a creative, problem solving mind, one that is more willing to cope and to persist until a solution is found. This is a realistic mindset, which recognizes that there will be challenges in life, that those challenges can be addressed and resolved, and that their resolution will lead to personal growth, greater autonomy, and goal accomplishment. Ultimately, a life challenge is where we learn about the resources we possess inside. It is when we have to dig deeper to solve life problems that we find new resources and develop new skills. It is also where we cultivate greater confidence. A key to empowered action is to see problems as challenges that provide opportunities for self-discovery and growth.

3. Control

The final characteristic of the resilient executives was that they also possessed a sense of personal control, or a sense of responsibility for the outcomes of their lives. This finding relates to the concept of locus of control, which was develop by psychologist Julian Rotter in the 1950's (Rotter, 1954). Locus of control is considered to be a personal psychological trait that we all possess. The basic idea has to do with how much we believe that we have control in our lives. There are two sides to the coin. A person with an *internal* locus of control (control located internally) believes that he or she has control or influence over what happens in life. That individual studies hard and then she gets an A. The person with an *external* locus of control (control located externally) believes that external forces, like karma, the will of the gods, fate, luck, are what cause events in life. The individual does not study hard, she gets a C, and blames the teacher for writing a bad exam. Individuals with an internal locus of control, because they take responsibility for outcomes, are going to be more likely to do what is needed to achieve their goals. They recognize that accomplishment is a function of their own thoughts and actions, no excuses.

Characteristics of Effective Goals

The following are things to consider when creating goals. Using these ideas will result in clearer, more powerful goals. The key characteristics include the following:

Personal and Relevant	Taskable/Actionable
Intentional	Written out clearly and visible for reinforcement
Values based	
Positive	Monitored for progress
Based on an initial assessment	Contingency plans considered
Realistic and subject to modification	Challenging
Specific	Holistic
Measurable	Acted upon
Timelined and proximal	Detached

Personal and Relevant

Research shows that personalized goals result in higher goal achievement (Levetan et al., 2002). Good goals are personal and relevant. They reflect what *you* (personal) ***really want or need*** (relevant). Given the limited and precious time we are given on this earth it is prudent to work on the highest priority goals and chuck the rest – ***I really want/need this outcome.*** Those goals, those deeply personal and highly relevant goals, will provide the greatest rewards in the long run. Focus on those.

There is no shortage of things we can do in a day, non-stop possibilities. Some of the possibilities available to us will be clear distractions (a waste of our time), some others will have potential merit, and a few will be extremely relevant to long-term happiness and success. If you are able to stay aligned with the short list of key personal life goals you will be much more likely to attain the awesome in your lifetime. The days, months and years will pass away before you know it, and then it will be too late.

Intentional and Values Based

In addition to having an understanding of ***what*** you want it is very helpful to have a sense of ***why*** you want it, to be intentional in your goal pursuit. Without a clear sense of the why, the motive for acting, it is easier to loose initiative. Without a clear motive it can be understandably harder to maintain motivation, and goals without motivation often sputter and burn out quickly. Ideally the basis for important goals also reflects personal values. If our highest goals are not built on the foundation of our deepest values then there is a greater chance that they will crumble. When we know our values, and select our key goals based on those values, then we have a foundation for strong and effective action that will persist in the face of adversity and endure through time.

Positive

Goals need to be stated in positive language. There is a classic Three Stooges line, "He's the most intelligent imbecile I've ever seen." On one hand it is a complement, but an obvious insult at the same time. Many people tend to state goals in a similarly negative sense. "I will stop being so lazy and try to get some work done this weekend." Wow, does that lack power and commitment. That goal needs to be restated in positive language. Turn "I will stop being so lazy" into "I am energetic and productive when I come home from school and I get 3 hours of work in." Turn "I will stop eating so much junk food" into "I love to eat fruits and vegetables every day." Rewrite "I get off my lazy butt and lose/gain 5 pounds," into "I am exercising 3 times a week and lose/gain 5 pounds and feel better than ever." A few, very few, goals will by default include a negative term in them, such as, "I will *stop* smoking cigarettes." "I am a ***non***-smoker." Or, "I am able notice and quiet my anger when it arises." There is no simple way to state certain goal in an exclusively positive fashion. If you are at the stage of stopping smoking or noticing anger then that is the goal.

That said, it is generally preferable to spin goals in a positive light. Positive phrasing shifts the focus from the problem (lazy, unproductive, pessimistic) to the solution (active, productive, optimistic). It shifts the focus from where you are (eating junk food), to where you want to be (eating fruits and vegetables). That future focus helps to build an image in your mind and heart of who you will become. Very importantly, positive is more encouraging and more rewarding than negative. Positive takes the focus off the lack, what is missing, what you regret or resent or are addicted to. It puts the focus on the goal, on what you want, where you want to go, who you want to be. That is more motivating. One example of this enhancing power was observed in a study on job satisfaction by Roberson. Satisfaction was found to be directly associated with an emphasis on positive work goals versus negative ones (Roberson, 1990).

Based on an Initial Assessment

People have goals because there is something missing, they are not at the desired state. A goal is where you are heading to – better health, more money, a loving relationship, improved sleep. In order to know if you are making progress toward the goal, or if you have reached the goal, you need to have a sense of where you started, the current state. Later in this chapter, and again in Chapter 8 on Continual Improvement, we will take a look at the Learning Life Problem Solving Model (PSM). The PSM is a useful tool for creating a solid plan to reach your goals. It is a core method we will be working with in this book. The model includes an initial assessment of the current state. How much are you smoking right now, how many hours of quality sleep are you getting each night, how much money are you spending on coffee and sweets per week. You cannot say, "My goal is to sleep 7 hours a night," if you do not know what your current sleep pattern is, the average, not one or two nights. Without doing an initial valid assessment how would not know if you needed to increase or decrease to reach 7 hours. We will discuss this more at the end of this chapter and in Chapter 8.

Realistic and Subject to Modification

Another key aspect of good goals is that they are realistic and subject to modification as needed. Besides being something that you really want (personal and relevant), they are also something that you can actually attain (realistic). That is an important consideration. If you want to perform as a solo pianist in Carnegie Hall that is going to require a lifetime commitment to music generally and to the piano specifically, not to mention a great deal of natural ability. For the sake of happiness and accomplishment it is useful to pick a goal that you can reach. If you set the bar too high it can be very frustrating and lead to abandoning the goal all together. Pick an attainable goal, reach it, then raise the bar to the next level with a new goal (create a new problem). If you recognize that the goal is too high, not attainable, not reasonable given your current resources of time, energy, or motivation, then you need to modify that goal. That is not a failure, it is a responsible decision that will allow you to be successful. Raising the bar to high for the horse to jump over does not teach the horse anything about successful jumping. It reinforces the perception of not possible. That only blocks learning and growth.

Remember, the value of goals is to not to just have goals. Who cares about that? That is like having money but never investing or spending any of it. The value of a goal comes from its fruits. The purpose of goals is to move forward, to climb higher, to have more fun, to grow as a human being, to achieve your dreams. I need to say that again, just to hear myself say it. The purpose of your goals is not to just to have goals. The purpose of a goal is to create a clear vision of where you want to go, to head out, and to get there. *The goal of a goal is to achieve the goal.* One more time for us slow learners. The purpose of a goal is not to have a goal. The purpose of a goal is to help us achieve the goal. So change the goal if it is not working. Drop the goal if it is not real. Otherwise live it, do it, make it happen.

Specific

Goals also need to be specific. It is insufficient to say, "I am going to be happy." Uh, ok? What is happiness and when will that happen exactly? The goal needs to be specific to you, your life, now and in the not too distant future. It is not just, "I will progress in my job," but specifically, "I will be promoted to assistant manager (specific what) by my next birthday (specific when)." Not, "I will improve my running time," but rather, "I will run an 8 minute mile (what) by the end of summer (when)." Not, "I will be more friendly," but instead, "This month I will say hello to at least three new people (what) every week (by when)."

In reality it is actually quite fine to have meta-goals like being happier, healthier, more financially stable. "I am going to be super healthy!" is an excellent goal. The main point is that a goal like that is waaaaaaaaay too generic, and as a result does not really mean anything at all. It is just too vague to actually give you any ideas about what to do next. It is not actionable, not taskable, does not give you a sense of the 'how'. If you do not know what to do, you do nothing, and you know what comes from that – NOTHING! *SIMPLE RULE* when thinking about writing a goal consider this – *does the goal, as written, give you a good idea about what you need to do next?* When you have a clear 'what and when' it is easier to come up with the 'how'.

A good goal has that kind of specificity. It gives you a sense of exactly what steps you will need to take to get there, because there is a there, there. You have a clear sense of where you want to go – promotion to assistant manager by next birthday. Clear, specified goals help to focus and motivate action because they point unambiguously at the target. You know what the target is and where the target is. You aim your bow and shoot. Each arrow gives you information on what you need to correct to get closer to the bulls eye. How could we ever expect the archer to hit the bulls eye if she did not know what the target was. Specific goals point in a specific direction, and that allows you to get up and start walking in that direction, step by step. Research shows that clear goals increase performance because they provide a basis for more accurate feedback on progress which improves the sense of self-efficacy (Bandura, 1988; Locke, et al., 1981).

Measurable

Good goals are measurable, an important aspect of goal specificity. They provide information on how much and by when, important for tracking and feedback. When a goal is measurable it is possible to see how close or how far one is from the bulls eye. Running an 8-minute mile by the end of the summer is specific and also easily measurable. "I will get a lot of reading done this month," is not specific and not measurable. What would you be measuring, how much is a lot? If, however, the goal is to read 8 chapters by the end of the month, then it is easy to count the chapters to see if the goal has been met 30 days later. It also helps with planning, 2 chapters a week would be a reasonable plan. With this new level of detail it is possible to count chapters each week, assess progress each week, and modify behavior accordingly. The open-ended quality of "get a lot of reading done" makes it harder to pace work – how many chapters per week. It also makes it harder to know when to stop – how many chapters is enough. Such a lack of goal clarity can create stress, because you do not really know what you are supposed to do, what is good enough. Goal ambiguity can also reduce the reward that naturally comes when you hit a clear target. When you clearly know what the goal is and you reach it there is a natural sense of accomplishment and pride. It is intrinsically rewarding. Also, when a bigger goal is broken down to subgoals – 8 books per month is 2 books per week – hitting subgoals allows for multiple rewards along the way and that can help to sustain motivation.

Making goals measurable also helps to make them realistic. If the count is too high (read 15 books) or the time frame too short (in one month) the goal can be become discouraging and counterproductive, a set up for failure. Creating measurable goals requires some forethought, but if done well it increases the likelihood that those goals will be more realistic. When setting goals it can be helpful to do some research to get a more realistic sense of parameters. How many hours does a typical student need to study each week to master Spanish or Arabic. Those are very different languages and for most students they would typically require quite different amounts of study times. Not knowing that information can result in goals set at the wrong levels. That is a common problem for many students the first year or two of college, they underestimate the amount of time they will need to devote to a particular subject in order to display the required level of mastery. Such information can often be found online or by asking a knowledgeable person, like a teacher or someone else who has mastery in the target behavior. The goal is to reach the goal, not to set oneself up for frustration and failure. Success breeds success.

Time-lined and Proximal

As described above, an important measure is time duration, when will the goal be accomplished. If you say you are going to run a mile in 8 minutes that is great, but by when are you going to do that? Good intentions can go nowhere fast if there is no deadline, no timeframe. A deadline makes the goal real as it puts it into the living matrix of time and space, where all change happens. (We will look at that in more detail in Chapter 9 when we examine change management). It is tremendously helpful to have a solid sense of when you plan to complete the task, and that timeframe needs to be a realistic. Specifying the timeframe, the 'when', makes goals specific and measurable. One of the reasons people fail, or do not even begin, is that they have unrealistic timelines. "I will read 15 books in one month. I will lose twenty pounds in two weeks." Good luck! Not going to happen for most people. It is very important to get into the habit of thinking about when you expect to be able to complete something, realistically, given all the other demands in your life, from work to fun. Look at your calendar and make a plan. Once you get a realistic sense of the timeframe make that information part of your goal.

Technique: When you want to estimate time to completion, your 'estimated time of arrival', try this. Sit down and close your eyes, get a sense of how much work is involved, what other obligations you have. Let your inner clock give you an estimated time to completion. Allow yourself to get a sense of the date and time of day. Do not think about it. Let it come to you. I encourage you to try this inner clock approach for a while. In time you can develop a reasonably good ability to ballpark the time to completion. I am often quite amazed at the accuracy of some of my time to completion estimates using this method, and I am talking weeks later, even months, not just a day or two.)

When considering your time-line it can be quite useful to focus on proximal versus distal goals, goals that are closer to home, more within reach. This is the small steps approach, breaking the long journey into shorter trips. A related study found that students given one of seven possible problems to solve in one session did better in terms of performance, interest, and self-efficacy than students who were given all seven problems to solve in a longer timeframe, a more distal goal (Bandura & Schunk, 1981). Lifetime goals are essential, crucial to living the big dream. If you only have big dream goals, however, it can be harder to get traction, to get real, to get moving. "I am going to be rich," is great, and big. "I will save an extra $1,000 in my ROTH IRA this year," is proximal and reasonable, and if you do that consistently over time and invest well you can get rich.

Most of us would be happy to have more money, even a bit more now and then. The person who actually saves the extra $1,000 is the one who is that much closer to reaching the goal of long-term financial freedom. For the sake of action it can be useful to work on small, practical goals, with shorter, more proximal end points, small steps. The journey of a thousand miles begins with a single footstep, and then the first mile, and then the first mountain, and so on. Do not just think of the final destination. Think of the next rock outcropping as you hike up the mountain. That outcropping is something you can see from here, the top of the mountain is not even visible yet, maybe it will not become visible until you actually reach the top. By choosing something closer as your next goal, something more visible, you will be more likely to reach it. That will make you feel like you are making progress, and that will help you to keep going all the way to the top of the mountain. Frustration is discouraging, success is encouraging. Small steps lead to success.

Taskable/Actionable

We have discussed the what and when. The next essential consideration is the how, the steps to make the goal alive, to make it real. A goal is where you end up, the destination. To get to that destination you have to take steps, perform a series of tasks, take action. Having clear goals helps in this regard, as it makes thinking about those specific steps or tasks more obvious. For example, consider the goal, "I will be healthier this year." What on earth does that mean, what steps would you take to do that? There are so many possible options, from food, to exercise, to attitude, to quitting smoking or cutting out sugar. Consider this goal, "I will run an eight minute mile by the end of the year." The specified goal makes thinking about the related tasks more obvious, much easier to visualize. It helps you to think about the 'how', how you will implement and accomplish that goal. The how, the specific tasks to reach that goal could include purchasing new running shoes, finding a group of local runners to workout with, creating a weekly running schedule, timing laps, and recording changes in time per mile from month to month.

In Chapter 8 we will consider the concept of small steps, an important part of the continual improvement process. One of the things that often stops people in their tracks is that the problem looks to big, the mountain appears too high. If you can break the process into smaller tasks, smaller steps, actionable tasks that lead to the ultimate goal, then it becomes much more manageable, much less daunting. It is very helpful to conceptualize the solution in smaller bites, the next actionable task, not the whole show. This is critical – think in terms of actionable (able to act on) tasks, the obvious next steps, small enough to know specifically what to do. Those are the individual stepping stones to reaching the goal, the desired state.

Written Out Clearly and Visible for Reinforcement

To be useful a tool has to be available. It is nice to have a top quality knife in your kitchen, but if it is so precious that you never use it then what good is it. It becomes a waste of space, a wasted resource, an unfulfilled potential. It is better to have a cheaper knife that you actually use. Your goals need to be like that. They need to be useful, which means they need to be practical, available, visible, memorable, real. It can be very empowering to have a short list of primary life goals etched in your mind and heart, memorized. Those goals will guide your life because you know them, because you are committed to them, because you live them. "I live my goals." It is a fortunate person who can say that. Creating a list of core life goals can take some time, but that is a very worthwhile project. The best goals are clearly written out and visible. They are carried in your wallet, or posted on your wall, or at the top of your daily to do list, or best of all – memorized, taken to heart, in your heart, by heart. Visibility and accessibility help to make them real, make them useful. Research has shown that explicit challenging goals increase motivation (Locke, Shaw, Saari, & Latham, 1981).

Monitored for Progress

As mentioned above, good goals are specific, measurable, and time-lined. You have a goal to run a 7-minute mile and you are trying to run five times a week. You go into action and you start running. An essential part of your training includes monitoring progress. Monitoring progress provides essential information on whether you are sticking with your plan and if it is working or not. Both are important, tracking implementation and outcomes.

So let us say you are running and monitoring your workouts. You notice that you are never doing more than 3 or 4 runs a week. The plan you originally implemented was to run 5 days a week. You look over the information you have collected and you can see that the problem is probably due to the time of day you set for training, running after work. Reflecting on that you recognize that you are often too tired for a run at the end of the workday. With this monitoring data you recognize the issue and you adjust accordingly, building in a few morning runs. Within a week you are now running five days a week, consistently. Every Saturday morning you do a time trial and you log that information on your tracking sheet. You decide to plot it so you can visually see what is happening. Over the next three months you see your mile times decreasing, getting closer to your goal of a

7-minute mile. Some weeks may actually show a slow down, but over, you are heading in the right direction.

Monitoring helps you to know if you are on task and if you are making progress. It can also be a source of inspiration and motivation as you see yourself advancing toward your goal day by day, week by week, month by month. Every day you run you mark a big X on your calendar. Seeing those visual cues of commitment and success can be quite encouraging. Formal self-monitoring and progress feedback has been found to be related to increased skill levels, higher self-efficacy, and greater skill maintenance (Schunk, 1983; Zimmerman & Paulsen, 1995). Research has also shown that simple tracking methods which allow one to see completion, taking steps toward a goal, can lead to improved performance (Shapiro, 1984).

Contingency Plans Considered

Another aspect of good goal planning is the inclusion of contingency plans, the Plan B. This is not necessary for every goal, but for some it can be a very good idea, especially where success is important, where failure would be a serious problem. The basic notion is that if things do not go according to plan you have a back up that allows you to continue to make progress. It is your plan B, in the event plan A crashes and burns. If you have pre-thought alternatives ahead of time you will be ready to make the swap as needed. When is this useful? If the cost of failure is high, or if there are unpredictable element in the process, then having an alternative can be something to consider. Let's say a parent is taking classes and needs to study after dinner, plan A. That parent has a daughter in second grade. Sometimes she requires help with homework at night, or just needs attention. That requires a plan B to reduce the stress of unpredictability and to maintain productivity. In that scenario, the contingency plan (Plan B) could include the parent and child studying together, the parent doing homework when the child goes to sleep, or the parent doing homework on the ride to work in the morning.

Challenging

Do your goals help you to grow? Another important aspect to consider is whether your goals, at least some of them, make you stretch. Do they make you a better person, healthier, wiser, more financially secure, smarter, more employable, a better parent, more confident. We all have room to grow, room for improvement. A good goal will facilitate growth. One of my mentors used to say that if you are always hitting the bulls eye then you are too close to the target. He would push the target further away so you had to pull deeper, find a new strategy, a new skill, a new level of composure. We do not grow so much when we do things we are already good at. We are already good at it! The place for greater growth is in some area of weakness, where we lack knowledge and skill, the place where we make mistakes. That is the obvious place for growth. There is clear room for improvement. The place we fall, is also where we rise. Realizing that simple fact can change a person's life completely. It is the root of never giving up.

When I first moved back to San Francisco I was teaching part-time in the SFSU Multimedia Studies. During that time I had the good fortune to meet Doug Engelbart, who was instrumental in the creation of the computer mouse and GUI. (GUI stands for graphical user interface. It is the interactive clickable icon format used in computers, tablets and phones that we are all familiar with today.) Prior to the creation of GUI a person would have to enter lines of text prompts to tell the computer what it was supposed to do. It was cumbersome and way not user-friendly. Doug Engelbart changed all that. I remember when he came to talk one evening to a small group of students and faculty about emerging technologies. Doug shared an experience from his life. He described coming back from the war with a dream of having a good job, nice car, comfortable home. One day he was driving from work, realizing that he had all that, and wondered if he could do more. He committed to doing more, to doing something that would change the world, and he did. His work revolutionized computing and telecommunications. Doug's goals were very big, world changing, not driven by a desire for fame or fortune, but by a desire to do something of value. He was quite an impressive chap.

Holistic

Good goals are holistic, they consider the whole person. If a single goal consumes a tremendous amount of life energy there will be a cost in other areas of life. There is only so much time in a day, in a life. We need to be conscious of how we allocate that time. If a person just chase the almighty dollar, all work and no play, health may be sacrificed. A singular focus on appearance and weight loss could cover the deeper need for self-acceptance. Life balance is an important idea to keep in mind when developing goals, considering all of the important domains of one's life.

Acted On

Finally, our goals are only as good as the actions that emerge from them. It is not just about having a goal that produces the desired result, it is about taking action on that goal as well. Goals are only as useful as the empowered actions that come from them. Action is what leads to attaining our goals. You can do all the imaging and meditating and praying and wishing and complaining in the world, but that will not get you to your desired state. You have to go after what you want in life. Pursue it with all of your energy. Every now and then you run into a person who really wants to change the world. They have a clear vision. They want to become a Supreme Court justice, or win a Nobel Prize. They may never attain those dreams, but you can bet that many of those individuals will make significant progress down their chosen path.

There is an old adage from the East, which says that paper cakes do not satisfy hunger. Goals only point the way. They are the first line in the story, "Once upon a time there was a small peasant child who dreamed of being the greatest magician of all time…" Things will not change or fall into place just because time passes and we get older. They fall into place because we make it happen, we take responsibility, we face the challenge with commitment to our dream and to our own life. The goal points the way, then one needs to start that journey, taking the first small step, and then the next.

Detached

One final thought. There is a verse in the Indian epic, the Bhagavad Gita, that captures much of the essence of the book. It states, " Fixed in yoga, do thy work, O Winner of wealth (Arjuna), abandoning attachment, with an even mind in success and failure, for evenness of mind is called yoga" (Radhakrishnan). The idea is that it is important to take our responsibilities seriously, but to not become to attached to the fruits of our actions, not to be overly attached to a particular outcome. When we get too attached to the goal it is possible to miss out on life, all of the beauty of the moments along the way. It can also cause stress and actually impair performance. It is important to live in the moment with an open heart and a clear mind. There is no reason to become obsessed with any particular moment. Each goal achieved becomes a memory. This too shall pass.

Academic and Personal Goal Clarification

Practices that have been found to facilitate student success include clear and committed goals, that are implemented and tracked; efficient management of time, social context, and stress; an internal locus of control, or taking responsibility for outcomes, positive self-talk, building on small successes, and ongoing reflection on the process (Bandura, 1997; Schunk & Zimmerman, 1994; 1998). We will cover each of these topics in this text, but importantly, you can see it all starts with good goals. Creating useful goals is an essential theme in this book. So this is a good time to take a moment and work on some goals of your own. We will approach this process by considering the basic questions of who, what, where, when and how. First some definitions and then some writing.

Core Values

The first step is to think about personal values. Values reflect the who in life, the who you are, what you stand for. If you value something you take care of it, you nurture it, you protect it, you want it to last. It is the same with our own values. The things we value in our life are the things we will nurture, protect and grow. Bernard of Clairvaux, the founder of the Cistercian monks once wrote, "That which we love we shall come to resemble." If you value someone, love someone, you we will protect them from harm. If you value a belief we will defend it from reproach. If you value health you will nurture and maintain it. We all have values, but they are not always obvious, because we do not necessarily think about them so much, they are just a part of who we are. Being more consciously aware of our values, however, can help us to choose the most appropriate goals, and to be more committed to those goals. Some people really value money, for others it is less important. It can be hard to motivate a person with the reward of making more money if that is not a high value for them. I once had a student who possessed a high aptitude for both math and writing. His parents valued stability and income and wanted him to be an engineer. He valued creativity and language and wanted to be a writer. I suspect he is writing today.

> **CORE VALUES**
>
> Write out a list of core values – what do you really believe in, what do you really value. When you are done with your list, prioritize them, rank most to least important. (You may want to do these activities on a separate sheet of paper so you have more room to think.)
>
> I value _____
>
> _____
>
> _____

Mission

Your mission is the *what*, what you are doing here in the world, your reason for being. Large organizations, from universities to corporations, typically have a mission statement. It is a short phrase that defines what the organization is about, their purpose for being. We can also have our own personal mission statement.

> ### REFLECTION
>
> Creating that statement can help you to think about why you are here, what your purpose is, your added value to this planet. A good mission statement can inspire a person to take bold action....
>
> **Education Mission**
>
> My purpose for getting a degree is _____
>
> _____
>
> **Personal Education**
>
> My purpose for being on the planet is _____
>
> _____

Vision

A vision considers the *where*, the sense of where you expect to be in the future, the desired state. In a vision statement you are describing what your life, your world, will look like at some point in the future. Moses and Muhammad both had visions that helped them to lead. In 1946 Mother Theresa had a vision to leave her teaching position and to begin caring for the poor and sick in the slums of Calcutta. Martin Luther King had a vision in which he hoped that his children would "... one day live in a nation where they will not be judged by the color of their skin but by the content of their character." A vision statement can also consider the when, the time by which the vision will become a reality.

> ### VISION
>
> The next step is to work on your vision statement, where you see yourself a few years from now. For this exercise work on a 3 to 5 year vision. That is far enough out to provide some room for creativity, and not so far into the future as to be essentially unpredictable. To begin the process start with these words and then fill in your response, "Within 5 years I will be..."

Goals

On the surface goals also represent the *what*. This is what I am going to do – run an 8 minute mile, get all A's in my classes, read two more chapters. At their core, however, bigger life goals speak to the *how*. They are the how, the way that you will fulfill your mission, attain your vision, live your values.

> ### GOALS
>
> Now take a moment to consider your future goals. These do not have to be carved in stone. The point is to just loosen up the thought process. For this exercise make a list of goals for each of the following four time blocks: (1) lifetime goals, (2) three to five year goals, (3) one year goals, and (4) quarter/season/semester goals.

Lifetime Goals

_____
_____
_____

3-5 Year Goals

_____
_____

1 Year Goal

_____
_____

Semester/Quarter/Season Goals

_____
_____

Core Life Goals

The final activity is to come up with THE short list of goals that you can memorize and review every day as the basis for your life decisions. These are your CORE LIFE GOALS. This is actually a process that will probably take the majority people a number of years to refine and complete. Now is a good time to start thinking about them and living them. Time for this task, as long as needed, years if necessary, yes, probably years.

_____
_____

Tasks

Tasks are the actual pieces, the small steps, *how* you get to the desired state, *what* you do next. Most goals are accomplished through a series of small steps, often implemented in some relative sequence. Goals are powerful, very important. That said, your goals are only as potent as the implemented tasks that emerge from them. You have to take action, and the relevant, specific next task is that action. To get clear on goal accomplishment it is important to think about the series of tasks that are involved in getting you there.

The Learning Life Problem Solving Model (PSM)

In this final section we are going to look at a very simple, useful, and powerful model for thinking about goals and creating a practical plan to achieve them – the Learning Life Problem Solving Model. The basic elements of the model include the following: (1) the current state, where you are right now; (2) the desired state, where you want to be; (3) the problem assessment, defining the problem, what is keeping you from being where you want to be; (4) the solution space, the way to get to where you want to be; (5) the monitoring plan to track your process and progress as you implement your chosen solution; (6) the evaluation of the outcome and preparing for the next step; and (7) celebration.

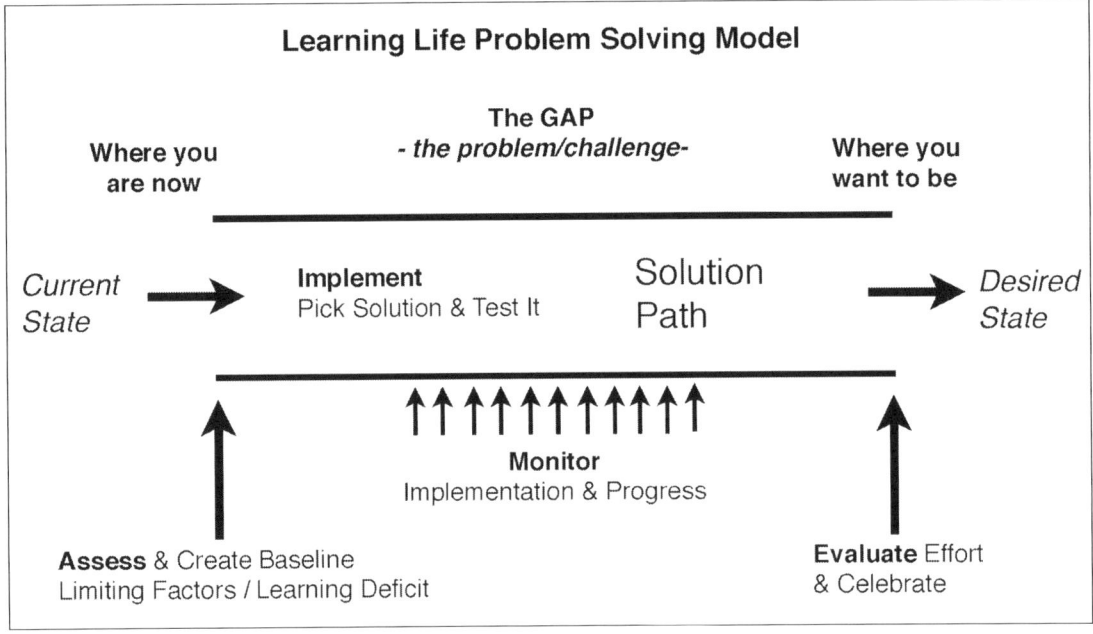

The PSM is a problem solving strategy. It follows a path – where you are, where you want to be, and the way to get there. It begins with the recognition that there is a problem, challenge, or issue. That problem/challenge is the gap between the current state and the desired state. Recognition of that gap might be the result of simple biology, we realize we are hungry. We want food (desired state), have no food (current state), need to get food (the gap). It may be social. A group of people recognize economic disparity resulting from racism, sexism, or some other societal forces. They want a fair days pay for a fair days work, they are not getting one, they organize to obtain it. The awareness might even come mystically, like the angel who appeared to Joseph in a dream saying that King Herod had died. On that news the family left Egypt and went back to Nazareth. Wherever your inspiration comes from, your body, your colleagues, an angel, there is an awareness of a desired state, somewhere you want to be that is different from where you are. If there is the possibility to act, and sufficient motivation to act, then solutions are considered, a path is selected, and the journey begins. The model flow, as represented in the figure below is the basic approach we will use to work with goals in this book. We will come back to it again in more detail when we start working with the principles of continual improvement in Chapter 8.

The Elements of the Learning Life Problem Solving Model (PSM)

1. Current State (Present Moment/Reality/What is)
The Current State is where you are at the moment. The Current State can be very good or very bad, or anywhere in between. Whatever it is, it is what it is.

2. Desired State (Goal)
The Desired State is where you want to be, something else is desired, something different from what currently is. The Desired State can be a source of great discontent, great inspiration, or both. The Desired State has the potential to become the goal if it generates sufficient motivation and commitment, or it can just be something we ignore, deny, or wish for, possibly for years, and never clarify or commit to as an actionable goal.

3. The Gap (The Problem)
The Gap is the difference, the space between Current and Desired States, between where you are and where you want to be, the space between wanting and having (Desired - Current = Gap/Problem). This Gap can create a tension (positive or negative) that can motivate action, trigger apathy or depression, generate self-loathing or envy, or simply be an observed experience in the moment. All of these options are fine, quite human, but the inspiration to act is what moves a person toward the Desired State.

4. Problem Assessment / Limiting Factors
Once you have a sense of the Desired State you need to Assess the Current State. The first assessment is to see if the Desired State actually merits your attention, energy and money. Does it fit your values, longer term vision, core life goals? Do you really need a new pair of shoes, a second latte, another night out with friends instead of studying? Goals that are driven by unconstructive dissatisfaction, unproductive social comparison (envy), or unconscious habitual responding (such as an addictive pattern), can lead to a desire for things that have no core value and as such result in efforts that are more likely than not to be a waste of time, money and energy. Those goals are not efficient, less value-based, less authentic, less enduring, less rewarding, less worthy of action. They do not serve your greater good or that of the planet. They do not fundamentally strengthen or improve you at a fundamental or core level. Another assessment is to determine if you have the resources of time, money, energy, now or in the future, to get to the Desired State. There is not much point in jumping through hoops in hopes of getting something that is clearly out of reach at this point in time. All things come to those who are patient they say.

If the Desired State appears to be a valid need, and if there are sufficient resources and motivation to consider acting on it, then the next assessment is to consider why you are not at the Desired State already. This is where we get into problem solving mode. What is the limiting factor? Is that limitation modifiable? Sometimes there is nothing you can do about it. If the Desired State is to be a foot taller so you can play professional basketball, that is not going to happen. One could use creative ways to meet that kind of Desired State, such as very high platform sneakers. That would solve the height need, but would still not open the door to the NBA, unless the shoes were made of flubber, and those are hard to find. Success in this Learning Life Problem Solving Model is based on things we can actually change, things we can learn to do differently.

One of the best ways to get a handle on the problem, why we are not in the Desired State yet, is to look for information that answers the question, "Why am I not there yet?" Are there things in the *environment* contributing to the problem? What particular ***behaviors*** keep you where you are? What is happening inside, at the *person* level, what are you thinking, feeling, what is your state of mind and body, your beliefs about self, others, life? Also pay attention to things that set the pattern off. If the desired state is to maintain your cool, you need to begin to recognize what triggers your anger. Another useful piece of information is to notice the consequences, what happens when you do get angry. This cause and effect information can be useful, both in terms of increasing motivation and potentially in terms of understanding the overall pattern. This helps you begin to recognize the root of the problem that needs to be addressed. Collecting the pieces of the puzzle can help you to get a better sense of the whole picture. This is a very important step.

So take notes on what the pattern looks like, when do you do what you do, think what you think, what seems to set it off, what are the consequences, who is involved, where are you, what is the state of mind and body before and after? As an example consider current state equals a real problem with procrastination. Desired state equals getting work done on time. Assessing why not there yet – look at procrastination – when does it happen, for how long, how are you feeling (emotionally, physically), what are you thinking (before, during, and after), how do you procrastinate specifically, and what are the consequences. As you collect these pieces of the puzzle in time you will get a much clearer picture of what is going on.

5. Solution Path

Once it is clear what the limiting factor is the next step is to decide on the best solution to get to the Desired State. This is another critical element. There are many roads you can take to get to New York City, but some would be terribly slow. You want to find the most efficient way to move forward, the most direct path. Finding the best path can be a process that requires some research and reflection. We will look at ways to approach this process in more detail in Chapter 8 on Continual Improvement.

One important thing to consider is that the solution is often not a single element. Let us say that the goal is to ride a bike. The solution space in learning to ride a bike includes pedaling, balancing, steering, sufficient velocity and so on. Maria procrastinates when she has a large writing assignment. The big assignment makes her feel uncomfortable (anxious). When anxious about work she tends to distract herself instead and spends time on the internet rather than working. By collecting some assessment data she begins to see the picture – anxiety triggered by large writing assignment leading to avoidant behavior. Her solution space might include a number of elements including learning some relaxations skills, practicing calming and encouraging self-talk, implementing some time management strategies such as marking specific study periods into her calendar, using rewards for task accomplishment, and breaking the big task of writing the large paper into smaller steps that are less threatening. The solution often involves multiple components.

6. Implementation and Monitoring

Once you implement your specific solution you need to collect some information to see how things are going. This involves two steps. First you need to have some baseline data to know where you start. You may already have this from the assessment phase. Second you need to collect data as you proceed to see if you are on task, consistently implementing the solution elements and to see if you are making progress toward the goal. Monitoring information will help with both. Is the solution you have chosen working for you? Are you getting dates, better grades, making more money, feeling more fit, having more fun? If the answer is no, or if those things are happening more slowly than you think they should be, or if some elements are working better than others, then it might be time to reassess the chosen solution and mix things up a bit. The monitoring process allows you to track your implementation (are you running every day, keeping up with homework) and evaluate your progress (what was my time this week running 4 miles, how much reading did I complete). This is a very important part of the model. It is like looking at the map – am I still on the right road, and how many miles did I cover today.

7. Evaluation

After a period of time you need to reflect on the process. What worked, what did not, if not, what is the next solution to try, what to salvage from the last trial, what new to bring in. If certain things worked well it is important to consider ways to standardize them, to make them part of how you will do business from here on out.

8. Celebrating

Need I say more. No matter what outcome, you tried. That is good. The next step is to enjoy the fruits of your effort and continue building from your new level of success, try again if it did not work, or to admit that this particular goal is not practical right now. All good. Nothing ventured, nothing gained. Tomorrow is another day.

SUMMARY

Goals are essential for a successful life. Good goals are the result of reflection and planning and help us to prioritize what is important. They focus energy. They inspire action because they lead to rewards, to a sense of accomplishment and meaning. They are a root to persistent action, especially in the face of adversity. Good goals can be characterized as being personal and relevant, specific and realistic, measurable and actionable. Powerful personal goals emerge over time as we more deeply understand our own values, vision, and mission. Once goals are clarified they need to be acted on, otherwise they are just wishes. A useful approach to putting goals into action is to think in terms of small steps, the sequence of specific tasks that lead to goal achievement. It is also to work on goals from a problem solving perspective. The problem is the gap between the current state (no goal accomplishment) to desired state (goal achieved). Having a specific strategy to map that territory and make that journey is a key to efficient and effective progress in life. The Learning Life Problem Solving Model is a very useful tool in this regard. Knowing what we need or want, and taking skillful action to reach that place, is a root to a happy life.

REFERENCES

Bandura, Albert. Self-regulation of motivation and action through goal systems. In: Hamilton V, Bower GH, Frijda NH, editors. *Cognitive Perspectives on Emotion and Motivation. NATO ASI Series Volume 44.* Dordrecht, The Netherlands: Kluwer Academic Publishers; 1988:37-61.

Bandura A, Schunk DH. Cultivating competence, self-efficacy and intrinsic interest through proximal self-motivation. *Journal of Personality and Social Psychology.*1981;41:586-598.

Elliot J, McGregor HA, Gable S. Achievement goals, study strategies, and exam performance: A mediational analysis. *Journal of Educational Psychology.* 1999;91(3):549-563.

Fareri DS, Martin LN, Delgado MR. Reward-related processing in the human brain: developmental considerations. *Development and psychopathology.* 2008;20(04):1191-1211.

Kobasa SC. Stressful life events, personality, and health: An inquiry into hardiness. *Journal of Personality and Social Psychology.* 1979;37(1):1-11.

Locke EA, Shaw KN, Saari LM, Latham GP. Goal setting and task performance: 1969-1980. *Psychological Bulletin.* 1981;90(1);125-152.

Roberson L. Prediction of job satisfaction from characteristics of personal work goals. *Journal of Organizational Behavior.* 1990;11(1):29-41.

Rotter JB. *Social Learning and Clinical Psychology.* New York: Prentice-Hall; 1954.

Schunk DH. Progress self-monitoring: Effects on children's self-efficacy and achievement. *Journal of Experimental Education.* 1983;51:89-93.

Shapiro ES. Self-monitoring procedures. In: Ollendick TH, Hersen M, editors. *Child Behavior Assessment: Principles and Procedures.* New York: Pergamon; 1984:148-165.

Jun T, Eiji H. Role of the lateral prefrontal cortex in executive behavioral control. *Physiological Reviews.* 2008;88:37-57.

Zimmerman BJ, Paulsen AS. Self-monitoring during collegiate studying: An invaluable tool for academic self-regulation. *New Directions for Teaching and Learning.* 1995;63:13-27.

Imaging Success 3

I can already see that this is going to be one of the best days of my life so far.

CHAPTER THEMES
- Imagery and Self Image
- Learned Helplessness
- Constructive Imagination
- Priming

Mental imagery is one of the ways that our brain processes information, understands experiences, and learns. A good deal of that imagery occurs as unconscious information processing. We also use imagery intentionally and consciously every day. Imagery is essentially imagination, using our imagination to see the outcomes we desire in life. A substantial body of research shows how this creative resource is being applied successfully in sports, the arts, education, medicine and other fields to improve effectiveness. In this chapter we will explore how to use mental imagery to achieve goals and build greater success in school and life. It is simply a matter of using our imagination to light the way.

Research on Imagery

Various models have been proposed to explain the phenomena of mental imagery. Some models suggest that visual mental imagery uses many of the same neural processes that we use in our normal visual perception (Farah, 1989). Other work suggests that mental imagery employs some unique neural processes (Bartolomeo, 2008; Ganis et al., 2004; Gardini et al., 2008). Despite a lack of agreement regarding underlying mechanisms there is great deal of evidence supporting the value of mental imagery for goal achievement, motor skill acquisition, improving health, and many other applications. It is, for example, becoming an increasingly important tool in healing, commonly used by cancer patients for managing anxiety, pain, the side-effects of treatment, and to enhance well-being (Bakke et al., 2002; Barnes et al., 2004; Carlson & Bultz, 2008; Kwekkeboom, 2001). Imagery also has a long history of use in sports. A review of studies of athletic imagery provides significant evidence of benefit for managing anxiety and coping with performance stress, improving specific sports skills, and increasing self efficacy and persistence (Driskell et al., 1994;

Martin et al., 1999; Martin & Hall, 1995). Mental imagery is also used effectively in education, including use for attention training, improving academic self-efficacy and performance, reducing test anxiety, and enhancing commitment to academics (Galyean, 1982; Oettingen, 2000; Sapp, 1994; Tartaglia et al., 2009).

Beliefs and the Nature of Self

Why use mental imagery as a tool for academic and life success? To help answer that question we need to briefly consider the nature of self, and the role that beliefs play in informing our sense of self. Philosophers and scientists have explored the issue of self for millennia. It is one of the fundamental questions of our human existence – what is the self? For the moment we want to consider two fundamental dimensions of self – the essential/ intrinsic/ inherent/ elemental/ indwelling/ native/ constitutional self and the social self. The essential self can be thought of as the self of the innocent infant – undifferentiated, egoless, simple, pure consciousness. Regaining that self is the goal of deep meditation. The social self, by contrast, is the constructed sense of self that emerges throughout the lifespan. It is the basis of our self image. That is the one what we want to look at now in relation to beliefs.

Self Image

The social self is a vast collection of experiences, ideas, and memories that have been gathered together over the course of lifetime. From these diverse inputs we build a framework of beliefs about self and the world, our multidimensional self image. The social self is sometimes referred to as the narrative self, because it is the story by which we know ourselves. It is the story in our heads that reminds us of who we are, where we are from, and how we should think and act. It is the "I am ....a tall, upper class, conservative, ex-smoking, female, lacrosse playing, Argentinean, who likes to travel" voice. It is central to our personal identity and to our interpretation of daily experiences.

This social self is like a piece of plain white cotton cloth that has been dyed orange. That orange color becomes an integral aspect of the cloth. Indeed, the cloth is now known by that label – the orange cloth. The label helps to differentiate it from other cloths in the bin, useful information. The labels we acquire over a lifetime, "slow learner, middle class, depressed," can be like that. We are no longer just a cloth, we are an *orange* cloth. Those labels become an integral element of self identity. The problem is that there is a good possibility that some of those labels were never correct in the first place, or if they were, they are not accurate now, or even if they are correct, it does not mean that characteristic cannot be changed. Those truths, however, can be hard to recognize and equally hard to change.

Does that matter? Yes, it matters. It matters because this conditioned mind, this mind that has picked up beliefs over time about self, others and the world, can be both powerfully facilitative and powerfully inhibiting. Beliefs about the inferiority of a race, gender, age group, religious orientation, or a culture can lead to very oppressive behaviors that are counterproductive for the oppressed individuals and for the society at large. The challenge is that because these beliefs are a fundamental part of who we perceive ourselves to be, and how the world expects us to be, they can be very resistant to change.

Revisioning Self

The good news is that these beliefs about self and the world are like any other beliefs. They are learned concepts, learned constructs. Because they are learned they can be unlearned, and potentially with dramatic effect. A wonderful tale reflecting this potential for revisioning is the story of the ugly duckling. As you may recall the ugly duckling was a swan, who came to believe that is was a duck, a basic case of mistaken identity. The unfortunate thing for that swan was that it was not a duck. So for its entire life it was vexed by a sense of difference, a sense of being unattractive, being too big, gangly, odd. Then one day as fate would have it the ugly duck came upon a family of swans and recognized itself as one of them. It was informed of its true nature by the image of those swans. That image awakened imagination, and new possibilities.

Can you imagine what the experience would have been for the swan in that moment, when it remembered its true nature? That was the moment of awakening to core self, transcending the memory of acquired social identity of ugly ducklingness. In that moment there was a recognition that everything it had always believed about itself, its inferiority, its imperfection, its not fitting in, was a misperception of self, a misunderstanding of true nature, an untruth. In that moment all of the past was immediately changed. There was an immediate and comprehensive shift into a new and positive re-memory of self, an instantaneous 'remembering' of self. In that *aha* moment it realized that, "I have always been a beautiful swan." Simultaneously, in that moment the possibilities of a new future vision emerged, a sense of self-pride, a sense of belonging to a community of equals, a sense of worth and worthiness. "I am a beautiful swan." This simple tale shows both the limiting and liberating power of belief and the malleability of such beliefs. One bird, two lives, based on two very different beliefs about what it thought itself to be – a duck and a swan. In the moment of realization of its real nature, in that instant, the swan's beliefs shifted creating a radical transformation of past, present and future. In that moment, everything changed.

Just like that, through a single, powerful insight, in a moment, all of time and space can change. Instant awakening, satori. Beliefs about self, others and the world are learned constructs. They are instruction sets that we have been given about who we are, about our place in the world, and about the role, place and value of others. It is what the Eastern meditation traditions call conditioned mind. Fortunately, because these are learned constructs we have the capacity to unlearn them. Certainly it can be a long road that will require a good deal of effort, but the potential for change is there. In some fundamental way everything in existence is relative. It all depends on our perspective, on where we are standing right now, on what we choose to look at, where we place our awareness and attention. That is why two people can look at the same thing and hold radically different beliefs about it. It depends on what you choose to see.

Learned Helplessness

Our beliefs about self, others and the world can be highly facilitative, such as beliefs that we are capable, lovable, and good. They can also be equally disabling and limiting, like holding beliefs that we are flawed, unlovable, or of little value to the world. Importantly, whether those beliefs are supportive or obstructive, they can be highly resistant to change. They form our identity, and that identity reinforces and protects itself.

Consider this for a moment. Imagine a child who is raised by a stay-at-home parent. The child will spend the bulk of each day with that person. By the age of five the child has had about 20,000 hours of contact time with the parent, 20,000 hours of one-on-one instruction. Now consider for a moment how the beliefs of that child would look if that parent were a damaged human being. The child would experience hour after hour, day after day of insult, humiliation, physical abuse, neglect, all manner of instruction about his or her unworthiness, incompetence, vulnerability, imperfection and unlovability.

What effect do you think that would have on the youngster? That parent is a very powerful and important source of information for that child. Compared with adults like you and me, that youngster has very few points of reference to assess the accuracy of the information he or she is receiving. If some stranger came up to you and told you that you were an idiot it is very doubtful that you would agree. Many of us would be inclined to think (possibly say), 'No, YOU are an idiot." So if that child gets 20,000 hours of instruction about his or her imperfection, that messaging penetrates the fibers of the cloth deeply. That cloth is now very orange. The child sees orange when he or she looks in the mirror. Many people in the world will also start to see orange when that youngster speaks and acts. The story, the orange cloth label, begins to reinforce itself, becomes the truth. That story deepens over time, the world begins to support the story, the idea of questioning it does not arise. That story will continue, like a dream, until something wakes that person up. Sadly, many individuals only wake up when something very negative happens, and many others never wake up at all.

Findings on Learned Helplessness

One powerful example comes from pioneering research conducted by Martin Seligman, a professor of psychology at the University of Pennsylvania. He was doing graduate work on animal experimental psychology, with an interest in depression. While conducting some conditioning experiments he noticed that the animals became stuck for a period of time. Thinking this was an interesting phenomena he devised some new experiments. The essence of those studies consisted of placing two dogs in harnesses and shocking them. One of the dogs was able to press a panel to end the shock. The other dog had no control over the experience.

Following this conditioning phase the dogs where then placed in separate shuttle cages. Each cage had two compartments separated by a low barrier that the dogs could easily jump over. One side of the cage was wired to deliver an electric shock via a grid floor. The other side of the cage was a safe zone. The dogs were placed in the cages on the electric grids. In this second phase of the study a light would go off. This signaled to the dogs that an electric shock was imminent. It did not take long for the dogs that had control in phase I to learn to jump over to the safe side of the cage and escape shock when the signal light went off.

By contrast, the dog that had no control in the first phase did not respond. Amazingly, time after time that dog just sat there. It whined, whimpered, and got shocked. It did not learn to jump. It did not learn a new behavior to improve its situation. It just endured the abuse, as it had before. According to Seligman and colleagues, the dog had learned that it was helpless, so it did nothing and just endured the pain. It did nothing about it. In subsequent replications of this research it has been found that the majority of animals do not learn to jump to escape pain despite that fact that they are actually free (Seligman, 1972; Seligman & Maier, 1967).

Constructive Imagination — A Tool for Success

We will now look at the use of imagination, of mental imagery, as a tool for purposefully changing the patterns of conditioned mind and body, for working with self image and belief, to enhance effectiveness and life success. Before we start, however, it will be useful to take a moment to understand what makes mental imagery such a productive resource.

Goal Clarification

Of all the benefits to be gained from regular imagery or visualization practice the two most valuable are goal clarification and goal reinforcement. Many people, maybe most, do not write down or meditate on their key life goals in any consistent fashion. If they do write them down, say on New Years Eve, that list of goals all too often finds its way into a folder on a laptop never to be seen again until the following December 31st. That is okay, better than nothing, but obviously goals tucked away cannot serve as powerful reminders of the desired state, cannot be sources of inspiration for a life waiting to be lived. The simple act of daily mental imagery, however, makes us think about important high priority goals on a daily basis. Related research has found that proximal goals, goals that are more immediate, more present in our awareness, are associated with greater self-efficacy and higher quality performance, in part because they are more accessible to real time feedback (Bandura1988; Karniol and Ross 1996).

Vicarious Learning

People frequently learn by observing others. That is called vicarious learning, learning by observing, rather than learning by doing it ourselves. For example, if you see someone unsuccessfully trying to pull a hot piece of corn from the grill you quickly learn that the 'bare-handed corn grab' approach can be a risky enterprise. Because you observed it, you did not have to get burned yourself to learn the lesson. You use the tongs to pick up your corn. Similarly, if you are traveling abroad and you see someone eat an unusual tropical fruit and then they immediately buy three more get a sense that the fruit might be quite enjoyable. Without ever having tasted it you now have a strong interest in trying it yourself.

Neuroscientists have discovered that when we observe someone performing a motor skill, like opening a jar, the same areas of our (observing) brain are firing, just like the brain of the person opening the jar. Those firing neurons are referred to as mirror neurons, like a mirror image. In some ways it is like the mirrors that you find in dance studios. The mirrors help the dancers see what they are doing. They provide time-space-body feedback, which facilitates learning. If your mirror neurons fire to neurologically mimic the activity of the person you are watching, it provides fundamental task information, it facilitates learning (Blanke et al., 2010; Deen & McCarthy, 2010; Miller et al., 2010; Rodrigues et al., 2010). In a similar fashion one can think of mental imagery as a form of vicarious learning. In the case of mental imagery, however, instead of observing an external performance you are observing an internal performance. Research has found that imagery can be an effective form of vicarious learning, and that vicarious learning can increase self-efficacy related to new tasks (Bandura, 1997; Neck & Manz, 1992).

Motivation and Persistence

Another advantage of this type of vicarious learning is that you get to practice the desired outcome, via visualization, as if the desired state was already a reality. That vicarious experience of the desired state, seeing what is possible, feeling the enthusiasm of that successful enactment, increases positive expectancy for the desired outcome, and increases the belief that it is possible. Increased expectancy has been found to be related to greater motivation and the willingness to persist in the face of obstacles (Battle, 1965).

If you watch the Olympics you will see world-class athletes doing mental imagery of the skill they are about to perform. Before the high dive, giant slalom run, or dead lift, you can observe many of those athletes, eyes closed, bodies moving slightly as if they were doing their reverse two-and-a-half somersault. Indeed, they are, in their heads. Highly effective, peak performing individuals, such as elite athletes, will often engage in mental imagery, internally visualizing and experiencing the desired state before they begin. It is a way for those exceptional athletes to enhance their expectancy for successful action, increase their motivation, reduce anxiety and build courage, and optimize their neurology by vicariously running the event mentally. When the athlete or artist performs the target behavior in their head, they vicariously experience a flawless performance. In their mind and body they feel the rush of success as they come out of the water, pass the finish line, hold their racket high taking a first in the Wimbledon. They hear the crowd cheering. They see the trophy.

Do athletes using imagery always cross the finish line first? Of course not. There are many factors involved. They might just be outclassed that day, be recovering from an injury, or be at the end of a long series of performances, so many things. But do they expect to do better because they have already seen the event successfully completed in their mind? Yes. That is why world-class athletes and other top performers use mental imagery. For individuals at the top of their game the mind becomes another resource. It has to be, otherwise it can become a source of failure. I sometimes wonder if that is why elite athletes sometimes appear to be so full of themselves when they are interviewed. On some level, possibly unconsciously, they are just enacting their positive mental frame, which leaves no room for doubt. They want to be the best and do the best so they know they need to use every tool available to them, and what better tool is there to use than a one's own mind. If a person does not believe that he will succeed, then he will be less likely to start and less likely to continue. If, on the other hand, that same person believes he will succeed then he will be more likely to head out in the direction of that dream and persist until it is attained. Seeing (the desired outcome) is believing, and believing generates hope.

The Priming Method

We use mental imagery all the time. Every time we use our imagination to see possibilities we are using it. We use our imagination as we wonder what might be in the box next to the birthday cake, or to imagine what the clueless customer service rep on the phone looks like, or to imagine what the weather will be like tomorrow when we go to the beach, or what it will be like to give a speech in front of 100 people. Imagination is a way we use our mind to look into possible futures, into the unknown. Mental imagery is one of the ways our brain processes information, yet a great deal of that processing is unconscious. What we want to do is to use mental imagery consciously and intentionally. Imagination and imagery can awaken enthusiasm and energize action. Imagining what might be in the box next to our birthday cake can generate a good deal of excitement. Imagining what the weather is going to be can elicit preventive action, like taking an umbrella to work. Using imagery and imagination thoughtfully gives us access to a very powerful inner resource.

Now we will learn how to work with that innate capacity to imagine our future and put that capacity to work on our behalf. The approach we will take for imagining the desired state in Learning Life is called Priming (Burke, 2004). It is a simple visual imagery method that is quite quick and easy to do. This particular visualization method provides an excellent foundation for living each day because it gets you to think about your most important goals (on a daily or regular basis), and it provides a chance to see those goals successfully accomplished. This helps to set a positive tone for the day by providing a vicarious experience of the successful accomplishment of important life goals. You vicariously experience an awesome day before you step outside of the house. The ultimate purpose of Priming is to increase the odds of having a rewarding, high accomplishment day – the best day of your life so far.

Instructions - Priming the Day

The instructions provided below are for Priming the day. These instructions will be followed with additional information on how to use the same steps to prime specific events, like imaging yourself successfully taking an exam, giving a presentation, meeting someone you are interested in, kicking the winning field goal, or anything else that is important to you in the moment.

Priming the day is best done before things get rolling, ideally first thing in the morning. Some people do it after meditating, or after they draw up their to-do list for the day, even on the bus on the way to work or school. No matter where, the goal is to vicariously experience the successful day before it begins, visualizing successful completion of a most remarkable day. Priming a successful day in this way, in the morning before heading out, provides a chance to reflect on key goals for the day and to set the tone for the day – clear goals, vision of success, positive expectancy, increased enthusiasm. It helps you start the day off with an "I can do this" feeling. Indeed, you already have done it, and you were awesome. Here are the steps.

Step 1 — Determine Your Goals

Priming involves internal visual imagery of the most important activities and goals for the day, seeing them successfully accomplished, having a vicarious experience of them as already complete. The goals can be anything of primary importance to you for that day, and they can change from day to day. As an example, they might include taking care of your health (eating well and exercising), meeting new people, being productive and getting work done, feeling more confident, or having a successful job interview.

A review of the literature on goal setting and performance consistently shows that specific and challenging goals lead to higher performance (Locke et al., 1981). Research also shows that using goals and having goal-oriented beliefs helps improve student academic motivation and self regulation (Pintrich & Schunk, 1996). A number of studies have been conducted to compare simple goal setting with imagery-based goal setting. These studies provide evidence for the additive value of goal-oriented imagery in enhancing achievement. One study, for example, randomly assigned 48 college students to one of two groups. One group was asked to make an implementation intention to accomplish a specific task (an implementation intention is a goal action plan that clearly specifies the how and when). The second group made the same implementation intention but added vivid imagery of their implementation plans. Significantly more of the students in the goal intention plus imagery group completed the assigned task compared with students who just set goal intentions. The imagery students had a vicarious trial run and achieved their goals, in their minds eye. Imagery improved performance. Finally, one study I conducted with students in my Academic Achievement class compared days in which students used Priming versus days when they just used To Do lists. All of the students did both methods on alternate days for several weeks and then the Priming versus the To Do days were compared for sense of accomplishment, stress and coping, and other factors. The study results showed that both methods helped students stay on track and provided a sense of accomplishment. The Priming (imagery) method, however, produced a greater sense of positive emotion and an increased ability to deal with daily stress (Burke, 2014). Those are two qualities that help individuals persist with goal pursuit even in the face of life challenges.

DO THIS

To get started pick one or two goals to visualize, something that you would like to do today or tomorrow that would give you a sense of accomplishment if you completed it. For this step you might want to refer back to your work on mission, vision, and core life goals from Chapter 2 on Goal Setting. Limit the number of goals you Prime to just a few, three to five max. This is not a To Do list. Picking too many items will water down the effect, less is more in this case.

Step 2 — Close Your Eyes And Relax

A good time to Prime the day is soon after getting up, before your day begins, or right after a morning meditation. No matter what time you choose to do it, always take a moment to relax before you begin the visualization component. Relaxation helps to drop the mind and body down into a more receptive space, a state of brainwave activity that facilitates imagery (toward alpha and theta brainwave levels). Related research has found alpha and theta EEG activity to be associated with relaxation and mental imagery ability (Batty et al., 2006; Cavallaro et al., 2010; Jacobs & Friedman 2004; Williams & Gruzelier 2001). Also, the adult brain tends toward beta and left hemispheric dominance during alert activity. Beta represents a more bioelectrically active state of the brain. The opposite end of the spectrum is delta, which is characterized by slower brainwave activity and sleep. Beta is your busy brain. Your busy brain is also actively engages the right hemisphere, which is involved in language. This is your brain talking, the voice inside your head. One of the ways to quiet the inner monologue, which helps to perpetuate beliefs about self, is to get quieter, to drop down out of beta and into alpha and theta. Alpha is associated with a quieter focus, like the mental state of meditation. Theta is characterized more by qualities of daydreaming and reverie. Taking a few minutes to quiet down helps to move the mind and body out of beta and right hemispheric dominance. One of the simple strategies, if you do practice meditation, is to do Priming immediately upon completion of your practice. That way your mind and body will be quiet and in an ideal state for mental imagery and the introduction of positive new ideas. The other simple strategy is a quick relaxation practice.

DO THIS

If you do not have time to meditate then another simple relaxation method is to count backwards from ten to one. Sit comfortably, close the eyes, take a few deep breaths, and relax the body with each breath out. Breathe normally and with each exhale count one number down from ten to one. When you reach the number one tell yourself that your hands and arms are warm, heavy, and relaxed. Let your shoulders and jaw relax completely, let the hands be very heavy and warm. Continue this process for a few minutes.

Step 3 — See Yourself in a Comfortable Space Looking Very Happy

If you are not yet skilled at using mental imagery you can just pretend that you see the image, even if you see nothing at all. Whatever you visualize is fine. It is the thought/intention that counts. Your skill with visualization will improve in time as you practice. Remember, you are just using your imagination, something you do all the time, it is really quite simple. A useful approach is to just pretend. You can ask yourself, "If I could see myself crossing the finish line what would that look like?" You can even just close your eyes and describe what that would look like to get things rolling.

DO THIS

It is the end of the day. You see yourself sitting in a chair at home (or some other relaxing place, maybe lying in bed). *You look happy*, very happy. *You feel happy*, because you have accomplished your major goals for the day. You are complete, *a real sense of accomplishment*, you are proud of yourself.

Step 4 — Imagine/Describe the Ideal Outcome As If It Has Already Occurred

Now you are going to imagine (see, hear) yourself completing each goal, the reason you are feeling so happy at the end of the day. Describe (in your mind, not out loud) what you are seeing. Even if you do not see images the verbal descriptions will provide the same information. If you do see images, then the words and the images reinforce each other.

> **DO THIS**
>
> Tell yourself that you feel happy/enthusiastic/grateful. Specify that you feel happy because you have achieved your goals. Imagine (see/describe) the goals the same way you would if you had already done them and were reflecting on them at the end of the day. For example, you can say, "I feel awesome because I exercised for an hour today, I got a tremendous amount of work done, and I talked with the person in class that I have been wanting to meet. *This has been one of the best days of my life so far.* I am stoked." Let yourself feel energized by the happiness and enthusiasm that comes from your success, from your accomplishments. The images and descriptions are not in the future, they are right now, in this imagined day that has already happened. You are 'remembering' this most incredible day. You are seeing and describing it to yourself repeatedly. The images and descriptions should be "I" statements – personal, positive, and in the present. "I am very happy right now. I feel great because..." Spend most of your time in this step. You may occasionally let go of the imagery and drop back into relaxation, then return to the images and verbal descriptions. That mixing of imagery and relaxation can help you stay in a more receptive state, which supports the imagery.

Step 5 — Create a Corresponding Positive Feeling

Your Priming will be much more powerful if there is a corresponding positive emotion, a sense of happiness and accomplishment. If you win a marathon, receive the top score in the class, get the phone number of someone you are crazy about, you will be jazzed, very happy. To make imagery realistic, that imagery has to have a matching positive emotional tone. For the imagery to be real, to be the most effective, then it cannot just look real, *it has to feel real*. If we give the image a strong positive feeling tone it will also be more memorable, as we tend to remember powerful emotional experiences, both positive and negative. Research also shows that goals are more likely to be unconsciously acted on during the day when they have a positive emotion associated with them (Custer & Aarts, 2005). If the goal feels good we will want to move toward it.

Certainly it can be hard to feel enthusiasm for something we lack confidence in, or something that does not intrinsically inspire us. That is where we just have to fake it, just pull the enthusiasm in from somewhere. If the imagery does not naturally evoke a noticeable positive feeling, then one simple strategy is to remember a past experience that was incredibly positive. When I need to bring positive energy into an uninspired image I just remember some powerful moment I had in nature, like body surfing at Pipeline in Hawaii or snowboarding in Tahoe. A memory like that will immediately drop you into the empowered mind-body state we are talking about. A memory like that has the say "Yes" to life quality we are looking for. That is the proper enthusiastic state needed to empower creative imagery.

> **DO THIS**
>
> As you image and describe each goal bring in a positive corresponding emotion. You can do this by telling yourself that you feel awesome, energized about the success of the day

– "I feel awesome, what an incredible day!" Pick the words or phrases that work for you. You can also take a momentary detour and think of something real from your past that was incredibly empowering for you, one of your life successes, rushes, adventures. You can even just sit up straight, pull your shoulders back, assume a very confident and strong posture, smile, take a big breath and expand your chest. Then do your visualization using that powerful pose for setting the tone.

Step 6 — Increase the Intensity

As you are reaching the end of the process you will want to make the entire experience more intense. Big stage musicians typically start and end their shows with a memorable number, something that makes you say, "Wow." That is the idea. We want to wrap up the imagery with some powerful, positive energy as the final imprint before starting the day.

DO THIS

Intensify the experience with positive self-talk – "I feel amazing. What an incredible day/feeling. I feel awesome. This has been one of the most incredible days of my life so far!" You can make the colors or images more vivid, the images bigger, closer. You can intensifying the body state, the energized feeling. Take whatever energy you feel and make it even bigger. Sit up straighter, bigger smile, more enthusiasm. This is the final shot for the day. One simple strategy is to imagine you are holding a sphere of energy in front of you. That sphere contains the goal imagery, feelings, and intentions. It is becoming brighter, the energy more intense. As you hold it the energy begins to fill your hands and flow down your arms until your whole body is radiating light.

Step 7 — Do an Integrating Breath

This final step involves integrating the imagery and positive feeling deeply into the mind and body for the day. You built it up, now you want to infuse that positive energy into your entire being, into your life.

DO THIS

This final integration process uses a four-part breath. Begin with a big inhale. With that inhale breathe all of the image/energy/light into your heart. Second, exhale the imagery/energy even deeper into your being, imagining it going profoundly deep, down into the very core of your being, infinitely deep. You see the light becoming smaller and smaller, like a comet hurtling into deepest space. Third, inhale the image and energy back up to the body surface, fill the entire body with that light and power. Fourth, release the light and energy out into the universe with one final, purposeful exhalation. Imagine that you are filling the entire creation with the energy of your most incredible day, with the most incredible day of your life so far. Remind yourself that from the center of your being to the furthest reaches of creation all of existence is filled with the vibration of the most incredible day of your life so far.

Step 8 — Conclude with an Anchoring Affirmation

The final step is to conclude with a powerful affirmation, a commitment to your success.

 DO THIS

Create an affirmation that reaffirms your commitment to your goals and to your most successful life, "I am committed to...." Reconfirm your major goals for the day. "I am committed to having the most wonderful relationship possible, to being incredibly healthy, to being financially free." Also, something I find very useful, is to tell myself that **"THIS IS GOING TO BE ONE OF THE MOST INCREDIBLE DAYS OF MY LIFE SO FAR."** I personally want to have a life filled with incredible days. I use Priming to help make that a reality. By making that claim, that today is going to be one of the most incredible days of my life *SO FAR*, it leaves space for my tomorrow to be even better. In that way each day can improve, there is space for even more good to come into life. Prime the day, then go out and seize it, live your life, follow the vision, be awake, be alive.

Summary of Steps
1. Determine goals to prime
2. Relax
3. See/describe yourself relaxed, happy and accomplished (at the end of day/specific task or event)
4. Imagine/describe the ideal goal outcomes
5. Create/experience a strong positive mind-body energy
6. Increase the intensity
7. Do an integrating breath
8. Conclude with an anchoring affirmation

Instructions – Priming Specific Events

In addition to Priming the day it is also useful to Prime specific tasks or events. For example, if there is an important meeting, phone call, test, speech, interview, performance, or competition it is always a good idea to Prime the desired outcome. Why not create positive expectancy and confidence for something important? It makes total sense to go into big events neurologically and psychologically primed for success. A key to success is to pre-set positive expectancy at the neurological level with imagery and positive self-talk. See yourself during the meeting/interview/performance being calm and focused (or whatever the most appropriate feeling/energy would be in that moment). See yourself after the event receiving applause, getting the date, signing the contract, scoring an A+, being accepted into law school. Image the before, during and after, or just the after, whichever makes the most sense to you. Bring the emotional qualities of happiness, confidence, and satisfaction into the imagery, or whatever other emotion/energy is appropriate. The bigger the event the longer you may want to prime for it, giving yourself more lead time. Writing a dissertation? Start Priming early. While others are struggling with writers block, overwhelmed by feelings of self doubt, you will be working away, small steps, making progress day by day.

Using priming before engaging in specific events gives you the vicarious experience of doing it and doing it successfully. It is a dry run, with a successful outcome, including the feelings of happiness, accomplishment and pride. When you Prime you are priming your neurology. Your brain has already done the task, and that task was completed successfully. Compare that person with the mind and body of the others in the room who have been worrying about the event all morning – VERY DIFFERENT. If you think of two athletes before a match, one seeing success, the other filled with doubt, it is obvious who has the edge. Priming uses your mind and body as a natural resource to increase your potential for success, every day, in any area of life that is important to you. You see your success, you feel your success, before it even begins. Using imagery, your imagination, in this way provides a very convenient, flexible, and potent resource.

Priming Key Life Destinations

Another useful Priming practice is to Prime major life goals, including life mission and vision. This type of imagery can be easily woven into life whenever you have a moment, like when you are entering that hypnogogic state of mind and body right before falling asleep. You want to be happily married, to have a loving family, to earn your first million (or first hundred even!), to be a highly effective district attorney, to finish the Boston Marathon under 4 hours, to surf a Maverick... whatever your big life dream is. Priming is a way to keep it alive over time. Priming big life dreams over the course of time also has the potential to help make that vision real, because as you hold it in your mind and heart you can become even more inspired to make it happen.

Priming and To Do Lists

One other useful practice is to use Priming and To Do Lists together. Research I have conducted on this topic showed that combining them together provided the specificity and detail of To Do lists with the encouraging success visioning of Priming (Burke, 2014). The two methods supported each other. A To Do list generally has too much detail for practical priming purposes. The Priming list probably does not have enough detail for remembering all the snigglebits that need to get done during the day. Creating a To Do list for the day and then Priming the top 3 to 5 primary – real sense of accomplishment items – is a practical way to get in the groove and get things done.

Best Quarter/Semester of My Life So Far

Another very useful life success strategy is to Prime a larger block of time, say the semester or quarter (or a season as a quarter, like the spring). The goal is to create a compelling, positive self-fulfilling prophecy that extends through time long enough to allow significant progress with key goals. To do this variation you need to look at a calendar and determine the date of the next solstice or equinox (or end of the semester, or other appropriate target date). Solstices and equinoxes are good general time-space targets as they are natural transition points, they mark the seasons, punctuated by the longest/shortest days of the year. They also tend to coincide roughly with things like the beginning and end of school years and major holidays. Solstice and equinox markers are also useful because they give you consistent three-month time blocks to envision, a good chunk of time to get some serious work done.

Self-Fulfilling Prophecy

Priming the quarter, semester, or season (winter, spring), is slightly different from the other variations in that you will be writing down a description of the desired end state. By writing it down you are committing to a vision. It becomes your roadmap, your self-fulfilling prophecy. So let's say you were going to use the summer equinox as the target date, generally around June 21st. Today, the day you are doing the Priming exercise, is March 15th.

On a clean sheet of paper or document on your computer write at the top of the page, "Today is (end of quarter/semester/season, about 3 months from the day of writing) June 21st, 2036 and I am very happy because…" Even though in reality today is March 15th, 2036 you are imagining that you are at home sitting on your couch and today is June 21st. You are thinking back on the quarter and writing a journal entry describing the incredible things that have happened to you during the past 3 months. Start writing a description of the events of the 'last three months' as if they had already happened, already occurred successfully, things that gave you a sense of accomplishment. You will only want to include things that are possible to accomplish during the three-month window, things that you have some control over, and things that would make you feel good if they really happened. At least one of these should also ideally be a bit of a stretch, not outlandishly so, but something that will require more physical or emotional effort to accomplish. Accomplishments for the period might be related to health and fitness, money, career, home, emotional well-being, spiritual life, school, family and friends, intimate relationships, adventure, fun, community service, whatever is important to you. By writing this information today, information of a possible future, you are a creating a self-fulfilling prophecy. You are writing your life story, your own life narrative. In this fashion you are shaping your life course more intentionally, the way you want your life to flow.

Remember to put the target date on the top of the page, such as June 21, 2036, and keep the document somewhere you can find it in about 3 months. Do not read it before the target date, just continue to Prime the best day of your life on a regular basis, ideally daily. On the target date read what you had written 3 months prior and see how it went. Will everything you wrote down come to pass? Maybe. More commonly you have done a good deal of it, some still in process, some a lot closer than they had been a few months back, and possibly some that became less meaningful and lost steam (also useful information). People who do this exercise are often amazed at how their vision becomes a reality. This is a very useful way to begin charting your own destiny in a much more intentional fashion.

> *I can already see that this is going to be one of the best days of my life so far.*

REFLECTION

Today is (date about 3 months from today, end of quarter/semester/season) _____

and I am very happy because _____

SUMMARY

Our mind is a very important resource in the journey of life. Unconscious and conditioned, the mind can be a habit reactor. It does not readily see new opportunities. It does not knowingly create new paths. The patterns of conditioned self image, of social self, repeat and perpetuate old patterns. One of the ways to modify this entrenched self image is with imagery. There is a substantial body of research showing the value of imagery to enhance sports performance, learning, healing, and well-being. Neurological studies show that areas of the brain related to the imagined activity are engaged during imagery. In essence we are getting to practice a new behavior without the risk of overt failure, and we can practice perfectly in our mind. Imagery is simple to do, free of charge, and produces results. One of the other big benefits, or regular imagery practice, is that it gets us to think about our primary goals on a daily basis. The method used in Learning Life is called Priming. Daily Priming provides a chance to think about what is really important today, what is important in YOUR life. Over time that builds a sense of control, of hope, of confidence, that you can have a dream, and that there is a chance that you can achieve that dream. It is a simple 8 step process that takes a few minutes. It can be done as a pre-set for the whole day, used to prime positive expectancy before specific important events, like a performance or big test, or to mentally prepare for a longer period of work, like priming an excellent semester.

MIND-BODY PRACTICE

Priming

For the week practice the Priming mental imagery method every morning. See the Priming instruction guide in the Resources section at the end of the book.

REFERENCES

Bakke AC, Purtzer MZ, Newton P. The effect of hypnotic-guided imagery on psychological well-being and immune function in patients with prior breast cancer. *Journal of Psychosomatic Research*. 53(6), 1131-1137.

Bandura A. *Self-Efficacy: The Exercise of Control*. New York: Freeman; 1997.

Bandura, A. (1988). Self-regulation of motivation and action through goal systems. In: Hamilton V, Bower GH, Frijda NH, editors. *Cognitive Perspectives on Emotion and Motivation*. Dordrecht: Kluwer Academic Publishers; 1988:37-61.

Barnes PM, Powell-Griner E, McFann K, Nahin RL. Complementary and alternative medicine use among adults: United States, 2002. *Advance Data*. 2004;27(343);1-19.

Bartolomeo P. The neural correlates of visual mental imagery: an ongoing debate. *Cortex*. 2008;44(2):107-108.

Battle, ES. Motivational determinants of academic task persistence. *Journal of Personality and Social Psychology*. 1965;2(2):209-218.

Batty M, Bonnington S, Tang BK, Hawken MB, Gruzelier JH. Relaxation strategies and enhancement of hypnotic susceptibility: EEG neurofeedback, progressive muscle relaxation and self hypnosis. *Brain Research Bulletin.* 2006;71(1-3):83-90.

Blanke O, Ionta S, Fornari E, Mohr C, Maeder P. Mental imagery for full and upper human bodies: common right hemisphere activations and distinct extrastriate activations. *Brain Topography.* 2010;23(3):321-32.

Burke A. *Self Hypnosis.* New York: Random House; 2004.

Burke A, Shanahan C, Herlambang E. An exploratory study comparing goal-oriented mental imagery with daily to-do lists: Supporting college student success. *Current Psychology.* 2014;33(1):20-34.

Carlson LE, Bultz BD. Mind-body interventions in oncology. *Current Treatment Options in Oncology.* 2008;9(2-3):127-34.

Cavallaro FI, Cacace I, Del Testa M, Andre P, Carli G, De Pascalis V, et al. Hypnotizability related EEG alpha and theta activities during visual and somesthetic imageries. *Neuroscience Letters.* 2010;470:13-18.

Custers R, Aarts H. Beyond priming effects: the role of positive affect and discrepancies in implicit processes of motivation and goal pursuit. *European Review of Social Psychology.* 2005a;16(1);257-300.

Deen B, McCarthy G. Reading about the actions of others: biological motion imagery and action congruency influence brain activity. *Neuropsychologia.* 2010;48(6):1607-1615.

Driskell JE, Copper C, Moran A. Does mental practice enhance performance? *Journal of Applied Psychology.* 1994;79(4):481-492.

Farah MJ. The neural basis of mental imagery. *Trends in Neurosciences.* 1989;12(10):395-399.

Ganis G, Thompson WL, Kosslyn SM. Brain areas underlying visual mental imagery and visual perception: an fMRI study. *Cognitive Brain Research.* 2004;20(2):226-241.

Gardini S, Cornoldi C, De Beni R, Venneri A. Cognitive and neuronal processes involved in sequential generation of general and specific mental images. *Psychological Research.* 2008;73(5):633-643.

Galyean B. The use of guided imagery in elementary and secondary schools. Imagination, *Cognition and Personality.* 1982-1983;2(2):145-151.

Jacobs GD, Friedman R. EEG spectral analysis of relaxation techniques. *Applied Psychophysiology and Biofeedback.* 2004;29(4):245-254.

Karniol R, Ross M. The motivational impact of temporal focus: thinking about the future and the past. *Annual Review of Psychology.* 1996;47:593-620.

Kwekkeboom KL, Cherwin CH, Lee JW, Wanta B. Mind-body treatments for the pain-fatigue-sleep disturbance symptom cluster in persons with cancer. *Journal of Pain and Symptom Management.* 2010;39(1):126-138

Locke EA, Shaw KN, Saari LM, Latham GP. Goal setting and task performance: 1969-1980. *Psychological Bulletin.* 1981;90(1):125-152.

Martin KA, Hall CR. Using mental imagery to enhance intrinsic motivation. *Journal of Sport & Exercise Psychology.* 1995;17(1):54-69.

Martin KA, Moritz SE, Hall CR. Imagery use in sport: a literature review and applied model. *The Sport Psychologist.* 1999;13(3):245-268.

Miller KJ, Schalk G, Fetz EE, den Nijs M, Ojemann JG, Rao RPN. Cortical activity during motor execution, motor imagery, and imagery-based online feedback. *Proceedings of the National Academy of Sciences of the United States of America.* 2010;107(9):4430-4435.

Neck CP, Manz CC. Thought self-leadership: The influence of self-talk and mental imagery on performance. *Journal of Organizational Behavior.* 1992;13:681-699.

Oettingen G, Hönig G, Gollwitzer PM. Effective self-regulation of goal attainment. *International Journal of Educational Research.* 2000;33(7-8):705-732.

Pintrich PR, Schunk DH. *Motivation in education.* Englewood Cliffs: Prentice Hall; 1996.

Rodrigues EC, Lemos T, Gouvea B, Volchan E, Imbiriba LA, Vargas CD. Kinesthetic motor imagery modulates body sway. *Neuroscience.* 2010;169(2):743-50.

Sapp, M. (1994). The effects of guided imagery on reducing the worry and emotionality components of test anxiety. *Journal of Mental Imagery.* 1994;18(3-4):165-179.

Seligman MEP. Learned helplessness. *Annual Review of Medicine.* 1972;23(1):407-412.

Seligman MEP, Maier SF. Failure to escape traumatic shock. *Journal of Experimental Psychology.* 1967;74:1-9.

Tartaglia EM, Bamert L, Mast FW, Herzog MH. Human perceptual learning by mental imagery. *Current Biology.* 2009;19(24):2081-2085.

Williams JD, Gruzelier JH. Differentiation of hypnosis and relaxation by analysis of narrow band theta and alpha frequencies. *International Journal of Clinical and Experimental Hypnosis.* 2001;49(3):185-206.

Mindful Learning
The Power of Self-Awareness

I am aware of my experience, of where I am right now.

CHAPTER THEMES
- Mindful Learning
- Philosophical Roots
- Seated Mindfulness Meditation
  - Basic Process & Technique
- Active Mindful Awareness
  - Basic Process & Technique

So this is it. This is the moment you are experiencing. You are reading words, possibly focused, possibly distracted, interested or bored, tired or cranked, recognizing or not recognizing the endless interplay of mind and body, behavior and environment. Whether the mind and body are lost in the past or wandering about somewhere in the future, in actual reality, this simple moment is where it is all happening, in each breath, in each heartbeat. Being present, in the moment, is the root of more effective learning. Recognizing the gift of each moment is the beginning of a happier life. Living completely, fully engaged in the potential of each moment is the key to success in all that you do. In this chapter we will examine the mind-body mechanisms underlying conscious attention and the benefits and practice of this thing called mindful awareness.

Mindful Learning

It is harder to learn if we are not aware, not present, not conscious. Of course we learn a lot unconsciously. Kids model their parents, picking up good and bad habits without any conscious instruction at all. Imitation is the highest form of flattery they say. That type of learning is very useful, an essential part of how we acquire new skills and ideas. Unfortunately it does not work as well for much of the learning we need to do as adults. For that we need to bring awareness and attention to the task at hand, being present, in the moment, engaged and on task. We need to be awake, to bring mindfulness, awareness to our learning. That is the first core practice of mindful learning – ***being present with the task at hand.***

The second core practice of mindful learning is to observe how we react to life experiences. Over time, through the simple process of self-observation, we begin to recognize our automatic responses, the habits of conditioned mind and body. With growing awareness of our patterns we can gain insight into how we deal with stress, how we study, how we interpret events in our lives, how we respond to success and failure, what pulls us off task and what keeps us on. By noticing and recognizing these habitual patterns we develop a new capacity for choice, change, and growth.

You might think, "I am already aware of my life experiences." Okay, agreed, certainly everyone is dramatically aware of pain when they bang their head on the corner of the cupboard door, "Ouch." We are aware of anger when someone makes an insulting gesture, or aware of frustration and impatience when running late for an important meeting. Awareness or heightened attention in such moments is a natural biological response to a threat, to potential harm. It is the body's way of alerting us to possible danger, helping us to survive. Awareness of that type, however, is more base level, automatically activated, not intentional. What we are talking about in mindful learning is not just noticing those in-your-face experiences that yank you off the couch, but rather being able to recognize the subtler changes in mind and body, and doing that intentionally. That is the core of mindful learning, the combination of awareness of the moment and ongoing reflection of our responses to the experience of life.

The Core Practices

Our approach to mindful learning in this text will involve two simple awareness practices. The first method is a *Seated Mindfulness Meditation Practice*. It is used as a foundation practice used to train the brain to be able to sustain attention with momentary experience. The second is an *Active Mindful Awareness Practice*, which is used to cultivate a more pervasive mindful awareness during daily activities. Both of these approaches, Seated Mindfulness Meditation and Active Mindful Awareness, are intended to increase our capacity to hold or sustain attention with the flow of life experiences over an extended period of time. Before we get into the mechanics it would be good to have a basic understanding of the roots of the practices, historically and philosophically.

Historical Perspective

Although mindfulness meditation is widely accepted today as a secular psychologically-oriented practice for cultivating greater self-awareness it is useful to consider the historical roots of the tradition. The essential ideas of mindfulness meditation are derived from the teachings of the 6th century (BCE) historic figure, Gautama Buddha. The Buddha was born around 550 BCE in Lumbini, now part of Nepal. He was named Siddhartha Gautama and belonged to the Gautama clan. His father was the leader of the clan and Siddharta enjoyed a princely life. As the young prince matured he came to find the pleasures and comforts of life incomplete. While exploring his father's kingdom with his charioteer he encountered the aged, the sick, and the dead. He was deeply moved by the suffering he observed. Fueled by a growing sense of futility for the life he had been living he decided to become a mendicant, a wandering monk. On the night of his 29th birthday, while his wife and child were sleeping, he quietly set off with his charioteer. At the Anoma River he cut his hair, donned the simple garb of an ascetic, and began his search for truth. He engaged in deep study and rigorous practice for the next six years and eventually came to a great understanding, he became the Buddha, the awakened one.

Philosophical Foundations

Understanding Self as Construct

In the mindfulness tradition the self is considered to be an artifact, another mental construction. In Buddhist philosophy there is no trans-temporal self, self does not really exist. A modern equivalent might be the materialist view that personality and self are biological epiphenomena, things that arise because of biological processes, but that do not inherently exist on their own. The question of whether there is a self or not, what the self is, are questions that have been debated from the days of the ancient philosophers to the modern neurosciences. Whether one believes in an enduring aspect of self or not is a matter for other texts, debates that will not be resolved any time soon.

The important thing for our purposes is the understanding that working with self as construct or idea can be very practical and enlightening. Like all things, the sense of self, experience of self, is changing. One of the main values of working with 'no self' is that it can help us to begin to take this changing self less seriously. If there is no self, then who gets insulted? If there is no self, then who is threatened? It is logical, that if there is no one to be threatened or shamed then there is a greater ability to move into life more powerfully, to be less reactive, to take more risks, to be more engaged. For me the main take away from the 'no self' concept is that if we take our selves (our self) too seriously we are asking for trouble. If there is 'no self' then it is less personal. If we take things less personally then our lives will be much smoother. So how to use this? First, forget about the question of whether there is a self or not, believe what you believe, there is no simple answer. Whatever *you* believe is right, done. Second, remember this simple rule – **Don't take it so personally**. If there is no self involved, less self focus, you will not take things so personally. That is a very good resilience strategy in general. If take things personally, it is much easier for the idiots of the planet to get under your skin, to get into your head. If you do not take it so personally, it means they cannot penetrate your energy field. You remain whole, you are still in control, and being in control of your own responses is power, that is called CHOICE.

Recognition of Impermanence

Another key concept of traditional mindfulness practice is cultivating an appreciation of impermanence, recognizing and accepting the changing nature of all things. Certainly it is useful to notice that we are upset with someone, or that we are depressed, or that we are exceptionally happy, or that we really, really want to smoke a cigarette. It is also helpful to recognize that everything is constantly changing. Change is inherent in all things, in all life, in each moment. Change is obvious as the golden leaves of autumn give way to the first frost and ultimately, once again, return in the spring with the wild flowers in and the robins. Change is day and night, life and death. How is that useful? If someone is trying to quit smoking it can be very helpful to remember the impermanence of all things, to remember that this urge I am feeling right now will pass. Reflecting on the impermanent nature of any experience can provide some helpful emotional space, a reminder that the unpleasantness of the moment will not last forever – this too shall pass.

Acceptance and Non-Judgment

Recognition of impermanence can also help to create a sense of acceptance. The Persian poet Rumi once wrote an essay entitled, "It is what it is." Indeed it always is what it is. What else can it be? Seeing that this moment is what it is, and whether good or bad, pleasant or unpleasant, it is going to pass, is a source of peace. That realization can help us to be less graspy with the good, and less pushy with the bad. From this centered position it is possible to experience each moment with increased clarity of mind, more balance, resulting in greater flexibility in life. With recognition of impermanence, and the practice of acceptance of the moment as it is, *we can cultivate a greater capacity to be ok with not being ok*. Acceptance strengthens our ability to maintain equanimity in the face of discomfort and challenge. That does not mean we tolerate injustice, or that we become passive or apathetic. It is more about increasing our capacity for self-management, greater rootedness in the face of life's insults and temptations, more composure, more flexibility and resilience.

Non-judging is another aspect of acceptance, just a bit more concrete. Undoubtedly, as we experience life there will come the good and the bad, the beautiful and the profane. In life the natural tendency is to withdraw from discomfort and to move toward comfort. In the mindfulness tradition, however, this tendency is seen as one of the roots of discontent and unhappiness. Why? Because life is what it is, sometimes ugly, sometimes not. If we are able to stay the course, maintain a steady state in the face of life's ups and downs, then we will be calmer and happier, stronger human beings. For that reason, one of the core practices is to allow our life experience to be what it is, and to reduce the tendency to judge things as good or bad. The deeper goal is to be without judgment, letting go of holding on or pushing away, just being with it, like a child holding a lady bug – observing, curious, experiencing it in the moment. The goal is to be a dispassionate observer of the scene, like "the fool on the hill" that the Beatles sang about so many years ago.

I. Seated Mindfulness Meditation

Meditation is becoming an increasingly common form of mind-body training in the United States. The 2002 National Health Interview Survey included questions on the use of complementary and alternative health practices in the United States. Of the 36,000 individuals interviewed in that survey there were 7.6% who had practiced meditation in the previous 12 months (representing approximately 15 million adults). Meditation was one of the most commonly used of all 27 methods assessed. Of the 11 mind-body methods measured, including hypnosis and guided imagery, meditation was the third most common. In a subsequent 2007 follow-up survey the number of adults who indicated that they had meditated during the previous year increased to 9.4%, a statistically significant increase (Barnes et al., 2002; Barnes et al., 2007). One of the reasons that people do meditate is for the wide range of practical benefits. Here are a few.

Benefits

Changes in Brain Structure and Function

One of the main reasons to use mindful meditation as a strategy for learning and achievement is the effect it has on the brain. Indeed, in recent years there has been a surge in the publication of research studies on meditation and the brain, with many of those studies examining mindfulness-oriented meditation. Regular meditation, both mindful and concentration approaches, produces changes in the brain over time (we will explore concentration meditation in Chapter 10). Much of this research is done today use magnetic resonance imaging (MRI) technology. MRI measures changes in the flow of oxygenated blood in the brain. One anatomical MRI study found that participants in a mindfulness meditation training course had increased density of grey matter in the left hippocampus, the posterior cingulate cortex, the temporo-parietal junction, and the cerebellum. These are regions of the brain associated with learning, memory, emotional regulation, and perspective taking processes (Hölzel et al., 2011). Greater density of grey matter has also been associated with better performance on intellectual tests (Kalat, 2007). Another MRI study revealed that the practice of mindfulness meditation increased connectivity between the auditory and visual networks as well as other regions of the brain associated with attention and self-reference. These increases in brain connectivity were associated with greater attention, insightful responsiveness, and improved sensory processing (Kilpatrick et al., 2011).

Improved Attention and Memory
Successful scientists, teachers, artists, lovers, athletes, parents, poets and entrepreneurs have the ability to focus and stay on task. Research shows that meditators have greater ability to maintain attention than non-meditators (Kerr et al., 2011). More experienced meditators are better able to catch a wandering mind, shift attention back to the task of meditation, and sustain that focus for a longer period of time (Hasenkamp et al., 2011). This ability to recognize task drift, move attention back on task, and maintain that attention over time, is obviously a useful quality for studying, taking exams, optimizing long rehearsals and performances, powering through a marathon meeting, having an important conversation, or completing large projects, just about anything requiring attention over extended periods of time, which is a lot of important life events and processes. Many related studies show that our attention is trainable and that one of the ways to train it is through mindful awareness practices such as seated mindfulness meditation (Chiesa et al., 2011; Lutz et al., 2009).

Studies have also found that practice leads to changes in brain structures associated with learning and memory. Clear changes have been observed in the hippocampus of both newer and experienced meditators, a region of the brain associated with long-term memory (Engstrom et al., 2010; Holzel et al., 2011). A review of studies conducted to explore mindfulness and cognitive abilities consistently found evidence that mindfulness meditation practices were associated with greater working memory capacity in addition to improved executive function and selective attention (Chiesa et al., 2011). It has also been observed that many of the associated benefits improve with practice over time (Barron et al., 2010; Luders et al., 2009; Lutz et al., 2009).

Reduction in Rumination/Worry/Stress
Rumination is the repetition of a particular thought, such as repetitively thinking about a bad grade on a paper, a missed line in an oral presentation, an argument with someone, a text message you received. Rumination is sometimes contrasted with worry – rumination being a repetitive thought about a past experience, worry being a repetitive thought about something that could happen. Both of these types of thinking can be clearly unproductive, associated with self-judgment, task avoidance, procrastination, less healthy coping strategies like drinking and drug use, and emotional upset contributing to anxiety and depression.

Research suggests that mindfulness mediation can be helpful in reducing rumination, worry, and cyclic anxious and depressive thinking. One study looked at the neurological effect of sadness and recovery from negative emotions in a group that underwent mindfulness training compared to a control group. Both groups experienced provoked sadness in a laboratory setting and then underwent an MRI scan to observe regions of the brain affected. Participants in both groups reported equal degrees of sadness. Interestingly, however, the neurological reaction was different between them. The mindfulness participants displayed a greater right-lateralized recruitment, including visceral and somatosensory areas associated with body sensation. This increased involvement of somatic brain regions has been associated with lower depressive scores (Farb et al., 2010). Mindful practices can also help change the nature of attributions, the way we think about ourselves and others, especially negative attributions, by fostering recognition that our thoughts are just thoughts, not truths. A review of the literature found that mindfulness practices helped to reduce stress, ruminative thought and anxiety, while also increasing empathy and compassion for self and others (Chiesa & Serretti, 2009).

Facilitated Habit Change
Finally, mindful awareness can also lead to insights into unhelpful habits, unproductive life patterns. There is a great saying – nothing is obvious to the uninformed. Trying to change an old habit can be like trying to get out of a labyrinth – bewildering – which way to go? When you are down in the maze you cannot see all of the paths, only the ones visible from where you are standing at that moment. That can make the challenge of solving the puzzle quite tricky. One strategy is to just give up – resignation – choosing to not deal with it. Another is to move helter skelter through the maze, without a plan. An alternate strategy is to bring awareness to the problem.

The value of employing a mindful awareness strategy is that the process of just noticing, in this case noticing an old habit, can begin to move it. How? In part because we are now engaging with the old pattern in a new way, simply by starting to really notice it. That is different, and anything different is good when it comes to habitual behavior. Just noticing can gradually bring in new light, from the simple observation of our thoughts, feelings, behaviors and environments. In some ways it is not that much more work than resignation, giving up, but the potential for benefit is vastly different. Over time, as we wander through the maze, stopping and noticing differences here and there, we begin to build a growing inner map of the maze and a sense of our momentary location in it. As the internal map of place grows so does our ability to navigate in that field. In time, with patience and persistence, we may even be able to find our way out once and for all. That will be a new day.

A Final (Critical) Thought
Does all of this sound too good to be true? Indeed mindful awareness practices can be very helpful. However, one medicine does not cure all ills. Mindful awareness is a powerful strategy for increasing effectiveness as a learner and as a successful human being. The vast majority of studies show its benefit, while some show no effect, and a few are negative. Personally, I have meditated a long time, and find it to be extremely helpful. I actually started practicing as an undergraduate. It quickly became one of the core strategies that moved me from not doing well to graduating magna cum laude and all the rest. Despite its clear value to me and countless others I would be the first to say it is part of a package, not the whole show. Today there is a lot of hype about meditation, often from people with very limited experience, many of whom are out to make a buck on it. Business is business, no problem there. The bottom line, however, is that humans are complex, life challenges

can be complex, and complex problems are often best addressed with a diverse set of tools useful for working with various pieces of the puzzle. If you are not sure of meditation, or if it feels uncomfortable at first, take a small step. Meditate for 2 minutes for a while and build from there.

The Basic Process

Although it is not essential that individuals using this book practice a seated mindfulness meditation practice, it is strongly encouraged, at least for a while. The reason for a regular seated meditation practice is that it can help integrate the concept and skills of mindful awareness more deeply than just doing the active practice alone. It is a concentrated dose, a focused experience. It is like sitting and practicing the piano alone, with attention, for thirty-minutes. So it is highly encouraged.

The practice of Seated Mindfulness Meditation can be broken down into five core activities: (1) an open awareness of momentary experiences; (2) selective attention for one of several principle types of experience; (3) a recognition of the changing nature of those experiences; (4) an accepting, non-judgmental attitude regarding those experiences and changes; and (5) a return to momentary awareness upon recognition of loss of attention. In mindfulness meditation the main point is to be mindful of the moment, to **be here now**. Through momentary awareness we can notice what is going on inside our own skin and outside in the world around us. Here are the details:

1. Intentional open awareness of momentary experiences

Mindfulness emphasizes an intentional awareness of experience in the moment. We bring intention to our awareness, seeking to be more consciously versus unconsciously aware, and to direct that intentional conscious awareness to our life experiences. The unconscious mind and heart are more reactive, responding from older, often very old, personal/family/community patterns. This is conditioned mind and body at work, the habitual way of doing and being. Unconscious and habitual responses to life can be quite limiting, even harmful. The antidote, to consciously bringing awareness into the moments of our lives. We can bring awareness to a more narrow experience, such as observing our breath, or a broader experience, like observing how hearing a particular song leads to a memory of an old friend, and that the memory produces an emotion of happiness, a flow of sensation, memory and emotion.

2. Selective attention

Meditation is a vehicle for training attention. In meditation practices there is generally some object that one attends to, selectively, selecting it versus other objects. In the Buddhist mindfulness meditation tradition, the object for that selective attention is our everyday experience. For purposes of practice these are broken down into five types of experience that we can use, awareness of five different phenomena. These are referred to as the *Five Aggregates*. These include awareness of:

1. Body (and all physical form/matter, including the external physical world)
2. Mental Experiences - thoughts, emotions, memories, imagination, habit
3. Perception - sights, sounds, smells, taste, touch
4. Drive - awareness of our sense of attraction, repulsion, or neutrality (evaluative aspect)
5. Consciousness - the field of awareness

In the mindfulness philosophy life is seen as an interplay of these five domains. Because of their centrality to our experience these domains constitute a natural focus for mindfulness meditation practice. The practice involves bringing our awareness to the experience of the moment within one or more of these domains. Like all things they are recognized to be transient, impermanent, changing. They are also inextricably linked together, interdependent, continually and reciprocally influencing and affecting each other, the web of life.

3. Recognition of impermanence

As described above in the philosophical foundations section, cultivating an appreciation of impermanence, recognizing and accepting the changing nature of all things.

4. Acceptance and non-judgment

As described above in the philosophical foundations section, acceptance and non-judgment are elemental aspects of the practice. It involves acceptance of self and others, life, our experience, the endless comings and goings of things. This is also related to the practice of Metta, or Loving Kindness, which will be discussed a bit more in Chapter 11 on Emotional Literacy.

5. Return to the object

Do not pass go, do not collect $200. When you realize that your attention has drifted, you return, without judgment, to being in the moment with full awareness on whatever object you have selected.

The Technique - Mindfulness of Breath

We are going to start by working with breath as the object of meditation practice. You will just sit, eyes closed, paying attention to the breath as you breathe normally through the nostrils. As you breathe you can notice the rise and fall of the abdomen, expansion and contraction of the chest, or the flow of air entering and exiting the nostrils. It can be challenging in the beginning months of practice to stay with the breath, but like in all learning, practice is a key to success. When you notice that you have lost your focus (and everyone loses their focus) then you just return to the breath without judgment or self-criticism. Do this for about 15 to 20 minutes.

Figure 1 provides a graphical representation of the process of mindful awareness meditation, for visual learners. The <><><> line represents the primary object of meditation, in this case the breath, awareness of breath coming and going. The other points in the line, the ...., indicated by various detours of mind, when our attention has drifted into other fields, such as thinking about that last conversation, or noticing an inner sensation like hunger, or being absorbed in a sensory moment, like hearing a bird singing off in the distance, or being pulled in an emotion, like joy, or boredom.

As you begin your meditation you are sitting there quietly noticing the breath, the primary meditation object, noticing inhale and noticing exhale. Eventually you lose awareness of the breath, pulled off into thoughts, emotions, sensations. Then you remember what you are supposed to be doing, awareness of breath. You could simply quietly return immediately to awareness of the breath, back to the main object. Another option would be to employ momentary labeling, which will be described below.

FIGURE 1: Visual representation of a mindfulness meditation breath practice

Aware of Breathing	<>...............<><>...........<><><>.............<><><><>........<><>			
Intervening Events	*Remembering a conversation*	*Noticing hunger*	*Listening to a bird chirping*	*Feeling bored*
Labeling	"Thinking"	"Sensation"	"Hearing"	"Feeling"

Working with the Object of Awareness

The vast majority of meditation techniques use some form of object of awareness. That object is the focus of attention, what is attended to, in order to help train the brain and mind to stay on task, on target. There are two common strategies for attention training used in meditation. One type involves more of a fixed focus, a *fixed attention* on a specific object of meditation to the exclusion of all others. That is the concentration type of meditation, which we will explore in Chapter 10. In that approach the object is usually a specific thing, such as a specific word or phrase, a specific mental image, or a physical object. One concentrates on that. The second type of practice, which is the one we are learning now, is more of an *open awareness* method. In this approach the object of meditation is the experienced moment, awareness of some aspect of the Five Aggregates, such as the experience of breathing (body), or hearing (senses), or thinking (mental activity). As an analogy, a bird might be targeting a piece of fruit, that is *fixed attention* on a very specific object, but it must also maintain an *open awareness* of the broader field (both in terms of not flying into something and not getting eaten). Both are important, fixed and open, both are essential.

In mindfulness meditation the breath is commonly used in the beginning stages of practice as a place to direct awareness, as the object. Actually it is both a starting point of awareness training and potentially a lifelong tool for maintaining presence. Awareness of breathing is a good object of meditation because it is always there, as long as you are alive. It is rhythmical (a naturally quieting quality, like the way a rocking cradle soothes a baby). It is internal (useful for a meditative focus). It is physical, not mental, and therefore does not have the same personal story quality that thoughts and feelings possess. Because it does not have a story it is less likely to pull us off track. Because it is simpler in this way it can also be used to help focus attention when the mind is active and wandering (see Managing Busy Mind below). Finally, breath is something we can consciously regulate if we need to, slowing it down, as a vehicle for intentionally quieting mind and body.

Using Labels

As mentioned above labeling can be another way to help bring the mind back to the main object. Research shows that increased ability to differentiate and label experience, such as labeling emotional states, improves capacity to self regulate those states (Barrett et al., 2001; Gyurak et al., 2011; Schultz et al., 2001). Labeling can also help with self-regulation during meditation, as a way to keep the process on track. During meditation it is natural for the mind to wander, especially in the beginning. The solution – mind wanders, bring it back. One nice method for bringing it back is to make a mental note once you realize you are off task, that you are off the primary object, such as breath.

Let us say you were using breath as the object of meditation, the primary object. There you are sitting on the river bank of your mind observing breath. After a few minutes you realize that you have been pulled off the river bank and have been floating in the stream of thought. As soon as you realize that you are floating down stream in thought, feeling, sensation, sensory experience, you can make a mental note of where you are. So, for example, you were practicing being aware of your breathing. At some point you drift off and are now totally engaged in the sound of traffic (the senses). As soon as you realize that you have been pulled of the breath by sound you can make a mental note, "Hearing, hearing, hearing," and then gently return to a focus on the breath. If you were noticing discomfort in the hip (the body), you could make a mental note, "tension, tension, tension" or "pain, pain, pain," and then quietly return to the breath. If an emotion pulled you away, once you recognized that you were off the breath you could repeat, "feeling, feeling, feeling," or "anger, anger, anger," "bored, bored, bored," "happy, happy, happy..." It is recommended to mentally repeat that label 3 times, so you can recognize and be present with that moment, before returning to the breath. See Figure 1.

Using labeling in this way helps to turn what might be considered distractions or failures into a secondary object of meditation. This is a very useful strategy. In mindfulness meditation awareness of momentary experience is the task, that is the training. We use techniques like watching the breath to provide more focus, to provide something specific to attend to. Although breath may be the primary focus of awareness, in the moment of noticing that you have shifted and are off somewhere else, that somewhere else can be labeled. Once recognized and labeled it becomes a secondary object of meditation, the new momentary experience. As a result there is no failure. Everything, once recognized, becomes an object of our attention, an object of our mindful awareness. Indeed, by mentally commenting on these momentary detours of attention the method allows any aspect of life, all of life, to be a *secondary* object of meditation.

That is one of the things that is so beautiful about this practice, it is inclusive. Although the awareness is on a primary object, such as the breath, all other experience can become secondary objects of meditation. The benefit is twofold. First, this approach increases the continuum of awareness, using primary and secondary objects, one following the other. Second, it provides a means to begin to see how things associate with each other, how one thought or feeling or sensation kick-starts the other. This is useful in its own right for insight into our habits, our life patterns.

Non-Judgmental Attitude
After a few minutes of meditating it is common to find that the mind has drifted off somewhere, lost in some story, some memory, listening to some sound, sensing some ache in the knee. When that happens, as soon as it is apparent that the mind has drifted off, then gently bring it back to the task at hand – awareness of the moment, such as the next breath. Do this without judgment, self-criticism, or despair. This is a mental training. It takes time. Remember - "I don't know how to do that yet, but..." The whole point is to develop attention and awareness. Those qualities have not been highly trained in most people. Meditation is a mental training, so it will take some practice, just like learning to play the violin or learning a new language. As with any skill, however, it will get better over time if done correctly. Self-criticism is also arousing of mind and body and will pull you out of a meditative state, less productive.

Posture

For mindfulness meditation a seated posture is the best. Lying down will probably lead to sleep if fatigue is present. Sit comfortably with the back, neck and head in a fairly straight line, erect but not rigid. It is fine to sit on a chair or couch. Meditation does not require any extreme yoga postures. If you do use a chair or couch then choose one that allows you to maintain a fairly straight posture, not a slouchy position, that is less ideal. Getting the posture right may require some adjustment. If you do elect to sit on a flat surface, like a bed or the floor, then it is a good idea to place a cushion under the buttocks for elevation. You want the buttocks higher than the knees. That puts a natural curve in the lower spine, which takes strain off the quadratus muscles of the low back and allows for more natural posture and longer sitting. If you are a sitting on a cushion you will need to cross your legs in front of you in some fashion. Ideally the knees touch the floor, no problem if not. You can cross legs at the ankles, pull one heal in to the groin region and place the other foot in front, or sit half or full lotus if you are so inclined (see your yoga teacher for instruction). Hands can be placed folded together on the lap, or resting on the knees. Allow the posture to be straight and still reasonably relaxed.

Eyes open or closed can work. In most traditions, however, eyes are closed. The reason for an open eye approach is to maintain greater mental alertness. It is not for seeing. You do not need to look at anything. It is generally suggested when using an open eye approach to look down a bit, with the eyes only half open. For folks new to meditation practice, however, my advice is to close your eyes as that reduces visual input and helps to quiet the brain/body/mind. It also reduces distractions.

Time

When – The very best is to meditate first thing in the morning before you get too busy. Get up, clean up, wake up, meditate. The Dalai Lama gets up at 3:30am for practice. That is probably too early for most folks, but early is good. Here in San Francisco if you are out and about early in the morning, say 5:30am, the air is sweet and the streets are pretty darn quiet.

How Long – The recommended amount of time is 15-20 minutes per session in the beginning, quality over quantity though. That said, 2 minutes of quality meditation is better than 30 minutes of lazy focus. It is also better to do something every day, even if only briefly, than to do large random spurts. Just like learning to play the piano, playing for 4 hours on Saturday is way less productive that playing for 30 minutes every day. It will require a bit of time management at first, but once you get in the habit it will become part of your routine. It will probably not take that long before you start to notice how much better you feel on days you sit and practice. Eventually it becomes something you look forward to doing. It is like regular exercise in that regard. Other timing factors include meditating before meals, but if you are starving it is okay to have something light so you are not too distracted by hunger.

Place

You can do the seated mindful awareness practice potentially anywhere and at any time. That is one of the beauties of the method. We will explore that more in the next section on the Active Mindful

Awareness practice. Seated mindfulness meditation practice requires, obviously, a time and place where you can sit and relax for at least a few minutes, with your eyes partially or completely closed. That does not mean you need pin drop silence or the solitude of a Himalayan cave. I almost always meditate when I am on any form of mass transit, be that plane, bus or boat (depending on scenery of course). If you able to find a more suitable spot, however, that is best, somewhere that is clean, quiet, and where you will not be disturbed during your session. Once you get a bit more comfortable with the method, however, you will find that you can successfully do the practice in a very wide variety of settings.

Managing the Busy Mind

Quieting the mind requires time and patience. If the mind is particularly busy, however, there are some simple things you can do, not technically mindfulness practice, but helpful. One method is to count backwards from 10 to 1 with each exhale, or to repeat the number 1 with each exhale, or to repeat the word 'exhaling' with each exhale. In all of these approaches, when you realize that the mind has drifted off somewhere else then just quietly return to the breath, accepting the momentary detour and starting again with '10' or '1' or 'exhale'. In terms of breath, you can put a bit more energy into really staying with the breath, tracking it along its path – inhale, transition at top of breath, exhale, pause at the end, urge to inhale, inhale, and repeating so on.

Final Thought

Although breath is often the starting place for teaching mindfulness, anything can be a focal point for a period of practice. One can sit and be mindful of sensory experience for 20 minutes, or sensations in the body, or thoughts. We will work with these as we go through this book. For now, however, a good place to start is to work on the basic practice by noticing the inflow and outflow of breath.

> **REFLECTION**
>
> Note your experience with sitting mindfulness meditation practice this week. You can use a meditation log to keep track of your daily experience.

II. Active Mindful Awareness Practice

The second core mindfulness method we will be using throughout this book is an Active Mindful Awareness practice. This is the out-in-the-world, driving the car, sitting in class, attending a meeting, talking with a friend, awareness practice. **"I am aware of my experience, of where I am right now."**

The sitting practice is a training to develop a more focused attentional capacity, the ability to remain more intentionally, consciously aware in the moment. The active practice uses that increased awareness and cultivates a capacity for greater real-time awareness of our life experience in the midst of activity. The point of a more active practice is to develop greater momentary awareness during the day, increased awareness of thoughts, feelings, sights, sounds, inner sensations, all of it. It means greater awareness of frustration and happiness, thoughts of worry or delight, the smell of the bakery and of the disheveled street person. Knowing where we are in the moment, what we are thinking, feeling, doing, allows us to have more control over our responses to life, it increases our choices.

The Learning Life Approach - Awareness, Inquiry, Response

The Learning Life approach to *active mindful awareness* builds on the basic skills developed in the sitting *mindfulness meditation*. It combines methods and philosophical concepts from the Buddhist mindfulness tradition, with elements of contemporary psychology, such as cognitive-behavioral self-monitoring, and ideas from the domains of continual improvement and cybernetics. The Learning Life approach to active mindful awareness involves three components – Awareness, Inquiry, and Response (AIR). Using the method is indeed like taking a moment to get some air, catching one's breath, getting some space. That is a helpful way to think about it and remember it, getting some AIR.

What really brings this method to life, as compared to conventional mindfulness practices, is the dynamic use of questioning. It involves the basic questions of daily life - who, what, when, where, how and why? Awareness relates to *what* – "What am I thinking, feeling, sensing, doing in relation to the world around me?" Inquiry relates to the *why* – "Why did I just do that, think that, say that?" Response is about the *how* – "How do I get it back together, quiet things down, speed things up, do that differently next time?" The *who* is obviously the person doing the reflection, you and me, all of us who are trying to become more aware and more effective in life. The ***when and where*** is whenever you are applying the AIR method, taking a moment to get some AIR.

1. Awareness

Awareness is the foundation. It considers the 'what'. It is awareness of what I am thinking, feeling, doing, in relation to the world around me. It is much harder to see the pattern of our habitual responses to life, and make necessary changes, if there is no attention, no awareness. This is where mindfulness practices become useful – ongoing, non-judgmental awareness of life experience, being with what is, in the moment. One of the differences in the Learning Life approach to mindfulness is the scope of our mindful awareness. Rather than observing and labeling the Five Aggregates the approach is to observe and note the elements of the Wheel. That can be both simpler and more informative.

As introduced in Chapter 1, the *Learning Life Wheel Model* represents the three primary levels of our human experience – Person, Behavior, and Environment. These are the inner circles. They are contained within the larger circle of life, the sphere within which they are experienced. From a mindfulness perspective, this outer circle also represents our awareness. This is the mindful awareness that notices the interdependencies and interactions of person, behavior and environment, of our lived experience. This larger wheel moves through time, past into future, and through space, from here to there. From one day to the next, from one room to the other, we can bring our awareness to our inner experience (Person), our outer responses/habits/actions (Behavior), and the contexts of life (Environment).

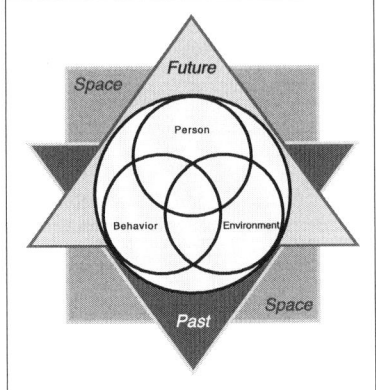

The *Learning Life Wheel Model* is a systems view of our experience, a holistic view. It recognizes life's innate interdependencies – triggers in the environment set off thoughts and feelings, which result in behaviors, which affect our environment – an endless loop. Each component - Person, Behavior, Environment – plays an essential, integral role in the circle of life. Our awareness allows us to recognize and learn as we move through time and space, the days and weeks and years of a lifetime.

Person includes everything happening inside of our skin, the endless ebb and flow of mind and body events. This would include the activity of our genes, our cells, tissues, organ systems and all physiological processes, cascading biochemical events, hormones, sensory perceptions and the interpretation of sensory information, thoughts, emotions, imagination, memory, self-awareness, unconscious neurological processes, consciousness, spirit, and all the rest. It is at the level of Person, for example, that we recognize our thoughts and feelings, an essential component of successful self-management. People who cannot recognize and control their feelings are going to be reactive rather than responsive. Reactivity can be the root of a lot of life problems.

Behavior includes all of our verbal, non-verbal, active and passive doings. It is what people can see when they observe us. That might be the body just sitting still with eyes closed. Or it could be some facial expression, a gesture of the hands, the tone of our voice. Behaviors are the things we do. The things that someone else can observe. No one can look into your heart to know if you are happy, but they can see the smile on your face, and hear the optimism in your voice.

Finally, *Environment* includes our physical, biological and social environments, the world around us. The *physical environment* includes inanimate materials and the physical forces of nature – wind, water, copper, zinc, light, heat and cold, barometric pressure, gravity, radiation, electromagnetic fields, acidity and alkalinity, humidity, and so on. The *biological environment* is the living world residing inside and outside of us. These are the viruses in our noses, fungi on our skin, bacteria in our clothes, insects and plants in the forest, animals in the trees, birds in the air, fish in the sea. Finally, the *social environment* involves our co-existence with other humans on the planet – texting a friend, holidays with the family, the annual homecoming, state park policies, race relations, gender roles, political identity, global cuisines, folk arts, fine arts, workplace hiring practices, international border disputes, economic strata, war, social movements, mass migration, and all the other forms of human social interactions and systems.

This Wheel of endless interdependencies and interaction provides a central framework for our active mindful awareness practices. The growing awareness of the relationship between specific experiences and their interdependencies will become a foundation for seeing our own habit patterns, both helpful habits and limiting ones.

2. Inquiry

Once the 'what' comes clearly into awareness it can be useful to inquire about its purpose or nature. This is the "why?" Asking ourselves the question 'why?' shifts us into a continual improvement orientation (more on that in Chapter 8). "Why did I just do that? Why did I say that? Why am I holding tension in my shoulders? Why am I late again? Why am I so happy?" The goal here is not necessarily to get an answer, but rather to start a process of inquiry, to simply ask a question. Also, it is important not to judge, or rebuke. At this stage the point is to simply inquire. Instead of, "Why am I late AGAIN!!! What an idiot," it is simply, "Why am I late again?" Done. End of inquiry.

What is the benefit of a moment of inquiry? First, it engages the learner in us. It begins with our awareness, noticing "tension, tension, tension" in the shoulders. But then it proceeds to seek insight through inquiry, "**Why** are my shoulders tense right now?" This awakens the quality of curiosity, an invitation to discover and learn. The simple question "why?" begins the process of considering what may be behind this pattern, this habit. Second, very importantly, inquiry reinforces the noticing, our self-monitoring, our mindfulness. Noticing is powerful, noticing and asking, is even stronger. You can notice you avoided homework once again – "I did not do my homework last night." Even better, is to notice as soon as possible, and in addition ask, "Why am I not doing my homework right now like I know I should be?" You can probably appreciate the fact that the answer to that question may not be immediately obvious. But asking it begins an exploration.

Every time you procrastinate and ask 'why?' you begin to look for answers, to explore what is going on in person, behavior, environment that contributes to this pattern. Over time a pattern of causes and effects may begin to become clearer. "Why am I in this part of the forest again?" With that question you retrace your steps and start to notice where you tend to take the wrong turn. In time that is corrected and you get to your destination much sooner. You become self-correcting. The final benefit of inquiry is that it implies caring. Strangers will notice you are crying. A friend will ask you why. Asking why implies a sense of concern and a desire to help. That in itself is healing. Again, this requires simply asking, not expecting answers, not knowing how to fix everything all the time. This is why the aspects of non-judgment and loving-kindness are important. It can take time to understand our ways of being.

3. Response

The final component of the Learning Life approach to active mindful awareness is Response – "How can I get back on track, stay on track, strengthen this positive flow?" You can practice mindfulness meditation until you are blue in the face. It is great to be aware that you are anxious, in pain, failing at math. What good is it to notice a problem, however, if you do not do something about it? This is where a continual improvement philosophy comes into play in our approach to mindful awareness. The goal is to apply an antidote, when practical and available. When that is not possible then it is useful to simply observe the process (awareness) and ask why (inquiry). Often, however, there is an antidote, and we know what it is. In small steps we can begin to apply that medicine and change the story for good.

The Technique

Now we will consider two types of active mindful awareness: (1) a general awareness method; and (2) a targeted awareness approach. Both are intended to cultivate a deeper understanding of the method and greater skill in application. In upcoming chapters we will look specifically at using the tools of mindful awareness for optimizing learning strategies and academic success.

1. General Awareness

The first Active Mindful Awareness Practice is a generalized approach. It deals with the whole picture. It essentially involves bringing intentional awareness to any aspect of the Wheel – Person, Behavior, Environment. The practice is simple. As you remember, at any point during the day, be aware of the things you are experiencing, anything, whatever you choose to be aware of. Be aware of what you are thinking or feeling. Notice sensory input, such as how the sun feels on your face, or listen to the sounds the bus is making, or explore the color of the sky. Notice sensations in the body, if you are hungry or full, tense or relaxed, energetic or tired, craving or satisfied, how you are standing or sitting. Make a mental note of some of your experiences, mentally label them, "angry," "happy," "walking," "standing," "eating," "hungry," "hearing a bird singing." When observing, it is beneficial to make a mental note of stronger, less productive reactions that are no longer useful. Conversely, if there is something that works well, then notice that, applaud it, and consider expanding it. Recognize it and praise it. In both cases you can bring inquiry to the awareness. In the case of success it may be better to ask "How did I do that?" to trace the steps that worked. In the case of challenges it can be good to ask "Why?" Another excellent general awareness question to ask at any moment is, "What am I experiencing right now, where am I right now?"

2a. Targeted Awareness – Body Practice

We will now look at two targeted active mindful awareness practices. In a generalized active mindful awareness practice you can notice the myriad things throughout the day, the endless flow of changing experiences. You can recognize feelings of frustration and happiness, notice worrisome or hopeful thoughts. You can listen to the sound of dry autumn leaves under foot or the quiet rumble of the subway. You can peel an orange and savor the taste, notice the feeling and scent of the orange skin and its oil on your fingers. Those are simple, clear ways to be awake, in the moment. That said, it is also impossible to be aware of the endless flow of changing experiences. There is so much, too much, and sometimes because there is so much, we forget to be mindful at all. As an alternative it can be helpful to pick one thing to be aware of during the day, some targeted thought or behavior that would be useful and motivating to track.

One such technique is to use a specific mindful awareness cue, like every time you touch your phone. You get in the habit of engaging your mindful awareness when you touch your phone. Another idea is to select certain times of the day to be mindful, similar to the practice of adhan, when Muslims pray, five times a day, facing Mecca. Practices like this build mindful awareness into life as a routine, and that means it gets done. Another approach is mindful awareness of a specific target, such as being aware of ***physical tension***. The value of this type of practice is that it can help to both develop momentary awareness as well as contribute to well-being. The way to do this practice is to pick some area of the body where you tend to hold tension. Shoulders can be a good focus for this practice for most people. During the day, randomly or at cued times, like when you are at a stop sign, notice your shoulders. Is there any holding that does not need to be there? That is called dysponesis, unnecessary muscle tension. High level athletes pay consultants a lot of money to help them recognize where they are holding tension, using muscles inefficiently. Dysponesis produces wear and tear and reduces performance.

Doing targeted mindful awareness practiced in this way provides two benefits, increased awareness, and increased physical well-being. This approach makes the homework of mindful awareness practical, useful, and motivating.

But can we do more? Yes! The point of Learning Life active mindful awareness is not just to notice, but to use that increased awareness to move toward new learning and greater happiness. How? First, **Awareness**, notice the tension, make a mental note if you are so inclined "tense, tense, tense." Then if you want to take it to the next level, take a moment and introduce **Inquiry**, a quick assessment, "Why am I tensing my shoulders?" No need for an answer immediately, just let the awareness of the question be the start of an exploration. Very important, do not stress over finding the answer, let it come. Third, **Respond**, move into relaxation, release the tension. Take a breath, breath into the tension, raise and lower the shoulders, move the tight spot, ask the tension, the body, what it needs right now, and let go as much as the body is willing to release in that moment. Finally, importantly, practice letting go of any judgment of the tension if it is there, instead bring in acceptance and even some kindness toward yourself, acknowledging what a good job you did noticing, releasing, healing and learning.

2b. Targeted Awareness – Judging Practice

In the Body Practice we were working with the physical plane, noticing and releasing tension. In this second Judging Practice we will work with the thought/emotion plane, focusing on a specific target — judging (self and others). This training is similarly practical for increasing mindful awareness generally and cultivating compassion specifically, making the method practical, efficient, and motivating. This method is related to another important element of the mindfulness meditation tradition known as *metta*, or loving kindness practice, which was mentioned earlier in the chapter. Our conditioned or habit-based mind can be quite reactive, such as being quick to anger for no good reason, anger directed toward self or other. Those conditioned habits can also be quite self-reinforcing and persist over a lifetime with minimal improvement. Observing and releasing judgment is an excellent foundation to developing loving kindness, the essence of *metta*.

The basic approach is to notice criticism, judgment of self or others. During the course of the day have the intention that you will be more selectively attentive to judging self and other. With that increased awareness notice that thought/emotion when it arises, or the behavior if it is expressed as critical speech about self or other. It can be helpful to label, "Judging, judging, judging." You can ask, "Why am I judging?" and notice what is going on inside and around you, what triggers that pattern. If you are inclined and able you can begin to respond, to apply an antidote of loving kindness to that mental habit. The antidote would be to drop the judgment or to look for the positive, to reframe the experience positively. Loving kindness is not about accepting evil or injustice, it is about recognizing that humans are dealing with their challenges. If you are human (and I suspect you are), then you probably have your own struggles too. It is easier to hold space for others' imperfections if we recognize our own. The New Testament speaks of removing the beam from our eye before remarking about the sliver in the eye of another. It is also easier to have compassion for our own imperfections if we recognize our potential for good. Which reminds me of one final core idea in the mindfulness philosophy – people are fundamentally good, they have just lost touch with that true nature and need to find their way back home. That is what a learning life is all about.

> **REFLECTION**
>
> Note your experience with mindful awareness practice this week. This will include observations of both general awareness and targeted awareness practices.

SUMMARY

It is harder to learn if we are not aware, not present, not conscious. Bringing some mindfulness to the present moment increases our attention, memory, and ability to acquire and integrate knowledge and skills. Mindful awareness is also a catalyzing tool for observing our own habits of body and mind so that we can more effectively and efficiently reduce what limits and increase what enhances. Mindful awareness is a key strategy for greater life success and happiness. To increase our capacity in this regard it can be highly useful to practice some form of seated mindfulness meditation. Meditation practice has been shown to change brain structure (positively related to learning), improve attention and memory, reduce rumination, and facilitate habit change. The practice is simple and involves using our momentary experience as the object of meditation, the object of our attention. In addition to sitting meditation it is especially important to engage in active mindfulness during the course of life. Momentary awareness can be implemented using the Awareness, Inquiry and Response (AIR) approach. Awareness is recognition of the 'what', what I am feeling right now. It is about observing the interplay of the Wheel elements of Person, Behavior and Environment. Inquiry is the 'why', an inquiry into reasons for that behavior, thought, statement. The final Response, is how we deal with any observed loop to pull self on track toward the ultimate destination. Taken together the sitting and active practices provide a solid foundation for greater awareness of life in each moment, the chance to be truly alive.

So this is how it all starts. Right here, right now.

MIND-BODY PRACTICE

Sitting Mindfulness Meditation

Focus on awareness of breathing (5min/day).

Active Mindful Awareness

During the day be aware of things that you take delight in, a color, a smell or taste, the breeze on your face, the way a song makes you feel. Check in periodically during the day and ask - "Where am I right now?" (in terms of mind, body, spirit).

Priming

Practice priming mental imagery to create a most incredible day/week and ideal outcomes with specific tasks."

REFERENCES

Barnes PM, Powell-Griner E, Mcfann K, Nahin RL. Complementary and alternative medicine use among adults: United States 2002. *Advanced Data*. 2004;343:1-19.

Barnes PM, Bloom B, Nahin RL. Complementary and alternative medicine use among adults and children: United States, 2007. *National Health Status Report*. 2008;12:1-23.

Baron Short E, Kose S, Mu Q, et al. Regional brain activation during meditation shows time and practice effects: an exploratory FMRI study. *Evidence Based Complementary Alternative Medicine*. 2010;7:121-127.

LF Barrett, J Gross, TC Christensen. Knowing what you're feeling and knowing what to do about it: Mapping the relation between emotion differentiation and emotion regulation. *Cognition and Emotion*. 2001;15(16):713-724.

Chiesa A, Calati R, Serretti A. Does mindfulness training improve cognitive abilities? A systematic review of neuropsychological findings. *Clinical Psychology Review*. 2011;31(3):449-64.

Chiesa A, Serretti A. Mindfulness-based stress reduction for stress management in healthy people: a review and meta-analysis. *Journal of Alternative and Complementary Medicine*. 2009;15(5):593-600.

Engström M, Pihlsgård J, Lundberg P, Söderfeldt B. Functional magnetic resonance imaging of hippocampal activation during silent mantra meditation. *Journal of Alternative and Complementary Medicine*. 2010;16(12):1253-8.

Farb NA, Anderson AK, Mayberg H, Bean J, McKeon D, Segal ZV. Minding one's emotions: mindfulness training alters the neural expression of sadness. Emotion. Feb; 2010;10(1):25-33.

Gyurak A, Gross JJ, Etkin A. Explicit and implicit emotion regulation: A dual-process framework *Cognition & Emotion*. 2011;25(3) 400-412.

Hasenkamp W, Wilson-Mendenhall CD, Duncan E, Barsalou LW. Mind wandering and attention during focused meditation: a fine-grained temporal analysis of fluctuating cognitive states. *Neuroimage*. 2012;59(1):750-60.

Hölzel BK, Carmody J, Vangel M, Congleton C, Yerramsetti SM, Gard T, Lazar SW. Mindfulness practice leads to increases in regional brain gray matter density. *Psychiatry Research*. 2011;191(1):36-43.

Kalat JW. *Biological Psychology*. Belmont, California: Thomas Higher Education; 2007.

Kerr CE, Jones SR, Wana Q, Pritchett DL, Wasserman RH, Wexler A, Villanueva JJ, Shaw JR, Lazar SW, Kaptchuk TJ, Littenberg R, Hämäläinen MS, Moore CI. Effects of mindfulness meditation training on anticipatory alpha modulation in primary somatosensory cortex. *Brain Research Bulletin*. 2011;85(3-4):96-103.

Kilpatrick LA, Suyenobu BY, Smith SR, Bueller JA, Goodman T, Creswell JD, Naliboff BD. Impact of mindfulness-based stress reduction training on intrinsic brain connectivity. *NeuroImage*. 2011;56(1):290-298.

Luders E, Toga AW, Lepore N, Gaser C. The underlying anatomical correlates of long-term meditation: larger hippocampal and frontal volumes of gray matter. *NeuroImage*. 2009;45:672-678.

Lutz A, Slagter HA, Rawlings NB, Francis AD, Greischar LL, Davidson RJ. Mental training enhances attentional stability: neural and behavioral evidence. *Journal of Neuroscience*. 2009;29:13418-13427.

Schultz D, Izard CE, Ackerman BP, Youngstrom EA. Emotion knowledge in economically disadvantaged children: Self-regulatory antecedents and relations to social difficulties and withdrawal. *Development and Psychopathology*. 2001;1:53-67.

Continual Improvement and Quality

I regularly ask myself if there is a better way.

CHAPTER THEMES
- Kaizen
- Continual Improvement Concepts
- Learning Life Problem Solving Model

In this chapter we will explore the concepts of quality and continual improvement (CI). A quality focus and a continual improvement orientation are essential Learning Life strategies. Quality can be associated with a product, person, event, process, or experience. Something of quality is well designed, well crafted, well executed. It predictably delivers what is expected. It can reflect a variety of attributes such as usability, reliability, high functionality, efficiency, consistent and enduring value, or desirable aesthetics, such a beauty. Continual improvement, on the other hand, is the ongoing task of moving toward greater quality in products, services, processes, and being.

Kaizen - Quality and Continual Improvement

We will begin our exploration of quality and continual improvement through the lens of Kaizen. Kaizen is an approach to continual improvement that came into existence after World War II, as part of the effort to help Japan rebuild its industrial base. The Japanese word Kaizen 改善 is composed of the two roots – *kai*, which means change, and *zen*, which means good. So Kaizen refers to change for the good, or improvement.

Although large scale change and rapid change can be part of the continual improvement process, the more typical approach in the Kaizen tradition is improvement via small corrections over time. Large scale, all at once change is often associated with innovation, such as change produced by the introduction of a new technology or a major new production process. That can be quite disruptive. For example, when the ARPANET (the original Internet) went live in 1969 it was a specialized technology used by a small group of government and academic research centers. Today there are about 2.5 billion people around the world using the Internet. In a relatively short period of time, some decades, this technological innovation has had a monumental impact on communication, commerce, research, entertainment, politics, national security, on so many aspects of the human experienced. Previously dominant media platforms, such as print newspapers and magazines, have been changed forever. Political campaigns and social movements are using new media in ways that did not exist a decade ago. Online shopping has significantly impacted sales in bricks and mortar stores and completely transformed the very nature of the modern shopping experience. That is a rapid and large scale change that has been simultaneously beneficial and quite disruptive.

Many individuals similarly pursue an all at once approach to change, especially on New Years eve. "I am going to quit smoking, start exercising, lose 25 pounds, and become a vegan." Good luck!!! Radical change of that sort is often impractical, unsustainable, and ineffective. Kaizen on the other hand focuses on ongoing, incremental change, nothing radical, just slow and steady, continually refining, continually improving, over the course of a lifetime. No yo-yo diets, no $400 treadmill sitting idle in the living room. The Kaizen process is like driving a car on the freeway. As you drive along you are making small ongoing adjustments. Small, ongoing adjustment while driving is way better than making a major adjustment when the car has crossed the median strip and is heading into oncoming traffic. Passengers in those oncoming cars will be freaked, not a good strategy. "Oops, sorry, my bad!" If the process involves a series of small, ongoing adjustments it will be more sustainable, less jarring and disruptive, something that can be carried out over extended periods of time, indeed a lifetime, with less wear and tear, with greater predictable ongoing success.

The History of Kaizen

At the end of World War II General Douglas MacArthur invited Edwards Deming to Japan to help work on a national census. Deming was a statistician, who along with Walter Shewhart, had developed some useful quality control measures for use in industrial settings. While in Japan, Deming was invited by the Japanese Union of Scientists and Engineers to teach these statistical process control methods to engineers and managers. One of Deming's core messages was to focus on quality as a means to achieve greater productivity and competitiveness. Ultimately, these ideas evolved into a Japanese business management philosophy known as Kaizen.

Deming's ideas contributed to a major transformation in Japanese business process leading to, among other things, Japan's global leadership in automotive manufacturing and sales. As a result of his contribution Japan's Prime Minister honored Deming in 1960 with the Order of the Sacred Treasure, one of the highest civilian awards in the country. Unfortunately, Deming's work was largely ignored in the United States until toward the end of his life, after Japan had become one of the worlds leading automakers, creating products widely recognized for their quality and reliability. I can say personally, having grown up in Detroit and witnessing the decline in reputation of American cars, that I came to appreciate the importance of Dr. Deming's work and his commitment to quality even more. I once actually had the pleasure of hearing Dr. Deming speak. He was quite elderly at that point, but that was not keeping him from getting out to talk about social reform through continual improvement. At that particular meeting he was talking about quality improvement in the US educational system. He was obviously passionate about his mission, and he continued to consult until the end of his life at the age of 93. He certainly did not need the money. He just believed deeply in what he was doing. One of Dr. Deming's main lessons was to, "Create constancy of purpose toward improvement," in other words, to make improvement a lifetime priority (Deming, 1986).

Some Key Kaizen/Continual Improvement Concepts

Quality Solutions

Rule number one – focus on quality. A quality focus helps to align goals and actions, and this helps to maximize the productive use of our precious time and energy. A quality focus places a premium on finding solutions that are effective, efficient, reliable, simple, sustainable, functional, usable, and beautiful. A particular solution may not have or need all of these characteristics, but they are aspects to consider. Is a quality focus essential, mandatory? No, of course not. Sometimes you just want to find any plug to keep the boat from sinking, a quick fix. In the long run, however, especially for important ongoing life processes, a focus on quality solutions will be very productive, fixing the boat the right way, so it will not leak again. An American ski prodigy, 18-year-old Mikaela Shiffrin, became the youngest person to win an Olympic gold medal in slalom. It was well known that Mikaela's strategy was not to focus on winning but rather to focus on continually improving (Meyer, 2014). If we focus on quality everything else will follow.

Root Cause of the Problem

Kaizen is interested in *getting to the root* of problems (if possible). An example from healthcare might help explain this. Katie had a frequent skin rash. She went to the dermatologist and was prescribed a medicated cream to apply to her skin. It helped a bit, but the problem would always come back. After some research and trail and error she discovered that her problem was a food allergy. She changed her diet and the problem went away, completely. The skin cream helped to address the symptom, the rash, but it could not really solve the problem, because the root cause was not being treated. The food allergy was the underlying cause, the root of the problem. Treating the symptom instead of the root resulted in an incomplete cure. Once the root was found and addressed the problem was resolved. In traditional Chinese medicine the branch and the root are differentiated. The branch is the symptom (that which is often visible and more easily recognized). The root is the underlying cause (often less obvious). It is generally considered better in traditional medicine to treat the root. If we merely address the symptom it may solve the problem, but in many cases such solutions can be incomplete or temporary.

Effective and Reliable Solutions

Is the solution effective. Does it work? Does it get the job done? Does it help you reach your goal, the desired state? That may sound obvious, but it is not. Many people pursue perceived solutions thinking they will bring happiness, but they actually take them further from it. As the old Vermont joke says, "You cannot get there from here." I once studied with a Tibetan meditation master. He would say that if your method (of practice) was not making you happier then it was either the wrong method or you were doing it the wrong way. I never forgot his good council.

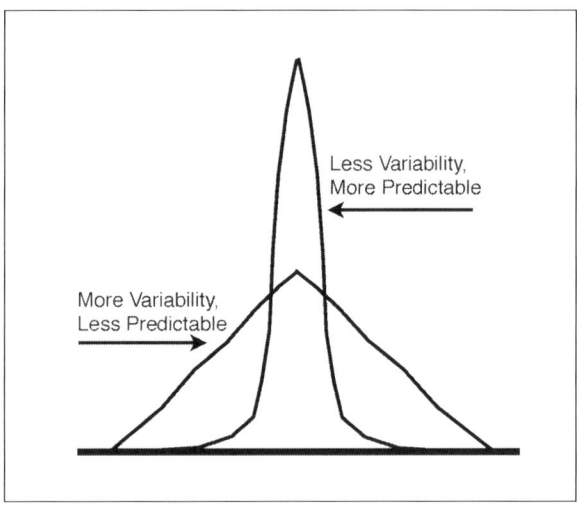

A related characteristic is reliability, does it work predictably, consistently. We want solutions we can count on, solutions that work consistently. Say you bought boxes of discount batteries from company A and company B for a wilderness program. On the packaging both companies promise that on average about 80% of the batteries will work, which means about 20% will be duds. Company A has lower quality control on its products. They are cheaper to buy, but sometimes the pack has a lot of dead batteries, that product has a lot more variability. Products from Company B are much more reliable, more likely that at least 80% of them turn on the lights, less variable. Product reliability for batteries from Company A, however, is more widespread. On average 80% will work, but there is more variability per shipment. In some shipments you get 100% effective batteries, in others you get 55% effective. They are more variable, less reliable (see figure). In life we want solutions we can count on, just like friends.

Simple Solutions

Another characteristic of optimal solutions is that they are simple. Indeed, simplicity is one of the guiding principles of Kaizen. Why do something that is complex if something simple will get you the same result? Superstition and ritual are often the product of not knowing which part of a behavioral sequence produces the desired outcome. We create simpler solutions by noticing unnecessary steps that can be eliminated or possibly combined. We want to trim the habitual, superstitious, redundant, superfluous, unquestioned elements and just use the pieces that really count (that said, picking pieces that actually count is often much easier said than done).

Functional and Usable Solutions

An ideal solution is also functional and usable. A solution that is functional does what it is supposed to do, allows you to complete the needed task you are using it for. Let us say you are buying a paper shredder. One of them can take 5 pages at a time and shred them into long strips, but you have to remove staples first. The other one has an auto feeder where you just drop in a stack of papers, it shreds up to 20 sheets at a time, staples no problem, and it cross cuts each sheet into confetti-sized pieces. Both shred but the second one has more functionality, it can handle more paper, including with staples, and shreds into finer bits, harder to re-assemble and steal data from. Usability has to do with how easy it is to use something, how useful, convenient, practical it is. If the second shredder had complex digital manuals that had to be reset each time it might be used less than the simpler version, lower usability, less useful.

Usability and functionality are not infrequently inversely related. As something becomes more functional, now able to do twenty things instead of two, it is often harder to use, harder to program, harder to remember the combination of steps. So, one size does not fit all. The key is to get a good fit for the job. It is like finding that go to jacket that is the first thing you reach for when there is chill in the air. It is highly functional – has the functions you need – warm, wind proof, water resistant, portable. It is also very usable – great fit, nice color, lightweight, folds small so it is easy to carry in a daypack for use when you need it. That coat is functional and usable, a good investment, a good solution.

Efficient and Sustainable Solutions

Quality solutions are efficient. What does that mean? It could mean many things, but it is essentially about saving precious resources. An efficient solution does not just get you to the desired state, it gets you there for less money, in less time, with less energy, with fewer materials, and with less waste. It is fine to have multiple routes to a destination – you drive to the mall via the country road on Tuesday, you use city streets on Wednesday, and then take the highway on Thursday. That adds color to your trip, which is great if you have the time. But if this is going to be your regular route to work every day then you probably want the path that gets you to your destination in the quickest time and with the least stress. An efficient solution results in less waste. The ancient Taoists recognized this as one of the keys of a long life – to *work with* nature rather than *working against* it. Ask yourself, "What is the most efficient way to get to the desired state."

An important related concept is sustainability. Is the solution sustainable? Does it require a lot of resources to be maintained? A high maintenance boyfriend or girlfriend, or food crops that need a lot of fertilizer and pesticide, are less desirable solutions because they are not easily maintained over time, they are less sustainable. Solutions like those use up your resources more quickly. A solution that is sustainable does what you need, is easy to use, is durable, and requires comparatively fewer resources over time to maintain.

Incremental – Small Steps

One thing that often snags people on their path to change is that they envision the whole journey at once. They look at the map and immediately see that it is a very long way from here to there. It is daunting, disheartening, maybe not even possible they think. That is why the old Chinese adage reminds us that a journey of a thousand miles begins with a single step. During the Tang Dynasty (618-907 CE), the noted Chinese Buddhist scholar Xuanzang spent 16 years travelling thousands of miles from China to India and then back in pursuit of his search for truth. He did not have the Internet to book hotels and restaurants, no guidebooks, no translation dictionaries. Talk about a daunting journey, a long journey, a perilous journey, but what an adventure, and for such a noble and transcendent goal, to understand life, to search for truth. How did he manage? One step at a time, one day at a time, moving forward slowly along his path, living his adventure.

Kaizen also recognizes that life's challenges can be daunting. Big problems can shut people down, stop a process. So one of the keys to success is to break large tasks into smaller, more manageable steps.

The Kaizen strategy is to break the problem into smaller piece and then solve the smaller problems one at a time. The focus is on small steps, incremental change, as compared to radical or abrupt change. The goal is to make progress along the path one step at a time. Continual improvement, however, also embraces change that is large and dramatic. The reality is that innovation happens, and sometimes that is the best way. It is like shaving your hair off for the Fourth of July. Sometimes a big change is just the right thing. Most of the time, however, Kaizen suggests small continual changes over time as the best way to stay on course for a lifetime of increasing excellence.

Final thought, *sometimes we just need to take that first step, no matter how small or seemingly inconsequential. It can be very liberating to just start, even if that first step seems very small, it is movement along the path.* That is how we build self-efficacy, one small step, one small success at a time. We take the first small step for the sake of doing something, for the sake of getting our life back. One small step after another is an effective strategy for sustainable growth. *Think Small Steps*.

The Learning Life Problem Solving Model

Kaizen and other approaches to continual improvement commonly employ a multi-step process. Deming was known for endorsing a four step Plan-Do-Check-Act (PDCA) Cycle (Gabor, 1990). We are going to focus on a 5-step continual improvement model that includes the following elements:

1. Identify the Problem – recognize and acknowledge, name, assess problem and its root
2. Consider Solutions – generate possible solutions that can address the problem
3. Pick One – consider the potential solutions and select the best fit
4. Try It – test the proposed solution on a small scale
5. Evaluate the Effect and Celebrate! – evaluate outcomes, reward effort, standardize solution

These five basic steps match the *Learning Life Problem Solving Model (PSM)* described in Chapter 3 very nicely. The PSM, as you may recall, looks at the current state, assesses deficiencies, and defines the goal or the desired state that you seek. The gap between current and desired is the problem. Once the problem is clear(er) the best solution path (the most efficient and effective route from current to desired) is selected. That path is implemented and data collected (trying out the solution to see if it works). When there is enough information about that implemented solution it is evaluated to see if it is the best path, the best solution. If it does indeed appear to be a good fit then a larger scale implementation can follow. If not, then it is back to the drawing board for reconsideration to determine the next solution to test, repeating this process until the way becomes clear. We will now look at these 5 continual improvement steps in relation to the *LL Problem Solving Model*. This is the problem solving approach we will be working with in this text. A template for working through the steps listed below is also located at the end of the book in the Resources section.

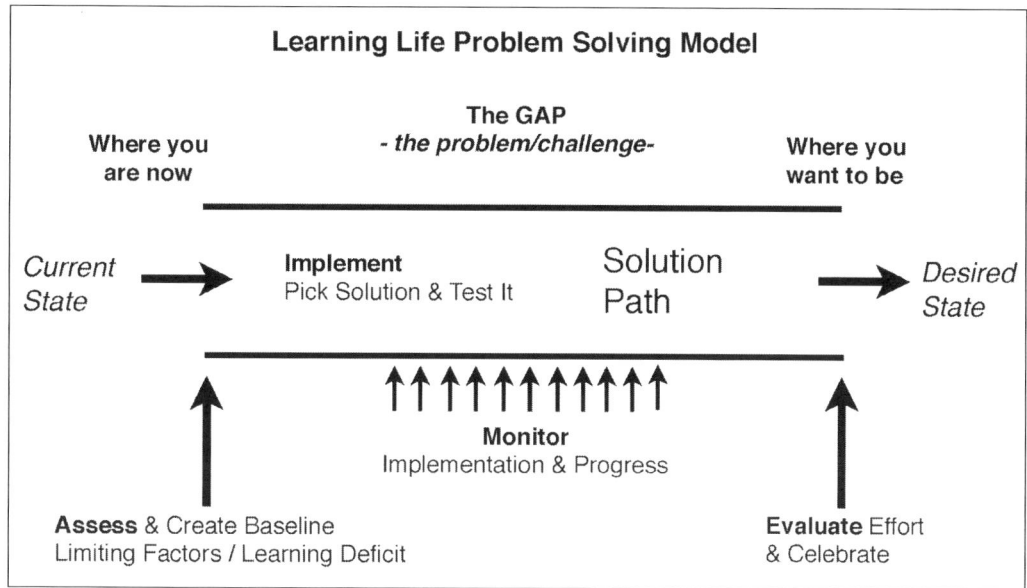

Step 1 — Identify the Problem

The first step is to identify the problem, the gap between current and desired. This step includes a number of aspects. These include: (A) recognizing the problem; (B) describing and labeling the problem – current state, desired state, and the gap; and (C) assessing the causes, including root causes, why am I here and not there.

A. Recognize the Problem

A problem is a gap. It is the space between current state (where you are right now) and the desired state (where you want to be). If you were already there, already at the desired state, there would be no issue, no problem. It would all be good. If, however, you are not at the desired state yet, then there is room for improvement. It all starts with recognizing that gap, noticing the problem, naming it, and thinking of how the situation could be better, envisioning the desired state. That may sound fairly obvious and simple, but there are certain behaviors that can block problem recognition and others that will promote it. Here are some things to consider.

Denial and Inaction

Admitting that there is a problem is often the very first step in an improvement process, admitting that something is wrong, or that things could be better. The opposite is ignorance and denial. Ignorance has to do with a lack of information. In the 1940's people did not know that smoking caused lung cancer. They used to give out free cigarettes to GI's during World War II. The army does not do that today. Back then society was ignorant of the harmful effects of smoking. While ignorance is lack of information, denial is intentional rejection of information. If someone smokes today and says it is not harmful, that is denial. It is pretty unlikely that anyone living today does not know smoking is harmful. Despite that information people can deny the facts. Denial is a dishonest response to self and others.

Why do people engage in denial? Because ignorance (denial) is bliss. People want to be happy and if they can successfully ignore or deny problems then their denial can provide some peace of mind.

Denial is also convenient, as it does not require action. If there is no problem then nothing needs to happen, simple. Ignorance and denial means we do not have to do anything about our situation. We can just keep watching television and eating macaroons, all good. Denying the problem also means we will not upset the apple cart, the status quo remains in place, no risk of disturbing powerful others if we do not question things. We just stay in our place, quiet and invisible. Finally, denial is a great way to keep getting high (in whatever fashion we find most compelling) and pretending that there is no consequence, or that we will take care of it manana.

How to deal with this challenge? Get help, get real, be honest, find your deeper motivations to change, recognize old conditioned body-mind habits as the collar that keeps you in the cage, respect yourself, honor your life, cultivate the gifts you have been given and use them for good. Denial can be part of an old story that often has to do with unworthiness, absence of love, fear and insecurity. Denial is one way to pacify these places of unhappiness. The problem with denial is that those old holding patterns may never change. They continue to limit our ability to become who we are capable of being, a whole person, happy and radically alive.

Invisible Problems and Inaction
The next challenge is invisibility. Many problems in life are quite obvious. You have no eggs and the recipe call for eggs. Your car runs out of gas on the way to the airport and your flight is in 30 minutes. You are 100 feet under water and the scuba gear you rented from the little shack on the beach suddenly stops working. Those are obvious problems, some more consequential than others, but all of them obvious problems. There are other problems, however, that are far less visible, possibly even invisible. Some problems can truly be very hard to see, like bacteria before the advent of the microscope. Because of invisibility we remain ignorant of the existence of such problems, ignorant of the root cause. These invisible roots can be beliefs, behaviors, or attitudes that have existed for a lifetime, maybe family norms or community norms. When a way of being is so pervasive, possibly part of a lifelong pattern, it may not be readily recognized as a problem. It is just the way it has always been.

> **STRATEGY NOTE:** A person needs to be much more vigilant, mindfully aware, to find those types of problems. One strategy is to pay attention to where the gap between the current and desired state persists, or where efforts to move forward keep stalling, or where stress or depression consistently pop up, or where other people are troubled by our actions, or where we just sense something is just not right. Those are red flags, good places to look.

Recognition and Inaction
When we move beyond denial and ignorance the potential for resolving problems begins to emerge. We now recognize that there is a problem, maybe we can even name it, identify it. That still does not mean we will change, however. A problem is the gap between current state and desired state. That desired state, however, may either be a place we *would like* to be or a place that we *need* to be. If the gap is between here and somewhere that we *need to be*, somewhere that we *have to be*, like getting the next breath of air to stay alive when the scuba tank malfunctions, then that gap

will more likely have the qualities of visibility and urgency. For any normal human being, reducing that gap between no air and air will be highly motivating, hyper-motivating. If, however, the gap is between here and somewhere we would *like to be*, such as having a healthier diet or getting better grades, then there is no fire under foot to close that gap. The gap between where we are and where we would *like to be* can simmer for years, in truth, for a lifetime. People can be aware of the fact that they waste too much time watching television, or exploring the internet, or texting. They may be depressed, not expressing their needs, maybe feeling taken advantage of. They may be smoking too much pot or drinking too much beer. A person can easily spend a lifetime with full awareness, fully mindful, of the gap between what they have and what they want, simmering in various degrees of discontent, but never actually doing a single serious thing about it to change the situation. A simple life truth is that our habits do not change until we do.

> **STRATEGY NOTE:** Same as for 'Denial and Inaction' above. The bottom line – we need to recognize that our tank is on empty and you are running out of gas, or even more motivating, running out of air. It needs to become important, potentially an appreciation of its urgency. It is our happiness, our success, our life which lies in the balance.

Recognition and Action
If the first step in problem solving involves acknowledging that there is a problem then the next thing that must follow for change to happen is the motivation and intention to move from here to there. The philosopher Krishnamurti once said that when we become truly honest about a problem it becomes harder to live with it (Krishnamurti, 1964). That is one of the clear benefits of acknowledging and identifying the problem. It can make the status quo less okay, and that can be motivating. When we see how something holds us down, hurts us or someone else, holds us back from our own life, it becomes harder to just let it be. The sooner the work gets started the sooner the sun will rise.

Problem Prevention and Problem Creation
In CI models like Kaizen, besides the invisible and visible problems, there is also an appreciation of preventable problems and created problems. The first involves thinking of problems before they occur, taking a preventive perspective. This is a core goal of preventive health practices and a key mandate in public health. Humans have a tendency to react to problems rather than to prevent them, being reactive rather than proactive. One example is the continual growth in national expenditure on healthcare, a significant contributor to national debt. One big cause of this growing expense is all of the money spent on the care of individuals with chronic preventable diseases, such as type 2 diabetes. A much better solution would be encouraging and supporting appropriate lifestyle habits related to diet, exercise, and stress management. A preventive lifestyle approach could improve the quality of health for millions of people, both young and old, increase productivity and wellbeing, and dramatically reduce healthcare expenditure.

Another CI approach is to intentionally create a problem by selecting a new standard or by setting a higher goal. In this situation we create the problem. Things may be working just fine, no gap between the current and the desired state. For example, last semester Martha was perfectly happy getting all B's in her classes, a big improvement from her first year in school. Desired state, desired goal, was achieved. Then she realized she could do better. She created a new desired state, getting all A's. She raised the bar, created a problem (challenge) were there was none before.

> **STRATEGY NOTE:** "Is there a better way to do this?" One very useful strategy is to ask the simple question, "Is there a better way to do this?" That is the mindset that will notice opportunities for improvement. That simple question can be used as a basic tool for exploring problem recognition.

B. Describe and Label the Problem – Current, Desired, Gap

Once you have recognized the problem the next step is naming and labeling it – problem identification. Naming and labeling things can be very illuminating, very helpful. "No you are not having a heart attack, that feeling in your chest is actually just some serious indigestion." Oh what a relief it is to know that. In the *Learning Life Problem Solving Model* we define a problem as a gap between the current state and the desired state. Hungry (current), wants to be full (desired), must find food and eat (the problem, the gap). Quite simple. It can be helpful to get in the habit of thinking of task management, life management, in these terms – current, desired, and gap. Just doing that quick assessment helps to put things in perspective. It provides an orientation in the problem solving flow, "This where I am. This is where I want to be. This is what the problem is." Having that map in mind can help us to more calmly and rationally move forward along the path.

> **STRATEGY NOTE:** A useful entry point to problem clarification involves a simple writing exercise - a description of current state (the way it is at the moment), another description of the desired state (how we would like it to be), a simple, succinct problem statement (this is the problem). Hungry (current), wants to be full (desired), must find food and eat (the problem). At the very least, get some clarity on the desired state. One of the reasons that people float about not know which way to turn is they do not really know where they want to go. Clarifying the desired state will go a long way to focusing the problem and potential solutions. What is the desired state, highest good for you and others. That can be a process to figure that out, but well worth the investment. Having this type of clarity about the endpoint is extremely helpful for planning. It allows one to start at the end and work backwards, to visualize the path that will be needed to reach that goal.

C. Assess the Cause of the Problem

First we recognize and label the problem – the current state, the desired state, and the gap between them (the problem). That is a big first step on the journey. The next thing to do is to assess the cause of that problem. Problem assessment is looking for the SOMETHING that needs to be corrected. Where is the deficiency. It seeks to answer the question, "Why am I not getting good grades, managing my weight, scoring more free throws?" The deficiency, the something that needs to be corrected, could be an attitude/motivation (I don't care), a behavior (drinking too much), a skill (poor note taking strategy), knowledge (never really learned algebra well), resources (missing text books), the environment (a noisy living space).

In the assessment we are looking for the cause of the problem, ideally the root cause. It is important to recognize that one symptom, like poor math grades, can be the result of various causes. If the goal is to get good math grades you need to have some idea of cause in order to pick the right solution. If you have 3 student doing poorly in a math class it could be because one is working the midnight shift, the second lacks interest in the class, and the third has language issues. Because there are potentially a wide variety of causes it is useful to keep the Wheel Model in mind and to consider if the cause is related to Person, Behavior, or Environment, or some combination. In order to resolve the problem we need to assess and isolate the cause. Treating the wrong cause will not solve the problem. If there appear to be multiple causes then there may need to be multiple solutions.

Finding the Root
If possible we want to find the root of the problem and work on that. If we just treat the symptom the problem may keep coming back. Zoe is missing her morning classes. She can buy two alarm clocks, but if the root cause of her missing morning classes is the result of low motivation, four alarm clocks will not make a difference, at least not for long. Again, using the Wheel Model can be a helpful way to analyze a problem and explore possible root causes.

The other truth is that problems at times can be multifaceted in their causation (several roots), or from a very distant past originating before a person can even remember. Finding the root of such problems can be challenging, even impossible. If that is the case there are some other strategies that can be of help. The first is to not worrying about isolating a root cause and to just focus on the goal, the desired state. The root is the past, and the past is the past. What we really want is a different future, the desired state, the goal. For that reason if the root cause is unclear then it is useful to just focus on the goal (the future) and work diligently on that. If the problem gets solved then the root often becomes irrelevant. We have reached the other shore, and a new adventure begins.

One final strategy for working with less visible roots is to just bring attention or mindful awareness to the problem. Be with the problem with acceptance, as it is, and apply kindness toward self. The goal is not necessarily working to change things yet, but rather learning to be with it as it is, without judgment. This brings the element of mindful awareness into the picture. Because the quality awareness is a new addition to the old habit it is by default being modified. It is being modified with the addition of awareness and acceptance. Even with less visible problems it is possible to get helpful insight in this way. Bringing awareness to the problem and observing our patterns over time can provide the basis for insights. Solutions can begin to emerge. It may take time, but it can be quite enlightening, and potentially better than doing nothing. Mindful awareness used in this way can be the beginning of a subtle but pervasive change.

Specify the Motive

One of the common deficiencies that can keep people from reaching the desired state is a lack of motivation or not having a clear motive. Reflection on the desired state relates to getting clear on the 'what'. What do I really want, what do I really need? In the next 4 steps we will consider the 'how'. How will I get there, how will I get what I want or need? Before heading down that path one very important final consideration is the 'why'. Why is this important to me. This element is generally not part of industrial models because the why is often presumed. We are doing this because we need to improve profit, reliability, customer satisfaction or whatever driving reason has been found. With individual change this aspect, however, is less clear or potent. There is no one above telling you this needs to be done, no organizational mandate, it is one's own journey. If there is no strong motive there is a good chance the effort will sputter and die in time. If there is a clear motive the probability of persistence and success are truly greater.

> **STRATEGY NOTE:** Collect Some Problem Assessment Data. Sometimes the problem is quite obvious, out of eggs, out of gas, out of air. Other times it is not. Even when it a problem appears to be obvious, the real cause might not be. The symptom is often obvious, the root, not always. So in many instances it can be helpful to keep tabs for a few days or weeks or months to get a sense of what is really going on. Look for the pattern and try to get ideas of where the problem originates, the root.

What are the best ways to gather this data? One idea is to start with a list – who, what, when, where, why, how. Do a simple brainstorm of these questions. Then keep tabs for a while. Jot down notes periodically to begin to get an image of what the completed puzzle would look like. Pay attention to the Wheel elements of person, behavior and environment. Is it a pattern of thought or emotion that is at the root, feelings of anxiety, worry, negative self-talk, depression? Is it a behavior, drinking too much, using the wrong study strategies, being too aggressive when you try to ask someone out? Is it the environment, noisy study area, not getting along with housemates, living far from school? When you get a sense of what may be the root then track it for a while longer to see if your hypothesis holds up. Keep an index card handy to note how much studying you did today, when and where, mark the days on your calendar when you are depressed, fill a bowl with beer caps for a month to see how much you are drinking. Collecting this type of assessment data will help you know where to intervene, where the greatest benefit will be gained, where the seat of the most enduring change resides, where the most probable area of success is, what aspect of the problem you have sufficient resources to deal with right now. Spending time here can be very productive in the long run. Einstein once said, "It is not that I'm so smart. But I stay with the questions much longer." Staying with the question can be enlightening. If you get really inspired, although beyond what we will be addressing in this chapter, there are more complex ways look for what the problem might be including cause and effect analysis, correlational analysis, cost-benefit analysis, comparative analysis (exploring options), and input for other sources including experts (Tague, 2004).

Step 2 – Consider Solutions

Seek the Optimal Solution Space

A problem is a gap, the unfilled space between here and there. It is into that space that we will insert the proposed solution to solve that problem. Hungry (current), wants to be full (desired), need food to eat (the problem, the gap). Solutions – go to the fridge, call for pizza, ride bike to grocery store, walk over to cafe. Once you have a sense of the problem, because it is obvious or because you have done sufficient problem assessment to get a sense of it, then the next step is to find the best solution to that problem. In the Kaizen approach to continual improvement we want to find a solution that is direct, efficient, and effective. We want to find the optimal path through the solution space from current to desired. There are a lot of potential 'solutions' in life that have little to no chance of getting us what we want. Wrong direction, wrong path, crazy detour, dead-end – those will not take us to the desired state any time soon. Poorly selected solutions can actually take us further from where we want to be, like getting on the wrong train!?! What we want to find are those solutions that get us to our destination in the most efficient manner, the straight path. So Step 2 involves some research and brainstorming to come up with a sense of which ones, out of all the options available to you, provide the optimal solution to work with right now.

Do Your Background Research

Doing some background research on the problem will give you more insight into possible causes and best solutions. Trying to figure it out without any guidance can be like shooting in the dark. Shooting in the dark means you have no idea of where the target is. To be successful you need to illuminate that space. Problems often exist because we lack information, knowledge, and experience (no knowledge, limited knowledge, wrong knowledge). Getting more of that information can dramatically increase efficiency in the change process and improve the quality of the final product.

One excellent source of information includes people older and wiser than you, or counselors of various persuasions, or people who have walked the path you are contemplating. Maybe even better, and possibly even more accessible, there are many very smart, hard working people who have spent the bulk of their adult working lives trying to understand the very issue or goal you may be working on. It can be highly productive to use their insights to help you get some practical ideas for addressing that issue. Go to the library, search the internet, explore online databases, get books on the subject, find the expert. I cannot tell you how many times I have recommended a particular book to someone, written by an expert in the field. Does that person go out and get the book? Often they do not. Too bad! Talk about an efficient source of potential spot on solutions. People need to find their own way though. You can take a horse to water, but you cannot make it drink, as they say. That kind of behavior can be a form of self-sabotage, another form of denial, maybe laziness or stubbornness, or perhaps that person is just not ready to change quite yet. Change can be threatening. It means losing something predictable for something unknown and presumably less gratifying, even if the current habit is clearly unproductive or harmful, blocking access to deeper happiness and greater autonomy. Has a wise soul ever given me sage advice I did not heed? Yes, sadly so. It is what it is. We learn when we learn, hopefully sooner than later. Final thought, when you start collecting background information, make sure it is of the highest quality possible, the most authoritative and well supported.

Brainstorm

After you have done a bit of research and gotten a better sense of what the possibilities are then it is time for a bit of creative brainstorming. Creativity is an important element of the solution generation stage. Look for ideas from diverse sources. Meditate on the question, ask friends, pray for insight, do some free writing on it, ask your inner wisdom self. Think about it then let it go for a while, swim, run, sleep, take some time to just let it percolate at a deeper level. Dream on it. When you are about to go to sleep pose a question to your dream mind, "What is the best possible solution to this problem?" Prime and see yourself waking up the next morning and during the day having an insight into the problem. Then go to sleep and see what happens. Use of intuition, non-linear thinking, has also been shown to be an important component of creative problem solving (Eubanks et al., 2010; Perkins, 1992; Simon, 1989). We will look at the process of creative intuition in more detail in Chapter 12 on decision making.

Also, reflect on your own life experience, "…the sense of security that resides within yourself," (as Milton Erickson once advised). You have done a lot of things in your life. Reflect back on solutions you have used in the past, strategies that have helped you deal with life challenges. Finally, remember that complex behaviors, like smoking, and conversely quitting smoking, are probably going to require a number of solution strategies, including changes to the environment (no cigarettes at home), changes in social behaviors (telling friends not to give you cigarettes when you ask), managing cravings, maintaining motivation and so on. Do not get stuck on one solution as being the answer, be open to doing what it takes to solve the puzzle.

Step 3 — Pick One

The next step recognizes the fact that there are often many paths to the same destination, a variety of solutions could potentially help with the problem. The goal is to find the best fit, the most parsimonious, practical, sustainable solution. The one that will work for you, right now. If you did your work in Step 2 you should have a sense of the cause of the problem, and some possible solutions in mind for addressing that specific problem.

Come Up with Criteria

A very useful next step as you prepare to pick one is to consider what your criteria are, what will produce a best fit solution at this point in time. The desired state is a new sleeping bag. You can just go out and buy a sleeping bag, mission accomplished. Or, you can do a bit of research first. In that process you learn important information on sleeping bags, that they differ by materials, weights, warmth, durability, cost and other factors. Background research can help you see things that might be important, but that might not considered if you are not informed about them (nothing is obvious to the uninformed). Solution 1 – I will go to the store and buy the sleeping bag that is on sale. As a result of limited information you may end up with a bag that a bit cheaper but not warm enough for your intended use. One freezing night in the woods and you clearly recognize the mistake, but too late to make a difference. Solution 2 - I will go to the store and buy the sleeping bag that can be used in three seasons, down to 20 degrees, is machine washable, and packs small. Listing some specific criteria for your solution helps to make the optimal solution more clear. It also helps to make it more real, giving you a sense of which solution of a possible variety, can actually be implemented, given your current resources of time, money and energy. You are clear of the functionality you need it to have to be useful to you.

With this information – sense of problem, solution criteria, possible solutions – you have the basics for making a reasonably informed choice. You also understand the Kaizen notion of small steps. You have accordingly broken the problem down into smaller workable pieces. Now after some consideration you pick one, you pick a solution to work on to make progress on that next step.

Of course, picking a potential solution can be more easily said than done in reality when the costs of a mistake is high or the way is still not clear. In the upcoming chapter on decision making we will look at more ideas on how to make decisions in the face of complexity.

Step 4 – Try It

After determining what the problem is, and which possible solutions might work best, and picking one to test, it is finally time to put that solution to work with a small-scale pilot project. If it is a larger problem in need of a larger solution, then try out smaller pieces of the solution first, small steps. As part of your test phase you will also need to decide how to collect data on your implementation in order to determine if progress is indeed being made. You will need to specify your measures, what type of data or information you will collect. You will need this type of objective information to know whether the solution is working or not.

Step 4 is like a mini research project. It is not sufficient to just assume your solution will work. There is a reasonable chance it will not. You need to collect a bit of information as part of your implementation to see if the specific solution does indeed produce the desired effect or not. Some years back a pharmaceutical company funded a large-scale study on hormone replace therapy for menopausal women at risk for coronary heart disease. Given the positive experiences of users with related products the company was probably confident that the findings would be positive. Unfortunately for them, when tested on a very large population, the results showed that their product was not beneficial and actually increased some risks, which resulted in a dramatic reduction in the use of the product (Hulley et al., 1998). Good quality information can be life saving. Obvious solutions are not always the best, maybe not even real solutions at all. It is important to evaluate the effectiveness.

Collect Some Information
During the implementation phase you will want to collect baseline and process data. In the final step of our 5 step model we will consider outcome data as well, but first we will look at baseline and process data.

Baseline Data
So you recognized and named the problem, assessed the cause, considered some solutions, and picked one to test. The next step is to collect some baseline data. The problem assessment data collection back in Step 1 was to help you figure out what the cause was, what to focus on in terms of a specific solution. If what you collected data on provided specific baseline information for the solution your are testing, then you have what you need. Often they are different and you need to collect some data specific to the solution you are testing. For example, Carol was getting a lower grade in her English class than usual. She collected some information on study time, motivation, work hours and class attendance. She came to the conclusion that it might be related to motivation

in this particular class. She came up with some possible solutions to test, like increasing positive self-talk and using rewards for completing work early. Before implementing the solution, however, she knew she should collect some baseline data. For two weeks she collected information on her motivation in her three classes and hours of study in each. That gave her some baseline information on her specific motivation levels at the beginning of her solution trial.

Why is baseline information important? Let's say you are working on procrastination and you try out one of your new solutions. A few weeks later you feel like you are actually getting more done, at least you think you are. That is where baseline data comes in. If you had collected some baseline data on number of hours spent studying each day you would be able to compare baseline with current levels to see if things were actually changing. If there is no record of where you started, no point of reference for comparison, then it can be hard to tell if progress is occurring. Trust me on that one.

Change can be gradual, incremental. A clear before and after record can help you confidently see if real change is happening. Evidence of change builds confidence and increases motivation. If no such record exists it is harder to evaluate the chosen solution. If you cannot remember where the starting line was how can you accurately determine how far you ran? Recording information for a few weeks to get a baseline, a sense of the starting line, is a critical step to getting evidence of whether the solution is working or not. In the long run it will help you to confidently know how far you have gone. How that data is collected can be simple or sophisticated. It can be a 1-10 scale, 1=I feel lousy, 10=I feel great, or writing a few sentences at the end of the day in a pocket notebook, tossing beer caps in a jar, a smiley or frowny face on a calendar each day for mood, or an up or down arrow for energy. Simple, Kaizen style, the simpler it is the more likely you are to do it. Having specific information of this type will show whether a change is happening or not, as well as potentially providing insight into why or why not.

Process Data
So you have a solution, you have collected some baseline data, and now you are putting the solution into motion. Once the solution has been implemented it is important to keep track of two things. First you want to track how often you do the solution, what we can call, *the intervention*. If you are trying to increase your energy level and mood (the goal, desired state), through exercise (the solution, or intervention), then it will be helpful to actually keep track of your exercise, such as how often, how long, and what type. The second type of information to keep track of is *the effect*, the evidence of whether you are moving toward the desired state or not. So if you were using exercise to increase energy you would want to keep track of the number of days you exercised and for how long, and some measures of energy and mood. Keep track the treatment/solution and the effect.

So let us say Serena has a large project and she is suffering from writers block due to her anxiety about it. She decided to try some stress management methods to help her deal with this challenge. She named the problem, assessed the cause, picked a solution or two, and set it in motion. She had a goal in mind, an outcome, a vision of the desired state – a completed thesis paper in ten weeks with an A grade. She planned on working for 2 hours each weekday morning on the project. The *intervention* was to use relaxation and imagery at the beginning of each session to help her manage anxiety around writing. She already had her baseline data, information on her anxiety levels causing her writing avoidance. She she was not working on the paper at all. During that ten-week period she kept track of how often she used her pre-writing stress management techniques. That was the *intervention* data. She also kept track of her stress levels related to writing and the number of hours she actually wrote each day. That was the *effect* data. She tracked this for an 8-week period. Over time it was clear to her that on days she did the pre-writing relaxation methods she was more relaxed and wrote for about twice as long. She finished her paper in time and got an A.

> **SIDE NOTE:** Because the paper was so good she got a job with the New York Times right after graduating. While working as a political reporter she was recognized as a keen political thinker and asked to run for State Senator back home. She easily won that race and eventually went on to become president. Being such a good president she was eventually canonized a saint. Children carried her picture and prayed to her for candy. And, it all started because she collected data and was able to use that data to help her change an old habit. See how valuable it can be to collect useful data! It can change your life too.

Step 5 — Evaluate the Effect and Celebrate!

Once the solution has been implemented on a small scale, and process data collected for a reasonable period of time, you can review your findings. This is the time to see if the particular solution has moved you in the desired direction and matches your other criteria of simplicity, efficiency and so on. If you get a thumbs up then it is time to implement on a larger scale. A solution is only useful if it is put into action. The bigger purpose in all of this is to act on your vision, find your way home, live your big life, and become more of who you were born to be.

Final Evaluation

Using the baseline and process information collected over an appropriate period of time, you can make a comparison between the beginning and end of the test period, the starting line and finish line, to see if there is a difference. If it worked, great. Was the effect big enough? If not, maybe another solution is in order. Or maybe a small effect is fine, as it will grow in time with patience. If at the end of the outcome evaluation, however, you conclude that the solution did not work then there are a few things to consider. First, perhaps it was the wrong solution. Second, it was an acceptable solution, but not the best one. Third, it was a good solution, but it was not implemented strongly enough or continued long enough to show a difference, the right medicine, just not enough. Finally, it is also possible that there is no solution (on a learning level). Probably for the kinds of changes most folks will be working on in this course/text, however, there is a learning-based solution. Often the limitation is the selection of a solution that is not the best fit or not enough time with it. What does one do then? Maybe take a break and try again a bit later, or jump right back in, back to Step 1 or 2. The stream will find a way to get past the boulder and make its way back to the ocean. We are all part of a timeless, vast and profoundly powerful life force looking for answers. It is in our nature to persevere. If there is a way, there is a very good chance we will find it, we just need to keep looking.

Party!

No matter what the outcome it is important to recognize your efforts, whether they 'worked' or not. It is time to remember that a step was taken on the path, and that commitment to change deserves some recognition. Thomas Edison was said to have tested over 1,000 filaments before he found an effective solution for the incandescent light bulb. One reporter asked him if he felt like a loser (paraphrasing) for having failed 1,000 times. He replied that he had not failed because he now knew 1,000 ways that did not work. He of course eventually found the way that worked, a productive prototype, which he retested and refined. Each step forward, whether a success or failure, is a step taken toward liberation from the weight of the past, from the habitual, from the unconsciously reactive life that so many people remained buried alive in. One step at a time is the way forward.

Reward and recognition are important aspects of Kaizen philosophy and practice. The emphasis in Kaizen is on small rewards. A worksite setting using a Kaizen approach would give rewards for three different types of accomplishment: noticing problems, generating solutions, and for the effectiveness of implemented solutions. Using rewards is actually a very good idea. Our brains like rewards, a perceived reward triggers a dopamine release, which makes us feel good. It is important, however, not to make the reward the driving factor, which is probably why the emphasis in Kaizen is on small rewards. The real reward we want to reinforce is the sense of our accomplishment, our progress, and our growth. That said, however, using rewards is useful as it helps us to recognize our efforts and accomplishments, it builds confidence and motivation, and it encourages persistence. Give yourself a pat on the back when you notice problems. Give yourself a pat on the head when you come up with and implement solutions, dealing with problems proactively. When that solution works, jump up in the air and give yourself a high five (just do not let people see you doing any of these things because they will think you are a little bonkers, no kidding, they will lock you up and throw away the key).

Standardize Solutions

Although the term continual improvement implies an endless process, it is actually pragmatic to find what works best and to standardize that for the time being. It would not be very efficient to be continually reworking your strategies if they are already working pretty well. So one of the main points, but not obvious, is that we want to find the best way and then make that our new habit, our new pattern. The science of cybernetics provides some useful ideas on this.

Cybernetics is the study of self-regulatory systems that use feedback to correctly navigate their environment and reach their goals. Norbert Weiner, an engineer, mathematician and philosopher, and one of the pioneers of the science of robotics, coined the term cybernetics (Weiner, 1948). He derived it from the Greek word for 'steersman', defining cybernetics as the science of communication and control. The cybernetic system acts, collects feedback on its status/process, and self-corrects until it reaches its goal. The *Learning Life Problem Solving Model* that we use in this text can be applied in the same fashion. Once a good solution has been found then it can be standardized, become the new habit. That new habit takes you, each time it is used, from current state (paper not written) to desired state (paper written). As you write you use feedback, mindful awareness of how you feel, what you are thinking, your behavior (are you on or off task), taking real-time corrective action as needed to help you stay on task with your writing objectives for that session. A cybernetic system is goal-oriented, aware, and self-correcting.

Continual Improvement Tools

Kaizen includes tools that can be used to assist in brainstorming and planning your continual improvement process. Three of the commonly used resources are provided here. These methods are relatively easy to work with and can definitely facilitate insight into causes, solution paths, and standardization of best practices. They can be applied in various ways but one suggestion is to use the Cause and Effect Diagram to assess possible root causes of the problem; use the Process Flowchart to graphically represent the problem and to plan the solution flow, including response strategies at various stages if challenges emerge; and use Checklists as a tool to help you to stay on track with implementation of the solution.

1. Cause and Effect Diagrams – Assessing Causes

There can be numerous possible causes to a problem, some more relevant than others. The Cause and Effect Diagram shows them all at once for consideration and comparison. The basic structure is a central line or spine. Along this spine on either side are diagonal lines. Because this framework can look like a fish skeleton it is also called a Wishbone Diagram. The central line is where you describe or name the problem that is under consideration. On the diagonal lines you list any major contributors to that central problem. Then from each of those branches you can make additional horizontal lines to list elements contributing to that aspect of the problem.

So let us say the problem is not being on time, always being late for class, meetings, events. That is the center horizontal line, main problem – Late!!! The next step is to list the possible primary causes of being late and to list those on the angled lines coming off the center. To brainstorm these primary major causes we can simply begin by asking, "*Why?* Why am I always late?" The primary causes of being late might include morning fatigue, poor time management, lack of motivation, home/office disorganization, and transportation issues. Each of these gets an angled line. Finally, from each these possible causes the same process is repeated, drawing horizontal lines from each one and elaborating specific reasons that come to mind. It is like a tree, the center is the trunk, off of which you have main branches, then finally the stems. So if the trunk of the tree is 'Always Late' then one main branch might be 'fatigued in the morning'. Coming from that branch would be a number of stems, such as 'staying up late studying', 'drinking too much alcohol', and 'eating pizza at midnight'. The other branches and stems are elaborated in the same fashion. One of the benefits of this method is that it now becomes possible to see common themes that might exist. In this case, for example, perhaps the individual recognizes that excess drinking is related to morning fatigue, lack of motivation, and transportation issues (DUI, lost license). That overlap would suggest something important to take a good look at. The Cause and Effect Diagram can be a useful way to begin brainstorming and disentangling problems, by providing ideas about most important causes and showing best possible places to intervene.

2. Process Flowchart - Mapping Solutions

A process flowchart is a diagram of any process with the key steps of the process presented in sequential order. The flowchart provides a visual depiction allowing you to look at the whole story at one glance. It can be an excellent way to visualize the steps involved in a particular process, to think about the process concretely, and even to show the process to others who can then add their intelligence to solving the problem. Because of this birds eye view the flowchart diagram helps in visualizing the process, making it easier to see where useful changes might be possible in the process, or where there is an unnecessary step, or where a key step is missing. It is a flexible tool that can be used to graphically represent any process – how to get a date, fill a customer order, get to work on time, write a research paper.

The elements of a process flowchart include activities, decisions, individuals, materials, services and other essential contributors. To create a flowchart decide on the boundaries of the specific process in question, how much of the process you want to represent (as some processes/problems can be very large and not practically represented on a sheet of paper). Brainstorm all the relevant steps of the process, then arrange the steps on paper. Think about the flow of the problem, where it starts, where it ends, and all the steps and decision points in between. For a personal flowchart of this type you can just use words. A more formal flowchart will use symbols to represent various aspects of the process. For information here is a list of some key symbols, but again, not necessary for personal application. The concepts are more important than the symbols.

3. Checklists - Standardizing Best Practices

Checklists are becoming increasingly important tools for use in a wide variety of settings, from airline safety to hospital operating rooms (Gawande, 2009). They are also super duper for making sure you have a happy vacation. Passport? Check! Suntan lotion? Check! A checklist is a comprehensive list, often presented in a sequential order, that can be used to inform you if you have the right tools to perform the surgery, whether all of the plane's essential functions are operational, or if you have all the provisions needed for your month long backpacking trip. A checklist can be easy to construct and once constructed can be used in future situations for related tasks (a simple, standardized efficiency tool). As an example, once you have an effective checklist for writing term papers you can reuse it as a simple process reminder on all future papers (see Resources section for an example created by the *Academic Success* class). Very efficient!

Creating a basic checklist is fairly straightforward. Start with a list of the actionable items that need to be done, the concrete steps to be taken for project completion. Once you have the list of tasks to be accomplished then prioritize them in order of importance, or in their natural sequence, or group them by category. Format the list so that it has all the key step/elements you need to remember and that you want to use it (functionality and usability). Try it out with the next related project and see how it works. Refine it over time, make it practical, and use it.

SUMMARY

In this chapter we examined concepts of continual improvement and quality, key elements of a academic and life success path. Edwards Deming, a pioneer in the quality improvement field, emphasized quality as the key to improved quality and productivity. The results of his work contributed to the Japanese quality model known as Kaizen or change for the good. Key elements of Kaizen include a focus on quality, search for root causes of problems, and finding solutions to problems that are simple, effective, reliable, functional and useful. Kaizen also puts on emphasis on incremental change, small steps. A five step continual improvement model is provided: problem identification, brainstorming solutions, selection, pilot test, and evaluation. Three useful improvement tools are described: the Cause and Effect Diagram for assessing causes of problems, the Process Flowchart for analyzing problems and considering solutions, and Checklists as a way to standardizing effective solutions for easy future use.

MIND-BODY

Sitting Meditation

Continue with the practice of noticing breath and pleasant sensory information, such as sounds around you. In addition, begin to pay attention to inner body sensations, like warmth, tingling, heaviness, warmth/coolness, pulsing of blood. Practice for about 5 minutes per day.

Mindful Awareness

Pay particular attention to something you do on a regular basis, like washing the dishes, or working on writing or reading activities. Ask yourself, before, during and after, "Is there a better way to do this, an easier way, a more efficient and effective way?"

Priming

Prime a most incredible semester of your life so far.

REFERENCES

Deming WE. *Out of the Crisis.* Cambridge MA: MIT Press; 1986.

Eubanks, DL, Murphy ST, Mumford MD. Intuition as an influence on creative problem-solving: the effects of intuition, positive affect, and training. *Creativity Research Journal.* 2010;22(2):170-184.

Gabor A. *The Man Who Discovered Quality.* New York: Penguin Books; 1990.

Gawande A. *The Checklist Manifesto: How to Get Things Right.* New York: Metropolitan Books; 2009.

Hulley S, Grady D, Bush T, Furberg C, Herrington D, Riggs B, Vittinghoff E. Randomized trial of estrogen plus progestin for secondary prevention of coronary heart disease in postmenopausal women. Heart and Estrogen/progestin Replacement Study (HERS) Research Group. *JAMA.* 1998;280(7):605-613.

Krishnamurti J. *Think on These Things.* New York: Harper Perennial; 1964.

Meyer J. Mikaela Shiffrin of Eagle-Vail wins Olympic gold in women's slalom in Sochi. *The Denver Post.* Posted February 21, 2014. Available at: http://www.denverpost.com/olympics/ci_25198471/mikaela-shiffrin-colorado-leads-olympic-slalom-after-first. Accessed October 9, 2014.

Perkins, D. N. (1992). The topography of invention. In: Weber R, Perkins DN, editors. *Inventive Minds: Creativity in Technology.* New York: Oxford University Press; 1992:238-250.

Simon HA. Making management decisions: The role of intuition and emotion. In: Agor WH, editor. *Leading and Managing Productively.* Thousand Oaks, CA: Sage; 1989:23-39.

Tague NR. *The Quality Toolbox.* Milwaukee: ASQ Quality Press; 2004.

Wiener N. *Cybernetics; or Control and Communication in the Animal and the Machine.* Paris: Hermann & Cie; 1948.

SECTION II

LEARNING STAGES AND STRATEGIES

6   Academic Skills – Acquisition

7   Academic Skills – Integration

8   Academic Skills – Display

Academic Skills
Acquisition

I know that learning requires efficient acquisition, persistent integration, and quality display.

CHAPTER THEMES
- Metacognition / Metawareness
- Three Pillars of Learning
- Acquisition
- Note Taking
- Reading
- Observation
- Open Inquiry

The next three chapters will provide essential information on academic strategies that contribute to efficient and effective learning. Each chapter will focus on one of three principle pillars of learning – Acquisition, Integration and Display. Acquisition, the first pillar, relates to getting new information into the mind, body and heart. Chapter 6 examines the second pillar, Integration, with its focus on getting that new information even deeper into long-term memory for greater access and understanding. Finally, chapter 7 covers the third pillar, Display, looking at how to optimally present our learning, showing our new knowledge and skills to the world.

How Humans Learn

Humans are learning organisms, it is hardwired into our nature. Indeed, one of the things that differentiates us from other living creatures is the amount of brain mass devoted to higher cortical functions. This includes complex language skills, symbolic thinking, self-reflection, creative problem solving, empathy, and other capabilities that allow us to do remarkable things, both remarkably good and remarkably bad.

Various theories have been proposed to explain how we learn. Behaviorism was the dominant view for much of the twentieth century. The work of behaviorists like Edward Thorndike, John Watson and BF Skinner shaped research agendas and beliefs about human learning for decades. As the name implies, behaviorism was a study of learning that focused on observable, measurable behaviors, not the unobservable things that happen inside the mind and brain. By the end of the twentieth century the dominance of behaviorism had finally waned and the study of human learning had expanded into more comprehensive and complex perspectives influenced by advances in cognitive psychology, research into the human-computer interface, artificial intelligence, behavioral economics and decision sciences, the exploration of human emotion and motivation, and the neurosciences. At the dawning of the 21st century we now have smartphones with personal assistants that answer questions and make jokes. The National Institutes of Health has completed the Human Connectome Project, a mapping of the circuitry of the entire human brain (Toga et al., 2012). Researcher at UC Berkeley are developing tools to reconstruct what a person is thinking based on scans of the visual cortex of the brain, a machine that reads thoughts (Nishimoto et al., 2011).

Strategies for Improving Academic Effectiveness

In the next 3 chapters we will look at how humans learn and how we can use that information to our advantage to increase success in school and life. Each chapter will provide key strategies for approaching learning more efficiently and effectively. What is a strategy? A strategy is a plan of action that is implemented to achieve a major goal. It is a game plan. Research shows that academic performance improves when students use the right learning strategies (Robbins et al., 2004). That makes sense. If you use the right tool for the job, like a hammer for pounding nails, then you will get better results. Academic success is not about working harder (although for some of us that might not be a bad idea), it is about working smarter. Working smarter includes using the right tools, the right approach. Is there a better way to do a reading assignment, take exams, organize class notes? Is there a more effective way to do a routine academic task that will get you where we want to go in less time and with higher quality? Using the wrong tool, no matter how hard one tries, will generally result in wasted effort and lower quality. If someone uses a broom to pound nails they might succeed, but it will be a very inefficient, slow, and frustrating process. We want to use the best resources available to us. An effective learning strategy is a powerful resource and a key to academic success.

Metacognition – Mindful Awareness in Learning

Chapter 4 introduced the concept of mindful awareness. We are now going to apply that concept directly to learning, to mindful learning, through the filter of metacognition. The Greek term *meta* means about, beyond, or above. Cognition has to do with our capacity to think, our ability to understand, solve problems, figure things out. So metacognition can be described as thinking about thinking, or being aware of diverse mental processes, such as being aware of how we approach assignments, how we read a textbook, take notes, solve math problems, or memorize a list of names. Being aware of how we approach learning is a very important element of academic success. Through increased mindful awareness of our learning strategies we can notice the effectiveness or ineffectiveness of those strategies. With that information we can begin to select approaches that are helping and eliminating those that are not.

John Flavell, a developmental psychologist, was one of the first researchers to study and advance the concept of metacognition. He described metacognition as a person's knowledge of their cognitive processes related to learning (Flavell, 1979). In terms of classroom learning the goals of metacognition include having a reasonable idea of what you already know (and do not know), what the learning task is (such as needing to review notes for a final exam), how best to do that task (best strategy, like the most efficient strategy for reviewing notes), and then applying that learning strategy effectively, and finally, assessing whether it worked or not.

Metawareness

Although the conventional concept of metacognition is extremely important and useful, we are going to modify it in order to incorporate the holistic perspective employed in this book. To this end we will use the elements of the Wheel Model as the objects of our Mindful Awareness, as introduced in Chapter 4. The term metacognition implies a focus on cognition, awareness of mental processes. In the Learning Life approach, however, we want to use our mindful awareness more holistically, by bringing awareness not just to cognition but to the three elements or cogs of the Wheel Model – *Person* (which includes cognitive functions), *Behaviors*, and *Environments*. We will refer to this as Metawareness, the mindful awareness of the interdependent elements of person-behavior-environment.

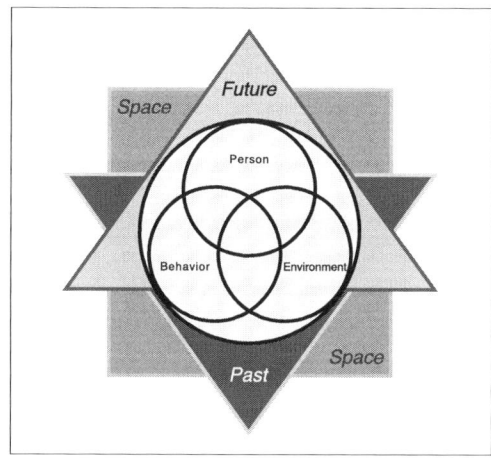

Metawareness recognizes life's interdependencies. Triggers in the environment activate our thoughts and feelings. Those thoughts and feelings lead to behaviors. Those behaviors have an impact in the environment. These interacting elements in this way creating an endless loop. For example, you see someone on the other side of the street (environmental trigger). You think, "She still owes me money," and a feeling of annoyance rises up (thought/feeling). You decide to cross the street and check in with her (behavior). She sees you coming and quickly heads around the corner out of view. You think, "What the ...." (thought/feeling). You now feel a bit of anger (emotion) and make some attributions about why she did that (thoughts) and begin to question your friendship (impact on future behaviors).

One of the keys to success in school and in life is self-management, which requires being able to recognize these interdependent forces at work in mind, body and behavior, and then being able to work with them creatively and constructively. We will use Metawareness as a way to explore and optimize our learning process. The goal is to increase awareness (to be more mindful) of these three spheres of life – Person, Behavior, Environment – to see how they interact in ways that either help or hinder our learning, and to make necessary adjustments in the moment and over time.

Dr. Burke's 8 Metawareness Questions

One simple way to apply metawareness to any academic task is to ask yourself some probing questions. Questions engage thinking. Asking the right questions can facilitate self-reflection, problem solving and goal attainment. The following 8 questions lay a foundation for greater mindful awareness of the learning process. In the Resources section at the end of the book you will find a printable list of these 8 questions. You may want to make a copy of it and put it in your wallet or notebook or on your wall where you study. These questions will help to make your learning process more productive and effective, keeping you on track, task focused, and moving forward. The questions facilitate useful insight into the learning process before, during and after any academic task.

Before a Learning Task

1. Task Clarity

What is the task at hand? What exactly am I supposed to do? What is the expected outcome or product (including how much, by when, and with what quality)? If there are options in terms of what you can work on then pick the most important item. Ask yourself, "What is the most important thing for me to do right now?"

2. Motivation

Why am I doing this, what is the purpose/value/goal (external/for others and internal/for me)? How does this activity fit with my personal and academic goals?

3. Strategy

What is my strategy? How am I supposed to do this? What is the best way to do this (including tools)? Where is the best place to do it? If this is a multi-party task, who else is responsible, and for which aspects?

During a Learning Task

4. Task Focus

How am I doing? Am I on task? Am I actually doing it? Really? Am I staying on task and on target (efficient, effective, most skillful)? How can I get more intense with it, really into it?

5. Task Reorientation

If I am not on task, or drifting, what one simple step can I take *right now* to change that? Consider the Wheel, use Metawareness, what can I change in person, behavior, or environment that will help me stay on task? (See Chapter 13 for ideas.)

After a Learning Task

6. Effect/Effectiveness

How did it work out? What was the grade, response, my sense of accomplishment? How was the quality? How could I improve and do even better next time?

7. Efficiency

How long did it take? How much did I get done? Is there a better way to do this? Could I have done anything differently, what should I repeat in the future, and what should I change in the future?

8. Holistic Reflection

What else? Consider the Wheel, is there something at the level of person, behavior, or environment that could be modified to improve the process? Sit down, close eyes, pause for a few minutes and ask "What else?" Sit in silence, reflect, and allow insights to come.

If you ask yourself these questions, before, during and after a learning process you will begin to see improvements in everything you do, whether that is asking someone out or writing a research paper.

Learning Strategies

At the beginning of this chapter we introduced the idea of using the right tool for the job, a hammer for nails. That is just smart, more efficient, more effective, easier. The same goes for learning. Reading a math book from the back to the front would be an obvious example of a less effective strategy, one that results in less efficient learning. In that light we will now consider specific tools or strategies for making learning more efficient, effective, rewarding, and fun, tools for greater academic success.

Learning strategies are basically things students do to accomplish learning (Gu, 2012). For the most effective and efficient learning it is useful to have an idea of what learning strategies are out there, which ones are best for specific learning tasks, and finally, how best to use each approach (Garner, 1988). In the next several chapters we will examine a variety of strategies. They will be organized based on the three stages of learning, around an idea of the information processing procedures of the brain. Information is taken in, encoded or integrated into long term memory, and then retrieved for display (Ashcraft, 1994). For understanding and recall we will describe this in terms of three phases of learning – Acquisition, Integration and Display (AID, like a study aid). Acquisition will be presented in this chapter, Integration in Chapter 6, and Display in Chapter 7.

Acquisition

Acquisition, the first stage of learning, is the point at which we *receive information*. The acquisition phase involves taking in ideas and experiences, which then become the building blocks for greater understanding and application. Examples of acquisition activities related to academic learning include attending lectures, taking notes in class, and doing reading assignments. In the acquisition stage information comes in through the senses and is stored very briefly in *sensory memory*. Pertinent information then goes from sensory memory to *working memory* or short-term memory. Our short-term memory has limits in terms of storage capacity and duration. That is why we have to repeat a new phone number as we search for something to write it on. Content in short-term memory has to be continually rehearsed, otherwise it is quickly lost. If the information is relevant (pertinent, useful, motivating), short-term and long-term memory begin to communicate with each other to encode and elaborate this new information, to help make sense of it, and to get it into longer-term storage.

Integration

The second stage of the learning process is *Integration*. In this stage we take what we have received in the first stage and integrate it even more solidly into long-term memory, weaving it into other pieces of knowledge to create a bigger picture, a more complex understanding. If the new material does not eventually get integrated into long-term memory then we will not have access to it in the future for use on exams, during a performance, at work, in life. Examples of the Integration stage of academic learning can include reviewing notes, doing additional research, thinking about and working on practice homework problems, comparing and contrasting articles and synthesizing ideas for a research paper, rehearsing material that has already been heard or read or played, organizing and linking concepts, generally deepening, refining and improving access, understanding and skill.

Display

The third stage of the learning process is ***Display***. One of the main reasons we learn anything is to display our learning, to use our knowledge and skills in the world for greater autonomy and effectiveness. If acquisition is input, and integration is through-put, then display is the output. In this stage the information has been received and integrated and is now ready to be retrieved and expressed. In relation to school the display phase includes taking exams, writing research papers, performing in a music recital, applying classroom knowledge in an internship, and all of the other myriad opportunities to show the world your stuff. Effective learning allows us to display competence in diverse domains of life, whether that is in a career, in relationships, staying healthy, investing and increasing earnings, all of it. Display can also include the synthesis of knowledge and the creation of new insights and innovations, taking understanding to a higher level. Display is why we learn, so we can be more successful at whatever we chose to pursue, to get things done, to give something back, to help the planet and its people.

Stage I - Acquisition

For the remainder of this chapter we will consider key learning strategies related to the acquisition phase. Why is acquisition a key step? One of the main reasons people do not succeed in life, cannot do certain things at all, or cannot do them correctly, is because they ***never received information*** on how to do it or they ***received incorrect information***. Simple, not complex. They were never shown at all or they were shown the wrong way. It is hard to get to New York if you do not have a map, you only have half a map, or you have the wrong map. The Acquisition stage of learning involves getting information into our senses, brain, body, unconscious mind, and conscious awareness. It is about input. With academic learning a good deal of the input of new information comes via lectures (both live and online) and through reading. Some information, especially motor skills, comes through observation and performance. Finally, discovery is another essential element of the Acquisition phase, learning by doing, trial and error. Now we will now consider some fundamental academic Acquisition practices – taking notes in class, reading, observation, and open inquiry.

1. Taking Notes

Note taking is a core practice for academic success, a key to effective acquisition of course content. First you write down main ideas and supporting information, then you make sure it is complete and organized. Your notes are a primary resource for study and review, for understanding of course content. Research shows that students who take notes (and review them) do significantly better on test performance than those who do neither (DiVesta & Gray, 1973; Kiewra, 1985). To get the most out of note taking it is useful to think of it as a three-part process – before the learning event, during, and after.

Before Any Learning Event

Mentally Prepared for the Session

It is important to be mentally prepared for class, the online lesson, or whatever learning event you will be engaged in. Let us take a classroom lecture as an example. Doing course readings, sample problems, and completing any written assignments before the lecture definitely improves learning. Assigned material has a high probability of being discussed in class. If you have not done the assigned tasks you will be less prepared to participate fully in class activities. Being mentally prepared contributes to efficient and effective learning. First, it means you are more likely to be engaged in the class lecture and discussion since you have some idea of what the instructor is talking about. That will increase motivation, your sense of belonging in class, relevance.

The next benefit of coming prepared is that the lecture will reinforce material you have already thought about, which is reinforcing long-term memory, recall, and understanding. That is efficient, and efficiency will save you time in the long run. If you have not read the material before the lecture, or at least reviewed it, then your brain will be busy with the *Acquisition of new information* versus the *Integration of familiar information*. Big difference. Because the unprimed brain is busy with the input of new information it may miss pieces of the lecture as it tries to understand concepts and decide what is relevant for notes. Lapses of attention result in lapses of information in your notes, and that can be a problem later. People also make the mistake of thinking, "I did not read so I will not go to class," or, "I need to read everything, and since I do not have time I will not read anything." If you do not have time to read the whole chapter then at least look at the summary and chapter headings before you go to the lecture. That gives your brain some scaffolding to build on. Something is way better than nothing. Going in cold to the onslaught of information is like the proverbial deer in the headlights, too much too fast. The reality is that most learning and competence is not all-or-none, rather, it is built in layers, in stages, so pre-exposure before the lecture, at any level, is adding a layer. That is a very good idea.

Physically On Track

On the bio side of preparedness, check in before class starts or before you begin a new online lesson. What is your current bio state? The goal is to be present, in mind and body. That means doing what you need to do to be fully present in class. Remind yourself of your goals and do some Priming for an excellent class. Are you groggy? Then you need to wake up your body. Get some water, take a quick walk outside, get some tea. Stretch a bit. If you are overly tired, especially if you are consistently overly tired, then it might be time to re-evaluate your sleeping pattern, exercise habits, diet, hours at work, or emotional well-being. All of these things can affect daily energy levels. Stay hydrated. It can make a world of difference, just try it. If you have a drooping plant in your house give it some water. In an hour it will be standing straight up. Water does the same for a human body and brain. Finally, make sure you are not too hungry. That can be a big distraction, as low blood sugar can result in reduced brain function and attention. Bring foods with you to campus to keep yourself going, like energy bars, raisins and almonds, an apple, a cookie, a can of cat food (well maybe not cat food), whatever you find works best for your body (and err on the side of healthy when you can, and usually, you can).

Motivated to Learn

Stay motivated during the semester and come to class with a commitment to learn. A great deal of learning is self-initiated. Success in this process depends on you. The Metawareness question to ask yourself is, "Why am I doing this, what is the purpose or benefit, how does this lecture/lesson/activity relate to my goals?" Enthusiasm for anything can wane after an initial burst of interest. Marriage, career, hobbies, everything in life has its ebbs and flows, ups and downs. That is normal. It is good to remember that all of life has highs and lows. It is the way of things. It is the way it is. That is why it is useful to periodically reflect on your motives for being in school, for taking a particular course, for getting good grades. *Recommit to your goals*. Tell yourself how this lecture, this course, this degree fits into your bigger life vision, your mission, your dream. Go back and re-examine your responses from the Goals chapter. Clear, motivating goals will increase persistence in the face of challenge. Remember your goals. Commit to your goals. *Live your goals*. Research shows a clear relationship between motivated learning and having clear goals, such as recognizing the value of getting an education, believing in yourself and in your dream (Zimmerman, 1998). Many people on the planet will never have a chance for a decent education. It is a gift to be used wisely.

Right Gear

Have the right gear. Bring what you need for the lecture, lab, online chat, or rehearsal. Bring your books, pens, recorder, laptop or tablet, smartphone, whatever the particular set of tools and required class materials might be. When taking notes it is also important that you have the right materials and the right method. Personally, I think that three ring binders are a great resource, because of their flexibility. You can insert handouts, add pages printed from the Internet or copied from books, rearrange items for study purposes, and do other handy tricks. If you are using a binder it can be helpful to write on just one side of each sheet so you can spread pages out later and see all of the notes at one time. If you are environmentally conscious (good thing), you can use the clean side of recycled paper (and X out the back side so you do not get confused). Many people like spiral notebooks. If that is your style then definitely consider getting notebooks with a pocket page so you can keep essential materials handy, like the course syllabus. Also consider buying notebooks with perforated pages so you can pull them out later and rearrange them for easier study. In addition, the perforated sheet approach allows you to use the notebook for class and then later to pull pages and store them all in a three-ring binder along with other materials you have gathered, the best of both worlds.

During Any Learning Event

Attend Class

Whether live or online recorded lectures, you need to get the material into mind and body. The team that does not show up forfeits the game. You must be present to win. The best students show up. They go to class, sit in the front row, pay attention, and ask informed questions. When they show up, it is not just in body, but in mind as well. It is possible to do okay while not regularly attending class, but it is harder, and not a good plan. Just recently I had another student, smart and capable, who was too engaged with other priorities in her life to come to class. She barely passed, because of all the work she missed, which she was not even aware of. When you do not go to class you do not hear material from an expert. You do not discuss ideas, see examples of problems, get reminded about assignments or upcoming quizzes. When you skip class you do not develop relationships with other committed students who can help you when you have questions about materials. You do not get to know the teaching assistants. You do not hear and think about ideas that will be on the exam. Importantly, you do not review things that you have already learned.

Speaking as a professor who has taught for many years I can honestly say that the students who do not come to class are often less committed to school, less clear on their careers, and doing less well academically (often they are the ones who flunk my class, which honestly makes me sad). Getting in the habit of attending classes, prepared and present, is a very good strategy for increasing academic success. One of the best ways to think about school and class is to consider it to be your job. Unless you are a lifeguard your employer will not pay you to go to the beach. You get paid when you go to work and do your work. ***Attending class***, ***ready***, and ***on task***, ***is good preparation for a future career***, and going to class will increase your chances of actually getting a desirable future career. Attending class is part of the job description.

Select a Good Seat
The best students are also the ones you often find sitting in the front of the classroom. Having your body at the front of the class can make it easier to read the board, hear the professor, or watch the movie. The students in the front rows are generally more likely to be prepared and to pay attention, as they are the most visible to the instructor. The ones in the back are often the ones chatting during class, texting, coming in late, and leaving early. These behaviors are remembered on grading day. (Interesting note: in my Academic Success class, the class this book is based on, I have freshman, sophomores, juniors and seniors taking the class, an occasional grad student, and sometimes an auditing elder. More often than not it is the juniors and seniors in the front rows and the first and second year students in the back. The seniors have a major, are preparing for a career, and see the world of work coming at them fast. They get it. They take it seriously. They are up front where they can learn the most so that they can be the most prepared for what comes next. They do not have time to be playing with toys in class. They are on a mission. They have work to do.

Listen and Observe (be mindful and stay on task)
Research by Van Meter found that successful students used note taking as one of their methods for staying attentive during class (Van Meter et al., 1994). Attending a class lecture is an excellent time for practicing active listening, a wonderful opportunity for mindful awareness. Naturally, minds wander now and then, but the overarching goal is to pay attention, to be present. Paying attention in class is like a meditation, a mental training. " Am I on task or off task?" Becoming distracted during a lecture is just like being pulled away by thoughts during sitting meditation. As soon as you notice you are off task you effortlessly come back to your 'object of meditation', your lecture notes. That is one of the clear academic benefits that comes from a sitting meditation practice. It trains the brain/mind to notice when it is off task and to then come back to that task more quickly. Indeed, research has found the practice of meditation to be directly associated with a higher GPA (Hall, 1999).

Decide What to Write Down
The goal is to identify what is the most important information and to capture that as succinctly as possible. It can include main points, any supporting information that helps you to understand

main points, and material that is likely to be on the exam. Jot down the key words. Note the main ideas, using the best way to paraphrase them (or word-for-word if needed at times). This again reminds us why being prepared for class ahead of time is so helpful. Advanced preparation helps you to know what the important points are.

Listen and observe. Listen to the questions the instructor asks, and the answers given by the instructor, or approved by the instructor. Write those down. This can provide information as to what might be on the exam, possibly actual exam questions and answers. Observe – always write down what is on the board. If the instructor writes it on the board then he or she thinks it is important. Also pay attention to points of emphasis in the lecture. If there is something the professor repeats or emphasizes then write it down. If the instructor says, "This will be on the exam," jeez, write it down. Those are all big clues. Make special notes for definitions, keywords, key dates, key formulas, that may appear on the exam. Notice if lecture content reflects the text. If it does it suggests that the overlapping material may be getting emphasis because it is particularly hard to comprehend or it is important for the exam, or both. Make a note. Guest lectures, films and other ancillary materials are often (not always) supplementary, so use your discretion with that content.

While you are taking notes also include your own questions. Mark items you do not understand so that you can look up the answer or ask the TA later. If you have an 'aha' moment during the lecture (I typically do when I am attending an interesting lecture) then write it down. Just make sure you separate your insights from the instructor's thoughts. The two of you may have very different views of the world, and the instructor's perspective is generally a good bet for the exam. Do not try to write the lecture word-for-word. You cannot write that fast and you will probably lose too much lecture content. Go for the main ideas, formulas, examples. Again, this is why being prepared for the session ahead of time will increase your efficiency and effectiveness.

Think Critically
As you take notes, especially if you are prepared ahead of time, you will be able to think somewhat critically about the material. Try to separate the wheat from the chaff, the important from the unimportant. Good critical thinking gets to the heart of the matter, not lost in detail or extraneous information.

Have an Organizational Scheme
It is important to have a scheme for organizing information from the lecture as you take notes. You will eventually want to be able to see the connections (you will do more of that level of processing after the lecture, so it is not essential to integrate at that level during class). There are many approaches to taking useful notes. Outlining, bullet points, arrows, underlining. Outlining the main points of the lecture, if it has some logic, can be one very effective strategy. Outlining is a way to hierarchically arrange information, providing a visual display of the order and relationships between elements. That can help to improve understanding and recall.

Three levels of detail are typically sufficient for outlining information – main topic, sub-topics that fall under it, and supporting details. You can mark each level with Roman numerals or some other symbols that you prefer. You can use symbols – star for the main topic, circles for subtopics, and a dash for supporting information. You can use indentation, different color pens, whatever you like. It is all fair game. The goal is to find an approach that works for you and then to use that approach consistently. There may be some experimentation until you come up with your preferred approach, a good use of time.

The first level is the major topic, so in a class on jazz it might be a lecture on jazz piano. That would be the major topic. The second level would be the subtopics within that category, such as artists, like McCoy Tyner, Hiromi Euhara, and Aldo Lopez-Gavilan. The third level would be supporting details, such as where the artists were born, where they studied, recording labels, important influences, and other relevant details.

Some teachers speak very fast. Some are not well-organized, or tend to go off on tangents. In those cases creating perfectly linear notes, real-time during lectures, can be hard to do as you do not know exactly where the lecture is going, or you are not sure how many levels there may be to any point. In those moments just do your best. Also, when you take notes it can be helpful to label them with the date and a page number. That will help you to order the pages in the event you take them out of the binder or notebook later for study. Dated pages can also be useful for comparing dates against the syllabus to match notes with readings and homework assignments. Finally, it is important to leave enough space in your notes to allow for modifications after class, such as adding more details for clarification, or inserting diagrams.

Connect the Dots
Some people like to take notes in different colors. That can be a good way to differentiate levels. You can also take notes in one color and use another color to underline key terms or to star concepts that you do not understand. Use visuals in your notes – arrows, circles, boxes – to direct you to related information or to emphasize key ideas. Remember to include any diagrams that are on the board, especially if they are not in your text (another good reason to have read the text). You may want to create your own diagrams as well. A visual depiction of an idea is a helpful way to represent things that may be hard to understand verbally, potentially quite illuminating. I remember once having a challenging time understanding a particular concept from a statistics class I was taking in my doctoral training. I asked my officemate about it, she was very good at statistics. She drew a diagram of the concept and it immediately made sense to me. It was very convincing evidence of the power of visual representation of ideas. Finally, if you use abbreviations then make sure you use standardized ones, including your own, so that you know what they mean when you come back to them later.

Cornell Method
One specific note taking method that you often see described in study skills guides is called the Cornell Method (Pauk & Owens, 2010). Whenever I mention it in class there will be a few students who have been taught the method in the past. Some people like it, and others groan when you bring it up. Whatever works best for you is what works best for you. If it helps, that is the good, if not, find another way. The goal is to get good notes, learn the material, and get good grades.

Study Skills (continued from last class.)	
1. Note Taking Skills	
a. Before class preparation	What can I do before class to maximize note taking effectiveness?
a1. Mentally prepared for lecture	
a2. Have right materials	
a3. Set motivation for effective class session	

To use this method you make a line down the page you are taking notes on, from top to bottom. The line divides the sheet of paper into a wide section (2/3^{rds} of the page), and a narrow section (1/3rd of the page). Personally, I like the narrow column on the right, typically it is presented on the left, do what works for you. Take notes in the wide section. After class go back and in the narrow section write in a key word, a short phrase, or a question that captures the essence of the main points. You can also leave space at the bottom of the page and write a summary of all the material on that page. Later when you go back to review your notes cover up the material from the lecture, the main notes, and use the cue words and questions in the column on the right for self-testing. Read the question or cue word and see what you recall, then read the class notes to determine what you remembered and what you still need to study. This approach turns notes into a helpful review/self-testing resource when used in this fashion, and that facilitates integration.

After Any Learning Event

Get Organized

Well-organized notes are more efficient and effective for studying and comprehension. Review your notes and organize them after class. Make sure you have the key terms and main ideas down. Consider summarizing the lecture. Immediately after class is the best time to do this if at all possible. Take a few minutes to underline or highlight key words or concepts, write some cue words or questions in the margins, add diagrams and images to help you understand visually in addition to verbally, draw arrows between related concepts, star things you are not clear about or that need to be double checked. This immediate review will help strengthen memory and recall (making for easier study later and improved test performance). A quick review soon after class also provides a chance to see what you captured and to make sure you have what you need. If not right after the lecture, then sooner is better than later. Consider making an outline of the lecture to add to your notes as well. If you recorded the lecture then listen to the recording and transcribe it as soon as possible. As needed, edit the content of your notes, make corrections, and add missing material using the text, online sources, supplemental class readings, and information from the teaching assistant or your classmates. Seek clarity on things you did not understand. If you had a question on something during the lecture and marked it down then make sure to get the needed information.

Assess Your Process

How did your note taking go? If you were mindful of your note taking strategy you might have noticed strengths and weaknesses. Take a moment now and then to consider how you could upscale your ability in this area. You will be doing a lot of it in school. Having an effective method will benefit you in the long run. Research on student note taking conducted by Van Meter and colleagues (1994) found that student note taking ability improved over time and that those skills especially improved in hard classes.

If You Miss Class

Make sure you get the notes. If you miss a class then get the notes from one of your classmates, preferably someone who is a good student and who takes organized, legible notes.

> **REFLECTION**
>
> Take a moment to reflect on your Acquisition process. Think about your learning process before, during and after a learning task. Were you clear about the task, motivated, were you able to stay focused and on task, did you work efficiently?
>
> _____
> _____
> _____
>
> Take a moment to reflect on how you approach note taking. Do you bring the proper motivation to the task? Are you prepared before class so that you understand the lecture and can take the most effective notes? Are your notes legible? Are you getting notes that you can use effectively for study and exam preparation? Do you organize and review your notes after the lecture? Do you fill in missing information? If there are one or more areas meriting attention, pick one and think of what simple next step you could take right now to move toward the desired state of well-organized, highly useful notes.
>
> _____
> _____

2. Reading

Confucius was reported to have said that you cannot open a book without learning something (we could presume he did not read cheap romance novels about Princess Quan and the Frolicking Sifu). A good deal of acquisition occurs outside of the classroom in the form of reading, such as reading the textbook and assigned papers, reading to get ideas for an assignment, or reading to research a topic. For the rest of your working life you will be reading materials. Effective reading strategies will enhance academic and life success.

Read Efficiently

People do a lot of reading in school and in many professions. Applying productive reading strategies will increase efficiency. A key, emphasized throughout this book, is to have a goal in mind, the desired state. In terms of specifics, one strategy that facilitates efficient reading, and increases understanding and recall, is known as the SQ3r method (Robinson, 1978). The acronym stands for Survey, Question, Read, Recite and Review. This is one of the methods that contributed to a significant spike in my GPA when I was an undergrad. The method is most useful for humanities or social science information. Even with math or physical sciences, however, applying some aspects of the method can be helpful for orienting to the material and preparing to read and study. You can sit in front of a book for hours, with the intention of reading the material, and not have a clue when you are done. That is a BIG waste of time. Better to spend the time cleaning the back of the refrigerator. SQ3r is a way to create an active reading experience, so that learning is optimized.

Step 1: Survey
The first time through, survey the entire book, quickly. Look at the table of contents, the index, any information at the beginning of chapters and summaries at the end. Once you have a sense of the whole then survey the section or chapter you are about to read in more detail. Look at learning objectives, section headings, diagrams, glossary terms, and sidebars. Get a feel for the chapter and what it is about, the general flow of information. If the author had a brain there is a logic to the material. This preliminary survey will prime your inner reader to extract what is important and to skim what is not.

Step 2: Question
In preparation for reading, turn the chapter headings and subheadings into questions. For example, a section in the text has the heading, "George Washington – The Formative Years." Turn that into a question, "What life experiences shaped George Washington's character as he was growing up?" The next section in the biology text has the heading, "Krebs Cycle," which becomes, "What is the Krebs Cycle?"

Step 3: Read
Read to answer that specific question. This simple step saves a huge amount of reading time because you are now reading to answer just one question. If the book was written logically, and if the headings match the content, then the heading should inform you about the essence of that section. If you turn that heading into a question, and read to answer that question, you are by default doing a search for a specific answer, the essence of that section of text. Unless you want to read every word, which seriously slows down reading, then the SQ3R method is a very effective way to reduce time spent reading filler and detail – all killer, no filler. This method takes you to the heart of the material you are reading, the prime cut, the essence. Turning the heading into a question and reading to find the answers to that specific question is a very efficient and effective strategy, making for much more productive reading.

Step 4: Recite
Next you want to test yourself to see what you have actually learned. Once you have read the section, cover the text, ask yourself that same question again, and answer the question. This provides *immediate feedback* as to whether you are beginning to move the material into long-term memory. If you cannot answer the question, then you do not have the material in memory yet. Simple, case closed. If the answer is not there immediately after reading the page it will certainly not be there three weeks later on the day of the exam. If you did, however, come up with an answer then check it. If the answer is wrong or not complete then repeat the read/recite/review process. Remember, the reasons that people cannot do something is because they never learned, they only learned a portion of the information, or they learned the wrong thing.

One other good idea is to underline or highlight that key answer. This is very helpful for later review, increasing the efficiency of your review process. By using these highlights during subsequent review sessions, or for cramming before the exam, you will be reviewing the essential concepts from the text and not wasting time on ancillary material. It focuses review, which again is a very efficient use of your precious study time.

Step 5: Review

Items fade from memory unless they are reviewed, rehearsed, and reflected on. People who do not use a new language lose it. It is much easier to remember the name of someone you interact with regularly compared with someone you see once a year. Review helps to consolidate the information, deepen the path, the neural track. If you highlighted the answers to the questions you asked in Step 2 (Question) then you can use that underlined material for a quick periodic review of main points. That is an efficient way to integrate information into long-term memory. Build a periodic review of reading materials into your weekly study schedule. It will raise your GPA. It really works.

Take Reading Notes

The information presented above regarding taking effective lecture notes can be applied to reading notes as well. Depending on how the reading material will be used it can be helpful to take notes while reading or to summarize reading when you are done with a session. Note taking can help with comprehension and provide a useful resource for review. It can also be a useful self-testing approach. At the end of reading a section do a brief summary and a quick check. If you cannot write something reasonable then you have not mastered the material.

Be Selective

There is an old saying, "Garbage in, garbage out." If you start with low quality ingredients, it will be harder to make a high quality meal. That is why junk food has to be fortified. It is junk, everything good has been removed. It is all filler, no killer. It has to be refortified to give it some nutritional value. They have to put synthetic vitamins and minerals back in, because they have taken all the natural ones out.

Similarly, in an academic sense, if you start with high quality it is easier to end with high quality. Why is this important? Because there is a lot of junk information out there, just like there is a lot of junk food. Easy to find, tastes good, make of garbage, not good for you. So if you have a choice of what you are reading, be sure you discriminate and go for quality. The amount of easily accessible information available to anyone with an internet connection today is staggering. Various reputable sources estimate that there are billions of pages of content on the Internet and the number grows every day. There are 35 million books in the Library of Congress. In the United States alone there are over 300,000 new books published each year. A lot of what is out there is of very, very low quality. Given the immense number of sources of information to select from it is imperative that we become discriminating consumers. The ability to discriminate between high and low quality information, fact from fiction, evidence from anecdote, is a sign of an educated mind, a mind that does not believe everything it hears. The goal – go to the best sources for information and ideas, the best scholarly articles, the most authoritative individuals, the most thoughtful and thorough reviews, the most balanced and comprehensive coverage of news, culture, arts, sports, science and all the rest.

Not sure what those sources are? "I don't know how to do that yet, but I will learn." Ask your professor (as one very good starting point), and ask in class so others can benefit from the answer. Ask the librarian, go to scholarly websites, learn how to use your campus library and public domain databases. Become intellectually potent. Use the good brain you have been given to discriminate the wheat from the chaff. The chaff is not nourishing. It is food for cows.

Which leads to the second important consideration – once you find good quality information, then make sure you get enough of it. If you only get a few facts on Nikola Tesla it will hard to write a very thoughtful paper about his life and contributions. He was a complex character. People do things poorly or not at all, because they do not have any information, they do not have enough information, or they have the wrong information. Success requires a necessary and sufficient amount of accurate information to understand how things work.

Read Faster

Another aspect of reading efficiently is reading more quickly. This is a learned habit, like all the other things we learn, reading more quickly is a skill that will improve with knowledge and practice. There are some basic rules. If you apply them you will increase your speed and have more time for review, for access to new material, and for fun (because you will be done with work before other people who read more slowly).

The Steps

1. Time your reading. You can do this by taking a readable book, maybe a piece of fiction, not calculus or some ponderous philosophical tome. Calculate the number of words per page (figure out the average number of words per line and then multiply by the number of lines). Set a timer and read for 1 minute at your normal speed. See how many pages you read in a minute and multiply that by the number of words per page.
2. Take something you need to read and consider its complexity and the level or comprehension you need to achieve. More complex material or something that requires higher comprehension will take more time.
3. Review what you are about to read, SQ3R style.
4. Start reading.
    a. Do not subvocalize (quietly speaking words) while reading. Reading is faster than speaking.
    b. Do not reread words, keep moving forward. Keep reading at a steady, faster than normal pace.
    c. Use your finger or the tip of a pen to guide your gaze. Place your fingertip or pen tip under the line you are reading and keep it moving from the beginning to the end of the line, one line after another, like a pacing machine. You want to pace your reading.
    d. Do not read individual words, read blocks, like in SQ3R, go for the main meaning, the heart of the matter, not individual words.
5. Do not worry about comprehension as much in the beginning. You are learning a new skill and you will improve with practice. Remember, "I don't know how to do that yet, but I will learn."
6. Time yourself periodically to evaluate progress.

> **REFLECTION**
>
> Take a moment to reflect on how you approach reading. Are you spending more time than you need to, reading superfluous material, unfocused and off task, not remembering what you read, lacking easy access to key ideas for use in preparation for exams? If there are one or more areas meriting attention, pick one and think of what simple next step you could take right now to help you move toward the desired state.

3. Observational Learning

Cognitive scientists talk about two types of knowledge. There is declarative knowledge, *knowing that* a dog is a mammal. This is factual information, something you can readily share with someone. The second type is procedural knowledge, *knowing how* to ride a bike. Procedural knowledge can be something you know how to do, but you might have a tough time describing the process to another person. A lot of our academic knowledge, facts and information, is declarative knowledge that we learn from lecture or books. Certain things in life, however, are not as easily taught or imparted in that fashion. You can learn about kung fu from a book, but if that was your only source of instruction you should probably not say to the armed bank robbers, "Put the money down, I know kung fu! I'm counting. I mean it..." If the learning involves more complex motor skills, like swinging a golf club, or driving a car, or typing, or playing a violin, or tying a knot, it can often be more productive to show (and describe) and then have the learner demonstrate what was observed (Weiss & Klint, 1987).

Acquisition of motor skills often comes through observation and performance. A number of factors can improve learning efficacy in this domain. Although seeing and doing are common methods of learning motor skills, it is also helpful to hear. Research shows that visual demonstration with verbal explanation results in superior learning compared with simply observing a model performing the behavior (Weiss & Klint, 1987). If you can get the person showing you to also tell you what they are doing that can be helpful (and not everyone can explain what they are doing, they just do it). Another option would be for you to write out the steps or speak them out in your head as they are being performed, a mental checklist. Research also shows that motor skill acquisition is influenced by motivation, background knowledge, expectations, and other cognitive (person) factors (Lee & Solmon, 1992). So being in the right state of mind and body are important elements for motor skill acquisition – relax, focus, make sure you know what you are supposed to learn, expect to be successful (Prime), and remind yourself, "I don't know how to do that yet, but..." Distributed training, learning in smaller bits rather than in one long session, has also been found to produce better results, such as in acquisition of a specific surgical procedures by healthcare professionals (Moulton et al., 2006). Finally, there are individual differences in learning motor skills, like learning anything, so being patient with self is important. Some people are born athletes (natural ability) and others have to work at it. As the sage Confucius said, with commitment and practice, however, all can improve.

4. Open Inquiry and Discovery

Sometimes everything is given to you – here is the assignment, read 10 pages, do these 4 problems, here is one example completely worked through. At other times you have to go looking for answers. This is discovery learning, where you are reaching out into new territory. You are not sure exactly where you are going, you are engaged in a process of exploration of a new territory. For that process, which can be both fun and frustrating, there are a few things to keep in mind. The approach a person takes can be efficient or inefficient, both are okay, just a matter of what you need. If you do happen to need find a solution sooner than later it is probably useful to go for efficiency.

First think clearly about what you need, what is the problem. Second, use your resources, and make sure they are good quality resources. It might be a matter of asking one very knowledgeable person and the problem is solved. Again, look for rigorous, high quality thinking, research, and writing, not some blathering fools nonsense. Do not waste your time with junk. Third, persist, be patient, enjoy the place of not knowing. Life itself is a process of discovery learning. Einstein once said that he was not that much smarter than other people, he just hung out with the questions longer. Be patient with the question. Once you really start diving into deeper self-knowledge you may find some personal puzzles that may keep you engaged for the next 30 years. Recognize it is a journey, an exploration, the core of a learning life. You cannot force a rose to bloom. It opens as it opens.

Learning typically begins with awareness, being alert, paying attention, engaging in mindful awareness. We learn a good deal by observing, taking in information indirectly, watching. Observe, listen, feel. Explore life. Hold questions, ask questions. Little children ask questions all the time. They are curious. They want to learn. They want to attain greater mastery and independence, so they have to acquire a great deal of information about the complex world they now inhabit. Research things you are thinking about. Be curious. Read, attend lectures, watch videos, talk to people, travel. Wonder why, how, when, who. Do not be afraid to ask the questions that others do not ask, because they are afraid of being wrong. Ask it. Look for people who have skills that you want to learn, model their behavior, apprentice with them, read about how they approach and solve problems. Never stop learning.

> **REFLECTION**
>
> Take a moment to reflect on your Acquisition process.
>
> How am I doing with class attendance and presence? What are my most effective learning strategies? What could I do better? How could I improve what is already working? Where can I get the information/skills that I need to improve my effectiveness?

SUMMARY

Chapter 6 introduces the three pillars of learning – Acquisition, Integration and Display and focuses on the first of these, Acquisition. This is the stage in which new information is taken into mind and body, the first step. One of the keys to learning that will be integrated into these three stages is metawareness, similar to metacognition, just more holistic in its scope. The concept of metawareness brings mindful awareness to our learning. It involves mindful awareness of person (thoughts, feelings, physiological states), behaviors (verbal, non-verbal), and environments (physical, social and biological). Keys academic strategies for effective acquisition are explored: note taking, reading, observation and exploration. Important in note taking is coming prepared mentally and physically, having the right tools and strategies, or refining those notes once completed. For effective and efficient reading the technique of SQ3R was introduced. This stands for Survey, Question, Read, Recite and Review. Increasing reading speed is another good strategy for efficient study and learning, more done in less time. Observation is another useful approach, especially for improving procedural knowledge. Declarative knowledge is related to information that can be described. Procedural knowledge relates to knowledge of things that we can do, but may not be able to describe, like how to ride a bike. Finally, exploratory learning can be useful way to build agency through the organic process of creative discovery.

MIND-BODY PRACTICE

Sitting Meditation

Continue with awareness of body and breath, and sensory information. This week add awareness of thoughts and emotional states. When you think of it remember to label some of these moments of experiences, "thinking, thinking", "sad or happy."

Mindful Awareness

This week practice targeted awareness, specifically noting body tension. Practice labeling it when you recognize it, "tension, tension, tension." The take a moment to relax if it feels like that would be helpful for managing your tension or stress.

Priming

Practice priming a most incredible day several days or more this week. Also pick some specific task you want to work on and prime ideal an outcomes with it, like getting a higher grade on an exam you have to take this week, or being more involved in class discussion.

REFERENCES

Ashcraft MH. *Human Memory and Cognition*. New York: Harper Collins; 1994.

Flavell JH. Metacognition and cognitive monitoring: A new area of cognitive-developmental inquiry. *American Psychologist*. 1979;34:906-911.

DiVesta FJ, Gray GS. Listening and note taking. II: Immediate and delayed recall as functions of variations in thematic continuity, note taking, and length of listening-review intervals. *Journal of Educational Psychology*. 1973;64:278-287.

Garner, R. (1988). Verbal-report data on cognitive and metacognitive strategies. In: Weinstein CE, Goetz ET, Alexander PA, editors. *Learning and study strategies: Issues in assessment, instruction, and evaluation*. New York: Academic Press; 1988:63-76.

Gu Y. Learning strategies: Prototypical core and dimensions of variation. *Studies in Self-Access Learning Journal*. 2012;3(4):330-356.

Hall PD. The effect of meditation on the academic performance of African American college students. *Journal of Black Studies*. 1999;29(3):408-415.

Kiewra KA. Investigating notetaking and review: A depth of processing alternative. *Educational Psychologist*. 1985;20:23-32.

Lee AM, Solmon MA. Cognitive conceptions of teaching and learning motor skills. *Quest*. 1992;44(1):57-71.

Moulton CA, Dubrowski A, Macrae H, Graham B, Grober E, Reznick R. Teaching surgical skills: what kind of practice makes perfect?: a randomized, controlled trial. *Annals of Surgery*. 2006;244(3):400-409.

Nishimoto S, Vu AT, Naselaris T, Benjamini Y, Yu B, Gallant JL. Reconstructing visual experiences from brain activity evoked by natural movies. *Current Biology*. 2011;21(19):1641-1646.

Pauk W, Owens RJQ. *How to Study in College*. Independence, Kentucky: Cengage Learning; 2010.

Robbins SB, Lauver K, Le H, Davis D, Langley R, Carlstrom A. Do psychosocial and study skill factors predict college outcomes? A meta-analysis. *Psychological Bulletin*. 2004;130(2):261-288.

Robinson FP. Effective Study. New York: Harper & Row; 1978.

Toga AW, Clark KA, Thompson PM, Shattuck DW, Van Horn JD. Mapping the human connectome. *Neurosurgery*. 2012;71(1):1-5.

Van Meter P, Yokoi L, Pressley M. College students' theory of note-taking derived from their perceptions of note-taking. *Journal of Educational Psychology*. 1994;86:323-338.

Weiss MR, Klint KA. "Show and Tell" in the gymnasium: An investigation of developmental differences in modeling and verbal rehearsal of motor skills. *Research Quarterly for Exercise and Sport*. 1987;58(3):234-241.

Zimmerman BJ. Academic studying and the development of personal skill: A self-regulatory perspective. *Educational Psychologist*. 1998;33(2/3):73-86.

Academic Skills
Integration

I practice intelligently in order to remember, understand, and grow.

CHAPTER THEMES
- Integration
- Effective Study Skills
- Strategies to Improve Integration
  - Why We Forget
  - How We Remember
    - Review
    - Organize Course Content
    - Make it Fun

The first pillar of learning we learned about in the previous chapter was Acquisition. Now we will consider the second pillar, Integration. Once information has been acquired the next step is to improve memory access, integrate that new information with existing knowledge, deepen understanding, and increase our capacity to display that knowledge and skill in the world. There are a number of practical learning strategies that can facilitate effective integration. We will consider some of them now, with a focus on improving study skills and enhancing memory and recall. There will be a lot of ideas presented in this chapter. Consider your own situation and pick the ones that will benefit you the most. Start with one or two, make changes as needed, and add on from there, building your academic success one small step at a time.

Effective Study Skills

Having effective study strategies is a key to successful learning. In a nutshell, the reason for studying is to help get material into long-term memory, including muscle memory, and emotional memory. If we cannot remember the term, the formula, the brush stroke, then we will neither understand it nor will we be able to use it effectively. The goal of learning is to be able to access knowledge and skills for exams, performances, all important life moments, personal and professional. In this first section we will look at ways to make study time more efficient, effective and even enjoyable, helping to move you to the next level of the game. Before we begin it should be acknowledged that study can be related to both acquisition of new material and subsequent integration of that material. In studying there is often some of both. A math or language homework assignment will probably introduce new material and build on and reinforces what you have already learned. So in reality the strategies we are about to examine affect both the Acquisition and Integration phases of learning.

Estimate Hours Per Week and Book It

The very first thing is to estimate how many hours to study per week. A general rule of thumb is 2 hours of study for each hour in class. If you are in class 9 hours then you should study for 18 hours. Some semesters will require more or less study time, depending on the difficulty of classes. Some courses will take more time than others. If you are learning a challenging foreign language or taking upper division science classes you may need twice the recommended amount. Integration of new material takes time. Indeed, it takes as much time as it takes. It is what it is. Be flexible, be honest. If you are working on a subject you find challenging it will take more time. That is not a personal flaw or shortcoming, it is just a reality. Different people have different aptitudes. If the subject matter is not your strong suit then you should expect to spend more time mastering the material. If you do not have a good foundation, which means you have not done much acquisition and integration of related material previously, it will take more time to get it into memory and understanding. Two of the big reasons students do not perform as well as they could in a class is the simple fact that they did not use the right strategies and they did not put in enough study and practice time. You must take the right dosage of medicine to cure the illness. *Sufficient study time is imperative, there is no way around that.* Lead programmers for the Chinese web service Alibaba work together in a small apartment about 13 hours a day, all week long. They get a lot done. Things take time, as much time as they take. Once you have a sense of the number of hours needed per course, per week, then block that into your calendar and your semester schedule. Do this at the beginning of the semester, and then revise as needed throughout the semester. A weekly check-in is also a good idea, to see if your initial schedule is realistic.

Decide on What the Next Task Should Be

You blocked your study time into your schedule. Now you are sitting there on Tuesday at 2pm, one of your designated study periods. This is a good time to check your calendar/schedule to make sure you are on track. A very helpful question to ask yourself at that moment is – "What is the most important thing for me to do right now?" Decide on the most important, most appropriate task that gets you closer to reaching your personal and academic goals. What should the next task be? People will often choose an easier item when they sit down to work and justify its value in their minds. Not so useful. Be honest. Do what needs to be done. Select the task that really matters. This is where study planners and calendars come in handy. Thursday from 2 to 4 is time for math homework. It is Thursday, 2pm. Time for math homework, case closed. However, this week, there is a major paper coming up and you are caught up on math, so you decide that the most important thing to do next is to work on that English paper. Ask yourself, "What is the most important thing to do right now?"

Task Clarity - Understand the Assignment or Task

Once you pick that next important thing to do, then you need to make sure you actually understand what you are supposed to do, what is the intended goal of the particular task, how is it supposed to be done. If the task is a reading assignment, then it is important to know how many pages, by when, for what purpose, whether the reading is primary material for an exam or secondary reading for richer understanding in the course. People often begin a work task without a clear understanding of the intended outcome. As a consequence of not clearly understanding the purpose, or the process, a lot of time can be wasted, inefficient use of precious time that could have been spent having fun, playing with the kids, making more money, working out. Lack of understanding can also really affect the grade for that piece of work. It is essential to have a clear understanding of the assignment – what am I supposed to do, when is it due, who else is involved? Read the instructions, underline important words or objectives. If it is not clear then look at the syllabus again, often it is there, or possibly in class notes or in online class materials. If still not clear after all of that then ask the TA or instructor, in class or email.

Determine the Goal for the Session - Work to be Completed

Once you have done your task assessment, what is the assignment, then describe specifically to yourself what you will do before you start. "I will read the 10 assigned pages of English for 1 hour using the SQ3R method, underline key concepts for later use in review, and answer the assigned questions at the end of the chapter when I am done reading, and any others if I still have time." That is a very clear statement of what you will accomplish, the micro-goal, and serves the larger goal of getting an A in the class. You know what you are doing and why. You know where you are going.

You remember from chapter 2 that good goals are specific. It is the same for study goals. You need to know what work needs to get done, how much, and at what level of proficiency. Getting clear on these details is essential for effective time management. How so? All of us have probably experienced sitting in front of a book with the idea of studying for two hours. Two hours pass and lo and behold you can not remember a single word. The 2 hours of scheduled study time passed, so you satisfied the time requirement. The problem, not an ounce of meaningful work was accomplished. The block of time is a useful container, but the purpose of that container is to fill it up with productive work. So before you start a task it is useful to set specific (and reasonable) goals for what is to be done – the specific task, the amount of work to be done, and the quality. That approach puts the emphasis on the ***task*** to be completed, ***not the time*** to be passed, which ironically, improves time management (as we will see in Chapter 9 on Change Management).

Set Length of Study Sessions

Another important scheduling consideration is how long a study session should last. When it comes to academic work there is no magic number. A one or two-hour block of study time is a good chunk. That is enough time to get things rolling, long enough to get some serious work done on reading, problem solving and practice sessions. It may be too long for some people, however, and too short for others. So doing whatever works best for you is the key. Everyone is different. You need to find your pace. The main thing is that you are able to stay on task and get the work done. So experiment and decide on what your more effective time blocks are and do that. Also recognize that those blocks may vary based on the day, the subject matter, your mood, energy levels and other factors. Work, take a break, refresh, come back for more. Find the pattern that allows you to do a solid block of work, to get things done. Also, if you do work for blocks longer than one hour, take a short break at least once per hour, specifically standing up and moving about a bit. Increasing evidence suggests that sitting for long periods is quite deleterious to health (Schmid & Leitzmann, 2014).

One of my students, who had some serious study anxiety, worked out a strategy of studying for 15-20 minutes and then taking a small break for 5 minutes. He was taking difficult science classes and this method worked for him. His approach allowed him to study instead of worry and procrastinate, he could focus because he knew he would stop in 20 minutes. That helped him manage his anxiety well enough to log in more effective study time. Other students would work for several hours in a row, alternating 45 minutes of work and 15 minutes of rest, and some would just sit for several hours at a time, no breaks (again, not a good solution in terms of health). It all depends on what works for you. As we shall see in Chapter 9 on managing time and change the point is not how long you work, it is how much work you get done and with what quality.

Pace Your Learning

Another consideration is your brain, the way it acquires and remembers new information. If you are doing straight memorization it is better to do 3 blocks of 15 minutes, with short rests of 5 minutes between each block, that it is to sit for one hour straight. In the research literature on this topic, learning where you pack it all into long block is called *massed learning*. This is compared to learning in smaller blocks separated in time. That approach is called *distributed or spaced learning*. The evidence tends to be pretty consistent in favor of spaced learning. Especially when it comes to long-term recall, studying the same or related material in chunks of time versus all at one sitting, is more productive for recall, often significantly more productive (Carpenter et al., 2012). Memory has a limit, just like there is a limit to how much weight you can lift over your head. Memory integration seems to be more effective in smaller packets. In terms of the interval between sessions the evidence suggests that the sooner you will be tested the shorter the study interval should be. If you were going to be tested in a week, you might review every day. If the test was in a month, review might be most productive on a weekly basis (Rohrer & Pashler, 2007).

Monitor/Stay on Task

Whether you are working for 12 minutes or 3 hours the goal is to be on task and get the job done. It is the work we complete on important tasks that carries us to our intended goal. A simple mindful awareness practice can help in this regard. Periodically check in, some mindful awareness of where you are right now during a study session, an application of the AIR (Awareness Inquiry Response) approach. The simple Awareness question, "Am I on task or off task?" If not on task the simple Inquiry questions, "Why, and what can I do right now to get back on task?" The Response – do that – do whatever it takes to get back on task, or *assess current state* and *consciously decide* if ut is time for a break or even time to stop working. Another guiding question, "What is the most important thing for me to do right now?" Turn this simple mindful awareness practice into a habit and it will change your life. I would bet money on that.

Key Point: Remember, it is not necessarily about the amount of time you spend studying, it is about how you study, what you do during that time, your task focus and persistence. Research on business students found that study time did not predict GPA, but rather study time moderated by the ability to concentrate, or stay on task. That was the critical factor (Nonis, 2010). The goal is to get the task done with the appropriate level of quality. If completed before the scheduled time then you are then free to roam about the plane, do more work, have some fun, your choice. This approach also fosters a continual improvement mentality. It gets you to start thinking about how can you can do the task faster and end up with an even higher quality final product.

Find Your Best Study Time

Another strategy to increase productivity is to determine the time of day that is optimal for productive work, not just work, but productive work. It is advisable to do the hardest projects, or to work on your hardest classes, when you have your best energy, clearest mind, and highest motivation. You would not want to go into the big prizefight if you did not feel your best. If you are a morning person then schedule your hard subjects and study times earlier in the day. Get to these projects when the power is on. If you are a night person, do the heavy lifting then.

That said, here is one important thing to consider regarding night work. I often hear students claim that they are night people, a common refrain at the beginning of the semester in my *Academic Success* class. In fact, they are often not night people at all. They are just mismanaging their time during the day (wasting time doing nothing terribly useful) and then as a result have to stay up late to get the work done. This leaves them tired the next day, potentially prone to missing morning classes, and doing rushed, lower quality work. I have had many students report that once they shifted to working earlier in the day they noticed a clear benefit in performance. Everybody is different, every body is different, finding out your biorhythms will help you succeed. That requires an honest assessment of energy peaks and valleys

Study in The Right Place

Work in the right environment. Many of my students find they do their best work in the study commons of our campus library. It is relatively quiet there, few distractions, and you see everyone else studying (misery loves company). There is a coffee shop on site as well. It is helpful to have a place where you can get work done, focused and free from distractions. It might be a school library, public library, café, an empty classroom, a random comfortable place to sit where you can put on your headphones and get focused. When I was an undergrad I had a favorite classroom I would sometimes use for study. It was often empty, always quiet, had the right academic vibe, and kept me in a productive work mode. Also, right place implies access to the materials you need to get your work done efficiently. That might mean bringing them with you. If you work at a desk keep it reasonably organized and free from clutter. That will help you feel calm and focused.

Minimize Distractions

If you are working at home or somewhere that allows you to have easy access to your cell phone, turn it off. You do not want to be texting, checking social networking sites, responding to emails, or engaged in anything that takes you off task (consider using phone time as a reward for completing a period of focused work). ***Stay ON TASK***. That is the goal. "What is the most important task right now? Am I on task?" If not. "Why am I off task? What small step can I take right now to change that?" Practice your Metawareness. Do a scan of mind and body. Do you need a break, some tea, a pep talk, a moment of relaxation, priming a vision of the finished product, a quick walk outside for sunshine and fresh air? If you have housemates or roommates let them know you are working and politely (or not) ask them not to bug you, tempt you, distract you. If you are clear about ***the*** *amount of work you need to complete* and *the amount of time you will be working* then it is easier to say no to friends. Finally, if you tend to distract yourself by always having brilliant ideas or thinking of things for your To Do list then have a separate piece of paper and jot those ideas down quickly, once out of the way get right back on track. You can come back to them later when you have completed your relevant tasks in your allotted time.

Create a To Do List or Checklist

Create a To Do list to remind yourself of the tasks you need to work on for a specific exam, paper or performance. If it is a repetitive task you can create a checklist that you can use repeatedly (we will work on checklists in Chapter 8 on Continual Improvement). The basic strategy is simple – create a list of the actionable items that need to be done. Once you have that list of tasks to be accomplished you then prioritize them in order of importance, or in their natural sequence. (For more ideas on To Do List strategies go back to Chapter 3 on Goals.) If tasks extend over a period of days or weeks you can schedule them into your calendar to help with your detailed planning. As an example, a test prep list might include – review class notes, write sample exam questions, meet with study group, prime getting an A on the exam, create flashcards for key terms, review and reread highlighted materials on Tuesday and Thursday, cram review morning of exam. These items would be prioritized or sequenced and then put into your calendar, mapping key events into appropriate target dates. Check them off as completed.

Optimize Study Moments

Another way to increase productivity is to use the bits of time that you have available throughout the day. A good seamstress can make a coat out of remnants of cloth. A house is built out of relatively small pieces of wood. Reservoirs are filled by the collected raindrops flowing down from mountain streams. The little bits of time in life, used wisely, can add up over the course of days, weeks and months, resulting in significant amounts of work completed. The time riding the bus, commuting in your car, waiting for your laptop to reboot or the television commercials to end, can be one more page of reading completed, three new words memorized, brainstorming for a paper thesis. Get in the habit of using those moments. It takes a bit of forethought to get it rolling, like preparing flashcards, or taking a book with you when you go into the bank, but once you get in the habit the impact on increased productivity will be obvious. I knew a chap in Santa Cruz. He worked in a bookstore. When the store was quiet he would often be standing by the cash register reading a book. He was one of the more well read people I knew, a page here, a page there. Guerilla warfare, used successfully throughout history, relies on a continuous series of small scale, intermittent events to fight an opponent that is typically much larger and more well-equipped. It is powerful to see what you can accomplish in small steps once you start to use the strategy.

Just Start

What is the next actionable task? Pick the task and do something. If the task seems overwhelming, pick a small step and just work on that for 12 minutes. Set a timer. When 12 minutes are up you can stop if you have to. Often by that point, however, you have gotten used to the cold water and you are now swimming. Many people just keep going from there. If you do stop, you will still be surprised at what you can get done. In 12 minutes you could come up with a title page. You could create a rough outline for a paper, do one problem, translate one sentence, memorize one short list of key terms. There is an amazing power in just starting. No significant human creation happens overnight (except maybe conception, but the credit for that really goes to nature, our part is pretty simple). Things take time, one step at a time. There is an old Chinese adage, that the journey of a thousand miles begins with one step (and then another and then another). That is the way of life. It is what it is. You just keep doing bit by bit and in time you will be amazed at what gets accomplished. The author John Steinbeck said that each morning he would sit in front of a blank page (and he was using a typewriter not a computer) and that he would feel sick knowing he had a 500-page book ahead of him. The only way he could proceed was to think about writing one page at a time. Big jobs need to be turned into smaller pieces, steps, stages. We will talk about that more in Chapter 8 on Continual Improvement.

Use Study Groups

A study group can be another good way to work on the integration of material into long-term memory. Each individual will come to the group with somewhat different notes, aptitudes, and backgrounds. When you do not understand a problem there is a chance that someone else in your study group will, or that the five of you together can figure it out. When you are about to give up someone else in the group will rally and keep you all going until you reach the end. So study groups can be very useful, but it has to be the right method for you, and the right group. If you are going to use a study group it is best to include people who are serious students, who want to do better in school, who can inspire you, and who can offer mutual benefit in preparing for exams and projects. If one study group does not work do not abandon them altogether. Most of us will have at least one 'group from hell' experience at some point. This is often a situation where one person in the group cannot work with the other members because he or she knows everything about everything, does not like humans, is not motivated in the class or in school, or whatever else is going on. No judgment, no problem. Chalk that up to experience – living and learning – and use it as an opportunity to practice emotional self-regulation and developing skills in managing difficult people (the goal in those situations might be damage control, keeping the ship afloat long enough to finish the project and getting a good grade).

Once you have your people then you can come up with an agreement on some basic parameters including when and where to meet and what the goals of the group will be. Create an agenda for each meeting, a list of things that you want to accomplish. You can use the group to solve problems together. You can assign each person to prepare a particular section of the book or a set of questions and then have them lead a group discussion on that section. You can use the Socratic method and ask questions to test each other. If using the Socratic approach you can have everybody in the group create test questions, with answers, and then take turns asking questions. You can also use the group as a way to compare notes from the class, prepare exam questions and answers, compare understanding of key concepts, and answer each others questions. Consider using a contract if the group work is graded. Agree ahead of time to anonymously grade each other on contributions and that you will attach that to the final document (whether the instructor requires any information on individual participation or not (you will find a sample Study Group Contract in the Resources section at the end of the book).

Keep Your Motivation Up

One final thought for improving study time effectiveness is understanding your reason for doing the work. Effective study requires motivation. If a person sees no value in a task it is hard to be motivated. Without motivation people give up sooner and more easily. If the motivation is strong, however, you will find a way. As the old India aphorism says, "If you hair is on fire, you will find water." For that reason it is good to remind yourself periodically of your reasons for doing the work. If you can see that your studying contributes to accomplishment of important personal goals and values, or leads to specific rewards, it will help you get to work and stay on task. Remembering why you are doing a task is a very good way to find motivation and to stay motivated. Assigned tasks can potentially be uninspiring, lacking obvious value. In those cases you need to find your motivation. Generic solution – any school task can be used as the basis for developing other important life skills, such as improved writing and critical thinking, increased emotional self-regulation, mental toughness, team skills. There is ALWAYS a benefit to be gained if a task is approached the right way. Another productive motivator is to think of the work as part of what you are giving to the world today, your contribution to a better planet. Then just do it. It will give you more grit.

> **REFLECTION**
>
> Take a moment to reflect on how you approach study time. Do you know how many hours per week you should be studying? Are you clear on what the task is, what to study next, and how best to do that? Do you set goals for your study sessions and distribute your study and review over time? Are you able to stay on task? Do you have a best time of day, best place to study? Do you use spare moments effectively? Do you ever use a study group?

Strategies to Improve Memory and Understanding

Creating a new memory is a building process. It changes things in your brain, creating new patterns, making new associations, linking new regions. All of that building takes time. What we want to look at now are some strategies that can be used to facilitate that process. First we will take a quick look at forgetting and then turn our attention to strategies to improve memory and understanding.

Why We Forget

There are a number of causes of forgetting. *Disuse* may be one of the most common. If you have not seen a particular person in several months it can be challenging to remember the person's name when you do bump into him or her on the street again. "Hey amigo!" works sometimes. That is one of the reasons periodic review is so useful. It is the antidote for memory loss due to disuse.

Interference is another reason we do not remember things. In the case of interference the actual mechanisms of memory are disrupted, interfered with. Causes of interference include emotional upset, anxiety and fear. These states create neurological changes that result in less effective memory processing. That is why test anxiety can affect performance. Chronic anxiety actually reduces memory storage in part because anxiety releases the stress hormone cortisol, which negatively affects the hippocampus and other memory structures (Henckens, 2009).

Another cause of forgetting is *retroactive inhibition* (retro, in the past, like disco and transistor radios). This is forgetting something you learned in the past because of new learning. For example, it might be hard to remember the words to a song you used to know because since then you have learned several new songs by the same artist.

A related cause of forgetting is called *proactive inhibition* (blocking the future). This is not being able to remember new information because of what is already in memory. One example might be passwords. A person is trying to remember a new password for their new tablet, but they have five old passwords they are still using. The old passwords are more completely embedded in memory and because of that may challenge the new memory.

How We Remember

We will begin with one of the most important strategies for integrating learning, deepening memory and understanding is REVIEW. Review, in all its forms, is the bedrock to success in school and life in terms of memory and retrieval.

1. Review, Practice, Rehearse (and Do It Well)

Deliberate, intelligent, mindfully aware review, practice and rehearsal is key. These are important foundations for longer-term memory, effective display, and ultimate mastery. A study of chess masters found that none attained international grandmaster status with less than ten years of intense practice (Simon and Chase, 1973). This same degree of intense and prolonged preparatory work has been similarly noted in mathematics, music, sports and other domains (Ericsson et al., 1993). The effect of practice on performance can be quite significant (Chi, Glaser, & Farr, 1988). Practice, rehearse, do more sample problems, seek to develop mastery. Find the areas of weakness and return to those for more work, as often as necessary.

One thing that is critically important to keep in mind regarding review and practice, however, is the quality of that practice. We will be discussing all of these topics in more detail in upcoming chapters, but in *Learning Life* we want to keep an eye on quality. If you make quality a principle performance criteria it will pull everything else along in the right direction. Learning is a problem solving game. *The goal is to progress from the current state of not knowing or not being able to do, to the desired state of knowledge and skill.* Using the right strategy with a particular problem makes solving it more efficient, like using a hammer to pound a nail. Effective problem solving also means taking the most efficient and effective path, the most direct route. In the world of music, for example, a 3-year study of over 150 music students found that it was the practice strategies students used that predicted achievement, not the amount of time they spent practicing (McPherson, 2005). Similarly, Williamon and Valentine (2000) studied four groups of pianists divided by level of skill. They found the best predictor of performance quality to be the quality and not the quantity of practice.

Characteristics of effective practice can include the following characteristics: the learner understands the practice/rehearsal task, gets feedback on performance (not always easy), repeatedly practices the same or similar tasks, can observe competent performers doing the task correctly, has been shown strategies for effective practice, practices thoughtfully, practices as if performing (quality emphasis), recognizes errors in practice and then rehearses and corrects them (repeated looping until correct form is achieved), and spends more time on areas of weakness (Duke et al., 2009; Fitts & Posner, 1967; Gagne, 1970). People often make the mistake on just looping on things they already do well. It is easy and makes the person feel competent (self-efficacy), but there is little new learning. It is important to loop on the tough spots in addition to reviewing what we already know periodically. In a study on gender differences in navigating 3D virtual space, it was found that women (who generally performed less well) performed as well as men when both used large screen displays. The large screen display provided more optical flow cues, more information to help the women navigate effectively (Tan et al., 2003). The point from much of this research is that if there is a sticky problem you need to slow it down, loop the tough spots, blow it up in size, have it explained, watch it being done, or do assorted other manipulations to get a handle on how to do it correctly. Whatever works, and often that means more than one strategy. Never forget the idea that, "I don't know how to do this yet, but I will learn." If there is a will, there is very often a way. Never give up.

Periodic Review
In a similar vein, your brain benefits from periodic review of lecture notes, poetry verses, piano scales, whatever needs to be learned, to get that into long-term memory. It is important to make reviewing a habit, doing it efficiently, and doing it sufficiently, to get the knowledge and skill into memory, into body and mind, making them increasingly accessible. Once you have taken notes in class, practiced the new swing, learned your opening lines for the play, then you want to review/rehears/practice. Research indicates that memory of information, like class lectures, drops rapidly within the first day and then more slowly thereafter, and that this memory decay is influenced by many factors including difficulty of the material, stress levels, and motivation (Baddeley, 1999). Research shows that when students are re-exposed to material they learned but cannot remember they master the material much more quickly the second time (Berger et al., 2008).

It is important to schedule review and practice time into your calendar each week, not just study time for *acquisition* of new material, but review time for *integration*. It is also very helpful to quickly review materials before and after classes. It is easy to do if you have breaks between classes or commute home after school. Even a few minutes right before or after a class will refresh the materials in memory. That builds long-term recall, access to material for the future, and deepening understanding (which also facilitates memory and more sophisticated display). Get in the habit of doing an end of the week review, such as Friday afternoons, all subjects. An end of week review also helps you to think about classes and assignments that will be coming next week and that supports thoughtful planning and scheduling. If you use SQ3R or a related method you will have highlighted texts. Use that highlighted material along with any outlined class notes for efficient review.

Consider making at least some of your review materials portable. If something is inconvenient, hard to reach, cumbersome, it is less likely to get used. Flashcards are a good solution. They are especially useful for facts, formulas, key terms, foreign language vocabulary, and other discrete bits of information. Put a question on one side of the card and the answer on the other. Carry a small stack with you in your backpack or purse for moments of review when in line or on the bus. You can also create test guides, outlines, and mind maps as ways to provide a snapshot overview of key ideas. You can make mp3 recordings of key ideas to listen to between classes or while commuting. Creating these resources is its own review process, and then you also have a final product that provides an accessible, portable, convenient means to review content.

Paced Review
Review does not have to be long and arduous. As described above research shows that distributed or spaced learning (smaller sessions spaced apart) is superior to massed learning (one big chunk), especially for longer term recall (Carpenter et al., 2012). It makes sense. Spaced review is like eating three smaller meals versus sitting down for one episode of massive face filling. The smaller meals are easier to digest and assimilate. You get more nutritional value, and it feels better. Healthy eating is a good example of a small steps approach. Do the same for learning.

Self-Testing
Self-testing is a most excellent way to review and deepen understanding while simultaneously preparing for tests. A study by King (1992) compared three methods of working with class lecture notes. One group summarized notes at the end of lecture, the second created self-test questions, and the third simply reviewed notes. Both summary and self-test students outperformed the reviewers in an immediate recall test. In a retest one week later the students who created self-test questions outperformed both groups. It makes sense. Summarizing materials and creating self-test questions would naturally require more engagement with material and thoughtfulness. The self-test questions approach has the added value of making you think like the instructor. You are reviewing the material like the professor looking for possible questions to put on the exam. You are also testing your understanding and recall of that material by asking and answering those questions. It is an excellent method.

You can use class notes, highlighted readings, and other course materials as the basis for self-testing. Ask yourself questions, based on key words, or chapter headings, or questions you added to lecture notes, and then see if you can come up with the answers. If you can answer them correctly then there is a very good chance you will get those answers right on the exam (especially if you review them periodically before the exam). If you answer incorrectly or cannot answer at all, then the information is clearly not in your head yet (wrong information or not enough information). This type of self-testing review strategy provides a very useful self-assessment, essential feedback on what you know or do not know.

Create your own sample problems or test questions, complete with answers. To prepare self-tests consider ahead of time what kinds of questions will be on the exam. What key terms, concepts, problems might reasonably be tested. Collect questions from the textbook and from class quizzes and lectures (when the professor answers a question that seems like possible exam material then write it down). If the instructor provides a study guide for exams then by all means use it, create answers to all items on the study guide. Work with a group of diligent students in a study group to generate a set of questions and answers to share. Teach each other. Find related sample test questions online, ideally with answers and detailed explanations so you can see how the answers were derived. Find equivalent material that has been translated, problems that have been solved, papers that have been written. Use them as sources of ideas for questions and answers for study.

Mental Rehearsal

We have already spent a bit of time on this, back in Chapter 3 on Priming. That said, it is useful to make the point one more time, for emphasis. Mental rehearsal, seeing yourself successfully performing the task, feeling that sense of accomplishment as if you had already succeeded, is a very helpful learning strategy. As described in Chapter 3, in relation to motor activities, mental rehearsal activates similar regions of the brain as if the person was doing the task or watching someone do the task (Cisek & Kalaska, 2004). Surveys of Olympic and elite athletes and their coaches found that the majority employed mental rehearsal as part of their preparation (Suinn, 1997). Evidence clearly supports its value (Driskell et al., 1994). Imagine yourself being able to do the task, solve the problem, shoot the goal, give the moving speech. See it, feel it, believe it. It is another resource to add to your kit of strategies.

Cramming

Research has found that in some circumstances cramming can be a useful review strategy (Vacha, 1993). If cramming right before an exam is the first exposure to the material that is obviously not review and not related to integration. That is Stage I, acquisition, and is in general a seriously suboptimal strategy. Cramming alone does not provide sufficient time or exposure needed for the brain to process the information adequately. Remember your brain is a physical structure, and like muscle, it needs sufficient time and repetition to build up a strong memory. Single exposure cramming is possibly better than nothing, but depending on the complexity and amount of material, it is often marginal. If it is actually a final review, however, it can be helpful. If cramming is not too anxiety provoking then doing a concentrated review immediately before test time can help. It reloads information into memory immediately before the event, making the material more proximal, more accessible. If, however, cramming is anxiety provoking, then it is best avoided.

Cramming is related to the memory phenomena of primacy and recency. Imagine you were at a large party and you met 20 new people. If you were asked to repeat names at the end of the event you would most likely remember the names of the first few people you met and the last few. This is known as the primacy and recency effect. The first few names (primacy, primary, first) were the ones you originally rehearsed the most. You were motivated to remember them. Eventually the list became too long to keep rehearsing all those new names. Toward the end of the night you met a few other new people. They were the last names you heard, the most recent (recency), the freshest in memory. What tends to be accessible for most people will be the first (primacy) and last (recency) few names. Repeated practice fills in the missing items.

Attending Class and Participating

Attending class is actually another great way to review. If you read the assigned materials ahead of time, and do the related homework, even partially, then the lecture will be a review of what you have already been exposed to in your preliminary acquisition activities. In addition, teachers will typically go over material they have already covered, explain things in more details, and answer questions related to content from the last lecture. In addition, attending class may also increase your commitment to getting your work done as you will be present and therefore more accountable, even if just a bit, and that is helpful. All of that supports long-term memory and deeper understanding of content.

> **REFLECTION**
>
> Take a moment to reflect on how you approach memorization. Do you review materials soon after class? Do you build in sufficient time for practice and review? Do you engage in periodic review? Do you use self-testing (creating your own questions)? Do you use priming, mentally rehearsing the desired outcome? Do you organize materials for greater understanding, such as using outlining, categorizing, or mind mapping? Do you use memory devices such as mnemonics or associational links? Do you make learning fun and personally interesting?

2. Organize Course Content

Another key strategy for the integration of learning is to organize the information you are learning. Organization creates categories and reduces the number of individual pieces you need to remember, it makes for more efficient information processing. The disparate pieces become part of one interrelated whole, like seeing one constellation instead of seven individual stars. One is easier to remember than seven. The process of organizing course materials, be that class notes, information from readings, or audio clips, serves a number of functions. First, it makes you look at the material again, a review. Second, it makes you look at the material more complexly, seeing the relationships between elements more clearly. Seeing the relationships helps with both memory and understanding (five thematically related ideas versus five random bits of information). Finally, the organized content, such as an outline of key concepts, can end up being a succinct, highly efficient resource for future review and exam preparation. Here are some organizing strategies.

Outlining

Outlining is always a useful way to review notes. It offers another chance to go over material, extract key ideas, and arrange them so you can see relationships more clearly. One common outlining strategy is to use three levels – major topic, subtopics, and supporting details. So if you were creating a study guide for your music class the first level, the major topic, would be jazz. The second level would be the subtopics within that category, including artists, styles, regions. The third level would be supporting details such as where the artists were born, where they studied, recording labels, important influences, and other relevant information. You just spent time putting together a nicely organized study guide. Creating the outline resulted in a productive review, possibly included some reflection, involved additional internet research on the artists and listening to music samples (more integration and added depth of learning). At the end of the process you also have an excellent exam review resource. It could even be the basis for an impressive attachment to a related assignment. You just learned a lot more about the topic than the average students who just read the assigned material, close the book, and head back to their videogames.

Categorizing

Categorizing is another productive way to organize information by time period, geographic location, form, function, or any other logical theme. One of the way the brain supports understanding is by organizing information into related categories, functional relationships, essentially concept clusters or nodes (Wickelgren, 1981). The strategy is to create nodes or packets of information, groupings of concepts that are related to each other. These are nouns, those are verbs, here are the adjectives. Categorizing can help you take something big and break it down into smaller parts or sets. That makes it easier to see relationship and functions more clearly. What do the elements in a category have in common? How are categories different from each other? Breaking it down into packets like this is also referred to as chunking. You are creating chunks or clusters or related information. Having information in nodes or bundles, items with related qualities, makes it easier to deal with large amounts of information. Biologist, for example, take the profoundly large and diverse domain of animal life on the planet and organize it into seven levels, a taxonomy going from kingdom, phyllum, class down to species. That allows biologists to sort animal life by groups, such as by class – mammals, birds, reptiles, amphibians and so on. This process of categorization helps to make the information more manageable and easier to work with and remember.

Mind Maps

Mind mapping is another way to look at the association between ideas, dates, events, and other facts. It is a fun and creative way to organize material, less linear. For this method you need a clean page. Put the main concept on a line in the center of the page. Then make branches from that starting line to outer nodes. The outer nodes are bundles of related information. Each node will have its own focus, maybe its own color, or images. It can links to other nodes as well. The idea is to create a visual relational map of the concept or domain, rather than just a string of words. This process can also help to make review a bit more fun as it is a different way of working with the materials you are learning.

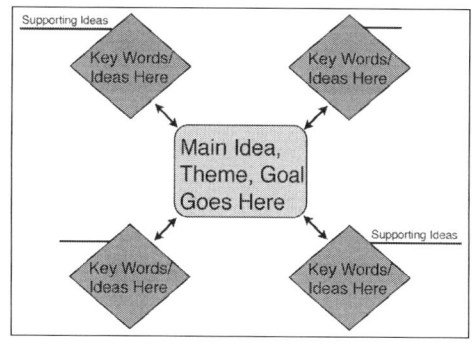

Study Crib Sheets

Make a sheet of key terms, concepts, rules, whatever it is you need to really understand, the essential bits. Put that all into a condensed format. That makes it easy to carry and review. It can also force you to remember more ahead of time as you may only have cue words that will be used to trigger more comprehensive recall.

Memory Devices

One of the ways to help integrate facts into long-term memory is through a strategy called elaborative encoding. This basically involves associating a new word or idea with something that is already well integrated into memory because it is already familiar to you, or is otherwise easy to remember. This approach includes mnemonics and linking.

Mnemonics

Roy G Biv, that person's name, in case you do not know, stands for the colors of the rainbow, the light spectrum - Red, Orange, Yellow, Green, Blue, Indigo, Violet. Acronyms are a useful way to organize strings of information that may otherwise be hard to remember. The acronym provides a cue or clue for each word. So instead of remembering seven words, in the case of the colors of the spectrum, you are remembering one person's name. The acronym stimulates recall of each word, triggered by the first letter. 'O', what other color could that be, ochre (which is heading to orange anyway)? Brilliantly, Roy G Biv, not only helps you to remember the color names, but also their correct order in the light spectrum, not a bad trick. Using acronyms like this is simple, efficient, and can be fun to create. Growing up in Detroit our fifth grade teacher taught us the names of the Great Lakes with the acronym HOMES (Huron, Ontario, Michigan, Erie and Superior). All these years latter, instant access. Rather amazing actually how effective these things can be. You can also create stories using the acronyms or turn them into songs. Goofy, yes, but can be fun, and more importantly, it actually can facilitate recall and lonnnnnngggggggggg-term recall.

Associational Links

Linking is associating a new word or concept with something already well known. This can be very useful for memorizing names of people for example. If you meet someone and the last name is Carpenter you can imagine the person with a pencil above her ear, wearing overalls, standing in a pile of sawdust. If the person's name is Carol you can imagine her with a red and white scarf around her neck singing her Christmas favorites. Your brain/mind has a lot more associations for carpenters and carolers than it does for those individuals you just met. You have no reference for them actually. You meet someone named Dylan who happens to have some qualities similar to your old high school friend with the same name. If you tie Dylan's name into your larger existing memory network you are more likely to remember his name when you meet him again. You can also use associational imagery. For example, you meet a woman named Scarlet and she has red hair, or a fellow named Bob who nods his head a lot. Just try not to snicker when you meet them again and say their names. In all these cases the name is anchored to something already quite memorable, possibly a bit funny.

Memory is an associational process. That is why having some trigger, like Roy G Biv (the first letters of the words) helps to make the whole memory accessible. The letters are like the file tabs that help you to locate and access (remember) the contents of the file. Each letter is associated with a name of a color that you already know very well. When you see the letter R and you are asked to name a color, where does your brain go? Rust? Raisin? Rioret? No Scoobydo, it does not! For most humanoids it will go to RED!

Chunking
MINI QUIZ – you will be presented with 4 blocks of letters and symbols. Each block contains 3 items. See how many you can remember. Ready, set, go – b4i | 8hu | nGR | Y!*U* | 2?? – done. If someone just read those to you quickly, and the goal was to remember all of them, it would probably be challenging (unless you figured it out). However, if it was possible to take those elements and chunk or group them in a way that took all the separate parts to create a few memorable clusters, it could potentially be a much easier task. The same list reorganized into meaningful chunks creates – b4i8 hunGRY! *U*2?? (Before I ate, hungry, you too?) Remembering that list would be a much easier task. Because of that new organization it is not hard to pull the information back from memory, weeks later. It is associated with words you already know, and indeed the entire new sentence is easily remembered as it is something we all understand.

Cognitive research has found that this is the way expert chess players think of chess, the way experts perceive problems (Chase & Simon, 1973). Instead of seeing the separate moves that a novice would see the chess master sees related clusters of moves. Because they are seeing larger chunks and not individual steps they can remember much more. That strategy requires less memory and results in easier recall (and is the result of many years of practice at their art). When you review materials and think about them with an eye for order and relationship you will very often begin to see it. Look for the order in things, the patterns. Your brain likes order. When you see the pattern it reduces the field. It is the single constellation versus the seven stars. It is parsimonious. It will improve memory and deepen understanding. Regarding chess masters Chase and Simone wrote, "Specifically, if a chess master can remember the location of 20 or more pieces on the board, but has space for only about five chunks in short-term memory, then each chunk must be composed of four or five pieces, organized in a single relational structure." What they are saying is that if your short-term memory only has space for about 5 items (normal memory load, and chess masters were not found to have larger memory capacity), and someone is remembering 20 chess moves (way more than the limit of 5 items), it means they are chunking 5 pieces on the chess board into one relational 'move' that they are already familiar with, which means they just remember that one thing instead of five, a single chunk comprised of 5 items.

3. Other Elements

Make It Fun

We learn more in general when learning is fun, interesting, and engaging. Stronger emotions, both positive and negative, facilitate learning. Nature wants us to remember events that get an emotional reaction. If a big bear chases you up a tree your heart will be pounding and your knees will be knocking. You will remember to keep your distance from bears in the future. If you find some berries and they are amazingly delicious you will come back to that spot again next spring. Fear, joy, love, strong emotions like these make events more memorable. It is natures way of helping us feel and remember that this is good and that is bad, and such memories can save your life at another point in time.

So how can we use nature's strategy, connecting emotion and memory? One way is to make learning fun, associate learning with a positive emotion. How to make it fun? Singing is one approach. Remember the alphabet song where you were a little child. When you are doing something repetitive like learning letters of an alphabet or formulas, something potentially quite boring, making it a song can be a strangely, comically useful learning strategy. You are singing, not even aware that you are learning. You are having fun. So sneaky! Studies also show that learning can indeed be facilitated by the association of rhythm. Another reason why making up memorization songs can be useful.

To make your own song just take key words or concepts and put them to music or if you do not sing them turn it into a story. In addition to making up your own songs also consider using music as a learning resource. Music has been shown to relax students and make them more responsive to learning (Giles, 1986; Savan, 1999). Listening to the right type of music while studying might also help to keep you motivated, like listening to a punchy rhythm while working out. For study purposes it is probably better to listen to music without words, something quieter in nature, and relaxing. Examples of that could be recordings of nature sounds, or music genres like ambient, smooth jazz, certain classical, soft rock, acoustic anything, whatever works best for you. We use a lot of music in the *Academic Success* class.

Use Your Body

It is also important to remember to relax when you are learning. A relaxed body and mind are more able to take in information, just like a relaxed body is better able to digest and assimilate a meal. Build in regular exercise. Exercise is a good break from work, keeps the body healthy, improves sleep, and produces beneficial hormonal changes to help balance emotions and maintain a positive mood in the face of a mountain of work. Exercise can also be a great way to contemplate an assignment while doing an aerobic activity like walking, running, swimming, yoga. Your mind and body are active, engaged in a repetitive physical task, allowing you to let go of consciously processing material too heavily. It can be a great way to activate the unconscious mind to assist with creative insight and problem solving. Just plant the seed before your workout begins and let things flow as they will.

Get enough rest as well. As a general rule, sleeping on things is a good idea. It also allows the brain time to continue to process and integrate information. Sleep is necessary for human growth and survival. It also facilitates memory integration. Motor memory in particular, body memory related to physical activity, like sports or performance arts, is integrated during sleep time. I knew a musician who would always practice for a bit at night. He said it noticeably improved his skill. If your mind and body are seriously tuckered out it will be hard to stay focused, comprehend easily, or remember. Check in, be honest, take care of yourself. Work when your energy is there, not too high, not to low. If overly cranked, drink a large glass of warm water or take a fast walk or run. If you are toast then take a serious break, watch a movie, or go to bed. Tomorrow is another day! Find a schedule that works for your body and your study needs. Same goes for food – garbage in, garbage out. Junk food is junk. More on all of that in Chapter 14 on healthy lifestyle, but for the moment, eat well whenever possible. Also remember to build in down time. There is a break after finals because people need to recover. After a big race the body needs to repair. Take care that body and mind.

Maintain Motivation and Seek Understanding
You are more likely to learn and remember the things you are most interested in, that is where you motivation will be highest. You meet 10 people at a party and one of them is particularly interesting to you. Guess who's name is most likely to be most easily recalled a week later. Look for the relevance in what you are learning, find the relevance, make it relevant. No drama, no complaints, just finding the way.

Final Thought

Practice, and practice perfectly. It takes as long as it takes, no way around that. In the end, however, you will be a different person, you will be bigger, more capable, have more agency. One potent strategy to consider – pursue your passion because when you do you will want to practice. Follow your deepest interests and your learning will be a source of your greatest joy.

SUMMARY

In this chapter we consider the second pillar of learning – Integration. This is the step of integrating learning into long-term memory for easier access and use. One of the keys to success in learning is the use of effective study strategies. This includes knowing how many hours you need to study each week and scheduling that time, keeping study priorities straight, understanding the study task, having goals for each study session, including length of time and staying on task, studying in the right place and at the right time, and using opportunities for quick study moments as they arise. We next consider why we forget and how to increase memory and understanding. First and foremost is review, a key to success in learning. Periodic review seems to be the best way to get things into memory for long term recall. Self-testing is an effective way to review. The second is to organize content employing methods such as outlining, categorizing, acronyms, and mind maps. Finally, make the process fun, using music and other creative approaches.

MIND-BODY PRACTICE

Sitting Meditation

This week continue with awareness of body, breath, senses, thoughts and emotional states. Particularly notice the evaluative mind, what you take delight in and what you have aversion to, especially related to school activities.

Mindful Awareness

This week practice the targeted awareness, specifically judgment of self and others. Practice labeling it when you recognize it, "judging, judging." Then take a moment to practice acceptance and metta (kindness) toward self and others as needed.

Priming

Practice priming a most incredible week, and an ideal outcome in a specific task or two.

REFERENCES

Anders EK, Krampe RT, Tesch-Romer C. The role of deliberate practice in the acquisition of expert performance. *Psychological Review*. 1993;100(3):363-406.

Baddeley AD. *Essentials of Human Memory*. Hove: Psychology Press; 1999.

Berger SA, Hall LK, Bahrick HP. Stabilizing access to marginal and submarginal knowledge. *Journal of Experimental Psychology: Applied*. 2008;5:438-447.

Carpenter SK, Cepeda NJ, Rohrer D, Kang SHK, Pashler H. Using spacing to enhance diverse forms of learning: review of recent research and implications for instruction. *Educational Psychology Review*. 2012;24:369-378.

Chase WG, Simon HA. Perception in chess. *Cognitive Psychology*. 1973;4:55-61.

Chi MTH, Glaser R, Rees E. (1982). Expertise in problem solving. In: Sternberg RS, editor. *Advances in the Psychology of Human Intelligence*. Hillsdale, New Jersey: Erlbaum; 1982:1-75.

Cisek P, Kalaska JF. Neural correlates of mental rehearsal in dorsal premotor cortex. *Nature*. 2004;431:993-996.

Driskell JE, Copper C, Moran A. Does mental practice enhance performance? *Journal of Applied Psychology*. 1994;79(4):481-492

Duke RA, Simmons AL, Davis C. It's not how much; it's how: Characteristics of practice behavior and retention of performance skills. *Journal of Research in Music Education*. 2009;56(4):310-321.

Fitts P, Posner MI. *Human Performance*. Monterey, CA: Brooks/Cole; 1967.

Gagne RM. *The Conditions of Learning*. New York: Holt, Rinehart & Winston; 1970.

Giles, M. A little background music, please. *Principal*, 1991;71(2):41-44.

Henckens MJ, Hermans EJ, Pu Z, Joels M, Fernandez G. Stressed memories: How acute stress affects memory formation in humans. *Journal of Neuroscience*. 2009;29(32):10111-10119.

King A. Comparison of self-questioning, summarizing, and notetaking-review as strategies for learning from lectures. American Education Research Journal. 1992;29(2):303-323.

McPherson GE. From child to musician: Skill development during the beginning stages of learning an instrument. *Psychology of Music*. 2005;33:5-35.

Nonis SA, Hudson GI. Performance of college students: impact of study time and study habits. *Journal of Education for Business*. 2010;85(4):229-238.

Rohrer D, Pashler H. Increasing retention without increasing study time. *Current Directions in Psychological Science*. 2007;16(4):183-186.

Savan A. The effect of background music on learning. *Psychology of Music*. 1999;27:138-146.

Schmid D, Leitzmann MF. Television viewing and time spent sedentary in relation to cancer risk: a meta-analysis. *Journal of the National Cancer Institute*. 2014;106(7):dju098.

Simon HA, Chase WG. Skill in chess. *American Scientist*. 1973;*61*:394-403.

Suinn R. Mental practice in sport psychology: where have we been, where do we go? *Clinical Psychology*. 1997;4(3):189-207.

Tan D, Czerwinski M, Robertson G. Women go with the (optical) flow. *Proceedings of the SIGCHI Conference on Human Factors in Computing Systems*. 2003:209-215.

Vacha EF. Cramming: A barrier to student success, a way to beat the system or an effectiuve learning strategy? *College Student Journal*. 1993;27(1):2-11.

Williamon A, Valentine E. Quantity and quality of musical practice as predictors of performance quality. *British Journal of Psychology*. 2000;91:353-376.

Wickelgren WA. *Human Learning and Memory*. Englewood Cliffs, NJ: Prentice-Hall; 1981.

Academic Skills
Display

8

I select the best strategy. I am committed to mastery.

CHAPTER THEMES
- Acquisition
- Foundations of Successful Display
- Taking Tests
- Writing Papers
- Performance-Oriented Display
- Knowledge, Awareness, Goals, Insight

Once you have acquired new information, and integrated it into mind-body memory, the next step is to use that learning, to display it. In this third phase of learning you are called on to show the world what you can do, to Display what you know. As with the other two phases of learning there are strategies that will improve that display, making for a higher quality performance in school and in life. We will look at some of the key strategies in this chapter with a special focus on taking tests, writing papers, and performing. We will look at some of the key strategies in this chapter with a special focus on taking tests, writing papers, and performing. Before proceeding to those specific topics, however, we will first consider some of the key foundations for successful academic display.

The Foundations of Successful Display

Work with Goals and Schedules

There are times in life when we need to put out your best product, your best performance. That requires starting with a clear goal, a well-thought-out schedule, and sufficient time to do the work that is required to reach that goal. Goals and schedules help you to see what you need to do and when it needs to be done. Successful people plan. It is the root of high quality display in all its diverse forms. If using goals and calendars/schedules is unfamiliar know that it that can be learned. It is a life changing habit worth the effort. Use your calendar. It is a brilliant piece of technology, used for millennia to increase productivity. Mark in important dates. When you complete a task then check it off. If you miss a target date then refresh the calendar. Stay on top of things. Keep your schedule current. Use a daily To Do List to maintain a productive daily task focus. Make a plan and once you have that plan stick to it.

Review, Practice, Rehearse - That is Essential

As discussed in Chapter 6 on Integration, this is a key step in developing the long-term memory needed for effective display. It is important to schedule review time into your calendar each week, not just study time for acquisition of new material, but review time for integration. It is also very helpful to quickly review materials before and after classes. It is easy to do if you have breaks between classes or commute home after school using mass transit. Even a few minutes right before or after a class will refresh the materials in memory. Those simple moments of review help to build long-term recall, access to material for the future. They also help to deepen understanding of material (which also facilitates memory and more sophisticated display).

Get in the habit of doing an end of the week review, such as Friday afternoons, all subjects. An end of week review also helps you to think about classes and assignments that are coming up and that supports thoughtful planning and scheduling. If you use SQ3R or a related method you will have highlighted texts. Use that highlighted material along with any outlined class notes as efficient review resources. Reviewing periodically, over time, is the best strategy for long-term recall and ultimate display.

Find the Weak Link and Loop There

The first time you encounter a new math formula, or play a new song, or learn a new baseball pitching grip, it is fresh material, brand new. It has not landed into mind and body to be displayed automatically and efficiently. Repetition, correct practice, is the way to deepen capacity. As you practice and start improving you will want to shift your focus over time. As you improve it is better to focus on the weak links, the places where you get stuck, and loop on those spots until you have developed more mastery with them. What is easy is easy. You have learned that part. It feels good to loop at that level, but there is less learning there. You already own that. Deeper level understanding, insight and display comes from working down into the nooks and crannies, the most challenging spots. That is a display strategy that is less rewarding in the short term, but much more powerful in the long-term, because your learning, understanding, and ability for skillful display will expand accordingly.

Also, always remember that *effective display requires sufficient review, practice, rehearsal.* You do not build a large muscle in one workout. It develops over time, and so does memory and skill. ***One of the biggest mistakes students make is not putting sufficient time into this essential step***. One the biggest reasons they fail to put sufficient time into this essential step is they have shaky goals and no plan. That is a formula for poor quality and poor results.

> **KEY:** If this is going to be your life work, or something that you really want to excel at, or an activity that you are truly interested in, truly passionate about, then engage in practice as if you were performing. Make it a performance, not a practice. Do the work with intention, awareness, quality and a focus on improvement, on efficient and effective improvement.

Keep Building Your Academic Self-Efficacy

Self-efficacy, as you will remember, is a belief in yourself, in your own effectiveness in doing something. The *Learning Life* goal is to develop greater self-efficacy for academic success in general, what researchers in education call academic self-efficacy. How to do that? First, use effective learning strategies. Second, practice metawareness of your academic process by paying attention and periodically evaluating how you are doing in class, how you are studying, reading, writing, what strategies you are using. Consider where you have room to improve and how. Finally, stick to your goals and your plan, stay optimistic and motivated, pick yourself up when you fall, keep moving forward, honor yourself, trust your vision, live your dream.

Maintain Motivation

Every journey has peaks and valleys. There are going to be dry spells. You need to hold on to your vision, your commitment. If the target event is a long way off, like a culminating exam in one year, there can be a lot of time for worry, a lot of room for self-doubt, fear, and avoidance. Mindful awareness, optimism, and application of self-management skills (Chapters 8-13), will make a difference. Do what it takes to keep the motivation alive. Give yourself rewards for small successes, keep goals in sight, use positive self-talk, associate with people who support you. With sustained motivation the chances of success are much higher.

Focus on Quality

One of the ways to end up with a higher quality final product or performance, one that you will be proud of and that others will notice, is to build a quality focus into the process. Is there a better way to do this? Is there a more efficient way? How can I improve the final product? What does it take to excel at this, to be great at this? We will look at quality in more detail in Chapter 8 on continual improvement. A quality focus in work and life will generally result in higher quality results, a more impressive display of knowledge and skill. Commit to quality and your life will change. It is not about beating other people. It is about being your best, at whatever you choose to put your energy into. If a person is willing to do the work it is amazing what can be accomplished. If you are going to put in the effort, why not focus on doing the best work you are capable of doing? Find your passion, whatever that might be, and put your heart into it.

Be Professional

Another aspect of quality display has to do with professionalism in final presentation. You want the final product to sound good, look good, feel good. Use the right gear and pay attention to detail. Do not waste time on excess detail, but get in the habit of doing quality work, putting your best foot forward, like you are a serious player, not a casual observer. Investing in the right tools can be a good use of money. Save up your pennies and purchase a laptop. A printer is another good investment. A black and white laser printer can be quite affordable. Most students do not need a color printer, too costly (replacement cartridges is where they kill you). Use campus printers for occasional color work. Finally, for goodness sake, buy a stapler and use it. Folding the corners together and gluing them with spit is not going to get you a great job any time soon (maybe sweeping the floor in a donut shop, maybe). Get a stapler and then learn how to use it. If you are not in the habit of using a stapler do not fear. Despite it being a somewhat advanced technology it is not that hard to operate, really, and if perplexed do a web search for "how to use a stapler" and give it a try.

Use Your Resources

If you want to do your best then you will need to use available resources effectively, a topic we initially explored in Chapter 1. Life is much easier if you have access to resources and if you use those resources appropriately. There are many resources available to improve learning outcomes. College campuses usually have some type of learning center. It may be in the library, in student services, part of career and academic counseling. Sometimes there is staff, other times the resources are primarily online. Ask your advisor or the campus librarian if you cannot find the equivalent at your campus, and just ask them about learning resources in general.

Many campuses offer non-credit courses on the topic (maybe the class using this text for example). Often you can get individual help in the form of tutoring. The tutors are often seniors or graduate students. Sitting down and getting some one-on-one time with a tutor can be a short path to understanding a math concept, improving writing, or enhancing learning strategies in general. If the tutor is a student that individual may also be a resource for information on other ideas about success in school and for academic self-efficacy in a particular area.

Resources exist on campuses to help you develop better study skills, learn how to take tests, improve your writing and math, and much more. There are also many campus resources to help with emotional well-being, such as managing anxiety, depression, or excess alcohol or drug use. Right now is a great time to begin to work on dissolving old limiting patterns, so that the energy spent managing those habits can be devoted to more effective and rewarding time in school and in life. Campus services can also provide assistance with financial aid, scholarships, study abroad, internships, job placement, resume writing and job interviewing skills, and a whole lot more. If you are a registered student then you are already paying for many of those services as part of your student fees. You are paying for it, so you may as well use it.

Celebrate

Appreciate your effort no matter what outcome. I have come in second more than once in my life. Actually I came in second place for teacher of the year at my university, three years in a row! Well there you go. Onward and upward bat fans. There is a great scene in the movie *Silver Linings* where the main characters are jubilantly celebrating their lousy dance competition scores and the judges are looking at them in a most perplexed fashion. They met their goal and that was what mattered to them. It is all relative. There is a concept that comes from the samurai tradition. It defines nobility as doing something wholeheartedly even though you know it is impossible to succeed. It is good to celebrate sincere effort no matter what the outcome.

Tests Taking Strategies

Life can be thought of as an endless series of tests and what we display in each moment is our answer to each question. Education and momentary mindful awareness can improve how many of those items we get right in our great adventure. In an even more obvious sense, school is an endless series of tests. Having a kit full of effective test taking strategies will make that part of the academic journey more efficient and rewarding. Here are some things to keep in mind.

Be Strategic

Before taking any exam always read the directions thoroughly. Most people do not like to read the fine print before they buy, but oh what a difference it can make. Read the questions completely, underline key terms, such as 'not' or 'compare' versus 'contrast'. "Which of these three is *not* true?" Missing the word 'not' changes the whole question. Ask the teacher/proctor if you are unsure what a word or question means (they will often clarify for you). If you answer the question in the wrong way because you misunderstood what was being asked, you will probably get it wrong.

Allocate time based on point value of each section of the text. If you did not realize that the section you just spent half of the test period on is only worth ten percent of the exam, you just made a big resource allocation error. Take your time. Use the entire test period. Do not leave blank items unless you are penalized for guessing. In some more sophisticated testing scenarios you get 1 point for correct answers, -1/2 for wrong answers, and 0 for blanks. In that case you are probably more likely to lose points for random guessing. On that type of exam, less common, it is better to leave the item blank than it is to just guess. Again, those are less common test situations, however, so in general filling in all blanks is a good idea. Put in something.

Finally, do not just go through the exam once and turn it in. Make sure you go over your answers at least once to make sure they are complete. One final check – all systems go – can be a grade changer. Then, after any exam, do a metawareness reflection to consider how the test went and why it went that way, what strategies (preparation and testing) worked, how to do better next time (effectiveness), and how to increase your test taking efficiency overall. Use your strategies, your game plan, do not be random.

Consider the Type of Test

One of the main things to consider when prepping for a test is what type of test it will be. Is the exam cumulative from the whole semester, or just the material from the midterm? Is it essay, item matching, multiple choice, true-false, or fill in the blank? Will you have to jump a horse over a fence, play a violin solo, or recite a lengthy poem. Different types of tests will require different methods of preparation. Getting ready for a marathon requires a different training regimen than prepping for sprints. Knowing what you are getting yourself into ahead of time will help ensure that your method of preparation is the best fit. Read the syllabus, ask the instructor, get clear. The students who read the syllabus and note that the final exam is open book have a very big advantage over the students who missed that detail and fail to bring their textbooks to class.

Multiple Choice and Related Exam Formats

If it is a *Multiple Choice* test here are a few basic rules of thumb. Only employ a multiple guess strategy if you truly do not know, no clue. If you have some idea, some clue (there might even be hints or reminders in the exam), but you are not one-hundred percent positive, then your first answer is more likely to be correct. Research suggests that when people second guess and change the answer it does not improve performance (Higham & Gerrard, 2005). Read all the choices and cross off the obvious wrong answers. Get down to the last two reasonable choices and reread the question. The exam may include *True/False* items. If any part of an answer is false then it cannot be true. Also, strong words, such as 'Always' or 'Never' are red flags. Those are often not the correct answer. For questions where you are asked to match items from a list it is a good idea to start with the ones you are most confident about. Use a process of elimination. Once an item is used cross it off the list. Continue working down the list in this way.

For *Fill-in-the-Blank* questions you have to actually *recall* information and not just *recognize* which of several choices is correct. With recognition formats, like multiple choice exams, the correct answer is on the page as one of the options. With recall formats there are no cues on the page, the answers have to be accessed completely from memory. Recall requires more deeply encoded information. So Fill-in-the-Blank recall items require more review, more study, more memorization. A good strategy for a fill-in test is to create you own questions and answers ahead of time. Doing this on your own before the exam provides another layer of study, review, and integration. You will be much more prepared (see Self-Testing in Chapter 6 for ideas).

Remember that other questions on the exam may also provide information or memory cues. Use the whole exam as a resource. If you are truly guessing on exams then just pick the answer that seems the most reasonable. Research suggests that individuals constructing multiple item exams will seek to vary the order of items with a slight bias toward putting incorrect items in the middle, in four-item multiple choice questions (Attali & Bar-Hillel, 2003). If you are actually guessing on a multiple choice test, no clue, then pick one choice and use it consistently, true or false, or item #4, all the way through on guessed items. If you guess and mark choices completely randomly there is a probability that you will miss every single guessed item. If you pick one response consistently then at least a few of them will probably be correct.

Essays
In the case of essay exams it is a very helpful to have thought of probable questions ahead of time and written responses to them. This will help greatly in your preparation. That is a much better plan than simply going to class and trying to remember, organize, and write a good response on the spot. Prewriting will increase your efficiency during the exam and give you more time for other areas of the test or for writing a better essay. If you are fortunate enough to end up with exam questions similar to the ones you prepared then you will basically be remembering and refining what you have already written.

When you do sit down to take an essay exam be sure to read the instructions. Be clear what you are being asked for – analyze, compare, define, explain, summarize, or contrast. If you are not sure what the question is asking then go up front and politely inquire. The instructor will often be happy to provide clarity (sometimes they will, sometimes they will not). If the essay asks for a specific response then that is what you need to provide, otherwise you are not answering the question and you could get the entire item wrong. Bad news! When you start writing it can be helpful to outline your answer first. That is a good use of time, a few minutes to organize your thoughts and provide a structure for your answer. That will also give you a moment to remember and reflect on what you want to include. Once you have started writing, since will probably not be crossing out big sections or moving paragraphs around, trying to make major changes becomes more challenging. If permitted, use a separate sheet of paper to organize your thoughts. When you have the basic outline down, with major topics and main details, then start writing. Have a clear thesis sentence, your main point. As a basic strategy, introduce the main idea in an opening section, explain it in more detail in a mid-section, and wrap it up with a good conclusion in a closing section. Consider incorporating terms or phrases from the question itself in your answer if appropriate.

Also, remember that it is always preferable to have a brief, well-written, thoughtful essay, than some tedious tome that paralyzes the mind and good spirits of the reader (aka grader). Someone has to read your essays to grade them. Most readers would rather see short and sweet versus long and rambling. Also, write as legibly as you can, and only on one side of the paper. Again, someone has to read these things and writing on both sides of the paper can reduce readability. The grader will like you less if your paper gives them a headache. Do not make the grader dislike you.

Computer Graded Exams
Read the instructions. Be neat. If the exam is going to be read by a scanner then make sure your marks are within the lines so the computer does not misread your selection. Similarly, if you erase then make sure that it is completely erased with no remaining pencil markings. Make sure you are answering the right question. Check numbers periodically to be certain that you are in the right section, question 25, bubble 25. I once put shingles on a roof (I was young). At lunchtime I came down from the roof and looked up. It was clearly not straight – serious bummer. Fortunately, the fellow paying the bill was an old Irish chap, Timmy O'Rourke, very forgiving soul indeed. Never did a roofing job again after that, except for one on my own house many years later, for my own learning and personal redemption. Finally, again, if there are no points for wrong answers then guess, even if you do not have a blessed clue. In that case give the same answer for each question. If you mark all 'D' responses then some of them will be correct. FYI, anyone relying extensively on a guessing strategy should *not* (notice the emphasis) expect to get a great score on the exam. That is way not an effective strategy for success.

Math/Science
On test day read the instructions. Make sure you actually understand what the problem is asking for. If the test requires the use of formulas then write down the formulas first, while your brain is fresh (remember primacy), then start the exam. Use a separate piece of paper for this if allowed. If open book is allowed then tab appropriate sections of the book before the exam for more efficient access of key sections, formulas, sample problems, table of contents, and index. Do not waste time searching for things in the book. Be prepared. Take any required/allowed equipment with you to the test. Use your resources.

Manage Mind-Body States

You want your mind and body to be allies during exams. Worry and physical anxiety can impede performance, affect recall, lower motivation. Get into a regular meditation habit, exercise, get enough rest. Be optimistic, realistically optimistic. Negativity will bring you down, dampen spirits, slow progress. Use positive self-talk, especially when negative thoughts start to get too loud. Remind yourself, "Everyone stay calm, I will handle this," then laugh out loud and run around the room. Use priming to keep the mind and body in balance. Priming is a particularly flexible resource in this regard. Use Priming as a way to prepare for exams, papers or performances (see Chapter 3 Priming). Imagine a successful outcome before you start. Sit down, close your eyes, see the results you want to achieve. See yourself looking very satisfied, feel the pride and a sense of accomplishment. If it is a very important exam then start Priming early, the more important the event, the earlier the Prime. Priming a specific target event over a period of time can help you to stay on track with study, manage anxiety, increase confidence, and improve final performance.

Determine the Best Way to Cheat on Exams

Study hard, then you will not have to worry about being unethical or getting caught. My favorite was a student in class a few years back, a business major, very involved in the campus religious community. He paid someone to write his final paper, good money, and that someone plagiarized another paper! Obviously not original work. Now there is someone you want running your bank. It was classic. He flunked.

Writing Excellent Papers

Learning how to write well is a very important life/career skill. Because of its importance to your success after college the university makes you do a lot of it. So having good writing strategies will result in a better product that is potentially generated in shorter time. When you get a writing assignment the first task is to select an appropriate topic. When choosing a good topic you should consider if the teacher will approve it, if there is enough information available from quality sources to be able to write something intelligent, and if you will find it interesting. Look for materials and information first, before you start writing, to assess the lay of the land. Is there enough out there to write about it. Determine if the information and topic will interest you sufficiently (an ideal if possible). If you are in the ballpark, but have any uncertainty regarding the fit with the class assignment, confirm with the instructor. Good idea to confirm anyway.

High Level and Detailed Outline

If you get a green light on the topic then start collecting pieces, such as research abstracts, or news articles, and make sure you note the full reference with each piece. You will want to be able to easily find the original source again. When you have enough material, and an emerging sense of the story, you can start to outline based on the information you have collected. Start with a *high level outline*, major themes, like the table of contents for a book. The high level outline provides the big picture view. Do not worry too much about details at this point. Once you have that outline, and have done some more research, enough to have a reasonable sense of what you want to say, then you can start creating the low level or *detailed outline*. The detailed outline takes the high level outline and builds on that skeleton, adding detail and refinement. The goal is to create an increasingly detailed outline as you progress. When you feel confident that the detailed outline will stand on its own, like the framing of a house, you can begin fleshing it out completely, putting in the doors, windows, sheet rock and trim.

Adding Content

Collecting pieces and building the detailed outline in this way allows for much faster final writing. Once you have enough pieces of information for a satisfactory detailed outline you can then take those bits and begin to fill in that outline. Take your abstracts, relevant quotes, related pieces of information and start pasting them in. Move them around like pieces of a puzzle, until they are in the right place, creating the image you want to see. At this point do not worry about grammar, punctuation, or fine detail. That slows down writing. Gather additional pieces as needed to fill in the gaps, to make a more complete and interesting story. As you add content to your outline the paper truly starts to write itself. It can be quite a rewarding feeling to see it coming to life, starting to make sense as a whole.

Editing

At some point you will have enough. At that point you can start to refine the prose and polish the final piece. Once complete set it aside and come back later for another edit, repeat as needed. As you edit have the courage to remove what does not belong, even if that bit seems very well written, is long, or took a fair bit of time. Each level of edit will produce a better product (and there is only so much time in the day, so avoid overkill, and do your best). If possible have someone else read it to provide additional feedback. Do a final word-for-word out loud reading. You will hear what you did not see after so many hours of looking at the same material. It is amazing what you catch doing this simple final check. ***Read the paper out loud***.

Use spell check and grammar check. This is one of those simple touches that adds to your professionalism. Get in the habit of using correct grammar and punctuation. Running a check will help in quality control while it also improves your spelling and grammar. It will make you look more professional, more like a serious player. I am always shocked when I get a paper from a student with obvious spelling errors. A few minutes would have corrected that. I would NEVER hire that person as an employee if I had any options at all. NEVER. I already know they are careless, not mindful, not motivated to do professional work. Those are not qualities I want on my team. Would you hire a lazy, careless person to work for you, manage your money, treat you if you were sick? I doubt it. We need to be able to trust our team members to help us all to do better. If he or she fails, we fail. Do final edits for grammar, spelling, and format. It takes three minutes to look more professional. Develop the habit and then you will not have to think about it.

One other idea, related to continual improvement, is to make your writing process efficient. You want to standardize strategies that work for you. For example, in the Resources section of this book you will find a sample checklist created by students in the *Holistic Approaches to Academic Success* class. It is a checklist for a typical research paper writing process. Try it out and modify it as you see fit.

Performance-Oriented Display

There are also times in life when the Display of our learning will be a demonstration or performance, such as giving a speech, playing an instrument, or performing CPR on a mannequin. For performance situations there are a few things to keep in mind. Here are some strategies to make successful display a higher probability.

Practice

Practice enough, practice well, evaluate your practice, and keep progressing. Bill Evans, a brilliant 20th century jazz pianist, said in an interview with Marian McPartland on the NPR program Piano Jazz, "It is better to practice one song for 24 hours than play 24 tunes in one hour." A serious musician knows where the challenge is in a piece he or she is working on, the part that needs the most attention, and that is what gets focused on. The goal is to loop on that piece, slow it down, until it can be played. Once competence is improved then that piece is integrated into the whole. The spot that brings us the most frustration and self-doubt is often where the growth is. The challenge is where the growth is. Learning how to play that really difficult measure well will probably improve your playing overall. Because practice is essential for successful display, scheduling and time management are crucial. Effective practice cannot be squeezed in at the last minute. It takes time.

Readiness - Be Prepared For All of It

The great blues guitarist B.B. King once said that, "You are only as good as your last performance." Every day of life is a new show and we are all on stage. This is not a dress rehearsal. This is it. Often we only get one chance to show the world who we are. One shot. "Thank you, next." "That's it?" "That's it. Goodbye." Being present, doing quality work, putting your best foot forward, on a regular basis, develops the habit of showing up and being ready for life. As the weatherman said to the marsupial in the classic movie *Groundhog Day*, "It's showtime Phil." For excellence in the Display phase you need to be ready in body, mind and behavior.

Prime / Stay Calm

As mentioned above in Test Taking, use priming to mentally prepare for the event. See it going perfectly before you begin. Imagine a successful outcome before you start. Prime during the period leading up to the performance and then again immediately before you go live. Use positive self-talk. Breath deeply and let go of tension and attachment. Focus on quality, not on winning. If you focus on doing something with quality, whether you win or not, you did it with quality. ***Maintain your equanimity***. If something does not work as planned, and at some point that will happen, do not blow a gasket. Stay in the flow. That is a characteristic of mastery. You adapt real-time. You do not lose the beat. If you are the accompanist for the solo soprano singing on stage, and the singer misses a bar, you have to jump ahead. If you are up to bat and you have two strikes against you it is not helpful to tell everyone in the audience how terrible you are at baseball and run home crying. You just keep going. It is like writing on water. You are in the moment, in the flow. No mark remains. Nothing persists, everything changes, you keep moving and work with it all. It is what it is. All good.

Meditate / Be Present

Meditate regularly and work on developing mindful awareness, greater awareness during the moments, the experiences of your day. Having a sitting mindfulness meditation practice and then applying active mindful awareness during the day will improve task focus and concentration during important activities like exams or performances. It will also help with relaxation during stressful times. Practice using breath awareness as a focus in sitting mindfulness meditation. Get in the habit of coming back to the breath, using breath as a home base. You can practice the method at convenient times during the day, taking a few minutes to close your eyes and being with the breath as you ride home on the bus.

You can practice active mindful awareness of breathing as you walk down the street, being aware of in-breath and out-breath. If stress is kicking in and you need to regain composure then do not just watch your breath, change it. Get hold of the breath, slow it down, take a series of slow, deep breaths. Slowing breath down will slow down body and mind. Finally, if the body is feeling cranked, you can reframe that arousal energy. Tell yourself that you are feeling charged and ready to go. See it as enthusiasm, as a sign of performance readiness, useful for sports for example (more on all of this in Chapter 10 on stress, coping and equanimity). Developing the practice of mindfulness meditation, active mindful awareness, and working with breath, can help bring greater balance and focus to all life activities.

Higher Order Display - Knowledge, Awareness, Goals, Insight (KAGI)

A final thought regarding Display has to do with making optimal use of what we learn, what we know, in order to continually improve our life and the world we live in. One of the goals of a learning life is to have greater agency, more capacity and personal control in one's life, greater effectiveness in the world. Learning is a progressive phenomena. Our abilities evolve over time as we learn new things, understand how the pieces fit together. We start as babies, held and cradled. In about a month we lifted our heads, in eight months we started crawling, latter standing on unstable legs, then learning to walk without holding someone's hand, and eventually able to run and play. *Learning is a progression through levels of understanding and competency.*

Educators have created a taxonomy or hierarchy of these levels of learning, each reflecting a higher order of display. One of the well-know versions, *Bloom's Taxonomy*, considers levels of learning in the domains of cognition (knowing), affect (feeling), and motor skills (doing) (Bloom et al., 1956; Clark, 1999). Bloom was an advocate of holistic learning which included all three domains – knowing, feeling, doing. Capacity in each domain ranges from basic to increasingly complex. For example, remembering the names of ten countries in Europe is basic. Understanding how national laws and policies support or obstruct economic cooperation between those ten countries is much more complex, a higher level of learning and display. Greater complexity and more sophisticated display require the acquisition and integration of more information and a deepening of understanding and skill. That evolution is reflected in the hierarchies of learning proposed in the Bloom's Taxonomy:

Cognitive Domain (knowing – knowledge)
Knowledge - memorization of terms, facts, basic concepts
Comprehension - ability to define, organize, describe, compare and contrast ideas
Application - acquired knowledge is used to solve problems

Analysis - things broken down into parts, causes determined, evidence provided as support
Evaluation - making a determination of the validity or value of things
Synthesis - putting parts back together in a new way, providing alternative solutions

Affective Domain (feeling – awareness)
Receiving - paying attention passively
Responding - paying attention and responding
Valuing - attaching value to different information/knowledge
Organizing - sorting and accommodating different values and ideas
Characterizing - particular values or beliefs become an individual characteristic

Psychomotor Domain (doing – goal directed action)
Perception - sense information is used to guide motor activity
Set - a mental, emotional and physical predisposition or readiness to act
Guided Response - response/learning is based on trial and error and imitation
Mechanism - movements are habitual and performed with some degree of proficiency
Complex Overt Response - complex motor response is automatic, accurate, coordinated, proficient
Adaptation - skill is well developed and can be adapted to various situations
Origination - new movements can be created to solve a problem or fit a specific need

The Knowledge, Awareness, Goals, Insight Model (KAGI)

One way to optimally work toward higher level display is to actively engage knowledge, awareness, goals and insights, the *Learning Life* KAGI practice. As an example, a woman wants to make sure the tingling in her hands and wrists improves (Problem). She knows muscle tension contributes to carpal tunnel syndrome and she has been reading up on proper body posture at the computer (Knowledge). She starts to pay attention to her posture during the day, and begins to notice that when she is tired at 3pm she really starts to slouch (Awareness). She acts on that insight to take a break at 3pm to see what affect it might have (Goal). She begins to notice a reduction in tingling on the days she remembers to get up from the computer and take a stretch and relaxation break (Insight). She now has a new understanding of her body, the ergonomics needed to keep it healthy, and her best work practices.

There is an excellent book, *The Art of Scientific Discovery*, in which the author describes how great scientific discoveries (insights) are often the product of someone with a well-trained mind (knowledge) and keen perception (mindful awareness) (Beveridge, 1957). These are also highly motivated individuals, with a commitment to quality science, and a passion for discovery (goal). When you combine their specific knowledge, awareness, and goal-oriented action, the foundation for insight and higher order synthesis and creation are there. Thousands of people will all see the same thing, but the person who is trained, paying attention with curiosity, and motivated to find a way to solve problems, will recognize some critical difference and have the capacity and desire to act on it. That is the person who will have the insight that just might change the world, creating a new pathway, a new way of thinking, feeling or doing, a new way of being. That is where new music comes from, new art, new scientific innovation, great architecture, inspired love making, beautiful poetry, transformative government and business.

Knowledge
When considering the role of knowledge in this holistic, cybernetic approach to learning there are at least three types of knowledge we should consider – knowledge of our personal goals, self-knowledge, and knowledge about the world. This first level – ***knowledge of goals*** – relates to knowledge of what we want in life, knowledge of our goals, of our dreams. Why? Because there is just too much to do in life, it is endless. By looking more closely into our own hearts and minds we begin to see more clearly our most important values, mission and goals. That understanding helps to clarify where we should put our precious life time and life energy to work, where we will develop our greatest capacities, our gift to give the world.

The next aspect is *self-knowledge* – know thy self. Self-knowledge is the recognition and understanding of our personal patterns. Self-knowledge requires us to increase our understanding of how we react to things, how we habitually think, feel, behave, how we limit or stretch ourselves, the nature of our conditioned mind and body, and the potential of our unconditioned mind. By increasing our self-awareness, the knowledge of our ways of being and doing, we can see how our inner world meets our outer world. By observing and noting this dynamic dance, over time, we begin to recognize the antecedents and consequences of our conditioned patterns. That awareness and increased recognition of patterns improves our chance of being able to choose how we will respond.

The third level of knowledge is ***knowledge about life***, the way things work. This is one of the reasons that education is so important. A good education provides us with foundational knowledge about life, about the way the body works, how the mind works, how humans form societies and govern themselves, the nature of aggression and conflict resolution, effective communication, problem solving, disease prevention, the laws of physics and biochemistry, how sound moves through space, how viruses mutate, how silicon wafers store data, and on it goes. Having a broader understanding of the way of life (a solid liberal education), plus understanding of domain specific content (such as molecular biology or accounting), provides a basis for seeing patterns more readily, more deeply, and that is the basis for a successful career, a greater capacity to contribute to society, and greater agency in life overall.

Awareness
Knowledge is a basis for awareness. Having some knowledge of local bird species would make a walk in the woods more engaging. You listen more intently to the songs because you have some understanding about the birds making those sound. You have a neural connection. Each bird song is already part of your embodied experience, your neural network, your embodied memory. Classically trained musicians hear more in a piece of music than non-musicians, their brains actually process the same piece of music quite differently than non-musicians (Bangerta et al., 2006). Knowledge can facilitate heightened awareness and engagement.

Similarly, awareness increases knowledge. Paying close attention to the sounds of the forest or a piece of music, over time, allows us to begin to differentiate and distinguish more and more subtle distinctions. You listen to a garbled phone message and after ten replays you can make out most of the message. Your brain has synthesized the content, filled in the gaps. You listen to a lecturer with a thick accent and after a few weeks you can understand most of what she is saying. Paying attention over time leads to a recognition of the patterns of life, whether that is greater understanding of a forest ecosystem or a piano concerto by Mozart or Saint-Saens. Knowledge supports awareness, and awareness deepens understanding. They support each other.

Goal-Oriented Action
The first two elements of KAGI – knowledge and awareness – become most useful when we are engaging the world through action focused on important life goals. The two legs of knowledge and awareness have the potential to carry us anywhere. Without clear goals, however, that can end up being a random stroll down a dark alley. That is nice once in a while (maybe???), but not so productive in the long run. Applying knowledge and awareness at any moment is valuable. Applying knowledge and awareness to important life goals is powerful. The combination will drive the process of growth and improvement in areas of highest personal importance. As we act on our goals, applying knowledge and awareness to our success and failures, we begin to recognize over time the patterns that lead to higher accomplishment in business, sports, communication, emotional self-management, anything that we hold dear. Knowledge and awareness applied to any moment of life is good. Knowledge and awareness applied to goal-oriented action in life is very, very good.

Insight
The final element in the KAGI model is Insight. Insight is the result of a deeply lived experience, a life lived with knowledge, awareness, and intentional engagement with the moment and with our goals. I studied hypnosis many years ago and one of my favorite practitioners was a psychotherapist named Milton Erickson. He had passed away before I had the pleasure of actually studying with him, but I did study with many of his principle students. I was impressed by how many of them spoke of his understanding of human nature (knowledge) and of his acute capacity to notice very subtle changes in his clients speech, physiological states, and mannerisms (awareness). Erickson would attend to the tone of their voices as they spoke about issues that challenged them, the changes in facial color, in breathing. He would use this as feedback, as part of their story. He would listen to those non-verbal 'voices' and he would speak to them as well. A deep sigh or a blushing of the cheek was unconscious information from the patient informing Erickson that he was on the right clinical track. He would indirectly comment about the sigh allowing the client's relaxed mind to know that Erickson was paying attention and understanding the real story, the deeper story.

Erickson had remarkable effects with patients, no doubt in large measure due to this capacity to notice what was changing from moment to moment, not the words they spoke, but those subtle unconscious body-mind changes they could not hide. Using information derived from paying attention (awareness), with his professional training and years of professional experience (knowledge), combined with his deep commitment to help his clients improve (goals), he was able to apply remarkable clinical insight (insight) that allowed him to guide a powerful therapeutic journey for his patients (patient insight and understanding, higher order learning).

Applying the Model

A final thought on the KAGI concept is its application in daily life. In upcoming Chapter 8 we will examine the concept of continual improvement. One of the key strategies in continual improvement is to be self-correcting, not requiring external feedback to correct our course, but using our own knowledge, awareness and insights as we head toward the goal, keeping oneself on course. In practicing self-correction while moving from current state to desired state we gather information, we learn, this works and that does not. These insights help us to improve our accuracy over time, allowing us to hit the target more effectively on future repetitions. By working toward committed goals, using knowledge of best practice, and bringing awareness and attention to our implementation and outcomes, we can gain insight into our process and improve our effectiveness. This is the essence of a profoundly alive learning life.

When Display Flops

"I don't know how to do that yet, but I will learn." Why did it flop? It could be a matter of aptitude, which means, that you will have to put more time and energy into it. It could be that you never learned how to do it, or you learned the wrong way. It could be a lack of motivation, low self-efficacy in that area, a lack of optimism and low expectancy for success. It could be the wrong learning strategy, like not putting in the sufficient amount of time needed for success in that particular subject.

It is the way it is. There is a gap. The solution to get to the desired state will require some thinking and effort, but it is often possible. Take fewer classes, get help from students in a study group, go see the campus tutoring service. In a study on high risk students, who were expected to drop out, it was found that when the students used tutors and took classes to improve reading and study skills they doing reasonably well by the end of their freshman year (Abrams and Jernigan, 1984). How? They learned effective strategies, were encouraged to keep going, realized there was a way, a path. Small success builds confidence and optimism, and that encourages us to keep at it, step by step, one day at a time.

> **REFLECTION**
>
> Take a moment to reflect on your Display process. How am I doing with exams, my writing process, performance experiences.

What are my most effective strategies?

What are things I could do better?

Where could I get the information/skills I you need to work on?

SUMMARY

In this chapter we examine the third pillar of effective learning – Display. The foundations of effective display include effective use of scheduling to provide sufficient time for mastery, review, locating deficiencies, building self-efficacy, and maintaining motivation. A common form of display is testing. The key to success is being prepared, knowing what type of test it will be and preparing accordingly, such as a recognition or recall exam. Writing papers is another common display product. A straightforward and effective approach to writing research oriented papers is to start with a high level outline, like a table of contents, gather information to fill it is, build a detailed outline, and then arrange materials on that framework. Performance oriented displays, such as recitals or presentations, require sufficient practice and state management to maintain focus of mind and balance of body. Meditation and Priming are good for that. The Knowledge, Awareness, Goals, Insight Model (KAGI) is presented as a way to think about working with the knowledge we acquire in life as a resource to help us achieve goals and gain greater insight into the nature of self and life.

MIND-BODY

Sitting Meditation

This week continue with awareness of body, breath, senses, thoughts and emotional states. Work with labeling thoughts, feelings and body sensations, "Thinking, thinking," "Anger, anger, sad, sad, happy, happy."

Mindful Awareness

Continue to pay attention to judgment of self and others. Notice what seems to bring it on, what feelings are associated with it, how you tend to respond emotionally and behaviorally to that internal messaging. The take a moment to practice acceptance and metta (kindness) toward self and others as it feels appropriate.

Priming

Prime, a most incredible week, ideal outcomes in specific tasks.

REFERENCES

Abrams HG; Louise Podojil Jernigan. Academic Support Services and the Success of High-Risk College Students. *American Educational Research Journal*. 1984;21(2):261-274.

Attali Y, Bar-Hillel M. Guess where: the position of correct answers in multiple-choice test items as a psychometric variable. *Journal of Educational Measurement*. 2003;40(2):109-128.

Bangerta M, Peschel T, Schlaug G, Rotte M, Drescher D, Hinrichs H, Heinze H, Altenmüller E. Shared networks for auditory and motor processing in professional pianists: Evidence from fMRI conjunction. *NeuroImage*. 2006;30(3):917-926.

Beveridge WIB. *The Art of Scientific Discovery*. New York: Norton; 1957.

Bloom BS, Engelhart MD, Furst EJ, Hill WH, Krathwohl DR. Taxonomy of educational objectives: The classification of educational goals. *Handbook I: Cognitive Domain*. New York: David McKay Company; 1956.

Higham PA, Gerrard C. Not all errors are created equal: Metacognition and changing answers on multiple-choice tests. *Canadian Journal of Experimental Psychology*. 2005; 59(1):28-34.

SECTION III

LIFE SKILL DEVELOPMENT

9   Managing Time & Change

10   Reducing Stress & Increasing Equanimity

11   Cultivating Emotional Literacy

12   Making Effective Decisions

13   Changing Habits

Managing Time & Change

> *Before acting I consider what is the most important thing for me to do next.*

CHAPTER THEMES
- The Nature of Time
- Change Management
  - Planning, Skillful Action, Insight
- Procrastination

In this chapter we will consider the nature of time, the concept of change management, and some simple strategies to get the most out of each day. There are only so many hours in a day and so many days in a life. We never know when our time will run out, and when it does, it will be too late to do anything more about it. Unfortunately it can come much sooner than expected. So taking advantage of the gift of life, while we have it, is the most prudent path.

The Nature of Time

So is time management the solution? There are scads of books written on the topic. There are time management gurus. There are systems, and planners, and apps, all designed to help you manage your time. But if you slow down and think about it for a moment a non-obvious question may arise – are we really managing time? Should managing time be our focus? What does it mean to manage time? If it is indeed time that we are managing then how do we actually go about doing that? To answer such questions my friends we must first consider the nature of time.

Time is Precious

In the Zen tradition time is viewed as a most precious gift, the precious moments of our lives. In San Francisco there is a beautiful old red brick Soto Zen temple. Down on the ground floor level, on Laguna Street, is the zendo. That is the space where the zen practitioners sit to meditate. In the hallway leading to the zendo there are some traditional instruments, a big taiko drum, a large ceremonial bronze bell. One of the items, used to keep track of time during meditation practice, is called a han. It is a thick piece of suspended wood that gets hit with a mallet, like a poor man's bell. The time keeper strikes the han 'whack-whack-whack' to inform residents that it is time to enter the zendo for sitting meditation, that the meditation is about to start, and that mediation has begun. On that particular han is a beautiful little verse. The black robed Zen priest standing in front of the han, keeping track of time, gets to contemplate the words…

> Great is the matter of birth and death.
> Life is fleeting.
> Gone, gone, gone.
> Awake, awake each one.
> Don't waste this life.

The point of the poem is to not waste one moment on the journey. The verse conjures images of Zen monks sitting in the still hours of the early morning, working intently on observing life, in order to understand the true nature of time and space. The American poet Ralph Waldo Emerson once wrote another provocative line about time. He noted, "How much of life is lost in waiting." What a great line that is as well. I suspect all of us can remember times when we waited, perhaps never taking any action at all, for fear of failure, because of self-doubt, lack of motivation – "How much of life is lost in waiting."

Time is a Subjective Experience

So what do we know about time? Well, from the ancient mystics and philosophers to contemporary experts in cosmological physics, the nature of time has received serious attention. Yet despite that effort we still do not have a clear understanding of what time really is. At the subjective level the perception of time is relative, some events appear to move painfully slowly, others astoundingly fast, and some just right. For example, two friends attend a lecture by a famous author. Both are in the front row sitting next to each other. The speaker comes out, opens her notes, and begins to read, head buried in her manuscript. One of the friends is highly engrossed, finding the speakers ideas truly brilliant, and enjoying the speaker's quirkiness, including the occasional spray of spittle. The other one is "OMG!!!" bored out of his gourd, but unable to walk out because he is sitting with his friend right in front of the speaker. For one or them, time will disappear. When the talk is over she will be surprised that ninety minutes had passed. For other person, however, it was an excruciatingly slow passage of time, like someone in a dream unable to run, unable to scream. It was the same lecture, the same ninety minutes (maybe?), but the subjective experience of time was so different for those two people.

Time is a Unit of Measure

Besides our subjective experience, we also have objective representations of time as a unit of measure. Did you know that the moon is about 1.3 light seconds away from earth (the number of seconds it takes light to travel from the moon to the earth). You are almost seeing the moon real time, just a 1.3 second time delay, rather amazing actually (both how fast that is and that there is a lag). The 1.3 seconds for the light to travel from the moon to the earth is a unit of time, like other measures we have created, such as days and months, which reflect a certain quality of order in the observed cosmos. Time is used to mark points along a path, to measure segments, from here to there.

Time Appears to be Linear

We have this idea in our human experience of walking a path from past into present and from present into future. We even describe the past as "*behind* us now" and the future as something we "look *forward* to." Meditation traditions place significance on the notion of being here now, being here (space), now (time). The implication of being in the moment is that we are upright, not falling back into the past or leaning forward into the future. All of these ideas reflect a sense of time moving along a linear continuum, the arrow of time moving through space. The Big Bang also suggests that time is linear. According to the Big Bang theory, before the physical universe manifested there was a single point of no-time and no-space, from which all things exploded into existence. Scientists measuring this cosmic emergence note that things near the center of the universe are closer together while things at the edges are more dispersed. This logically suggests that matter near the periphery has been moving out for a longer period of time, it is more spacious, more stretched out in a sense. It is like slowly pulling on a curled up garden hose. The part closest to you is getting stretched out first and will be more extended than the hose near the faucet.

Time is Real

Time is also a thing, an integral function of the physical universe, often described as the fourth dimension, along with the three space dimensions of height, width and length. The dominant theory in physics is that space and time are woven together in a single fabric, giving rise to the concept of a space-time matrix. Physical time is affected by motion in space, acceleration specifically. The faster an object moves through space the slower it moves in time. If an object approached the speed of light then time for that object would slow down to a near standstill. A person travelling on a very fast spaceship, for example, would age more slowly than her sibling living on earth, time would literally slow down for the person on the speeding rocket. We also know that physical time is affected by gravity (a concept known as time dilation). Hani goes up to the very top of Mauna Kea on the island of Hawaii, 14,000 feet above sea level. She calls her friend Kailani who is standing on the beach in Kona, eighty miles away. They compare time. Hani's watch, up on the mountaintop, would be faster (measured in nanoseconds) because there is less gravity pulling on time at that height. Finally, although we know something about the effects of acceleration and gravity on time, we do not know if time is discrete or continuous, similar to the issue of light as a photon (discrete particle) or a wave (continuum). Researchers studying this phenomenon have measured time down to about 10^{-15} of a second and at that rarefied level time is still a continuum (a nanosecond, 10^{-9}, is one-billionth of a second). Which, FYI, suggests that you should never tell anyone with an atomic clock that you will "be there in a nanosecond." You will always be late.

Conclusion from all of this – time is big, time is real, and it appears that we still have some very fundamental questions to be answered concerning its nature.

It is Not About Time, It is About Change

Well then, if time is so imponderable, why deal with it? Because, we have to deal with it. It is part of the package, part of the physical universe that we inhabit, an essential thread in our fabric. We are expressed in a space-time matrix. We are time. That said, I would suggest that the emphasis on time and time management in our day-to-day experience is misplaced. By emphasizing time we are neglecting the other half of the package – space. Recall that our current understanding is that time and space are inter-stitched, woven together, warp and weft. They are part of one cloth. Obsessing about time and neglecting space is a fundamental mistake. The two belong together, like the hand and the glove, like yin and yang. Focusing on just time is like running a race on one leg. You can do it, it is just less efficient.

Instead, rather than just thinking about managing time, consider managing time and space together. What does that mean when we manage time and space together? It means we manage change. Think of it this way. A person is dreaming. In the dream he enters a room. There is an apple on the table. He leaves the room and comes back some time later. How would he know that time had passed in that dream room, in that dream space? He would know because the apple had withered down to a small, dark, shriveled stub with a stem. Change happened. That apple, a form in space moved through time and it was modified, *it changed*. In time, space changes. Time and space are inextricably interwoven and their commingled process/product is *change* (*impermanence*). So the heart of the issue is change, not time. Life emerges from the co-existence of time and space, the place of contact in each moment, with the end product of that contact being change.

The Main Game

So the main game is not managing time. The real job is to manage the inevitable *changes* in life that result from the interface of time and space. *The goal is not time management, it is change management*. (FYI, the term *change management* is conventionally used to describe institutional restructuring, like downsizing a manufacturing plant because the owner can get cheaper employees in a foreign country. In this book, however, we will use the term change management to refer to managing the changes in life related to this interface of time and space). So why focus on change management? There are three important reasons why it is essential – entropy, perceived control, and productivity.

1. Entropy

The first reason to focus on change management is the undeniable truth that change happens, and that change often results in greater disorder. Consider the second law of thermodynamics, which states that in a cyclic process the entropy (increasing disorder) will increase or stay the same. Entropy represents a decrease in energy available for work. For example, if you put a gallon of gas in a scooter you can drive it for sixty miles. The gas is consumed and heat is produced as a by-product. Both the gas and heat are forms of energy. However, the heat energy released (hot engine, tailpipe, exhaust) is not readily available. It cannot as easily be put to work for useful purposes. It is entropic energy. It is lost. An ice cube takes energy to create, and it takes energy to maintain. Without energy to maintain it there is increased disorder, melted cubes in your glass, a sign that time has passed.

2. Predictability, Perceived Control, Reduced Stress

The second reason for change management is that change can be threatening. Humans prefer to have some sense of what is coming, some sense of predictability and control. If something can be predicted then it can be controlled or at least managed more effectively. A sense of predictability and control reduces stress. If change is random there is not much you can do about it. On the other hand, a lot of change in life follows a more predictable pattern, like the change of seasons. It was human insights into the cycle of seasons and plant life that lead to the development of agriculture, understanding seasons, and correspondingly, when to plant. That knowledge increased the predictably of crop output and reduced the stress of food supply uncertainty. Research consistently shows that perceived control reduces stress, both psychological and physiological (Glass, 1973). One of the probable motivations for the creation of the calendar and other astronomically oriented devices, like ancient stone henges, was for more accurate prediction of the seasons. The calendar is a fairly brilliant technology to increase our sense of predictability and control.

3. Improved Productivity

The final reason for managing change is that if we can manage change skillfully it can help us increase productivity and well-being. Using the agriculture example again, humans have been cultivating crops for about 12,000 years. Prior to that time our species lived a nomadic lifestyle in small hunting and gathering groups that had to migrate to stay with their food sources. Agriculture and related changes allowed humans to establish more permanent settlements. Complex societies and cultures emerged as a result of an increasing ability to work constructively with time and space, to manage change. The human story is indeed one of using intelligence and evolving understanding of the patterns of life to create predictable and ideally constructive change.

Change and Academic Success

In terms of academic performance and academic success it also make sense to think in terms of change management rather than obsessing about time. First, it makes sense in terms of entropy, control, and productivity. If you read a book but never review the notes, the memory of that studied material will decay and eventually be lost. Reviewing is a task that takes energy. That input of energy increases order in neural memory, and facilitates long term recall. By applying energy in the form of study and review we counterbalance entropy (forgetting or memory decay). That work, the maintenance of order, increases the predictability that the information you need will be there on exam day, and that reduces stress. It also increases productivity, as you will have quicker access to answers and greater confidence in their accuracy, and an increased ability to use that information productively in the future.

The second reason why change management is a more useful than time management has to do with the nature of academic work, any work for that matter. *This is a KEY idea*. If you think about academic work there are two primary points in the time-space continuum to consider. The first is the here and now, the current state – paper not written, book chapters not read, sale not closed. The second is the changed state, the desired state – a finished paper, a book that is read and highlighted, a closed deal and a signed check. The main purpose of problem solving is to move from the current state to the desired state. We want to *change* from where we are to where we want to be.

The goal, the desired state, is having a finished paper, the desired change. Whether it takes you 3 hours or 3 days, the amount of time, is not the main issue. Change is the main issue, the finished product. What is important is not time (3 hours or 3 days). What is important is change, getting from here to there. We need to manage the change from current to desired. Successful change is a function of both time and space and resources and vision and motivation and anything else that it takes to get it done.

> **VERY IMPORTANT** – the main point of work is not the time spent, it is the successful completion of a desired change. This is the most important point in this chapter, so please take note. People often make the mistake of focusing on time instead of change. Let us say Katrina spends her weekly 3-hour block of reading time to finish an assigned 20 pages. She feels good for having a weekly study period and for using it to read 20 pages. The potential problem with that strategy is that it can reduce efficiency. If the emphasis had been properly placed on change, reading 20 pages as quickly and effectively as possible, she might have completed the assignment in 1 hour instead of 3, a net gain of 2 hours for other activities, like sliding down the snowy hill on a cafeteria tray. When we focus on time it can be easy to lose track of the real goal – change – from unread to read, from unwritten to written, from no commission to commission. For the greatest academic and life success it is imperative that we focus on managing change and making effective use of time and space as part of that change process. (**IMPORTANT NOTE:** *If this did not make sense I would encourage you to reread this paragraph repeatedly until it does. If you understand and apply this concept it will change the nature of your academic life forever.*)

Principles of Change Management

It would now be useful to look at some strategies for managing change to increases success. Our approach to managing change will be to apply the elements of the Learning Life Problem Solving Model: get clear on the desired state, decide on your solution path, implement and work to stay on track for efficient and effective accomplishment, and conclude with an evaluation of the process. Those elements will be presented in relation to the three phases of change management:

1. Thoughtful Planning - Develop and Maintain Goal/Task Clarity

2. Skillful Action - Stay on Task, Focus on Quality, Accomplish Priority Goals

3. Reflective Insight - Review and Improve the Process

1. Thoughtful Planning - Develop and Maintain Goal/Task Clarity

The first step in managing change is to consider the goal, the desired state, the *where* you want to be (space) and by *when* (time). Based on your goal you select the most appropriate steps that you will take to get you there, the priority task(s). The goal is the desired state, the thing that you want to accomplish, the place you want to be. The tasks are the steps that get you there, the steps that take you to the desired state. This is like step 1 in the continual improvement process, defining the problem, thinking about the gap between current and desired, and clearly specifying the intended outcome.

Know Your Goals

In Chapter 2 you did some work listing life goals. That was the warm up. Now we want to look at ways to put those goals to work. Even if you wrote out your goals in Chapter 2 you may want to do this process again. The objective is to get closer to a working list of long term, intermediate and short term goals to guide your life.

> **REFLECTION**
>
> Create a short list of your *core life goals*, things you want to accomplish. The list can include good health, a happy marriage, having kids, owning a successful business. This list is for the big dreams that inform your life. Coming up with a list that truly inspires you, that feels deeply aligned, can take time, something that might evolve over the course of several years. It is something you can start now and refine over time. Ideally this is a fairly short list, maybe five bullet points. You want a list that you can memorize, know by heart, small enough to put on a card and carry in your wallet. If you memorize your short list of life goals they can become a beacon light to guide your daily decision making and life journey. That list will increase your efficiency on your journey if you take it to heart, into your heart, and listen to it. It is the straightest path to the desired state. Spend about 20 minutes on this.

> **REFLECTION**
>
> Next, create a working list of key *3-5 Year Goals*. That is a reasonable chunk of time to move things significantly along toward long-term goals. Beyond 5 years the picture can start to get a bit more fuzzy, life changes, technology changes, jobs change, relationships change. So create a 3-5 year list. Again, this is a shorter list of key goals, key life outcomes, desired state outcomes – health, relationships, finances and work, spiritual/emotional well-being, civic contribution, whatever is most central to your success and happiness, and your contribution to a better world. Spend about 20 minutes on this.

> **REFLECTION**
>
> Next come up with a list of *1 Year Goals* (the calendar *year*, so if this is October it is a shorter list). This is a list of key goals to accomplishment. It is a very good exercise to do every December 31st. At the beginning of each *quarter/semester* do the same thing for the next few months. Similarly, at the beginning of each *month* and for each *week* and *day*. These should be short lists of key items, the focus should be on the things that will give a real sense of accomplishment. "What will give me a sense of accomplishment this year?" That is a useful question to ask when creating such a list. Spend about 20 minutes on this.
>
> _____
>
> _____
>
> _____
>
> _____

Try to list the key items for the year, month, and week on just a few lines (not bullet points, but goal 1, goal 2, …one after the other). By limiting your space you are more likely to come up with a final list of items that are all killer, no filler. It is like moving into a very small room, you only take the essentials with you. The process of creating lists at the beginning of the year, month, and week will help you to prioritize and plan *key activities* for each time period. It also provides useful content for your calendar. Again, these are short lists of ***key outcomes, key goals to be accomplished*** for a specific time period. Each list points to the mountain top, orients attention for the day, week, month, year ahead. The purpose of these short lists is to have a handy way to remind yourself of the next most important task. You may want to create one sheet that includes life, year, month goals in one spot. The idea is to have a simple, accessible reminder of your guiding goals. Also remember that you want to make your goals concrete not abstract. You want goals that help you know what the next task is, taskable goals. These goals should make it clear what you intend to accomplish.

Make an Action Plan
When you have a goal, for the year, month or day, you then need to make a plan for reaching it. The goal is the desired state. Reaching that desired state requires taking specific steps, doing one or more tasks, that will allow you to reach that goal. For example, if the goal is a good dental check up in 6 months then the tasks leading to that would be daily brushing and flossing, taking a toothbrush to work to leave in your desk (and using it), and starting to cut down on sodas and replacing them with more water. Start with the goal and then list the steps or tasks leading to it. Sequence those tasks, also considering their start and completion dates. That is your action plan

Book It – Use Calendars and Planners
A goal without action is like hidden gold – of great potential value, but with little practical use. Once you have determined your goal, related tasks and action plan, you then need to schedule it all and put it to work. Trains run on time because they follow schedules. Without schedules there would be chaos, inefficiency, low productivity, risk of crashing. Scheduling a goal makes the goal

real, embeds it in the space-time matrix, on track to reach its destination in a specific time. It helps to make the goal/task action plan real.

As an example, the goal is a final review paper due May 18th. The tasks sequence might include preliminary research, selection of a topic and thesis, collection of background information, detailed outline, rough draft, revised draft, final proofing and edit. Some or all of these tasks could be entered on appropriate dates to provide a map for your journey. If you start with a major due date, like May 18th, you can work backwards from that date and put the key tasks in the timeline leading up to it.

That detail will help with timing and tracking progress, to see if you are on schedule, or if you need to make adjustments. Breaking things up into smaller pieces is the way also helps to make any unmanageable job much more manageable.

An essential scheduling element is *a working calendar* that is populated with specific goal due dates, supporting tasks, and other key events for the day, week, quarter/semester and year. We take calendars for granted, but they represent a brilliant technology that significantly enhanced predictability and human productivity. To use a calendar effectively you need to post dates for key events/goals/tasks – May 18th, final review paper due. Do not put non-date specifics on your working calendar, things like "take uncle Sammy to lunch some time." Put non-date specific items on a reminder list or some other information bucket. Use the calendar to mark deadlines for all important goals, to inform you of the day you are supposed to be at the desired state, when the train should be in the station.

Use To-Do Lists
In addition to having your succinct *Goal Lists* for the year/month/week it is also very helpful to have a corresponding *To-Do List* for the day. Many students find that to-do lists improve organization and help them use time more productively (Burke et al., 2014). Some people like them, some do not. You need to try it for a while, and see what works for you. In addition to providing an accessible reminder to what you have to do (memory jog) they are also a source of gratification. It is a great feeling when you see the check marks next to each completed task for the day, a reward in its own right, and rewards motivate action. To be most effective a to-do lists should note the important things that need to be done for the day. These items can come from your calendar, from your month or week goal lists, or from life on the fly. There are various ways to format to-do lists, a matter of personal preference. Here are some practical variations.

Open Lists
The simplest is the open list, an approach used by many people. It is just an off-the-top-of-the-head listing of the things you think you need to do that day. It is the classic laundry list approach. You cross things off as you go. It can include an infinite number of things to do. Open To-Do Lists can get very long, with way more things on them than anyone could possibly do in a day, or week. Also, they do not necessarily provide any sense of priority or importance. It is because they are somewhat random and often very large that they can actually contribute to a sense of stress and a

reduced sense of task completion and effectiveness. If they work for you fine. If they stress you out there are better options.

Closed Lists

There are a number of ways to make a to-do list more useful. The first is to make it a Closed To-Do List. An open list, what people often think of when you mention to-do lists, is just a container for holding ideas. Because the container is as big as the space you are writing on, potentially large, anything and everything can flow into it. That makes the open list never ending, like Sisyphus pushing the huge boulder up the hill. Once he got it to the top it would roll down again and he would have to start anew. In a similar fashion the open list provides no real sense of accomplishment or progress. At the end of the day you are often left with a huge pile of to-do's left undone. There is no end-of-day sense of closure.

That can be frustrating, and reduce motivation, as no sense of progress means no feeling of success, no reward. A solution is the closed list. The difference between the two is that the closed list takes the most important items for the day, probably 3-5 things, and puts those at the top of the list in their own closed section. They are the most valuable jewels in the vault. These are the items that will give you a real sense of accomplishment at the end of the day, the ones that take you to your bigger life goals. In addition, it can include things that MUST be handled, like the visa application that must be mailed by end of day. Items in the closed section should be the primary activities for the day. The remaining items are listed below on an open list. The open list items may get addressed or not. If incomplete it will not be a major disappointment as key goals for the day were given primary energy and attention. Completion of closed list items will lead to a greater sense of satisfaction and greater progress toward most important life goals, the ones you will remember when you are old and gray.

Prioritized Lists

Another practical strategy is to organize items by priority. When prioritizing you look over your whole list and rank each task as a *H*igh, *M*edium, or *L*ow priority (three levels is probably sufficient, like in class note taking). The high priority tasks are similar to the items on a closed list. If you can physically manipulate your list you might want to pull all of the top priority items to the top of the page, and create a closed list box for them. The medium priority tasks are the other things that would be nice to get done but not quite as essential to having a successful day. The low priority could possibly even be pulled from your to-do list for the day and put on a separate Time Permitting or Weekend list.

Time Specific Scheduled Lists

In addition to the closed and prioritized lists another productivity booster is to take priority items and arrange them by time of day, creating a scheduled list. This is handy as it puts actionable items into a specific timeframe. The value of this approach is that it can help you get a sense of how much you can actually accomplish in the time available. When you look at a train schedule you can see when the next trains depart for New York City, DC, and Atlanta. Could you imagine a train system without a functional schedule? How could people plan their travel? How could trains be prevented from running into each other?

Blocking by time in this way clearly helps with planning the day. It shows you what you will be doing and when. It also helps you estimate whether you can actually do all of the things on your list for the day. Since you are booking them before you begin execution you get a sense of what is possible in time and space. That can help make planning real, and that helps with decisions about priorities and managing time. It is a concrete way to see that there is only so much time in a day and in a life. Another benefit of this approach is that over time, if tasks are repetitive, it can help you develop a fairly realistic sense of how much time it usually takes for completion. That information can then be used as a basis for thinking about better ways to do the same task in less time.

Here is a related strategy that can be used as a training strategy for task focus and time management. Try this for a few months, doing this method periodically during the week. One of my colleagues has her own PR business. She tracks her activity every 15 minutes when she is working. She understands the value of her time, because she is charging customers a lot per billable hour. They want to see results and they want to know what they are getting billed for. She is highly accountable. To use this strategy create the time specific To-Do list just described above. You might list 9-10 for writing a report, 10-11 for working on a project outline, and so on. As you are working on those tasks make a note on the To-Do sheet every fifteen minutes indicating what you just accomplished. In a few days you will get a sense of your work pattern. It will also help you to stay on task as you are getting regular feedback about state of mind, body and accomplishment.

Project Folder & Project Task Lists

You can also create separate lists for specific goals, events, or projects. For example, your goal is to create a new website for your business by the end of the year. It is a good idea to create a specific task list for that project. The goal of the project is to complete a website, user tested and posted by June 20th. There are major milestones, various aspects to the job, and each of those with their own subtasks. A larger, more complex project with more moving pieces merits its own project task list and folder.

If you are a college student, each course you are taking should have its own project (course) task list and folder, as one example. Consider a research paper due on May 18th. That is in the History 101 folder. That folder has a History 101 Task List. One of the tasks is the final research paper. That paper has its own task list with corresponding dates, and those key tasks are entered into your working calendar. That may sound like a lot, but it is actually pretty simple. Bottom line, do whatever works best for you, but certainly having a folder for each course, and possibly having a corresponding Project Task List can be a helpful. Both could be hard copy or on computer, but having an actual paper folder is a good idea for keeping course materials organized, in a central location, easy to find.

Lists in Practice

Finally, no matter how you do your lists always think in terms of ***actionable items***, be specific. It is hard to act on "Be healthy!" What on earth does that mean? It means a million things. You can, however, easily act on "run two miles today (at 4pm)." That is actionable, down to the time of day. You know what you are supposed to do, what the action or task is, and when (if you choose to time block or calendar your tasks). Some goals will be broader, like "Clean the house on Saturday." Sometimes a goal like that is fine to put on the calendar, rather than the multiple actionable tasks related to it, like emptying the trash, folding the laundry, washing the kitchen floor. The main point is that you recognize and implement the actionable task, not a vague goal.

Also remember that *actionable means doable.* If a goal is large then break it into smaller tasks. A goal like, "write a 20 page research paper," is not a today item. It will take most people at least several weeks or probably longer to do a good 20-page paper. Completing the 20-page paper is the desired state, the result of a number of smaller tasks, such as choosing a topic, doing background research, creating an outline, and so on. Consider creating a separate project page with a detail list of tasks for larger goals of this type, and a project folder for even bigger projects.

One way to come up with specific actionable items is to simply ask yourself, "What are the five most important tasks for me to accomplish today?" or "What are the five most important tasks I need to act on to make progress on this goal?" If one of the answers is, "Get more reading done," then you can determine what reading, how many pages, when, and for how long. That specificity makes it concrete, clear and actionable. In order to stay on track you can also ask yourself periodically throughout the day, "*What is the most important thing for me to do right now?*" Get the answer and then take action. [For more ideas on the most important goals in your life you might want to reread Chapter 2 on Goals.]

Create your To-Do List at the beginning of the day (or the night before). *Carry the list with you* so you can remember what your priorities are for the day, when you will do them, and what is still left to do. One of my students had a major issue with procrastination and ADHD. He found that putting his items on an index card each morning and carrying that with him in his pocket was the best practice for remembering the next most important task and staying on track. Once he completed an item he crossed it off. Crossing off items helps to create a sense of progress, a sense of accomplishment. Also, remember that there is no perfect or standard To-Do list. Develop an approach that works for you. That can take some experimenting, and may vary depending on the application, but in the long run you will probably find To-Do lists to be quite helpful as a resource for improving daily productivity.

KEY: Goals are vital, but it is not about the goal, it is about the actionable tasks that help you move forward on that goal. Equally important, it is not about any actionable task, it is about actions that efficiently and effectively move you closer to your goal accomplishment, your desired state, step by step.

Consider Productivity Tools
There are a lot of productivity tools to help with scheduling, planning, and task management. These include paper-based, computer based, and mobile tools. Finding the method that is the most appropriate for you might take a bit of trail and error, but that can be time well spent if it makes you more productive. One of the ways corporations increase profits is not by adding more workers but by increasing the productivity of each worker currently employed.

One suggestion. Some students use the calendars on their smart phones as one productivity aid. Great idea, a very useful resource for mobile access to schedules. The one limitation of small handheld devices, however, is that it is harder to easily view the week or month at a glance, or to enter much information. Ideally you will want to look at your big picture schedule now and then, getting a sense of what the whole week or month looks like. Aside from that potential limitation, there are a lot of productivity apps out there, such as To Do apps, reminders, inspirational messages. If you want to see what is available do a web search for 'productivity tools'.

> ★ **DO THIS**
>
> When you finish this chapter please go to the Schedules activity in the Resources section to complete your Week Template, Semester Schedule and Graduation Map.

2. Skillful Action - Stay on Task, Focus on Quality, Accomplish Priority Goals

The first step in effective change management is knowing your goals and scheduling the tasks that will get you from here to there. The second step is to work skillfully to stay on task so you can get the job done, and to do that efficiently and effectively, producing a quality final product. Goals are essential, but goals are only as powerful as the actions that come from them. People can have beautiful, inspiring goals, but if they are not acted on, they are just empty words, of little real value. *Successful goal attainment requires skillful action*. We will approach skillful action, skillful goal accomplishment, from the perspective of the Wheel – Person, Behavior and Environment. Let us start with environment factors.

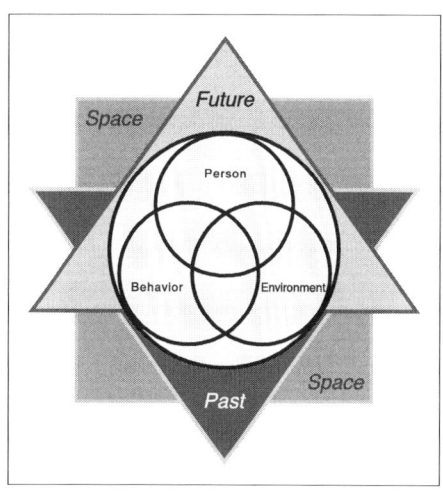

I. Environment

Environments can be chaotic, including environments at work, home, school, or your neighborhood. Chaos can appear in the form of dysfunctional co-workers, noise and grunge, crime, clutter, disorganization, lack of privacy, cramped quarters. Chaos makes effective and efficient change management more challenging. Although not always possible, it is much better to have the environment work for us, rather than against us. We want it to be a resource rather than a drain. Here are some strategies to make that happen.

Find Your Optimal Space

First of all, if possible, work in the right environment. Pick the best environment for the task at hand. If your living space is too noisy for productive study then go to the library. A campus library is an excellent resource for college students, public libraries are equally awesome. If your housemates are chronically piggish, then have a community meeting and make a plan, or consider moving. Sometimes the best solution to a bad work environment, an unhealthy boss or housemates, is to find another job or a new apartment. I know a good number of folks who have found peace via that path, and I honestly have never heard one of them express any regrets.

Be Organized
Make sure the environment is organized, and organized in a way that increases your efficiency. If your gear is in the right place you will get more things done, period. An environment that is orderly and reasonably neat will increase your sense of calm. The inner and outer environments affect each other. Create a place for everything. When you are done using something, put it back in its place. It takes a bit of discipline at first, but then it becomes a habit. Have a container for each class or major project (a simple folder can work just fine). If you worked in a shop where you used small metal parts all day long you would have a bucket, tray or bin for each part. The parts would be sorted and organized by size, frequency of use, or some other rule to help maintain order and increase efficient use. No time lost finding a part. No thinking about where to put an unused part. When you returned to work the next day you would know where all the parts were. When the people on the next shift came in, they would know where all the parts were. Effortless. No time wasted in searching, thinking, no energy lost in self-contempt. "What an idiot, where are my keys???" You will often find that highly productive people are very organized. They know where things are, when things are due, who to call next.

Manage Communications
Today it is so much easier for people to communicate with us, often with nothing of real value to add. That makes it imperative that we learn to manage communications efficiently. That includes emails, text messages, phone calls, letters, all of it. The key to managing communications is to have a good system, a good process, a clear what, when and where. The *what* and the *when* are what you do with it and when. The *where*, is where things go.

What
The *what* is about dealing with communications efficiently and effectively. This means having a process in place. If you do not have a good system yet, no worries. It will take some time to find the one that works best for you. It is what it is. When you do find your method, even the early versions, you will begin to notice greater efficiency in your work. In the beginning it will be a discipline. What is discipline? It is energy applied to create and maintain a new order, a new organization, implemented to reduce entropy and decay. Lost bills, unanswered emails, none of that will change until a process is chosen, implemented, and maintained over time. In time it becomes a new habit, with less discipline involved, just enough to avoid falling back into old habits. Having a good system will help you to respond in a timely manner, and that shows respect for other people. They will see you as professional and respectful, and they will appreciate it. You will stand out from the crowd.

When
The next consideration is when. The first step is a quick assessment. Is this something I can/should do now, soon, sometime, or anytime? Many things can be handled immediately. This is clearly junk mail – no further action required – trash can. Simple emails, a few word response answers the question, push 'send' and done. There are quite a few things that can be handled quickly, in 1 or 2 minutes, boom, boom, done. That piece is now out of mind. You will not have to handle it again. Keep the responses simple and professional, do not waste time on perfection. Get it done and move one.

The next levels are the items that will either require more time than available at the moment, or are of lower/low priority and can be postponed. They should all have their place and time, their where and when. For emails that could be a folder and process for each level of urgency. For 'today' items it can be useful to block a time of day for handling all the non-urgent responses. Responding to such items throughout the day can really break the work flow and be a big waste of time. Picking a time of day when your energy is lower and using that as an opportunity to catch up on all those texts and emails can be very efficient, maybe 3pm. Same thing with the 'Friday' level inquiries. Three o'clock on Friday they get their hour, and then you try to do as many as possible during that specified time block. Make it a game.

Where
The where speaks to the question where do things belong. As an example, you could have a file folder labeled 'Bills'. Then as soon as a paper bill or email bill comes in you put that in the Bills folder. Now you know exactly where to find the gas bill, no looking through a massive pile of papers on your desk. Even better, you have scheduled a biweekly 'Pay Bills' time on your calendar. On that day you open your folder, pull out the bills, pay them all, and file the records. Another very handy strategy is to label 12 folders, creating one for each month of the year. Keep those 12 folders at the front of your filing system and insert documents as appropriate. If you have a grant application that is due in three months, with no early submissions accepted, you put it into a folder one month before the due date. When that month comes, you open the folder, take out the items, including your grant application, and schedule those tasks. You know where your concert tickets are, the ones you bought 5 months ago when they went on sale. On October 14th you pull them out of the October folder as you head out the door to the concert, congratulating yourself for being so organized and so smart.

Manage Documents
Living in a modern society we all acquire paper and electronic documents, some of which need to be maintained for a period of time, such as tax records, vehicle registration information, birth certificates. Having a process to documents efficiently is important. The simple strategy is to get a label maker (great investment), some file folders, and a filing cabinet or box to store the documents in. Label the folders appropriately and neatly. That is a key to success and happiness, and the reason for getting a label maker. Then arrange the folders in an order that makes sense to you, possibly by related areas, such as your financial folders for receipts and banking, or a section of folders for each class you are taking. Do not just toss vaguely named folders into the abyss. Organize your files so you can find them when they are needed. Design the system based on the most logical organization. In your kitchen drawer, if you used soup spoons the most you would put those in the front. A little pre-thought up front will save you a lot of time later. If you have a suspension filing cabinet you can put related folders together, like all the financial folders, alphabetically organized in one hanging file section. Some folders might be temporary, while you are working on a specific project with a deadline completion date, others may be more long term, like your banking records.

Once you have a system the next thing to do is to use it. You want to minimize handling. You can use this same approach for clothes, kitchen items, tools, keys. Whether it is email, magazines, new pair of socks, a bill, extra blankets, process it and put it where it belongs. Find a home for things, a place where they logically fit, and put them there. You car keys are in the bowl next to the front door, ready to grab on the way out in the morning. Always in the same place. No thinking involved, less chance of misplacing. We apply energy to maintain order and reduce entropy and decay. If it is an efficient system it will require less thought and energy to maintain, it will be more efficient and sustainable. That is the nature of change management.

Keep it Simple

Again, establish a system for keeping things organized. Keep it simple. Do not let things accumulate. That is a root of entropy. It can create stress and lowers productivity. Decide how long you will keep magazines around. If not read, too bad, not going to be read, toss them. Keep records as long as they need to be kept for legal or practical reasons. Seasoned travelers pack light. The higher you want to climb the lighter you need your gear to be. Avoid clutter. Throw things away, give them to a charity or a friend, a still river becomes stagnant. Clear out what is not useful, keep what is. As for information and document storage, given the easy access to materials on the web, it may be out there stored on someone else's website, make a quick decision on whether you actually need to keep a copy. Do what works.

II. Behavior

The next cog in wheel of skillful action is creating a good workflow. There is the old Taoist tale of the wood carver who never needed to sharpen his tools. He was so skillful in knowing where to apply each cut that he met little resistance. He could work all day without tiring, with little wear on his tools. That is skillful. That is mastery.

Choose High Priority Tasks Based on Core Goals and Values

At the end of the day most people do not jump up for joy because they worked on twenty grunt level tasks. They jump up for joy because they made serious progress on a few important tasks, even more so when those tasks brought them closer to reaching their core life goals. One way to work on those kinds of tasks during the day is to ask yourself, ***"What is the most important thing for me to do next?"*** If you are on your computer wasting time on some social media site, and you ask this question, it is doubtful that the answer will be "to spend more time on this site." Social media, which is so often a life-energy-down-the-drain-time-sink would equate to a lost opportunity, a lost chance to work toward your dream. People stay in their little cages because they are not mindful, because they lack clear goals, because they do not recognize that they have the power to choose. So many think they still have a collar around their necks and that they are helpless, that they cannot jump to the other side of the cage, cannot get out of the cage. So they sit there distracting themselves. What a pity. The truth is, that more often than not, we have the power to choose. We have the right to dream and embrace a vision. It is a process. Change takes time. But one small step toward freedom can be the beginning.

Execute

Get work done as soon as possible. This is the way to create and maintain order in the environment and to feel supremely productive. Just handle things. When you put it on your calendar, you are done thinking about it. When you complete one task, one more piece of the project, you are done with that piece, and that much closer to the finish line. Book it, do it, move on. Keep it flowing. Periodically reflect on the process and consider if there is a better way, a way to do it even more quickly with less expenditure of time, money or energy.

Stay On Task
People have good intentions, but they get pulled off track, often quite easily. The key to getting it done is to just stay on task. "*Am I on task?*" This is perhaps the core mindful awareness centering question for students, for any human who wants to get things done and make a difference. "Am I on task." It is an honesty question, an integrity question, and the answer is usually obvious and simple. *You are on task or you are not on task, simple*. The light is on, the light is off, simple. If you are not on task then you have a choice, a decision to make. If you are not mindful about your current reality you could waste three precious hours on some useless activity. Staying on task can take a lot of deep breathing, patience, kindness, mindful awareness, positive self-talk, small rewards, discipline, and blocks of work time alternated with rest. When you have a commitment to task completion, and a plan of how to deal with distractions, you can apply energy to reduce entropy and manage change efficiently. With practice it becomes a new habit

Protect Your Time
Another important aspect of managing tasks is to protect your time. Just say "No." That can be a life changing exercise in self-respect and assertiveness. Do not let unimportant things chip away at your minutes, hours and weeks. Write emails that are polite but to the point (your readers will appreciate that as well). I once had a colleague who would write voluminous email responses, a waste of time for him and his audience. Keep it simple. Have a schedule and honor it (this is actually one of the benefits of clear schedules, it helps you to say no to distractions). Stay on task. When you work, work. When you play, play. Also, be mindfully aware of transitions. People lose a lot of time in their transition moments. Someone comes home from work or school and putters around. Before they know it three hours have passed. Again, chill time is good, essential, but to not lose time because of unconscious transitioning. The flip side of protecting time is being open to life's demands, like your kid's request for extra assistance with homework or spending some time for someone on the phone who just needs to talk about a problem. We need to be flexible, another part of skillful means.

Use the Right Tools
Another important behavior for managing change effectively is using the right tools for the job. As we have discussed before, you can pound nails with a broom handle, but it will be inefficient, slow, and frustrating. Use the tools you need for your success. If you are a student you need some variation of a computer and a printer. Those are solid investments that will increase your productivity and professionalism. Given the current costs you should be able to save up and buy a laptop or tablet and printer for a reasonable price, but do research and read reviews first. One suggestion, most students do not need a color printer. Color printers use expensive color cartridges that need replacing all the time, a big waste of money. Those printers are often sold at a discount because the companies know they will quickly make up the loss with significant margins (profits)

on the ink cartridges. For the occasional piece of color work that you may need you can go to the copy shop on campus. They have it all.

III. Person

The final cog in the wheel of *skillful action* is managing the internal state of thoughts, emotions and physiology. A person who can maintain a relatively steady state in mind and body, maintain their composure, is much more likely to complete the race, to manage change effectively, and to reach the desired state.

Practice Mindful Awareness

Practice mindful awareness of person, behavior and environment – metawareness. Observe the interplay of these life elements and notice how they interact to support or to block your use of time and space. Look for areas where you can make small adjustments in order to adjust your path to reach the desired state sooner. Observe and learn, observe and change. Be mindful of the feedback from inside and outside. Feedback is an essential part of learning.

Remember Your Goals / Maintain Motivation

We will all experience ups and downs in life. It is what it is. One of the ways to keep from spinning out when things get hard is to remember why you started in the first place, why reaching your goal is important. Remember your goals, and do what it takes to stay motivated. In a long race you might wonder, "What was I thinking? Why on earth did I sign up to do this stupid race at all!" Maybe at that point the only thing keeping you going is your pride, that you will finish no matter what. Was it worth the effort? Often yes, as those tough battles are the ones you remember for the rest of your life. Other times, it is better to learn from the experience and pull out. Sometimes the car just breaks down, end of race. Not possible to finish. Indeed, from an evolutionary perspective, never giving up includes fight AND flight. The purpose of having both options is to enhance the probability of longer term survival, never giving up (on life).

Manage Your State

To manage change you need to manage your internal state, to regulate your inner reality so that you can stay focused, stay intense, stay on task, finish the race, get it done. It is important to manage the anxiety or boredom that leads to avoidance and procrastination. Be mindful of apathy, fear and burnout. Make sure you take care of the whole being. All work and no play, not good. Get enough rest. Avoid over-caffeination. Eat well and exercise. Take care of yourself. Have fun. The dog in us needs to run and chase a squirrel. I am not sure what the squirrel in us needs, however? Actually, if feeling squirrelly, good to run as well.

Toughen Up

Develop some mental toughness. Create a quality of mind that drops worry, prefers realism to perfectionism, is optimistic, accepts responsibility, and appreciates challenges as a chance to grow in capacity. Pull your shoulders back, sit up straight, take a deep breath and tell the day to "bring it on," or "this is fun," or "I am learning something new and that is great." Open your arms and embrace life. Let your skin be a bit thicker. Learn to regulate emotions. Guide dogs learn to remain composed. If they can, we can. Do not let your chain get yanked so easily. Cultivate equanimity, balance. Learn to be gracious with fools. If people cannot flip your switch they cannot control you. Nelson Mandela had self-respect and he asked for respect from others (in prison). He did that graciously and with dignity and he got it. Be physically healthy, build your qi, your life force. Being vital physically will help you to feel stronger mentally. Research has found that competitive athletes cultivate mental toughness through mental imagery, thought regulation, and optimism (Nicholls, 2008).

Use Priming

Use mental imagery. Use your innate capacity for imagination and imagery to see the desired outcome you seek. Seeing is believing. Before beginning important tasks use Priming to see the outcome that you want to manifest. Experience it vicariously in mind and body before taking that first step on the path. See the goal, the desired state as if it has already been successfully completed. Priming in this way will reduce anxiety and resistance, increase creativity, and lead to a better final product. See it, feel it, let it be real. Then begin the task with enthusiasm and a sense of what is possible. Refer to Chapter 3 on Priming for review.

3. Reflective Insight - Review Your Process and Improve

After clarifying goals and your action plan, and taking skillful steps to implement that plan, the third and final step to effective change management is a time for review and reflection on the process. Deliberately, intentionally, consciously reflecting on your change process is critical for optimal impact. Periodically evaluating your process – how it is going and how it went – is a key to greater success. Are you working efficiently and effectively? Is change heading in the desired direction, optimally? Is there a better way to do the work?

Pick a time that works for you for your periodic review. During your review ask yourself if there is a more efficient way to do the work. Are there tools you could be using that would help you get more done, and done more easily? Are there resources, including people with specific skills or connections, you could tap into? Are there other strategies you could be using, like different study methods, or note taking techniques that would help you? The key question to ask periodically is, "Is there a better way to do this? Am I being efficient, effective?" More generally, it can be useful to do an end of day review reflecting, constructively, on where there are areas for improvement, and recognizing what went well.

Standardize and Create New Habits

Once you come up with a good process, a task approach that seems to work well, then standardize it. Use it like a recipe. If appropriated you can even write it down and apply it to related tasks. For example, if you have a checklist of steps that you use for exam preparation you can use that for all future exams. The basic steps probably do not change that much from test to test. You now have a simple rubric for exam prep. Using that checklist each time you prepare for an exam will increase your efficiency and productivity. Do not reinvent the wheel. There are a lot of them out there. If you come up with a good process, use it.

Use the KAGI Approach

You may remember the KAGI concept from Chapter 7, on Display. KAGI stands for Knowledge, Awareness, Goals and Insight. *Knowledge*, your knowledge base, is what you bring to any new goal, any new problem in life. You already have a lot of prior experience and understanding. *Awareness* is the mindful awareness that will help you gather the information you need, the feedback you need, to know if you are on course or not, and if not, to pull yourself back on track. The *Goal* is your goal. It is the change you are seeking to manage, getting from current state to desired state. As you implement tasks to reach your goal you apply knowledge, you are aware, getting feedback about whether on track or not. As you act on your goal with knowledge and awareness, and a commitment to success and quality, you will gain *Insights* into what works best, what is the optimal solution. You will learn more about life. Mistakes and successes both provide insight into more and less effective ways of managing change. They are both useful aspects of learning. Through this ongoing process of knowledge, awareness, goals and insight it is possible to establish and standardize best practices that make for a much smoother ride over time.

Procrastination

Procrastination has been called the thief of time. I had one student who took this course, about 24 years old, who said he had procrastinated his entire adult life. For his Integrative Learning Project he decided to work on that habit. By the end of the course he said he was no longer procrastinating on important things in his life. He described a sense of exhilaration that came from the accomplishment of tasks that were important to him. He was now clearly moving along the path of his life, intentionally, with passion and commitment, not afraid if he made a mistake or if he embarrassed himself. He was alive. He had thrown away the collar.

Causes of Procrastination

Research consistently shows that procrastination is associated with lower academic performance (Zarick & Stonebraker, 2009). It needs to be addressed if academic success is to become a reality. The research literature on procrastination lists a large number of potential causes. Personally, I think of procrastination as a symptom. The real story is the underlying causes, the root. I once had a student who took my class, did her final project on procrastination, and guess what, did not finish the paper. She took an incomplete. Incompletes turn to F's after one year at our institution. Well a year passed, she did not hand in the work, and the grade automatically turned to an F. Because of her F her GPA went down and she could not get her student loan. Well guess what happened? She turned in her paper a week later. She **never** had a problem with procrastination. When she needed to get the work done she finished it, with good quality, in short order. I believe she had a problem with self-worth, she was not worthy of personal success. That was what unplugged her motivation and commitment. There was not enough commitment to self. That is what really needed to be worked on, not procrastination. Procrastination was the branch not the root. My bet is if she worked on her own self-worth that the symptom of procrastination would spontaneously disappear. In the continual improvement philosophy, which we examined in Chapter 8, one of the key ideas is to get to root causes. Do not worry about procrastination. That is often just a symptom of something else. Focus on root causes and the procrastination will begin to shift on its own. Here are some potential root causes to consider:

Anxiety
Apathy
Depression
Disorganized environment
Fatigue and low energy
Fear of failure – shame, embarrassment, loss of face
Habit
Impulsiveness
Indecision
Lack of commitment
Lack of assertiveness
Lack of resources and right tools
Lack of self-confidence
Lack of vision and clear goals
Low motivation
Low self-efficacy or expectancy
Low self worth – do not deserve success
Low tolerance for frustration
Overwhelm – the task is too big
Perfectionism
Poor planning and change management skills
Project scope – will take too much time, cost too much, is too complex
Secondary gain – using procrastination to manipulate others

Task Aversion

Research suggests that a common correlate of procrastination is task aversion (Ferrari et al., 1998; Ferrari & Scher, 2000). People procrastinate on tasks as a way to avoid something unpleasant, what we can call task aversion. Let us consider an example using the Wheel model – Person, Behavior, Environment. The assignment is a 20-page research paper to work on, or end of year taxes to complete, or a phone call to make that is going to be very difficult. These are all pending tasks in the *Environment* that have to be dealt with. Most people will probably have some resistance to these kinds of tasks. Some people will have a very strong resistance. For the latter group even thinking about the big paper generates a significant amount of anxiety, despair, self-doubt. Those feelings arise inside, the *Person* level. They are unpleasant feelings, aversive feelings, which most people would want to get away from, quiet down somehow. The procrastination solution – watch television, start to clean the fridge, eat some ice cream, or any other million-and-one possible distractions and avoidances. Watching television or eating ice cream is the *Behavior*, the avoidant behavior, avoiding the thing that generates the feelings of anxiety. The procrastination pattern: *Environment*, the 20-page paper; *Person*, the aversive feeling of discomfort in the body and mind; the *Behavior* of avoidance and procrastination.

Pleasure and Pain

Two forces strongly reinforce human behavior – a reduction of pain and an increase of pleasure. Both are rewarding, reinforcing. If I reduce pain (anxiety) by not working on math homework, the action of avoiding math is rewarding and reinforced (avoiding math makes me feel better, which is a reward versus a punishment). If I eat ice cream, pleasurable, instead of working on math homework, that action of avoiding math becomes associated with reward, eating ice cream. Since we seek pleasure and avoid pain what is being strengthened in these cases is the avoidant behavior. We avoid doing math and we feel less stressed. Instead we go eat ice cream and we feel even better. The avoidance of math is doubly rewarded in this case, reduction of anxiety from abandoning homework and increase of pleasure from ice cream. It is like paying your kid to not do her homework. Obviously not a great idea.

The obvious problem with this task avoidance procrastination solution is that you do not get the math homework done. When you do finally get to the homework, often because it is last minute and you absolutely have to, there is less time to work on it and as a consequence it is probably not the best quality effort and there is less learning (not understood, not remembered). You get a B instead of an A on that assignment and you are less prepared for the midterm exam. It is easy to rationalize the behavior. "I got it done, a B is not bad, and I always work better under pressure." That is all spin. The reality is that time was not used effectively because of the underlying root cause of avoidant behavior related to the desire to reduce uncomfortable feelings. No judgment. It is what it is. It is, however, a less effective study/life strategy.

Solution

Mindful Awareness

So how does one deal with that? The first thing to do is to recognize that we are putting off work that will have to be done at some point. That is why we need to ask the core mindful awareness centering question, "Am I on task?" As soon as you notice that you are off task, procrastinating, or heading in that direction, then is a good time to become mindful of thoughts and of the feelings in the body. This is not a time for self-criticism. It is rather a time for recognition of the habit, acceptance of self without criticism, and beginning to build the commitment to change.

It begins by being mindful of our experience, noticing when we are veering off task. If that is because of anxiety or some other less pleasant feeling then it becomes an opportunity to practice being okay with not being okay. A key to overcoming procrastination is learning to be okay with not being okay. It is important to stay. Just stop and stay there, even for one extra minute. That develops our capacity to stand in the middle of the mess. Take slow, deep breaths. Be aware of your posture, sit up straight, pull shoulders back, smile. Go drink some water. Remind yourself of your commitment to quality and your goals. Use positive self-talk. Laugh. Recognize the natural impulse to avoid pain and seek pleasure. Remind yourself that the work will have to get done anyway. Ask yourself, "What is the most important thing for me to do right now?" or, "What is one simple thing I can do right now to move forward on my goals?" Then think about the next actionable task, something small enough to actually do, and do it. Find ways to keep yourself in the game, and if you need a break, take a break.

Twelve-Minute Rule

One of my favorite strategies for anything I have resistance to doing is to work on it for 12 minutes. In the past I did not like to do dishes. Now I have a dishwashing monkey. (I am kidding, I do not actually have a dishwashing monkey. I tried that for a while but the monkey made an even bigger mess in the kitchen.) So as a solution, instead of letting my dishes pile up for a week, to the point where I am eating out of cans with my fingers, I just wash dishes for 12 minutes. I set the timer and when it rings I run from the kitchen. It turns it into a game, how much can I actually get done in 12 minutes, quite fun. I have come to learn that you can get a barrel full of dishes washed in 12 minutes if you really crank on it. Why 12 minutes? It can be any shorter time period. I like 12 because I had a trainer that I worked with once when I was rehabbing a shoulder from a sports injury. Prior to that experience my brain was set to doing 10 reps on an exercise. Her rule, 12 reps. Made sense, since we are naturally geared to 10, 10 fingers, 10 toes, shooting for 12 is just a bit more of a stretch. The extra 2 feels like an accomplishment. Funny how the brain works. Actually any short period of time will work, 10, 12, 15 minutes as you like. Beyond that you are starting to move into real work time. Less than that and you will probably not get enough steam to move many dishes. One other thought, once you start the activity, with the 12-minute timer on, you will often stop the timer once it rings and keep going. It is like getting into the lake. The cold water keeps a lot of people from going in at all. The ones who do jump in swim around for a few minutes and realize it is not that bad. Soon they are actually having fun, so they just keep going.

Other Ideas

It is important to just do something, to just get started. Any little step is a beginning. Another very useful idea is to remind yourself of how the action fits into your life, and how it will move you toward your goals. Remind yourself of your commitments. One of my students, a very productive pre-dental student, would remind herself that the work was going to have to be done at some point so why put it off. You can address the pain now or later, either way, there will be a bit of pain, so why not get the work going now. Stalling just makes things harder later. Do it now and get it done. Another excellent mental frame is to think in terms of quality. If you bring a quality focus into your life and work then everything will begin to change, guaranteed. Research shows that students with higher GPA's are less likely to procrastinate, and more likely to turn in higher quality work, on time, and receive higher scores (Senecal et al., 1995; Tuckman 1998; Zarick and Stonebraker, 2009). Finally, use positive self-talk, encourage yourself, remind yourself that you are awesome (not a time for humility), get pumped. Positive self-talk can be very empowering.

Final Thought

Here is a simple strategy for overcoming procrastination. Develop a clear vision, a positive attitude, and good work habits; recognize your accomplishments; reward yourself for your progress; have fun; love people and life; do as much good along the way as you can; never give up (on life).

SUMMARY

In this chapter we considered the nature of time. We also examined how a focus on time management can actually lead to less efficient use of time. The ideal is to focus on change management, the accomplishment of desired goals, desired changes. The process of change management was approached as a three phases process: thoughtful planning, skillful action, and reflective insight. Planning involves knowing ones goals, working with calendars and scheduling, using to-do lists (open, closed, prioritized, and time specific). Skillful Action employed the Wheel model to look at effectiveness from the level of: (1) Environment (organized space, effective communication processes, and good document management); (2) Behavior (maintaining a task orientation); and (3) Person (methods for maintaining balance of mind and body, such as mindfulness and priming mental imagery). Reflective Insight emphasized evaluation of efforts and standardization of the most effective. A final section on procrastination looked at root causes and strategies for creating change, such as the simple 12-minute rule.

MIND-BODY

Sitting Meditation

This week continue awareness of body, breath, senses, thoughts, emotional states.

Mindful Awareness

During the week be mindful of your use of time. Notice particularly the simple experience of being on task or off task. One strategy is to take an assignment and keep track. Periodically check in and make a mental note (even better on paper) whether on or off task. If you are off task check in and ask, "Why am I off task?" Think of one simple thing you can do to get back on track.

Priming

Set your goals for the week. Use Priming mental imagery to create a most incredible week and semester of your life so far. If you find that there are areas where you tend to procrastinate, such as before writing assignments or math homework, take a few minutes before starting the assignment and see yourself having completed it successfully, staying on task, and even being surprised by how much you accomplished.

REFERENCES

Burke A, Shanahan C, Herlambang E. An exploratory study comparing goal-oriented mental imagery with daily to-do lists: supporting college student success. *Current Psychology*. 2014;33(1):20-34.

Ferrari JR, Keane SM, Wolfe RN, Beck BL. The Antecedents and consequences of academic excuse-making: Examining individual differences in procrastination. *Research in Higher Education*. 1998;39:199-215.

Ferrari JR, Scher SJ. Toward an understanding of academic and nonacademic tasks procrastinated by students: The use of daily logs. *Psychology in the Schools*. 2000;37(4):359-366.

Glass DC, Singer JE, Leonard HS, Krantz D, Cohen S, Cummings H. Perceived control of aversive stimulation and the reduction of stress responses. *Journal of Personality*. 1973;41(4) 577-595.

Nicholls AR, Polman R, Levy AR, Backhouse SH. Mental toughness, optimism, pessimism, and coping among athletes. *Personality and Individual Differences*. 2008;44(5):1182-1192.

Senecal C, Koestner R, Vallerand RJ. Self-regulation and academic procrastination. *Journal of Social Psychology*. 1995;135(5):607-620.

Tuckman BW. Using tests as an incentive to motivate procrastinators to study. *Journal of Experimental Education*. 1998;66(2):141-147.

Zarick LM, Stonebraker R. I'll do it tomorrow: The logic of procrastination. *College Teaching*. 2009;57(4):211-215.

Reducing Stress & Increasing Equanimity

10

I maintain balance. If there is a problem I work diligently to manage it and resolve it.

CHAPTER THEMES
- Theories of Stress
- Stress and the Body-Mind
- Coping and Equanimity

Scenario 1: Speeding down the highway, from out of nowhere a police car pulls in right behind you with red lights flashing. Scenario 2: Two people on the bus look like they are going to get into a fight and you are sitting in the row right between them. Scenario 3: Hiking along a very narrow trail you momentarily loose your footing, almost falling sixty feet to the rocks down below. If you were not in a coma when any of those things happened you would almost instantaneously, without a single thought, have experienced a racing heart, faster breathing, some sense of anger or fear, and a body in action mode. That is the stress response. The evolutionary purpose of that response is to prepare for action, for fight or flight. It is nature's way to help us stay alive.

We need a stress response. It is essential for our survival, both for the individual and the species. What we do not need is to get locked into a chronic stress response, into a place where we let fear or anger run the show. The challenge, if people do not possess the skills and resources to cope effectively, to self-manage, to work effectively with life problems, they can get stuck in a stress mode. Stress is what it is, an essential psychophysiological response loop that nature has embedded to protect her children when she is not watching. We need it. We just need to learn to work with it.

In this chapter we will look at the causes of stress, the mind-body response patterns, consider different theories of stress, and learn how to manage it to survive and thrive. Ultimately, our goal in the Learning Life approach is to be able to work with stress constructively, as a key to a more empowered life. Since our objective in this book is not just surviving, but ideally thriving, we will move beyond the concepts of stress management and coping and into the domains of skillful means and equanimity.

Theories of Stress

To better understand this concept of stress and coping it would be useful to review some of the seminal work done by several pioneers in this field of study. Reflecting on their ideas can increase our knowledge. Knowledge plus awareness can provide insight. Greater insight can help us navigate life more skillfully. Becoming more skillful in life is why we learn.

Before we begin it would be helpful to clarify one point, how we will think of stress in this chapter. We typically think of stress as something that is happening to us, like getting stuck in traffic, being short of funds when the rent is due, or having an encounter with an angry customer. Certainly, all of those events can be very stressful. The scientific study of stress, however, refers to those *external events* as *stressors*. What happens inside, the *internal* mind-body response to those stressors, is what they call *stress*. The pounding heart, rapid breathing, sweaty palms, sense of fear are all possible aspects of this mind-body stress response. External stressors are the cause of the internal state of stress, the internal mind-body effect.

> External *stressors* (the cause) ⟶ internal *stress* response (the effect)

Walter Cannon - Homeostasis & Fight-or-Flight

Walter Cannon is a key figure in the development of our modern concept of stress. An intellectually curious person, Cannon was interested in biology, psychology and philosophy. After completing his medical degree at Harvard, he was hired by the university to teach and do research. His initial research focused on the physiology of digestion. While conducting those studies he made an important observation. Cannon was using x-ray technology, an innovative new tool at that time, to observe the movement of food through the gut. This is a process known as peristalsis, a series of muscle contractions in the digestive tract. One of the unusual things he came to notice was that if the animals were calm the food would move through the gut normally. By contrast, he noted that when the animals were in states of fear or rage the movement was impaired. He published an important paper describing the relationship between fear and anger, activation of the sympathetic nervous system, and the release of adrenalin. He observed that together these changes energized the organism preparing the animal to respond to threats, which increased the probability of survival in the face of that threat. He defined this as the fight-or-flight response, one of Cannon's major and lasting contributions to this field of study. In 1915 Cannon published a full account of his findings in a work entitled, *Bodily Changes in Pain, Hunger, Fear and Rage: An Account of Recent Researches into the Function of Emotional Excitement.*

Following the end of World War I Cannon shifted his focus to explore the process by which the body maintains a state of relative internal constancy or equilibrium. He called it homeostasis, or the ongoing, dynamic process that regulates the delicate balance of water, salt, oxygen, temperature (98.6 degrees), blood pH (7.4), and other vital factors. He noticed that readjustments were continually occurring in the healthy organism to maintain a homeostatic balance. When the body got too hot it would start to sweat, if dehydrated a sensation of thirst, too much water resulting in urination. Similarly, when we the organism has a stress response the system will seek to rebalance that state of high activation. In an important article published in 1929, entitled *Organization of*

Physiological Homeostasis, Cannon defined physiological homeostasis as a process that maintains a stable similar state, homeo-similar/like and statis-stable/steady. It seeks a state of balance, not going too high or too low, a state of physiological equanimity. He listed four characteristics of physiological homeostasis. (You may notice how these four characteristics of homeostasis mirror key concepts of the Wheel model. They also parallel the small changes strategy of Kaizen, smaller changes made in an ongoing fashion to prevent the need for radical adjustments later).

Cannon's four characteristics of homeostasis:
1. The body is a highly developed open system interconnected to its environment
2. Changes in the environment activate changes within the individual
3. Ongoing automatic adjustments typically keep these changes within a narrow range
4. This prevents wide oscillations keeping internal conditions relatively stable

Hans Selye - Physiology and Stress

Hans Selye was the next historically significant contributor to our modern understanding of stress. Selye was a medical student in the city of Prague in the 1920's. While working in the hospital he observed that many of the patients being treated shared common symptoms including loss of appetite, fatigue, joint pain, and fever. He mentioned this to one of his professors who advised him to ignore what they described as side effects of being sick. Selye knew enough to trust his own intuition, that this represented something important. Completing his medical degree in Prague he continued his studies at Johns Hopkins University as a research fellow and then in 1932 went on to McGill University in Montreal to do endocrinology research.

Selye's research at McGill focused on the isolation of a new sex hormone. He would inject rats with ovarian extracts and then look for changes in their sex organs. Instead of changes in the sex organs he observed enlarged adrenal glands, shrinking of the thymus, and bleeding ulcers. He also noted that prolonged injections resulted in death. At first Selye thought he was on to a new hormone and so he continued his inquiry. Working with other substances he eventually came to realize that the observed changes were actually the result of the toxicity of the substance injected into the rats. The application of any toxic substance, such as formaldehyde, produced the same three physiological changes – enlarged adrenal glands, shrinking of the thymus, and bleeding ulcers. Selye knew that this represented a fundamental biological response. He named this phenomena the General Adaptation Syndrome (GAS).

In 1936 Selye published a brief article on this finding in the journal *Nature*, an article that would mark the beginning of a very important new field of psychological and biological research (Selye, 1936; Szabo et al., 2012). Selye introduced the specific term stress into this body of work in 1950 (Selye, 1950), ultimately defining stress as "the non-specific response of the body to any demand upon it" (Selye, 1956). The stressors could be "any demand" such as toxins, x-rays, high temperature, starvation. All of them would produce the same response in time, the General Adaptation Syndrome (GAS) – enlarged adrenals, shrunken thymus, and bleeding ulcers. These symptoms would emerge over time as the organism's physiology responded in an effort to cope with a stressor. These symptoms were the result of a system seriously out of balance, unable to return to a quiet state. Selye portrayed GAS as a three-stage process:

Stage I – Alarm

Stage I begins when some stressor triggers the organism's survival mechanisms. This stage is similar to Cannon's fight-or-flight response. Activation of the nervous and endocrine systems help to mobilize energy and produce other physiological changes needed for a quick response and survival, for fight-or-flight. The mouse sees the shadow of a hawk. A jolt of epinephrine is released into its blood stream, the heart speeds up, pupils dilate, neural impulses constrict vessel and shunt blood to the muscles of the legs, the mouse makes a run for cover. If it is a good day, the mouse will be hiding in its burrow as the hawk passes overhead. Safe once again, the mouse's physiology quickly returns to a state of homeostasis.

Stage II – Resistance

At this stage the stressor is persisting and the organism has to stay in high gear to survive. One example would be an experiment where a mouse is dropped into a tub of water. Somewhere in the tub is a little island that is just below the surface of the water. The mouse gets dropped into the tub, plunk! Survival alarms go off, the mouse swims around, it finds the little island, all is well. The body systems settle down and return to normal, homeostasis at work. The next day, the routine is repeated, with one exception – there is no island today. The mouse has to just keep swimming to stay alive. There is no turning off the alarm, no rest. The mouse is on full alert, trying to find a solution. The biological system remains out of balance, in fight-or-flight overdrive, using a lot of energy, a lot of resources.

Stage III – Exhaustion

If Stage II persists long enough eventually the organism will start running out of juice. The system is taxed beyond its limits, the engine can only run so fast for so long, then things start to fall apart. The signs of that breakdown, various diseases of adaptation, get expressed. If it is prolonged, death ensues. The engine has revved too high, gotten too hot, burned up its lubricant. It overheats and the engine block cracks. No more driving that car. Off to the junk heap. For humans, unremitting chronic stressors can result in a similar system crash and contribute to health problems such as arthritis, heart attack, kidney disease, cancer, and other serious illnesses.

Three Stages of the General Adaptation Syndrome
Invoked by any Stressor

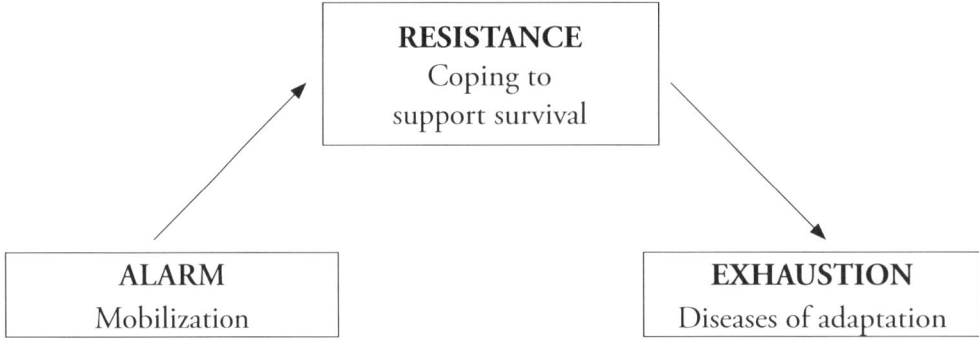

John W. Mason - Emotions and Stress

A third contributor to this body of research was John W. Mason. He was an investigator at the Walter Reed Army Institute of Research. Mason disagreed with Sale's notion that the stress response was the result of generalized stressors. Unlike Selye, who used unavoidable stressors that invariably triggered a stress response, such as injecting a known toxin or inducing physical trauma, Mason looked at the biological effects of different types of stressors, such as avoidable, unavoidable, and unpredictable stressors. He did not believe that stress was a nonspecific response to a wide variety of stimuli. Rather, he argued that the stress response, or lack of it, had to do with how the organism reacted emotionally to different types of stressors (Mason, 1968).

Mason believed that Selye's biologically-oriented model did not sufficiently consider the psychological aspects of stress. Importantly, he noted that emotional arousal was one of the most common reactions to many types of stimuli. In Mason's view, neither environmental events nor the person's internal state necessarily explained the stress response. He proposed that an individual's perception of the situation and the resulting level of emotional arousal was the key. Emotional activation was the trigger that set off the stress response. It was a mediating factor, between the stressor and the stress response. Working in a military research facility Mason had the opportunity to study frontline medics. He found that the level of corticosteroid response, a stress hormone, was not dependent on how dangerous the situation was, even during life-threatening events. He attributed this to psychological strategies such as perceived invincibility and religious beliefs. These buffered the individual's experience, quieting emotional reactivity, and thus quieting the stress response.

Richard Lazarus - Cognition and Stress

Another major contribution to the evolution of the stress concept came from the work of Richard Lazarus, a psychologist at UC Berkeley. Like Mason, he recognized that physical mechanisms and adrenal secretions did not answer the psychological questions about the stress response. Lazarus hypothesized that an individual's psychological perception (cognition) of the situation was the root of the stress experience. In his model stress was a transaction between the person and the environment that involved an appraisal of the situation. Lazarus argued that a situation must be perceived and appraised as threatening, challenging, or harmful for it to be stressful. For Mason, emotion was a key element. For Lazarus, cognitive appraisal of some stimuli as a threat was instrumental.

Lazarus described the first level cognitive assessment as primary appraisal, an evaluation of the stressor, whether it is seen as a threat. The individual makes an assessment - how big is it, how close is it, how important is it. After that first glance comes a secondary appraisal. During the secondary appraisal the individual considers the controllability of the particular stressor and individual capacity and resources to cope with it. Once the situation has been appraised a person can engage in various coping responses to address the appraised threat (Lazarus, 1966; Lazarus and Folkman, 1984).

Stress and the Body

When a stressor is encountered and perceived as a threat the body goes into a fight or flight mode to prepare us to respond. Whatever state of homeostasis the body was in is immediately disrupted. Rapid neurological and hormonal changes send information and resources to organ systems, muscle groups, the brain, to facilitate our survival. Mother nature at work to keep us alive (p.s. thanks mom, where would we be without you, uh, dead!). One key player in this bodily stress response is the autonomic nervous system. It is called autonomic because its processes are largely automatic and outside of conscious control, such as regulation of heart rate, respiration and digestion.

The autonomic nervous system is composed of two branches, the sympathetic and the parasympathetic nervous systems. The sympathetic nervous system (SNS) is located in the thoracic and lumbar segments of the spinal cord (mid and lower back). Branches from these spinal segments go out to innervate key target organs such as the heart, kidneys, and liver. During times of stress the sympathetic nerves release the messenger chemical epinephrine to activate these organs for appropriate fight-or-flight activity. The resulting sympathetic responses include making the heart beat faster and stronger, both of which help to get blood and energy to large muscles. The SNS also constricts blood vessels of the skin to reduce bleeding from trauma, releases glucose from the liver for increased energy, and decreases digestive activity to conserve energy. All of these prepare the organism for action. The *para*sympathetic nervous system (PSNS) is the counterpart. It is like a *para*medic, coming to the rescue to help quiet thing down. PSNS activities include slowing the heart rate, facilitating digestion and increasing sexual arousal, all things chill. The PSNS nerves begin at the cranial and sacral segments of the central nervous system, neck and sacrum/tailbone region.

The other key player in this process is the body's stress hormones, especially epinephrine and cortisol. When a stressor or threat is perceived the hypothalamus, a small neuroendocrine organ in the brain, activates the sympathetic portion of the autonomic nervous system, which then stimulates the adrenal medulla. The medulla is the inner portion of the adrenal gland, which is a small endocrine organ located on top of each kidney. When the medulla is stimulated it secretes epinephrine into the blood stream. Epinephrine is a hormone that helps to prolong the general sympathetic fight-or-flight response (it keeps things revved up). In addition, the hypothalamus triggers the pituitary glands, which then release a hormone into the bloodstream stimulating the adrenal cortex, the outer portion of the adrenal gland. The activated cortex releases hormones used in food, water and electrolyte metabolism to help the body cope with stress. One of the most important of these is cortisol, a major stress hormone. Cortisol tends to be pro-inflammatory. That is one of the reasons you get swelling around a physical wound. Today researchers see inflammatory responses in the body as one the roots of many types of serious diseases, including heart disease (Libby, 2006). When cortisol release persists over prolonged periods due to chronic stress it can have a significantly damaging effect on the body, the result of a system out of balance.

Stress and the Mind

Stressful situations often feel unpleasant. The knots in the stomach, the anxious or angry thoughts, none of that is fun. Maybe one of the reasons stress is designed that way is to make sure we learn.

If everything is neutral, if dangerous things are emotionally neutral, there is less memory residue, less of an imprint, less of a reminder to avoid that place again, to watch out when that animal is within sight, or to not eat that plant. The amygdala, an important part of the limbic system, is intimately involved in learning (Gallagher & Holland, 1994). The amygdala helps give a memory its emotional tone, especially fear. If fear imprints with an experience, a sense that something is not so safe, possibly a threat, it is more likely to be remembered. We learn. In this way the mental and emotional layers of the stress response help to keep us alive. The problem with this emotional aspect of stress, however, is that it can also ultimately keep us from doing things that are good for us, like learning how to ask someone out, or speaking in public, or risking shame by taking another challenging math class.

Our minds can be a great resource or a great liability, depending on how they are trained and used. If the conditioned mind associates a particular event with fear then a natural behavioral response would be avoidance, and avoidance means no new learning and no change. By gaining some basic knowledge of how this mind-body system works, we can begin to work with it more skillfully over time.

Stress and Disease

Learning how to deal with stress is essential for well-being. There is a clear association between stress and chronic disease (Cohen et al., 2007; Selye, 1976; Thoits, 2010). The CDC reports that half of US adults have one or more chronic health conditions like heart disease, cancer and diabetes. It is estimated that about $1.13 trillion dollars was spent on healthcare in 2007 and that about half of that was for individuals with one or more chronic conditions. Health expenditures for individuals with multiple chronic conditions is about five times more than for individuals with one chronic condition (Conway et al., 2011; RWJ Foundation, 2010; Ward et al., 2012). For many common chronic diseases stress can be an important contributor. Stress also affects emotional health, contributing to chronic anxiety and depression. These emotional states are often associated with less productive coping behaviors, such as smoking, drinking and drug misuse, that can also contribute significantly to negative health outcomes and other consequences to society.

Coping with Stress(ors)

Coping is the effort we make to manage the appraised challenge or threat (real or not) and the activated fight-or-flight response (our physical and mental arousal). There are many ways that coping strategies have been organized. Two common organizational themes you find in the literature are problem-focused and emotion-focused coping strategies (Carver et al., 1989; Skinner et al., 2003; Lazarus and Folkman, 1984). For our purposes we will use a slightly different way to consider coping strategies: (1) how to deal with the stressor, ***the problem***; and (2) how to deal with the internal stress response, ***our state of mind and body***. We will refer to them respectively as – *problem focused coping* (how we deal with the problem, the cause of stress, the stressor), and *state focused coping* (where we deal with the mind-body state, the internal response to the stressful situation). We could also think of them as *stressor*-oriented coping and *stress*-oriented coping, managing the cause and the effect.

> *Problem focused coping* (the stressor) *State focused coping* (the stress response)
> (How we deal with the problem)   (How we deal with the mind-body state)

Problem-Focused Coping (Managing the Stressor, the Cause)

Problem-focused coping occurs when the individual focuses on the problem, moves toward the stressor, the source of stress. Problem-focused approaches can be equally effective and ineffective, like any attempted solutions. If we were to look at the Wheel Model these solutions would more typically be related to working at the Environment level. As an example, you are driving your car along a country road and suddenly you hear a loud thud. You just hit a deep pothole filled with water. In about a minute your car is making a thumping sound. Your heart is probably going a bit faster, some muscle tension. You pull over to the side to see what happened. A quick walk around the car reveals a flat rear tire. This is a problem, a challenge. You reflect on your resources – no cell phone, little cash, probably spare tire and jack in the trunk, limited experience changing a tire. As with many things in life there are options here. Sitting in the car cursing your fate and weeping inconsolably, torching the car and walking away from the blazing heap like an action hero, waiting for someone to come by to give you a ride to town, or changing the tire. A problem focused coping strategy is to focus on the problem at hand and deal with it, to address the stressor directly. In the case of the flat tire one of the more effective problem focused coping solutions would be to change the tire. Another proactive solution might be to signal other drivers to see if someone could help out, possibly a lift to town or a cell phone to call a garage. If you are really good at problem focused coping you will have limited emotional activation around such an experience, you know the problem has to be handled, so you go about handling it as efficiently and effectively as possible. It is what it is. "I don't know how to do this yet but I will learn." You think to yourself, **"I maintain balance. If there is a problem I work diligently to manage it and resolve it."**

State-Focused Coping (Managing the Stress, the Effect)

The aim of state focused coping is to bring the internal state back into balance, to modify or manage the internal stress response, return to relative homeostasis, the pre-stress state. This includes bringing down physical arousal (body), quieting unhelpful thoughts (cognition), and calming fear and other negative feelings (emotion). In the Wheel Model this would be related to the Person level. Some typical state-focused coping methods that people use include drugs and alcohol, shopping and food. These methods temporarily distract the individual from the source of their unhappiness and provide some comfort. If we are in a coma we do not perceive threat. If we are anesthetized we do not feel pain. There is a time and a place for everything, but there are several shortcomings with using methods like drugs and alcohol for coping. The first is that they can have their own negative consequences in the long run. The second is that they do not work on actually resolving the problem. Finally, they can actually impair our ability to solve the root problem, because they can keep us stuck where we are. The Learning Life goal is to find methods that help to reduce stress but not with these limiting costs.

As an example of state-focused coping, Kathryn has a very important exam coming up in several months. Passing the exam is required for her to continue in the program. This is an elimination exam. If she does not pass it is all over, no second tries. High cost, high stress. Preparing for that big test brings up fear for her, thoughts of failure, uncertainty about her future, doubts about her ability. There is a growing sense of anxiety, resulting in more avoidant behavior. Instead of studying, which would be an effective problem-focused strategy, she is avoiding studying, cleaning the house, going out with friends, sleeping more. She knows this is not helpful, but the idea of studying is too distressing. This is the time for productive state-focused coping, using strategies to take the edge off, strategies to regain composure, to become grounded, to reduce drama, to get her head back in the game. Useful state-focused coping strategies could include building meditation or relaxation practices into her daily schedule, using exercise to burn off anxious energy, engaging in positive self-talk, and using imagery to build more positive expectancy. Such methods do not work on the problem directly – studying for the exam – which is the stressor. They do, however, help with the response, the internal stress response, and that can help her get back to a state of mind and body where she can once again study productively.

Coping Strategies – A Holistic Approach

Having a stress response is a good thing. It is part of nature's strategy to ensure our long term survival. Having an uncontrolled long term stress response, however, can be harmful to health and happiness. So what is the best strategy for effectively and efficiently coping with stressors and stress? It depends. One helpful way to look at coping with stress is from the Wheel perspective of Person, Behavior, and Environment. Each one of these aspects plays an important role in our approach to stress response and in our coping effectiveness. Learning to work constructively with these three spheres of life is a key to successful coping, skillful action, and thriving in the face of adversity.

I. The Environment

Recognize and Avoid Stress Triggers

On the Environment level of the Wheel there are many useful strategies for dealing with stress. One of the main things is to learn about what is out there that triggers your stress response, what your stressors are. Once you know those triggers you can avoid those sources of stress or learn to deal with them more effectively through reappraisal or new learning. Basic rule of thumb – if sad movies stress you do not go to them, same for all the rest. Reduce triggers. If you know you tend to get anxious before exams then do not set things off with a cup of strong coffee that morning. If you need coffee, then moderate your intake.

> **REFLECTION**
>
> Here are some things to think about in terms of understanding and coping with environmental triggers more effectively. Take a few minutes to answer the following questions and start building a map of your triggers, your typical responses, and some ideas for working with those patterns skillfully.
>
> 1. What experiences, things, events, places, thoughts, feelings did you find stressful, challenging, threatening, agitating, upsetting during the week or past month?

2. Why were these things stressful, challenging, threatening? What was it about them specifically? Think in terms of appraisal – resources, skills, personal history, reality, your strategies.
3. Do any of your beliefs about the world influence your perceptions?
4. If they do, where did those beliefs come from?
5. How do life stressors affect you – physically, emotionally, mentally, behaviorally, socially?
6. What do you do to cope with your life stressors? Specify the type of stressor.
7. How effective are those coping methods? What are the benefits? What are the costs?
8. What other resources/methods could you use to manage your life stressors?
9. What makes you feel relaxed, happy, optimistic, confident, generous, capable?

Use Your Resources
Cultivate your resources – people, places, things, skills, attitudes. Social resources, like close friends, are a great way to help reduce stress in life. Find places where you are productive, associate with people who support you, avoid what brings you down, move toward what makes you strong. Keep your environment clean and organized. Make your environment work for you.

II. The Person

On the level of the Person coping relates to what is going on inside, under the hood, the internal experience. The internal stress response includes body response (like heart and breath rate), stress related cognitions (thoughts like doubt and worry), and feelings, emotional experience (like fear and anger). Let us consider coping strategies for body, thought and emotions now.

Body
To deal with body stress, those jittery, queasy, cranked, me-no-like feelings, there are a number of useful and simple things you can do. First and foremost – relax. The word relax comes from the Latin *re-* again and *lax-* loosen. Relaxing is loosening again and again. Think of untying the knot, getting some space between the tight threads, loosening, letting go, letting blood and healing comfort begin to flow in and warm you, opening you. You want some space for the light to come through. Simple muscle relaxation can be a quick and simple first step to putting some chill into that stress response. If there is an unexpected loud noise behind you, the natural response is to momentarily freeze, stop breathing, and orient. The system locks, becomes tense. Letting go and relaxing is part of returning to balance. It is part of the ***para***sympathetic response. The paramedic is here. It is ok to relax now. One quick key to dampening arousal is to activate the parasympathetic system through relaxation. Relaxation moves us out of survival mode and back into a state of rest, recuperation and recovery. There are a number of simple ways to accomplish this.

Relax Your Shoulders
Here is one relaxation practice that is brief, simple and convenient. It takes about 5 minutes, and longer is good if you have more time. To do it sit or lie down comfortably. Close your eyes. Be aware of your shoulders, jaw and temples. First give yourself permission to relax, to feel better (sounds funny but it helps). Then with each exhale let the shoulders soften and relax. Give yourself

a gentle direct suggestion, "My body is relaxed. With each breath out my shoulders are softening, relaxing." The body listens to this type of direct suggestion. Do the same with the jaw. Let the jaw be loose, even let the mouth be slightly open for a minute or two. Tell yourself, "My jaw is completely relaxed." Then close the mouth but keep the jaw loose. Repeat the process with other areas of the face – eyes, temples, and forehead. Let the small muscles of the face really relax. Finally, integrate all three. On each exhale think to yourself, "With each breath out my body is becoming more and more completely relaxed. My face is relaxed, my jaw is relaxed, my shoulders are relaxed, my whole body and mind are completely relaxed." Let your mind and body enjoy any qualities of relaxation, feelings of heaviness, warmth. Be mindful, pay attention to any sensations of relaxation in the body. Feel the relaxation sensations. Let the mind penetrate and explore those feelings of relaxation. Spend some time there. This is also an excellent place to do some positive self-talk or some Priming. Describe the desired state, imagine it. When you are ready then take a moment, pull your shoulders back a bit, smile, and step back into the adventure.

Another version is to close your eyes, be present for a moment, then take several slow, deep breaths. With each breath in gently raise your shoulders toward your ears (this increases the sense of muscle tension in the shoulders). As you exhale let the shoulders drop down (this provides greater awareness of the contrast between tense and relaxed, and that reinforces the sensation of letting go). Tell yourself that with each breath out you are becoming more and more deeply relaxed. Do this for 10 deep, slow, refreshing breaths. If you want to incorporate imagery you can imagine breathing in courage, confidence, happiness, success and exhaling out fear, doubt, failure (inhale brilliant light and exhale rusty grey smoke). End with an affirmation, positive self-talk, and a positive Priming image.

Warm Your Hands
Another simple strategy is hand warming. When we are relaxed, in parasympathetic mode, the blood vessels in the periphery of the body (hands and feet) will be dilated, or more open. (One of the ways stress causes high blood pressure is by constricting the blood vessels resulting in less space for the same volume of fluid, so more pressure). During times of stress the blood is shunted from the periphery of the body (skin, hands, feet) to the core (brain, heart) and large muscles for fight-or-flight activity. That is why stress can cause cold hands and feet. (The expression "getting cold feet" indicates fear. It means the sympathetic nervous system has been activated to support survival in response to a perceived threat.) So one of the ways to shift the nervous system from sympathetic to parasympathetic is to make the hands warmer (to open the peripheral blood vessels).

To do this method, sit or lie down and get comfortable. Close your eyes. Rest your hands on your lap or at your sides, relax your arms and shoulders. Repeat to yourself, "My hands are warm, heavy, and relaxed." Consciously let go. Be mindfully aware of the surface you are sitting on – chair, couch, floor. Let go. Let that surface support you completely. Be mindfully aware of gravity gently pulling down on you. Continue repeating the phrase, "My hands are warm, heavy, and relaxed," and let go. You can also use your imagination. Visualize that you are resting your hands in a beautiful copper basin of warm water. You can also apply the same concept to the whole body. Starting at your feet tell yourself, "My feet are warm, heavy and relaxed." Work up the body in this way. "My calves are… My thighs are… My low back is…" Say it, feel it, let go.

Work with Breath

There is an area in your brainstem (base of the brain) that regulates breath, heart rate and blood pressure. Most of the core biological functions regulated at this level of the brain are automatic, generally outside of conscious control. Breath, however, is partially within our control. Using breath to modify bodily states is a powerful and effective approach to self-regulation. In ancient India there was an entire body of practices devoted to it, the science of *Pranayama*, or breath restraint.

One simple breath method that puts a dent in an overly activated mind and body is the **Fog Breath**. This is the same kind of breathing you do when you want to fog a mirror or clean your glasses. You close your throat slightly and breathe in and out, as if you wanted to talk like Darth Vadar (and who doesn't, seriously). You might even want to try it out, "Luke, I am your father." When you do the Fog Breath method you should be able to hear your breath. Take long, slow audible inhales and exhales, like fogging a mirror. Keep count in your head so the in-breath and out-breath are about the same length. Keep that going for 3 to 5 minutes. Most people will feel much more relaxed after you doing this for a bit. Finish with Priming mental imagery. See the desired outcome. Feel relaxed and confident.

Another simple breathing method, also useful when out in the world, is to breathe in healing energy, empowering energy, and breathe out fear, doubt, and stagnation. This is an old Taoist practice. You can imagine the empowering energy as sparks of copper light or warm mist and the exhaled energy as rusty gray sooty smoke. You can also inhale through all the cells of your body bringing positive energy in from the earth and sky. Then exhaling out where it immediately dissolves into nothingness.

Thoughts and Feelings

The next Person element to consider and work with is the mind, our thoughts and feelings. Negative thoughts and feelings can be one of the big reasons that people get locked into less constructive state-focused coping strategies. Everyone wants to feel happy. Some people turn to things like drugs, alcohol, sex, shopping, gambling, eating, and other distractions, to quiet the critical voice, numb the pain, stifle the self-doubt, lessen the anxiety. The obvious problem with those approaches is that they can have negative consequences in terms of health, relationships, work. A bigger problem is that these approaches do not get to the root of the problem. They also do not teach us how to become more skillful in managing the ups and downs of life. Thoughts and feelings can be a heap of trouble or a great resource. We want them to be resources. *The key is to recognize (be mindful) of these states, remember choice, drop the negative, and build the positive.* Here are some useful strategies.

Reappraise the Situation

Remember the work of Richard Lazarus? He observed how our stress response was influenced by how we appraised things. That is a BIG KEY. If we see something as a threat that will activate a stress reaction. If we do not perceive as a threat, no button gets pushed, no alarm goes off. If a four year old says, "Your hat looks funny," you will probably think its cute. If a forty year old gives you a look and says your hat looks funny, you will most likely not think its cute. Your blood pressure is likely to go up a bit, stress alarm has been signaled. A different appraisal happened, different attributions. Children do not have manners yet, do not really know what they are saying at times, do not understand social norms. Forty-year old adults should know better.

One way to keep the switch from getting flipped is to work with appraisal. Strategy number one and rule number one – do not take it personally. Who is attacked? You are attacked, threatened, insulted, accused. You, the big I (I-dentity). If we do not take things so personally, there is no one to be threatened. If no one is threatened there is no stress response. Good idea in life, do not take yourself so seriously. Strategy number two – remember your resources, such as remembering that you are a learner and a problem solver. "I don't know how to do that yet, but I…" You can figure it out. Strategy number three – make it fun, let it be a challenge, an opportunity to learn. "I am having fun now." "I am going to learn a lot working on this." Laugh and have fun with challenges when possible, why not! Even if things are difficult you may be able to find something to laugh about. Way better than complaining. Strategy number four – develop thicker skin. No drama. Remind yourself this is not big deal, reduce or eliminate drama, take care of business, do not let your chain get yanked easily, be professional, do it.

Reframe the Problem
When you are having a good time, like when you are chugging along in a 10k trying to beat your old time, or when you are speeding along in a go-kart racing with friends, your body will be in a fight-or-flight stress response mode. You are dealing with physical and mental 'threats', challenges, demands on the system to respond. It will be producing similar hormones as if you were being chased by a bear. The big difference – you did not ask the bear to chase you, so that is not fun, you might actually die. You did, however, choose to drive the go-kart. The two states of body chemistry have a lot in common. A big difference is how we interpret and experience the event. Both are stressors, but one is a source of negative stress or distress, and the other is what Hans Selye referred to as positive stress or eustress (Selye, 1974).

Image two students, one loves speaking in front of the class and the other is scared to death. It is the same event but experienced very differently because of how the two students differ in their perceptions of that single event. One sees it as simple, or fun, or a growth opportunity. The other sees it as a place for shame, a reminder of a previous failure, or any other number of negative associations. One strategy that can be productive in such cases is to take the 'negative' and spin it into a positive. That is called reframing. It is a process of looking for the good, making it work. Sure your body is feeling some extra energy. The reframe on that is, "I am jazzed, pumped, ready to rock." That is indeed what the stress response energy is there for. It is there to help you rock and roll with the bear (heaven forbid). "Let's do this bear!" So you can recognize that and remind yourself that the energy you feel is actually good. It is "let's do this" energy. The mind is a very flexible tool if used accordingly, make is a resource to help you. Remember the executives who did the best is Kobasa's studies? They looked at their life problems as challenges, places for growth, improvement and accomplishment. That was a big reframe of their personal experience.

A final reframe strategy is to have a few phrases in memory, at your disposal, to help you quickly change perspective. That is one of the reasons we memorize aphorisms in this book. Each one of them is a very specific phrase for use in moments when we need to shift perspective because we are stuck in an unproductive point of view. Here are some useful reframe lines that students in this course have found productive:

"I don't know how to do that yet, but I will learn."

"It is what it is."

"It is okay to not feel okay."

"If there is a problem I will work diligently to manage it and resolve it."

"I will handle this."

"This too shall pass."

"Never give up."

"This is fun/great/interesting! I am learning something new."

"No drama."

Work With Your Goals

Remember your goals. If you have strong, clear goals they will pull you through a lot of tough times. Develop your goals and then live them. Recommit to those goals on a regular basis, daily is best. Think of your key goals when things are tough. Let your goals inspire you, keep you going. When people have important goals they are less likely to let obstacles in their path stop them. They just keep looking for ways to get to where they want to go. They find a path.

One of the goals for a successful Learning Life is to learn to handle stress more gracefully, learn to maintain composure, maintain equanimity. Easier said than done, but a good skill to cultivate over time. People who stay cool in challenging situations will usually do better in the long run. I once met a fellow in the tiny town of Makawao, up in the mountains on the island of Maui in Hawaii. He had been successful in business and was able to retire young. He was a friend of a friend and I wanted to meet the chap and talk. We got together for tea. He told me, quite sincerely, that one of his goals was to see how relaxed he could become. I suspect he has succeeded at that too.

Employ Targeted Imagery & Priming

Mental imagery is another productive way to cope with stress. We learned about Priming in Chapter 3. You can use this approach to Prime your day, if it is going to be stressful. Or you can Prime specific stressful events, like preparing for a big speech. Think of the desired state. Get relaxed. See yourself in that desired state. See the scene the way you want things to work out. Bring in positive emotion, confidence, even if you need to bring it in from some previous positive experience, that is fine. See it, feel it, release it, then go do it.

You can use your imagination to help you manage stress. Just see yourself in a beautiful place in nature, looking relaxed and very peaceful. Listen to the sounds of nature, describe to yourself what is there, see it, enjoy it. This can be an imagined place or an actual beautiful place in nature you have been to. Take a moment to really be there in your mind again. In short order your body will be there as well. If your mind recalls a specific memory the physiology of that memory will return as well in your body. That body memory is part of the recollection. Right now, if you close your eyes and think of a beautiful sunset you will probably notice how the body becomes calmer.

A related imagination method is to have a conversation with your inner warrior self or with an inner ally or wise teacher. You could converse with an inner power animal, which brings you strength and protects you. Even today in modern India people will make offerings to the elephant headed Ganesh to get support for new journeys and important activities. To do this type of imagery practice you begin with relaxation, closing the eyes and getting quiet for a moment. Start to see and describe, mentally (or out loud if you wish), the image of your inner warrior, ally, teacher. If you get no image you can say to yourself, "Just pretending, if there was an image of my inner wise teacher what would I see," then just start describing, pretend. It will be there, an image or a sense of what the image would be.

A final technique is to work with the stress sensations in the body, combining mindfulness and imagery. Here is how it is done. When you are stressed do a body scan. Find the strongest stress sensation in the body. Let the attention go there. Concretize that sensation. With eyes closed ask yourself, "If it had a color, what color would it be? If it had a shape, what shape would it be? If it had a temperature, what temperature would it be?" Allow yourself to sense those qualities of color, shape and temperature. Then ask yourself what the antidote or opposites of each of those would be. "What is the antidote color, shape, temperature? What would be soothing?" You will know what color calms and which temperature soothes. Once you get that information then start to breath in those antidote qualities until they are overflowing from your body. Breath in the soothing color, temperature, sound. Then just sit in that space for a moment.

STOP and Get Your Perspective

Whenever you need it apply the acronym STOP. No matter what four-letter word usually comes to mind when you are stressed, consider adding this one. This little device has found its way into many industries and applications – Snowmobile Trail Officer Patrol, Sort-Toss-Organize-Put Away, Security Tracking of Office Property, Stack Overflow Protection, and on and on. Here is another translation that is useful for more skillful in-the-moment reappraisal, self-management, and coping.

STOP

Stop -	Just stop, really, just stop. Think "Stop." Then do that, just stop. Then remind yourself -
	"If there is a problem I will work diligently to manage it and resolve it."
Take a breath -	Key, not watching breath, that can provoke anxiety. Take some *deep* breaths!
Orient -	Get a sense of where you are, what the challenge is, what your resources are. Appraise. Ask yourself, *"What is the most important thing for me to do right now?"*
	If the answer is run, then you might just want to get up and do that. Run!!!
Proceed -	Fight, flight, freeze, push, pull, laugh, breathe, reappraise, any appropriate response.

Get Creative
Sometimes there can be something in life that is a fairly consistent cause of stress. You may work for one of them, por ejemplo. This is a great opportunity to apply the Learning Life Problem Solving Model. Current state, you are anxious when you have to give a talk in class (which it seems you have to do a lot this semester). Desired state, you want to be able to get up there, relaxed and calm, and give an excellent talk. That is clearly a learning opportunity. Possible solutions could include both problem-focused coping, like taking a class that focuses on communication and public speaking, getting some books on managing shyness and public speaking, and being very prepared for the talk. Other solutions could be state-focused, like priming an excellent talk, using positive self-talk before giving the speech, and starting a meditation practice to reduce anxiety in general. Use your big brain and come up with creative ideas to get a grip on life stressors. Manage them, reduce them, and eliminate them with transformations in Person, Behavior and Environment.

Recover From Crashes
Do top level athletes connect every pass, make every hole in one, dunk every basket? No, no way, in the land of time and space there are too many variables intervening for perfection to last. Change is a defining characteristic of the time-space matrix. It is built into the DNA of all life, into the very nature of all things. Nature is a process of decay and rebirth. Mother nature is **_Mother_** nature. Reproduction, recycling, renewal, rebirth is part of it all, endlessly. Will you make mistakes and fail. For goodness sakes we hope so. The person who does not make mistakes is living in a shoe box under the bed. The goal is not to be perfect all the time, that is a pipe dream. The goal is to have a vision, to go for it, to do your best, and when you do crash, to recover as skillfully, gracefully, and quickly as possible. Get back on the horse, giddy up, go. If it is important, and you sense you can continue to improve, then onward and upward. If you realize you are out of your league, good information, on to the next adventure. No shame, no problem, it is called learning.

III. Behavior

Adopt a Physically and Mentally Healthy Lifestyle
The final cog in the Wheel is Behavior, the things we can do, actions we can take, to address the stress in our lives. Constructive behaviors can include targeted problem-focused behaviors, like quitting a toxic job. They can be targeted state-focused behaviors, like using emotional self-regulation when dealing with difficult customers. Beyond that there are general behaviors that we can engage in that will increase our overall ability to cope more effectively. These include regular exercise and having a healthy diet. There is a large body of research on the physical and emotional benefits of exercise (Haskell et al., 2009; Penedo et al., 2005). Exercise will make you feel better, and when you feel better you cope better. You have more energy, you are more optimistic, you hang in there. Healthy diet and sufficient rest will also improve your ability to cope. That is one of the reasons that torture includes sleep deprivation. It wears a person down. It is a stressor. The fatigued person is ultimately less able to cope, more vulnerable, more compliant.

Be Assertive
Learn to stand up for yourself, move toward what you see as true and important, be assertive (being assertive has nothing to do with being an aggressive jerk, it has to do with speaking your truth,

saying what you need to say, doing what you need to do). A lot of people are less assertive than they realize. They do not go for what they want. *So much of life is lost in waiting.* If that is a weak link then get a book and learn about assertiveness, practice it, get better at it. If someone in your life talks trash to you, educate them to do otherwise. Let people support and encourage you. Find people who love you. Respect self, respect others, be respected. You deserve to be loved.

Practice Positive Self-Talk
Practice positive self-talk. When you see pro athletes of television sometimes it seems like they are quite arrogant, quite full of themselves. Maybe they are, but on some level what they are doing is using positive self-talk to increase their sense of self-efficacy. They need to believe they are the best. They do not want to have room for doubt. It is part of their practice, maybe unconscious in many cases, but useful for them. Pay attention (be mindful) of the mind stream. Notice what the internal voice is saying. If it is not helpful, change the channel. "I am not my thoughts." "I no longer accept that thought." Habits are learned. Habits can be changed. *Habit is conditioned mind, not true mind. True mind is quiet, clear and powerful.* True mind has the capacity to deal with life in the moment. More on this in Chapter 11 on Emotional Literacy.

Talk to Someone
Talking to someone about challenges can be a source of some good ideas as well as comfort. Find a friend you can confide in. Book a session with a therapist. Get ideas from your professor. Just telling someone who cares about you that you are having a tough time can be liberating. People are often much more willing to help than we give them credit for. Talking to people who have a few more miles under their belt. (older, been around), more specific knowledge in the area in question (training and expertise), can be very productive when looking for ideas in stuck places.

Take Action
Do it. Apply the 12-minute rule, take a small step, get started. Do something, just start. Get up, lift one finger and put it on the project for one second. Then praise yourself for taking a step. Never give up. Believe in yourself. There is an up after the down, everything changes. Work on solving the problem directly, a problem-focused approach. Work on creating a more resilient inner state of mind and body that is able to stay in balance when the waters get rough, a state-focused approach. Do not let fear keep you from living your life. Start with a small change right now.

Cultivate Equanimity

There is a great term in the Tibetan Buddhist tradition – calm abiding. It refers to a particular form of meditation, but it is also a useful concept, a nice image to keep in mind. Calm abiding is the essence of equanimity. It is being in the storm, but not of the storm. You are abiding in calm. You are in a place of equanimity. You have peace in your heart and mind. Composure. You are focused. You remain steady. When things are crashing and others are running blindly you are able to stay calm and find the way. Managing stress and coping are good. Composure and equanimity are better. No drama.

Meditate

Integrating meditation into your daily schedule is a great plan for longer term mind-body resilience. Twenty minutes in the morning is probably the best, but any practice is better than none. Refer back to Chapter 2 for information on Mindfulness Meditation for more specifics. If you do practice Mindfulness Meditation with some regularity you can cultivate awareness of breathing, returning to the breath over and over. In times of distress you can get out of your head and go back to that centering place, returning to awareness of the breath. Some find that helpful. You can be mindful of stress building in the body, or thoughts and emotions starting to spin. As soon as you notice you can start to tap the brakes on that spin.

That said, for some people, at certain times, being mindful of mind-body stress just highlights how out of balance they are. Mindfulness might not be the ticket at that point. Fortunately there is another profoundly helpful meditation techniques that focuses attention on an 'object' other than the stress. These types of concentration methods (compared to open awareness methods like mindfulness meditation) are helpful for developing the ability to stay on task, the ability to concentrate on one thing. That means being able to focus on something other than the feelings of stress. That narrowed field of attention reduces the other noise signals and helps to quiet things down. Concentration meditation techniques train the mind to maintain a stable, narrowed focus on a specific object. An animal in the wild needs to be able to focus attention on the piece of fruit hanging from a branch, while maintaining a broader awareness of the canopy above, if it hopes to eat and not be eaten. A prize fighter defends a small sphere, which extends the length of an arm or leg, while simultaneously recognizing and using the bounded space in which he or she is fighting. Both forms of attentional capacity, narrow and broad, have obvious survival value and are part of our natural neurological capacity. Just like muscles can be strengthened, our ability to focus can be trained and made stronger, and that strength will contribute significantly to learning and growth. Here is a simple and effective method in the concentration method category. It is called the *Hum Sah* mantra meditation.

Hum Sah

The word *Hum Sah* is a mantra, or mind object. The goal of a concentration meditation is to simply focus the attention on the object of meditation. Those objects can be images, body sensations, words and other vehicles. In this particular meditation the object is a sound, the mantra, *Hum Sah*. The word 'mantra' is an ancient Sanskrit term that can be translated as mind vehicle. So a mantra is the vehicle one rides into deeper meditative states of concentration. If the mind wanders then the task is to gently bring it back to the object. In this way the attention is trained to stay on target, to stay on task. In time the mind becomes more capable of sustained single pointed focus, a very useful quality.

To do this particular method you will sit quietly, eyes closed, paying attention to the breath. Breathe through the nostrils. With the inhale think the word *Hum*. With the exhale think the word *Sah*, or a repetitive "*Sah, sah, sah.....*" for the duration of the exhale. If you like you can imagine a sphere of light in the heart region or between the eyebrows. The light can be any color, but a traditional color at the heart is green and at the brow a darker blue. As you inhale the light expands slightly and as you exhale it contracts. Stay with the sound and breath but do no not force it. Let it be easy, almost spontaneous. Do this for about 5 minutes in the beginning and work up to 20 minutes over time.

Final Thought on Meditation

Why meditate, either style, mindful or concentration? Major reviews of meditation research, all types of meditation, over the past several decades tend to report positive benefits of meditation for physical and mental health and overall well-being (Chiesa & Serretti, 2010; Goyal, 2014; Luders, 2009). Cognitive benefits included greater capacity for sustained attention, and fewer intrusive thoughts. Physiological studies showed that during meditation there is reduced need for oxygen, reduced heart rate, respiration and blood pressure go down, and coherence between heart rate and breathing go up. All of this correlates with greater perceived calmness and relaxation. Changes in electrical activity of the brain, measured in EEG, include increased alpha and theta activity, hemispheric synchronicity, dehabituation, and specific cortical control (all good). Effects on the cardiovascular system include changes in heart rate, blood pressure and hypertension, and redistribution of blood flow. Studies measuring blood chemistry noted beneficial changes in adrenal hormones, thyroid hormones, total protein, lactate, white blood cells, red blood cell metabolism, and cholesterol. Effects on metabolism included beneficial changes in metabolic rate, muscle tension, skin electrical resistance, brain metabolism, salivary changes, body temperature, and exceptional body control.

Studies on meditation also showed benefits in the treatment of a variety of illnesses including cancer, chronic pain, asthma and other problems. Psychological changes included shifts in perceptual ability, reaction time and motor skills, deautomatization, field independence, concentration and attention, memory and intelligence. Psycho-emotional changes included increased empathy, creativity, and self-actualization. Transpersonal changes include greater equanimity, detachment, energy and excitement. Meditation is probably good for most people, but like everything, may not work for all. There are many types of meditation and mind-body practices out there. You just need to find the one that works best for you. One study comparing four common approaches found that novice meditators showed equal preferences for both mindfulness and Hum Sah concentration styles of meditation (Burke, 2012). There is no one right way. The right way is the one that works best for you. No matter what approach, the idea is to cultivate more of an ongoing quality of ease in life, a quieter mind and heart.

Be Mindful

Skillful means refers to the Buddhist concept of dealing with life effectively. One aspect of skillful means is responding less stressfully. Keys to that – practice mindful awareness, cultivate equanimity, and apply continual improvement principles in all that you do. Being mindful is a foundation, a key to managing the ups and downs of life. Some helpful mindfulness questions that can improve our coping effectiveness include the following:

1. Where am I right now? What am I thinking, feeling, experiencing, doing?
2. If stressed, why am I stressed out?
3. What is the perceived threat? What am I afraid will happen? What is the problem (visible or not)?

4. Is there a better way to do this? What are the best problem-focused and state-focused strategies to use?
5. What can I do in body, thought, emotion, behavior or environment that will make a difference here?

Notice what aspects of conditioned mind and body may be contributing to the experience of being 'stressed'. What old response patterns are operating that may no longer be useful. This can be quite subtle, but as you pay attention over time you will begin to see which responses are productive, and which are not. That simple process of recognition begins to build in choice. The responses that are less productive can be removed over time, step by step.

SUMMARY

In this chapter we considered the important role that the stress response plays in protecting us from harm throughout our lives. We also considered how this response can become over-active leading to less effective learning and reduced well-being. Major theories of stress, based on the work of Canon, Selye, Mason and Lazarus, were presented. Two approaches to coping were presented – problem focused coping and state focused coping. Ideas for addressing the sources of stress and the mind-body responses to stress were examined from the perspective of the Wheel – Environment, Person and Behavior. Methods ranged from body relaxation, to mental reappraisal and reframing, to modification and removal of triggers from the environment. The final section on equanimity proposed a practice of meditation and encouraged the cultivation of quiet mind and heart.

MIND-BODY

Sitting Meditation

This week focus on body scanning. During meditation let the mind move through the body and experience physical sensations, both ones you find positive and negative. Be with them. Notice how the mind reacts to them, the stories that emerge. If you find one that is less pleasant practice remaining there for a bit, learning to be okay with not feeling okay. Then breathe into it and move on. Find any place of relaxation and similarly allow the mind to linger there and to go deeply into that sensation. Go deep into the physical place of relaxation and see what happens.

Mindful Awareness

Pay particular attention to tension in the body this week. Periodically STOP, take a breath, scan the body. If there are any places of tension, straighten up a bit, take a deep breath, then let it go. Remind yourself that you are cultivating more equanimity in your life.

Priming

Plan your goals for the week. Use priming mental imagery to see the most incredible week semester of your life so far. Also, take some area in your life that may be a source of stress right now, like an upcoming exam or a phone meeting. Take a few minutes each day to Prime a successful outcome. See yourself managing that confidently and effectively, accomplishing your goal and moving forward in life.

REFERENCES

Burke A. Comparing individual preferences of four meditation techniques: Zen, mindfulness, qigong, and mantra. *Explore: the Journal of Science and Healing*. 2012;8(4):237-242.

Cannon WB. *Bodily Changes in Pain, Hunger, Fear and Rage: An Account of Recent Researches into the Function of Emotional Excitement*. New York: D. Appleton; 1915.

Cannon WB. Organization For Physiological Homeostasis. *Physiological Reviews*. 1929;9:399-431.

Carver CS, Scheier MF, Weintraub JK. Assessing coping strategies: A theoretically based approach. *Journal of Personality and Social Psychology*. 1989;56(2):267-283.

Chiesa A, Serretti A. A systematic review of neurobiological and clinical features of mindfulness meditations. *Psychological Medicine*. 2010;40(8):1239-52.

Cohen S, Janicki-Deverts D, Miller GE. Psychological stress and disease. *JAMA*. 2007;298(14):1685-1687.

Conway P, Goodrich K, Machlin S, Sasse B, Cohen J. Patient-centered care categorization of U.S. health care expenditures. *Health Services Research*. 2011;46(2):479-490.

Gallagher M, Holland PC. The amygdala complex: multiple roles in associative learning and attention. *PNAS*. 1994;91(25):11771-11776.

Goyal M, Singh S, Sibinga EM, Gould NF, Rowland-Seymour A, Sharma R, Berger Z, Sleicher D, Maron DD, Shihab HM, Ranasinghe PD, Linn S, Saha S, Bass EB, Haythornthwaite JA. Meditation programs for psychological stress and well-being: A systematic review and meta-analysis. *JAMA Internal Medicine*. 2014;174(3):357-368.

Haskell WL, Blair SN, Hill JO. Physical activity: health outcomes and importance for public health policy. *Preventive Medicine*. 2009;49(4):280-282.

Lazarus R, Folkman S. *Stress, Appraisal, and Coping*. New York: Springer Publishing; 1984.

Lazarus R. *Psychological Stress and The Coping Process*. New York: McGraw-Hill; 1966.

Libby P. Inflammation and cardiovascular disease mechanisms1,2,3. *American Journal of Clinical Nutrition*. 2006;83(2):456S-460S.

Luders E, Toga AW, Lepore N, Gaser C. The underlying anatomical correlates of long-term meditation: larger hippocampal and frontal volumes of gray matter. *NeuroImage*. 2009;45:672-678.

Mason JW. Organization of psychoendocrine mechanisms. *Psychosomatic Medicine*. 1968;30:565-808.

Penedo FJ, Dahn JR. Exercise and well-being: a review of mental and physical health benefits associated with physical activity. *Current Opinion in Psychiatry*. 2005;18(2):189-193.

Robert Wood Johnson Foundation. Chronic care: making the case for ongoing care. Princeton, NJ: Robert Wood Johnson Foundation; 2010:16. http://www.rwjf.org/content/dam/farm/reports/reports/2010/rwjf54583 . Accessed December 23, 2013.

Selye, H. A Syndrome produced by diverse nocuous agents. *Nature*. 1936;138:32-32.

Selye H. 1950. The physiology and pathology of exposure to stress, a treatise based on the concepts of the general-adaptation syndrome and the diseases of adaptation. Montreal: ACTA Medical Publishers; 1950.

Selye H. *The Stress of Life*. New York: McGraw-Hill; 1956.

Selye H. *Stress in Health and Disease*. London: Butterworth-Heinemann; 1976.

Selye H. *Stress Without Distress*. Philadelphia, PA: Lippincott Co; 1974.

Skinner EA, Edge K, Altman J, Sherwood H. Searching for the structure of coping: a review and critique of category systems for classifying ways of coping. *Psychological Bulletin*. 2003;129(2):216-269.

Szabo S, Tache Y, Somogyi A. The legacy of Hans Selye and the origins of stress research: a retrospective 75 years after his landmark brief "Letter" to the Editor of Nature. *Stress*. 2012;15(5):472–478.

Thoits PA. Stress and health. major findings and policy implications. *Journal of Health and Social Behavior*. 2010;51(1):S41-S53.

Ward BW, Schiller JS, Goodman RA. Multiple chronic conditions among US adults: a 2012 update. *Prevention of Chronic Disease*. 2014;11:130389.

Cultivating Emotional Literacy 11

I recognize thoughts and feelings.
I am not my thoughts and feelings.

CHAPTER THEMES
- The Nature of Emotions
- Emotional Dysregulation
- Emotional Literacy
  - Person, Behavior & Environment

Humans experience emotions. Our emotions can be a very rich resource. When perceived and displayed unskillfully they can also be the root of many problems. One thing is for certain, an absolute key to success in life is the ability to recognize and work with emotions constructively. In this chapter we will consider the neuroanatomy of emotions and emotional dysregulation, explore the elements of emotional literacy, and learn strategies for displaying greater emotional competence.

The Neuroanatomy of Emotions

There are a number of structures in the brain that are intimately involved in our emotional experience. One area of central importance is the limbic system. Key structures in the limbic system include the orbital frontal cortex, cingulate gyrus, hippocampus, hypothalamus, amygdala, and related areas of the thalamus. One of the jobs of the amygdala is integrating various areas of the brain involved in emotional experience. Projections from the amygdala to the brainstem allow unconscious activation of basic body functions like heart rate and sweating. Projections to the prefrontal cortex allow us to be more aware of and think about how we feel, "I am mad, but I will not raise my voice because that will not be helpful right now." The hippocampus, another part of the limbic system, is located in the medial temporal lobe (side of the head by the ear). It is involved in long term memory and learning.

The Nature of Emotions

Understanding our emotional experience is essential for optimal success in life. Although the jury is still out on what constitutes the core set of universal human emotions there is a good deal we do know. One contemporary model of human emotion describes it as being comprised of five key components (Scherer, 2005). The first component is *cognitive appraisal*. We make an assessment of the experience. "Jeez, did that person stumble or did he just push me on purpose? No, he definitely pushed me." The second component is the *subjective experience*. A feeling of anger rises up. Anger is a clear subjective experience. Generally you know when you are happy and you know when you are angry. These states of body-mind are subjectively very different from each other. Third, there are *physiological changes* associated with emotions, we feel our feelings, feelings are visceral. An emotion is associated with a corresponding change in physiology. Fourth, there is a *motivation to act*. The word emotion actually comes from the Latin *ex-* and *movere*, which means to move, move from, or something resulting from movement. Walter Cannon described emotions as the energy that moves an organism to action, fight (rage) or flight (fear), for the purpose of self-preservation (Cannon, 1915). Emotions are activating, anger makes us move toward, fear makes us move away. This an essential element of Nature's strategy to keep us alive. Fifth, the *emotion communicates information* essential in the complex social context of human interaction, the social environment. The other person sees your smiling or your furrowed eyebrows. Both of those emotional expressions convey important information to everyone who can see them.

In his book, *The Expression of Emotions in Man and Animals*, Charles Darwin had similarly argued that emotion was an important component of human communication as it helped us to understand each other, to know what the other is thinking and feeling. One question that has persisted, however, has to do with the universality of that emotional expression. In an effort to understand whether the information provided by emotion was universal or influenced by cultural differences psychologists Paul Ekman and Wallace Friesen conducted a simple cross-cultural study exploring human emotion and facial expression. Travelling to an isolated region of Papua New Guinea they presented a group of pre-literate tribal people with a series of pictures of faces and stories. The study participants had to match the emotion of the face with the story. Ultimately, the participants matched faces with stories the same way any New Yorker would (Ekman & Friesen, 1972). All around the globe, in some very isolated locations, individuals recognized and correctly matched the pictures and emotional content of the stories. Through their work, Ekman and colleagues came up with their core list of human emotions - anger, disgust, fear, joy, sadness, and surprise.

So the individual who perceived that he was pushed, made the appraisal, "That jerk did that on purpose." That perceived push was unconsciously interpreted as a threat. A subjective sense of anger comes into awareness. His physiology has changed, his stress response switch got flipped, preparing him to respond, heart rate and blood pressure rising. There is a motivation to act. "I should tell that idiot to not be pushing people!" He is now communicating this information through non-verbal cues including tightened eyes and a more erect posture. He feels anger and non-verbally communicates that message.

Emotional Dysregulation

The way individuals works with their emotions can impact career potential, success in intimate relationships, productivity, how happy they feel from day to day, their sense of self-worth, health, and even the length of life. Consider anger and fear, the core emotions of fight-or-flight. Research has found that people who show more hostility and cynicism in stressful situations tend to have poorer health outcomes. One study looked at mortality rates related to anger and hostility over a 20-year period. Individuals who ranked in the top 20% for hostility had a 42% greater overall mortality rate (Shekelle et al., 1983).

Anxiety, another very prevalent mental health challenge, can have similarly deleterious effects. Test anxiety, as one example, is a common problem with obvious implications for academic success. Research has found that in stressful test situations it is not uncommon for most students to initially get diverted from goal directed behavior. First contact with the stressful test can evoke feelings of frustration and doubts about self-efficacy. Students with lower test anxiety soon recover, however, and return to task focus. Students with high test anxiety, by contrast, experience an impulse to withdraw completely from the perceived threat, the test (Carver and Scheier, 1988).

Depression is another common emotional experience. Although most people will experience periods of sadness in their life, for some the experience can be quite deep and persistent. National survey data examining both one year and lifetime episodes of major depression found rates of 5.3% and 13.2% respectively (Hasin et al., 2005). Depression is common in the 18-29 age group. A study by the American College Health Association found 30% of college students reported experiencing significant depression at some point during a one-year period (ACHA, 2012). Factors contributing to depression (and other emotional challenges) can include genetic factors, life experiences including abuse, stress and loss of a loved one, hormonal changes, chronic illness, diet, drug and alcohol use, medications, and other roots. Symptoms of depression include feeling sad, hopeless, alone, having a sense of guilt. Physical symptoms include fatigue, disturbed sleep, impaired memory, changes in eating habits, and loss of interest in normal activities.

Emotional Literacy

Emotion is universally experienced by humans, in every country and culture. It supports survival by informing us of possible reward or threat and preparing us for action. Through facial expression and other paths it also provides information to others, helping to maintain social systems. When emotions are dysregulated, out of balance, it can dramatically impact our effectiveness and well-being. If we appreciate the central role that emotions play in our human experience, then we can recognize how important it is to understand and work with emotions constructively. For that purpose we need to build our emotional literacy.

The practical measurement of intelligence began in 1905 when Alfred Binet published the Binet-Simon Scale with his colleague Theodore Simon. Since that time many others have contributed to our understanding of the construct of intelligence. Princeton psychologist Howard Gardner published the book *Frames of Mind* in 1983. In that work he broadened the conventional definition of intelligence. His model included a variety of types of intelligence, including verbal/linguistic, logical/mathematical, visual/spatial, musical, bodily/kinesthetic, interpersonal, and intrapersonal intelligence. In 1990 two psychologists, Peter Salovey and John D. Mayer, wrote a seminal paper on emotional intelligence, contributing yet another idea to this list of human intelligences. They defined emotional intelligence as, "the subset of social intelligence that involves the ability to monitor one's own and others' feelings and emotions, to discriminate among them and to use this information to guide one's thinking and actions" (Salovey and Mayer 1989-90). The concept of emotional intelligence was later popularized by Daniel Goleman in his book of the same title published in 1995.

Cultivating Emotional Literacy

Although emotional intelligence is a term you generally see in this area of research, it might not be the best choice of terms. Literacy is probably a better word. Intelligence is often associated with a more innate capacity. You are naturally good at it or not. The standard measure for IQ is an example. If you measure IQ at different points in time the score will be fairly stable. Literacy, on the other hand, is something that is more open to change. A person can go from being completely illiterate, unable to read his own name, to fully literate and well read. The purpose of this chapter is to provide strategies for the cultivation of emotional literacy.

Emotional literacy as we will explore it includes the following:
- Recognize our emotions as they are arising
- Discriminate and label what emotion we are experiencing
- Regulate our emotional states, such as the intensity and duration of a particular emotion
- Choose our behavioral responses to emotions
- Observe emotions and not act on them
- Convey appropriate emotional information to others
- Recognize the emotional states of others
- Work with other peoples' emotions appropriately
- Be able to influence others' emotional states.

Emotional literacy is about working with emotions effectively. It is basically about being able to recognize, regulate, and work with our emotions and those of others. Building emotional literacy is a continual improvement problem solving practice. To learn more about deepening emotional literacy we will look at some core strategies in relation to the Wheel perspectives of Person, Behavior, Environment.

I. Emotional Literacy - Person

Embrace Self-Confidence and Self-Respect
"I can do this!" Say it loud and proud. In previous chapters we have looked at the concept of self-efficacy. High self-efficacy is important for academic and life achievement. Self-efficacy, however, is about perceived competence related to something specific. A person might have high self-efficacy for bowling, but not for cooking. Self-confidence, by comparison, has to do with a broader sense

of competence, self-acceptance, and self-worth. A self-confident person believes in his or her ability to tackle problems in life. It is a form of personal optimism. When a person says, "I don't know how to do that yet, but I will learn," they are not arrogantly saying, "I can do anything." They are recognizing incapacity in the moment, but expressing a willingness to try, and a belief that mastery will come as a result of persistent, creative effort. Implicit in that statement is a recognition of self as learner, self as competent and capable, needing training to get there, but able to get there in due time.

There is some evidence that self-confidence is partially influenced by genetics (Saphire-Bernstein et al., 2011). Uh, okay, so what is not influenced by our genes? It is also very much a function of learned behavior and belief. Low self-confidence is a state of conditioned mind and body. It can be an old story that a person learned a long time ago, "You are not good at that (or much of anything). You will never be good at this. Other people do not expect you to be good at it. So don't even waste your time putting in any half-baked effort." The low self-confidence body-mind is geared to fail from the get go. There is no hope. No hope means no juice. No juice means insufficient energy, incomplete follow-through. Self-confident people are more willing to take a risk because they know they will figure out a way. Self-confidence is being willing to risk making a mistake, failing, looking stupid, and then doing it all over again the next day.

How to build it? Embrace your capacity to succeed in life – "I don't know how to do that yet, but I will learn!" Take small steps. Build on your incremental successes. Acknowledge your success. Use positive self-talk. Believe in yourself. Respect yourself. Self-respect has to do with our sense of worth, our value, our acceptability, our goodness, our lovability. When we respect someone else we listen to them when they speak. We hear what they have to say. We would never belittle, embarrass them, shame them, or intentionally hurt them. We would want to help them if they needed assistance. We would enjoy being with them. We would recognize that they possessed the potential to be highly competent. If we really respected them we would want to associate with them and learn from them, maybe even be like them. Directing those same attitudes and behaviors to self is self-respect.

Practice Mindful Awareness of Emotions
Emotional regulation has been defined as a conscious or intentional process that requires self-monitoring and results in greater insight and awareness (Gyurak et al., 2011). It is hard to work with emotions constructively if we do not see them, in ourselves and others. This may sound odd, but just pay attention to peoples' behaviors for a bit, to their emotional behaviors. You will begin to see how out of touch many people are with their emotions, and in some cases, how poorly they manage their emotional responses. They can be envious, jealous, angry, cynical or sarcastic, fearful, depressed, resentful and not have a clue (all of these have a strong emotional thread running through them). You observe mean-spirited, passive aggressive behavior from the same person at every work meeting. She may be totally clueless, just reacting, unconsciously, habitually, like a puppet on a string. A person's emotional patterns have roots, and those roots can be very old, very unconscious, and very strong, and can contribute to behavior that is very poorly regulated and unhelpful to them or others.

People can change, however. When we practice mindful awareness we let a little more light into the room. We can see more clearly, recognizing what is present. In time, with practice, we grow in our ability to notice emotions as they begin to unfold. We learn to step back and observe the feeling of rage or fear, without having to act on it, more able to choose, more able to be okay with not being okay. Over time, as we observe the same emotion arising consistently in response to certain triggers (people, places, things), we may begin to recognize a pattern, maybe even a sense of a root cause. Through observing in this way we also begin to understand the emotional patterns of others as well, the individuals we live and work with. This ability to navigate the emotional landscape of self and others is a very, very useful skill. It increases our ability to work more effectively with people, in addition to increasing our range of tolerance, patience and compassion.

Mindfulness Methods

One of the basic ways to work with sitting or active mindfulness methods for the cultivation of emotional literacy starts with noticing our emotions. Sounds easy and obvious, it is not. Pay attention when you notice an emotion, especially less productive emotions. Notice the triggers in the environment, listen to the story in your head, watch the responses you make or want to make, note the consequences of that pattern. Label the emotion. "I am glad, sad, bored or baked," (baked is not really an emotion, but it sounded good in the sentence). Then once you have noticed and labeled, do as the Zen monk says, "Don't just do something, sit there." *That* is a key to high-end emotional literacy – learning to witness and not act, to be okay with not being okay. Just hang with it. Notice and feel the anger or fear, and let it pass. If you can notice fear and not run, even if it is just taking that first small step of waiting an extra 30 seconds before shuffling off, you are pulling up the root.

Another very helpful practice is to get into the habit of noticing sensations in the body, during sitting or active practice, when you are having an emotional experience. You can notice and label the emotion. You can also notice the body sensation associated with the emotion. Emotions are embodied experiences, they are visceral. They are called feelings because we feel them. When a powerful emotion comes up you can get out of your head and into the corresponding sensation in the body. Why? Because it gets you out of your head, out of the story, and into a non-verbal, less gripping level. It can be a very useful practice for diffusing the emotional urge to act.

Remember Compassion and Forgiveness

A related practice from the mindfulness tradition is to bring in some compassion for self and other. This practice is known as metta. One of the roots of emotional upset is judgment, criticism. People pick this up from somewhere, family often, and then internalize it. They become their own biggest critic. If you could listen to their thoughts you would quite possibly hear criticism of others as well. Neither of these is hugely constructive. These are habits, habitual mind, conditioned mind. Such judgmental thinking locks confidence and happiness out of the house. Replacing them is a good idea. Replace with what? Acceptance, quieting of critical mind, praise, positive self-talk. What would a loving godparent say to the young child. It is that kind of encouraging voice. Does this mean papering over the mistakes? No, honest evaluation is essential, the main point is that you can evaluate and you can also obliterate. Both of them may even be presented as 'helpful' criticism. What is important is the energy behind the words. Joseph Campbell, a great scholar of world mythology, once said to not pay attention to what you say but to the feeling behind the words. What he was implying is that it is important to be conscious of what is driving our thought, speech and action, driving us from a deeper level. What we want to do is to bring more kindness into the picture, more acceptance, more encouragement. A simple starting point is taking a small step increase in positive self-talk every day, maybe in the mirror first thing in the morning.

Develop a Productive Relationship With Thoughts and Feelings
THIS ONE IS MUY IMPORTANTE. PLEASE PAY ATTENTION. It is important to reduce or remove the negative soundtrack in our heads, the negative self-talk, "You screwed up again, what an idiot." It is important to find the garbage hidden in the dark corners and to clear it out, to clear out the negative self-talk and negative imagery. It is especially important to mindfully be aware of any recurrent negative thoughts that diminish self-respect and self-confidence. Those are the voices that keep the dog from escaping electric shock. The dog hears, "No hope," so it does not even try. Sadly the collar may have fallen off many years ago, but the dog never relearned, the old conditioned body-mind pattern persists, because no new disconfirming information is allowed in.

When you hear the voices of negative self-talk the first thing to do it to recognize that they are not yours. They were probably put there a long time ago by someone else, does not really matter who put them there, what matters is that they no longer serve. They are a voice from the past. It is old learning, a pattern that is no longer useful. It is time for spring cleaning. The practice of mindful awareness is essential in working on this type of self-limited, conditioned thinking. Why? Because even recognizing those self-critical, self-limiting messages can be challenging. If those inner stories are long standing 'truths' they may be hard to see. Because they are the way it has been so long they become part of the landscape, they blend in. Again, the strategy with those less visible roots it to use mindful awareness. Start by noticing when confidence and self-respect get shaky, when judgment of self or other is raging, when anger or fear pop up, regularly, bigger than they should. That is a good place to look for old limiting beliefs, conditioned mind and body at work. Simple check, "Is this how I would treat a best friend?" If it is not, then there may be something to look at there.

When you do find some consistent, obviously no longer useful pattern of thought/feeling then just start by bringing mindful awareness to that space, with kindness. When you notice it simply say to yourself, "There it that thought again." Just notice, no judgment, no despair. The goal is to become less reactive to the old pattern, to not get engaged, tangled, to just let it flow through (takes time). It is like a student learning to play music by ear, noticing when she hears the C chord versus a D minor. It takes some time to train the ear. In time she begins to recognize the C more consistently. Since it is just a musical note there would be no judgment of the C, it is just a sound. "There is C again."

With mindful awareness and acceptance we slowly become less agitated when that voice, that message, comes through the neighborhood again. In time we learn to observe without judgment (again this takes persistence and patience, it is a learning process). The good news is, however, that each single time we engage in that practice we are building a new behavior, a new pattern, we are beginning to shift the old. What was automatic and unconscious is now slightly more visible. The flight path has been changed. *Transformative self-awareness is now engaged. It is no longer habitual.* New learning is occurring. Now there is light where there was darkness, maybe just a tiny bit, but even that helps us to see more than we could before.

So instead of being pulled into a tussle and kicked around, we just stand back a bit removed from the experience, and observe it. Like all things in the time-space matrix the moment will pass and the voice will change into something else. Over time this practice of mindful awareness and non-engagement with the old pattern can begin to shift things. The habitual body-feeling-thought loop starts to wobble. Instead of just getting angry we begin to notice anger arising, stepping back and observing the cause (maybe old habits), reflecting on the consequences (and a more skillful way of being), and we watch it fade. Instead of being afraid we begin to notice fear arising and fading. We do not step into the river, we just watch the waters rise and fall.

The strategy is simple, and the changes do not happen overnight. With patience and persistence, however, there is a good chance the loop will begin to soften and loose some of its grip because we are no longer responding in the same way. We are moving on, no longer dancing with that partner. Like ending a passionate dysfunctional relationship, a week after the split it is painful to see your old flame, two months later, a twinge and mild longing, two years later, much more clarity about why it did not last, quite possibly some gratitude for your wisdom and self-caring choice to abandon such an unproductive and harmful connection.

Label Thoughts/Feelings

One specific and highly productive mindful awareness strategy for developing a more productive relationship with thoughts and feelings is simply labeling the experience. Any unproductive thought or feeling that arises can be labeled, "I am worrying. That is an anxious thought," "I am feeling angry right now, having a mental argument with Melanie," "I am bored, tired, confused." Studies have found that the simple act of labeling helps to reduce activation in the brain's emotion centers (Hariri et al., 2000; Lieberman et al., 2007). Giving something a label creates a space between the thought or feeling and our conditioned behavioral responses. We have identified it, and that bit of information provides some degree of control, and control reduces stress and threat. That momentary buffer can provide enough breathing space for right action to emerge. The idea behind this strategy is to begin to call the thoughts/feelings out, to name them. "Claudine, I know that is you wearing the mask." This simple act of labeling helps us to recognize what is present. If what we see if not good for us, the more often we observe that loop the harder it will be to sustain it. We will want to change. In Learning Life this is the attainment of a natural clarity. In that light the old patterns will naturally begin to dissolve, like snow in the sun. That is true insight.

Besides labeling the thought exactly as it is – anger, fear, jealousy, worry, envy, shame – you can also apply more general labels. These general labels can then be applied to any thought or feeling. We will consider four types of labels, which can be used separately or together on the same target. That *first label* response, "That is a thought/feeling," is a very good place to start and possibly stay for quite some. Do not move through to the next levels expecting to dissolve patterns faster. You will know when to transit to the next level if you pay attention. Spending several months at each level, or more, is the best training strategy. The first level, "That is a thought/feeling. There is that thought again" (just noticing, not despairing).

After working for a few months with the fist level, the *second label* is, "That is a thought (or feeling). I am not my thoughts (or feelings)." The benefit of this phrase is that it helps you recognize and remember, that indeed, a thought is just a thought. **"*That is a thought. I am not my thoughts.*"** Now you are really beginning to deconstruct the pattern. You are laying bare the old disembodied voice, that thought, installed in the past, programmed to go off when presented with certain triggering events. It is conditioned mind and body pattern. It has kept a particular story alive, through time and space. Like a decommissioned satellite orbiting a distant moon, long out of service, it continues sending out occasional streams of data – "I will never be any good at this. They do not really want me to be part of this group. I can't figure this out, I give up." That satellite needs to be brought back to earth an unplugged. A variation on this label could be, "That is a thought. That is not my thought." If it is clear that the thought/feeling was an old message coming from someone else, not something one would ever be inclined to say about him or herself, recognition that it is not one's own thought can be helpful. The outside message gets recognized as someone else's unhelpful projection.

After six months or a year the *third label* is, "I no longer accept/embrace/support that thought/feeling/behavior." The benefit of that phrase is that it helps us to slowly separate from the pattern. It helps us to be less identified with it, to take it less personally. This third labeling practice could be applied to a particular inner story after working for some time with the first two labels, the labels of noticing and confirming that the old voice is just a thought and that we are not our thoughts. Again, that can take a while. No need to rush. Cultivating mindful awareness and non-judgment takes time and practice. The third label is a process of starting to disengage from that old inner relationship, you and the voice from the past. It is noticing the thought, recognizing it as just a thought and that you are not your thoughts, and then acknowledging, "I no longer accept or support this thought." End of story. Let it go. Very important. Do not get into an argument with the voice. Say your piece and let it be. If the voice needs to persist, no problem, you have already said what you needed to say. You have begun to change the relationship. This is an acknowledgement to self that the particular thought does not fit with your new commitment to self-respect and life success. Another variation on this level is to include the phrase, "That is not my thought." You are dealing with an old message, outdated, no longer useful, the type of thought that gets into our head and heart from family, media, history. It was never our thought. Over time we identified with it because it was pervasive and strong, but now it no longer serves us. "That is not my thought. I no longer accept that thought." No self-respecting one year old would speak negatively about herself (not that she would have much to say at one, but you know what I mean). Negative messaging is information acquired over time. It is not part of the original instruction set.

The *final label* is, "I no longer need that thought." This would be the last level to implement. It might start to feel natural after working with the first labels for a year or more, if you working on very old patterns. It is a statement of recognition and transition. The recognition is that the old pattern has shifted, whatever role the old thought/feeling had no longer exists. Time has past, things have changed. Learning, self-respect, increased agency/capacity, and growth are now the objective. There is no longer a need for the old thought/feeling. You say it and allow yourself to experience the feeling of not needing it. You say it and let it be. Things take time, but piece by piece a new foundation is built.

Any of these labels, from naming the specific thought or emotion to general approaches like recognizing we are not our thoughts, can be empowering because they move us from victim to agent. We are no longer letting the waves pound us into the sand. We are responding *like an aikido master* – no anger, no fear, *just working with the energy*. That is a thought, not good or bad, it is just energy, and I let it flow through. I experience this moment, touching the wild ocean, sensing the beauty of it all. That is Zen. No judgment, just labels. Noticing it the way we notice leaves falling from a tree, it just is, notice and release, non-attachment, non-engagement.

Develop A Positive State of Mind – Optimism and Gratitude
Another root of emotional literacy and resilience is a positive outlook, an "I can do this" attitude. Optimism is the foundation of positive mind. Being optimistic is not about being unrealistic. It is about being positive. Optimists believe that they have the capacity to make a difference and succeed. They recognizing that things do not always work out, but they understand that if they do not they can move on and try the next approach. Research shows optimism to be associated with better physical and mental health, better coping, and better academic achievement (Affleck et al., 2001; Andersson, 1996; Chemers et al., 2001; Scheier, 1987; Scheier & Carver, 1992; Taylor & Brown, 1988; Yates, 2002). Optimist are more likely to keep trying. The person who keeps trying is the one most likely to get into the castle.

Gratitude is another potent vehicle for regaining emotional balance. Gratitude is a recognition that we have enough, that we are enough. It is root of contentment, and a true foundation for peace of mind. "I love my job, I love my family and friends, I love my life." A very simple way to engage gratitude, as a vehicle for changing how you feel, is to do a quick reflection on what you are grateful for. Consciously look for the good in things and for the good in your life. "Look for the good and praise it," as the old bumper sticker says. Kobasa's hardy executives saw their life challenges as opportunities for growth. Another option is to make a list of all the things you are grateful for in your life. Do this once a week until you get into the habit of recognizing the good. Studies have found that a focus on gratitude versus hassles has a significant positive effect on subjective well-being, optimism, life satisfaction, and satisfaction with school (Emmons et al., 2003; Froha et al., 2008). Another simple but powerful little method can be done just before you fall asleep at night. It is a reflection of the day. Ask yourself, "What was the nicest thing that happened to me today?" Find one or more experiences and then let that sink it, feel a sense of appreciation for the gifts of the day. It will give you a sense of the generosity of life. It is also good for sleep hygiene as it helps you to look for the good at the end of the day and to fall asleep with a sense of abundance. It can be a great exercise with young children before putting them to bed at night, or to do as a couple if you sleep with someone, asking each other what the nicest thing of the day was for them.

> **REFLECTION**
>
> Take a few minutes to list some things you are grateful for in your life right now.
>
> _____
>
> _____
>
> _____

Finally, remember reappraisal. Stress is the mind-body response to threat, and threat is a function of our perception and habitual response patterns. The stress alarm goes off when we perceive something as a threat. Research shows that reappraising the experience, changing the way we frame it, can be a very effective strategy (Entman, 1993). The faster you grab the rope the faster you break the emotional free fall. Reappraisal can include reappraising the situation – is the 'threat' big, close at hand, likely to happen, what resources do I have to manage it, what has happened in the past (Gross, 1998b). As discussed in other chapters, engaging the prefrontal cortex early, which is related to control and thoughtful behavior, can help regulate the activation of the limbic system, and that can help to quiet the fear response (Goldin, McRae, Ramel, & Gross, 2008; Ochsner et al., 2002)

Just Have Fun

I remember when I first decided to start teaching publicly. I thought I would do a weekend workshop and enlisted a colleague to co-teach and host the event with me. Having an ally provided some moral support, as I was not feeling one-hundred percent confident about the whole thing (lower self-efficacy with a new undertaking). She agreed, we created our agenda, divided the work, and prepared for the training. I created marketing materials, put the word out, and people started to sign up. We rented a nice space for a residential retreat, hired a cook, and paid the deposit. We were ready to go. About a month before the event my colleague got cold feet and dropped out. I began to wonder if it made sense to do the event at all and started thinking about cancelling. I asked another friend for advice (a resource). She had quite a bit of experience in corporate HR, involved with hosting plenty of events in the past. Her suggestion was to do the course and to just have fun, to let it be fun. I thought, "I like to have fun." That was all I needed to hear, "Yes, do it, and have fun." I was back on track and off to the races. It turned out to be a great event and the beginning of a long stretch of work in training and consulting. I do not think I would have done it just for the money. When I realized that it could be fun, however, for both me and my guests, it immediately reduced my stress. It made the event intrinsically rewarding! Certainly, having fun cannot be the motivation for all of our work. Some of our life tasks can be a grind, maybe stressful, dangerous, or at the least thankless and unremarkable. But if it is possible to do so, then consider making it fun. When life becomes mere drudgery there is a greater risk of bogging down in the mud and snow and freezing to death. Joy is a positive, motivating emotion. Fun equals enthusiasm. Fun equals play, not work. Fun equals, "Where did the time go?" It makes any task lighter. In the face of some dull, routine task, remind yourself, "This is fun!" You may actually believe yourself long enough to get through the next stack before lunch.

Work with Imagery, Imagination & Priming

Although a big fan of mindful awareness I also feel that the method can be too passive at times. You notice that you are angry or in fear, great, now what. To be sure, just the process of bringing awareness to the moment begins to shift possibilities. However, is someone wanted to take that up a notch then bringing in some other strategies would be warranted. This is one of the reasons we use imagery in the Learning Life approach. It is self-directed, easy to do, highly flexible, and effective. To kick off this next level of working with old patterns one can simply notice the old pattern. When it is on the radar you can implement the AIR strategy with a series of questions. Start with *Awareness*. Ask, "What am I feeling/thinking?" That engages awareness. You label what is up, and also possibly localizing it, noting what it is and where you feel it in the body. Once you get a sense of that you can engage *Inquiry*, "Why am I thinking/feeling this?" You do not need to know the answer. Just ask. You can also ask the localized sensation in the body, "What do you need?" See what comes to mind. The third level is *Response*. This is where we can apply some imagery techniques to begin to work more assertively with old loops.

Modify the Sensation

As described in the previous chapter, one technique involves working with the sensations in the body that correspond with the target thoughts, feelings or behaviors. Again, the first thing is to note the thought or emotion and its corresponding sensation in the body. One big value of finding the sensation and centering on it is that it shifts attention away from the thought and emotion and into the non-verbal impersonal level of sensation in the body. Non-verbal means no story. That can be helpful sometimes. Once you have located the body sensation then ask yourself, "If this sensation had a color, temperature and sound, what would it be?" Imagine those one after the other (pretend, if it had a color what color would it be, what temperature, what sound). Be with that for a moment. Then ask yourself, "If there was an antidote color, temperature and sound for this sensation what would it be?" Just pretend that you know. It will come to you. Then begin to fill that body space associated with the old thought/feeling with the antidote color, temperature and sound. Let that space overflow with the antidote energy. Be filled with it, soothed by, empowered by it, healed by it. This practice provides a degree of control over the previously habitual response pattern. You start with representations of the stuck energy and you reverse their polarities. You are manipulating imagery-based attributes of the old pattern. Research shows that perceived control reduces stress (Glass, 1973). A related method is to locate the sensation and then ask the sensation, "What do you need right now?" Let your mind receive that message. It can be quite informative and get you to the root of what is needed in that moment to feel loved, safe, relevant, whatever else may be going on in mind and body that is causing imbalance. This can be especially useful if the current imbalance results in a negative projection of thoughts and feelings onto a current relationship, but based on an old emotional wound. If that might be the case it is helpful to recognize that pattern/theme, and work on healing that old stuck place, bringing in what is needed now to become complete and even more capable. This is a way to illuminate old limiting beliefs and moving more powerfully into the present.

Taoist Approach

A simple related practice is to first recognize the thought or emotion, then notice the internal corresponding sensation, and finally, breathe very deeply into that sensation. Imagine breathing in healing qi, healing energy, empowering energy, dissolving the old knot. Re-Lax, to loosen again and again, to untie the knot. Breathe in light and energy, and then exhale out whatever needs to removed. Breathe in fresh, breathe out stagnant. Like the method described above, this simple approach allows you to do something, to be proactive, bringing in something new to disrupt the habitual. It also provides some sense of personal control. It might seem insignificant, like a small step, but small steps help to make the journey. When we change our body we change our mind. When we change our mind we change our body.

Work with Inner Allies

One other creative imagery approach is to work with your inner coach, inner wise person, inner power animal, inner accomplished self, your favorite saint, angels, whatever speaks to you. These allies can offer encouragement, provide sound council, be a positive inner voice, bring calm or inspiration, or just be present. To set the stage the first step is to close your eyes, relax, and ask to meet your inner resource. Let the image come to you. You might be surprised. If nothing comes to mind drop into play mode and just pretend. You can ask yourself, "If my inner wise person had a form what would he or she look like?" You can then start describing to yourself the image starting at the feet and working up. You also might already have an image. If you work with a historic figure, like Jesus or Buddha, you have some idea or possibly even a picture or statue you can use. Once you have a sense of the form you can then start working with questions. You simply ask the question and see what information you get. You can also do this with a laptop. Ask the question and type down the information you get, not thinking about it, just entering the information to read back later. The inner ally can even be the adult-you protecting and guiding the child-you. Find out what that child needs, and let the adult-you provide it.

> **REFLECTION**
>
> Take a few minutes to describe an image, if you could see your inner ally right now what would that person/being look like?
>
> _____
> _____
> _____
> _____

In addition to doing this in your head you can also do it out loud (just keep an eye open for the mental health folks). You could get your own one-inch Buddha or plastic Jesus at some novelty store and have conversations with your miniature advisor. It sounds funny but it can be quite a useful process, and definitely entertaining. My one-inch Buddha sits on my kitchen table, has breakfast with me every day. He cracks me up. "How come YOU get two pancakes?" he asks, really quite funny. I just laugh, usually do not say anything back. When he is not looking I eat his pancake as well! I also work with crows. Whenever I hear them call I pay attention to what I am doing, saying or thinking. They offer me good advice in the moment in this way, making me more mindful of where I am, what I am doing and thinking. Wind spirit is another resource when out in nature, recognizing the profound presence of life moving every tree in the forest. When you work with these kinds of resources then you are never alone. You also can get a picture of someone you admire and ask the image for insights. Let that person be a coach, and ally, a true supporter. If you listen they will have something to say. Ultimately, where does that information come from? For some it might be divine intervention, and for others it will be a non-linear access to a creative inner resource, like the dream mind. You may be surprised at the value of the information you get. Allow the avenues of your imagination, your creative inner universe, to be an ally in your life.

Use Priming
Finally, use Priming mental imagery. Prime and see yourself as confident, calm, assertive, doing what you need to do. Prime your core life goals every morning. This general daily Priming practice will remind you of your dreams, and help you to carry those dreams deeper in your heart, where they can affect everything you think, say and do. Prime self-confidence and self-respect. Make imagery a regular part of your daily practice.

II. Emotional Literacy - Behavior

Keep a Journal
Reflective writing can be quite enlightening, a great way to get some clarity on questions. Keep a journal. This can be a daily log, perhaps at the end of the day, reflecting on successes and areas for improvement. It could be jotting down an insight or experience that seems important, or recording life successes. If there is an old pattern you want to work on another strategy is to pick the issue and spend about twenty minutes twice a week writing on it. Just sit and write. Do not edit. Do not worry about grammar and spelling, just write. When the twenty minutes is up, stop. When you start again in a few days for the next round just start writing again. Do no think about what you had written before. Just write. The main goal is to just get things on paper. The benefit of this kind of practice is that it provides a way to get things moving, to get it 'off the chest' and create a bit of space, dissociate it, make it less personal. This is also a helpful way to process things you may not be ready to talk about with someone. If it is too personal then maybe write it out in code and then burn it when you are done if you need to (make it a ritual). Research has found that individuals who journal about challenging events, including related feelings and thoughts, often end up with more insight than those who just write about their emotions or who do not write at all (Ullrich & Lutgendorf, 2002).

Use Positive Self-Talk
Self-talk is just that. It is talking to yourself, in your head during the exam, in the mirror before the job interview, out loud in the car before your recital, quietly under your breath on the baseball diamond. It is a very useful aspect of state management, self-regulation of thought and feeling. The goal of positive self-talk is to strengthen the positive voice, the coach voice, the ally voice, the best friend voice, the encouraging godparent voice. Most people have plenty of self-talk, inner dialogue, but most of that is not intentional and often it is negative. That is the voice of conditioned mind. The voice we are referring to here is positive, intentional, motivating self-talk, and research suggests it is useful (Bandura; 1997; Hardy, 2006). Some self-criticism, realistic self-appraisal of performance, is important for quality improvement. If we want to do better, or if we want to do our best, then we need to critically appraise performance (constructively, not negatively). Performance appraisal of that type is not a negative judgment, or self-criticism. It is a reflection on quality and a consideration how to do things better, how to make the process more effective and more efficient.

That is Kaizen. So we want to switch, "You screwed that one up" with, "The first approach worked but the second did not. I wonder what I could do differently next time."

Implementing self-talk is essentially talking to yourself as if you were your own best friend, as if you were a highly paid personal trainer or coach hired to get the client to the next level of the game. Self-talk can be praise, encouragement, a reminder, advice, a commitment, a reprimand. They can be very specific, "You are calm and will get this putt." They can be general, " I accept who I am. I love who I am. I continually work to improve who I am." You can write your very own inspirational pep song that you sing in the shower every morning. Karaoke for one! If you have a challenging job or are just not plugged in for the day the 'shower song' can be a good morning practice. Whatever helps you get ready for the day is good.

However you do it, the bottom line is that self-talk emphasizes self-respect and encouragement. When you succeed at something, maybe even opening a jar of peanut butter with flair, give yourself a high five, a pat on the back. Catch yourself in your successes. *Absolutely do not let the big accomplishments go by unnoticed*. Give yourself a medal, a reward, a "Job well done!" Recognize your success and remind yourself that "you did good," the way a loving parent would recognize the success of a child. That type of recognition and reinforcement is what builds agency and self-respect in a child. Do the same for self. There is considerable research on the role of self-talk as an important element in building self-efficacy in life (Bandura, 1997).

> **REFLECTION**
>
> Take a few minutes to come up with some positive self-affirmations, positive self-talk statements you can use during the day to keep you going.
>
> _____
> _____
> _____
> _____

Use Your Body

When people are depressed you can see it in how they hold their bodies. When they are afraid, same thing. Remember, part of emotion is our physical communication via body language. Indeed, some theories of emotion even hypothesize that it is the body that informs the mind as to what we are feeling, that the body is a key to our perception and understanding of emotion. Whatever the causal path, the body does play a big role, including the posture. If there is a posture of fear, there must be an equivalent posture of courage. If there is a posture of depression, there must be a posture of joy. If there is a posture of self-doubt, there must be a posture of confidence. If you go into any significant Asian art museum, like the Rubin Museum of Art in New York, you will find statues in very specific postures, and those postures have very specific meanings. In the ancient East these postures were referred to as mudras. Each mudra was said to activate certain energies, like the idea of crossing your fingers to bring good luck. This is a very old idea, that certain postures awaken protective qualities.

This is a method you can use all day long. Try it yourself. Adopt a depressed face and posture. See how that feels. Then shift into a joyful face and posture. Sit up straight, pull shoulders back a bit, put a smile on your face, maybe even stretch and raise your hands up above your head like you were shouting for joy. Feel the energy. Feel it. Bring it in. This is a way to use body posture to communicate to self (as well as to the world).

Do Good
Another way to increase positive emotion is to develop kindness and to use your gifts to improve the world. There is a simple Buddhist phrase that speaks to this practice. I first encountered it when I was finishing some post graduate studies and doing a bit of part-time teaching at SFSU to pay the bills. I shared an office with George Araki, wonderful chap who started the program I now direct. George was an admirable human being, very committed to changing the planet through empowering people to heal themselves and each other. He passed away some years back. I can still see the little colored plaque on the wall above his desk. It read...

"Cease doing harm. Seek to do good."

The full version from the Buddhist Canon reads:
'Cease to do evil, learn to do good, purify your heart,'
This is the teaching of all the Buddhas.
The Dhammapada, v. 183 (Fronsdal, 2005)

The notion of being uptight implies that everything is wound up together and not moving. It is stuck, not alive, not flowing. The goal of a learning life is to get unstuck. One way to do that is to think of others (because one of the potential roots of being stuck is being too self-focused, not selfish, just too self-absorbed). So how to become less self-absorbed? One simple strategy, actually a great strategy that we will come back to in the final chapter, is to ask yourself, "What will I give to the world right now?" As soon as you do that you become a bit bigger, you are not as focused on your limits, you are now thinking of your resources and strengths, and you are thinking of others. In that specific moment what you give to the world might be a simple act of generosity such as smiling or encouraging someone. The size of the act does not matter, it is more about the direction in which the energy is flowing – out into the world, no longer locked inside.

Meditate and Cultivate Mindful Awareness
As mentioned above, sitting meditation practices, both mindful and concentration methods, will quiet the mind and body, help to cultivate greater emotional awareness, and generally increase happiness. Develop a regular meditation practice, or at least do it before times of high demand where emotions are more likely to get rolling.

III. Emotional Literacy - Environment

Associate with the Right People, Places and Things
We are affected by our environments. Our emotions are affected by the people, places and things around us. Find the ones that support you, heal you, make you stronger, build your capacity.

Create an encouraging social environment. Find people who support, love, and respect you. Create an encouraging physical environment. If you get a trophy for eating the most ice cream put it out there where you can see it. Hang up that photo of you and the king of Nolandia shaking hands. If you drew a nice circle with crayons, sure put in on the door of the fridge. What the heck. Let yourself know you are good – through the eyes of others and your own.

Also, take advantage of the power of modeling. Observe and copy the behaviors of others. It is a very efficient way to learn. It employs the time tested strategy of monkey see, monkey do, a big part of human learning. If you want to be better with emotions then find emotionally literate people and model their behavior. They could be diplomats on the news, spiritual leaders like the Dalai Lama, Pope Francis, Nelson Mandela. They might be people you work with. Very effective managers and business executives often have refined people skills, including being able to moderate their own emotions. See what they do, how they respond, get their vibe. Think of what they would do in your situation.

Use Emotions for Learning

Plato, the ancient Greek philosopher, once said that all learning has an emotional component. Emotions are part of the human package, part of who we are. The problem/challenge is that our emotions can support or obstruct our learning if we are not mindful and working with them consciously. As an example, consider Lizet, she has some anxiety (fear) about math. Math is perceived as a threat. How human is that! Could a dog ever see algebra as a threat? Not likely. Why is math a threat, what is threatened? Self-esteem most likely is under threat, due to some failure in the past, resulting in a loss of self-efficacy and a reduction in self-worth related to math. So for Lizet math is a threat, anxiety arises. Threat activates her stress response, which moves her toward the flight side of fight-or-flight. Emotion, e-movere, to move away or toward, is a motivator. Emotions motivate action, they are one of the drivers of the organism. That emotional energy leads to avoidance, resulting in limited learning, and reinforcing her belief that she has no math ability. The reality, however, is, "I don't know how to do that yet, but I will learn." Research has also found that some emotions can impede learning and memory on a physiological level. People with serious PTSD, who are often in a chronic state of anxiety, can actually experience shrinkage of the hippocampus, which is part of the brain related to long term memory (Shin et al., 2006).

The goal is to recognize that emotions are affecting our learning and to work with those emotions intentionally and constructively. In terms of a learning strategy, cultivate positive emotions in relationship to learning, and associate learning with positive states. Use rewards, play music that you like when you study, use positive self-talk, make it fun, work with a study group of people that you like, keep track of your academic accomplishments, like a sheet on the wall for all of your gold stars, be proud of yourself, be committed to your life goals and note your progress on them, do your best and give something to the world. All of that will make you feel good about yourself, about your learning, and will inspire you to do even better. Go get em!

SUMMARY

In this chapter we examined the role of emotions in the human experience and in learning specifically. Emotions provide information to self and other, and they help to activate the system, emotions move us. The limbic system plays a key role in our emotional experience, with the amygdala being of central importance, especially in the perception of fear. Emotional dysregulation is the root of poor mental health and other physical problems as well. Learning the foundations of emotional literacy is a key to happiness and greater success in life. Emotional literacy involves recognizing our own emotions and emotion in others, and being able to work with emotions constructively. Ideas for working with emotions from the Wheel perspective included working at the level of Person, especially recognizing that we have thoughts and feelings, but we are not our thoughts and feelings. At the Behavior level, journaling and positive self-talk were two important techniques proposed for increasing emotional literacy. Finally, at the level of Environment, association with supportive others was recommended.

MIND-BODY PRACTICE

Sitting Meditation

This week focus on body, breath and thoughts/feelings. Be especially aware of thoughts and feelings, notice any tendency to get pulled into the story. Label the thoughts and feelings, generally or specifically, "Thinking, thinking, planning, planning, feeling, feeling, or anger, happy, bored…" If it is a recurrent thought/feeling be sure to make the mental note, "That is a thought, I am not my thoughts." You can also notice the sensation in the body related to the feeling, and get out of the thought and into the body sensation. Notice it, breathe into it, let it go.

You can finish your meditation with a Metta practice. Visualize someone that you care about. Think to yourself, "May (name of person) be safe, healthy, successful and happy." Repeat a number of times. Think of other people in the world you know but are not close to, think, "May these beings be safe, healthy, successful and happy." Then visualize yourself. Think, "May I be safe, healthy, successful and happy." Finish with a visualization of the globe and think the same for all beings, all creatures, on the planet.

Mindful Awareness

Pay particular attention to thoughts/feelings this week. If you find yourself getting pulled into the story then just STOP, take a breath, scan the body, ask yourself what you need right now to get back on track, take a few deep breaths, proceed. Remind self, "That is a thought/feeling. I am not my thoughts/feelings." Also remind yourself that you are cultivating more equanimity in your life.

Priming

Think of your goals for the week. Use priming mental imagery to see the most incredible week/semester of your life so far. Notice if there is any habitual thought/feeling that does not serve your highest good. What does that aspect of self need to be complete. Using Priming imagery to see that whole self as if already complete, happy and successful.

REFERENCES

Affleck G, Tennen H, Apter A. Optimism, pessimism, and daily life with chronic illness. In: Chang EC, editor. *Optimism & pessimism: implications for theory, research, and practice.* Washington: American Psychological Association; 2001:147-168.

American College Health Association. *American College Health Association-National College Health Assessment II: Reference Group Executive Summary Fall 2011.* Hanover, MD: American College Health Association; 2012.

Bandura, Albert. *Self-Efficacy: the exercise of control.* New York: Worth Publishers; 1997.

Cannon WB. *Bodily Changes in Pain, Hunger, Fear and Rage: An Account of Recent Researches into the Function of Emotional Excitement.* New York: D. Appleton; 1915.

Carver CS, Scheier MF. A control-process perspective on anxiety. *Anxiety Research.* 1988;1;17-22.

Chemers MM, Hu L, Garcia BF. Academic self-efficacy and first year college student performance and adjustment. *Journal of Educational Psychology.* 2001;93(1):55-64.

Darwin C. *The Expression Of The Emotions In Man And Animals.* London: John Murray; 1872.

Ekman P, Friesen WV. Constants across cultures in the face and emotion. Journal of Personality and Social Psychology. 1971;17(2):124-129.

Emmons RA, McCullough ME. Counting blessings versus burdens: an experimental investigation of gratitude and subjective well-being in daily life. *Journal of Personality and Social Psychology.* 2003;84(2):377-389.

Entman RM. Framing: Toward clarification of a fractured paradigm. *Journal of Communication.* 1993;43(4):51-58.

Froh JJ, Sefick WJ, Emmons RA. Counting blessings in early adolescents: an experimental study of gratitude and subjective well-being. *Journal of School Psychology.* 2008;46(2):213-233.

Fronsdal G. *The Dhammapada.* Boston: Shambala; 2005.

Gardner H. *Frames Of Mind: the theory of multiple intelligences.* New York: Basic Books; 1983.

Gerhard A. The benefits of optimism: a meta-analytic review of the life orientation test. *Personality and Individual Differences.* 1996;21(5):719-725.

Glass DC, Singer JE, Leonard HS, Krantz D, Cohen S, Cummings H. Perceived control of aversive stimulation and the reduction of stress responses. Journal of Personality. 1973;41(4): 577-595.

Goldin PR, McRae K, Ramel W, Gross JJ. The neural bases of emotion regulation: reappraisal and suppression of negative emotion. *Biological Psychiatry.* 2008;63(6):577-586.

Goleman D. *Emotional Intelligence: why it can matter more than IQ.* New York: Bantam Books; 1995.

Gross JJ. Antecedent- and response-focused emotion regulation: divergent consequences for experience, expression, and physiology. *Journal of Personality and Social Psychology*. 1998b;74(1):224-237.

Gyurak A, Gross JJ, Etkin A. Explicit and implicit emotion regulation: a dual-process framework. *Cognition and Emotion*. 2011;25(3):400-412.

Hardy J. Speaking clearly: A critical review of the self-talk literature. *Psychology of Sport and Exercise*. 2006;7(1):81-97.

Hariri AR, Bookheimer SY, Mazziotta JC. Modulating emotional responses: effects of a neocortical network on the limbic system. *Neuroreport*. 2000;11(1):43-48.

Hasin DS, Goodwin RD, Stinson FS, Grant BF. Epidemiology of major depressive disorder. results from the national epidemiologic survey on alcoholism and related conditions. *Archives of General Psychiatry*. 2005;62(10):1097-1106.

Lieberman MD, Eisenberger NI, Crockett MJ, Tom SM, Pfeifer JH, Way BM. Putting feelings into words: affect labeling disrupts amygdala activity in response to affective stimuli. *Psychological Science*. 2007;18(5):421 428.

Ochsner KN, Bunge SA, Gross JJ, Gabrieli JDE. Rethinking feelings: An fMRI study of the cognitive regulation of emotion. *Journal of Cognitive Neuroscience*. 2002;14(8):1215-1229.

Salovey P, Mayer J. Emotional intelligence. *Imagination, Cognition and Personality*. 1989-1990;9(3):185 - 211.

Saphire-Bernsteina S, Way BM, Kim HS, Sherman DK, Taylor SE. Oxytocin receptor gene (OXTR) is related to psychological resources. *Proceedings of the National Academy of Sciences*. 2011;108(37):15118-15122.

Scheier MF, Michael F. Dispositional optimism and physical well-being: the influence of generalized outcome expectancies on health. *Journal of Personality*. 1987;55(2):169-210.

Scheier MF, Carver CS. Effects of optimism on psychological and physical well-being: Theoretical overview and empirical update. *Cognitive Therapy and Research*. 1992;16(2):201-228.

Scherer KR. What are emotions? And how can they be measured? *Social Science Information*. 2005;44:693-727.

Shekelle RB, Gale M, Ostfeld AM, Paul O. Hostility, risk of coronary heart disease, and mortality. Psychosomatic Medicine. 1983;45(2):109-114.

Shin LM, Rauch SL, Pitman RK. Amygdala, medial prefrontal cortex, and hippocampal function in PTSD. *Annals of the New York Academy of Sciences*. 2006;1071:67-79.

Taylor SE, Brown JD. Illusion and well-being: A social psychological perspective on mental health. *Psychological Bulletin*. 1988;103(2);193-210.

Ullrich PM, Lutgendorf SK. Journaling about stressful events: effects of cognitive processing and emotional expression. *Annals of Behavioral Medicine*. 2002;24(3):244-250.

Yates SM. The influence of optimism and pessimism on student achievement in mathematics. *Mathematics Education Research Journal*. 2002;14(1):4-15.

Making Effective Decisions 12

I have a choice. I make informed decisions and I act on them accordingly.

CHAPTER THEMES
- Why We Avoid Making Decisions
- Foundations of Decision Making
  - Remember Choice
- Decision Making Methods

Decision making at its core is a process of considering options and making choices. A person can make decisions with great confidence and certainty or with trepidation and doubt. Decisions can be made carefully and thoughtfully or carelessly and without consideration. In our journey through the time-space matrix there will be endless forks in the road where a choice will appear. Usually these will be small choices, whether to eat something, or drink something, spend time with someone, answer a text and stop studying, choices to do this instead of doing that. Is one choice better than the other, the right choice? Not always obvious. What is important is the recognition that these endless choices build over time, layer upon layer, and shape our way of being, shape who we become. We are to a large extent the product of accumulating choices we make over a lifetime. So learning to recognize choice, and learning to make good decisions, is indeed a key to success and greater happiness. Skillfully adjusting direction as we sail toward the other shore requires effective decision making strategies. Let us consider some key strategies.

Competing Realities

Every day, all day long, we are making decisions. When life offers us options we have to make a choice. If you own one pair of socks, no decision. You are wearing boots today, you put on those socks. But you just had a birthday and grandmama gave you two new pairs, different colors, wow! You now have three pairs, which means you now have options, and that requires making a decision. What program to watch on television, whether to have toast or cereal, which jacket to wear, how long to study, when to go running, all day long, endless choices and decisions. In the majority of those instances, involving the simple choices we make, we typically operate out of habit or convenience or custom or some other rule of thumb, some guiding principle like black socks with black shoes. There is typically not much tension or conflict involved. Those are pretty easy decisions for most people to make.

It is also the case, however, that even simple decisions, like which television program to watch, can become quite difficult. When? When there are competing intrapersonal or interpersonal demands, some type of conflict or tension, inner or outer. Inner conflict, Cathy wants to get in shape and there is an aerobics class on television right now. She also has a desire to just sit and watch her favorite detective show, which is also on. Outer conflict, the apartment has one television, and there are two big games on at the same time. Ryan, Kamal, and Zach have had issues with each other around the television before. The decision about which game to watch could become a source of serious discontent for at least one of them. Take those examples up many notches to large-scale decisions, big cost decisions, life-or-death decisions, and one can appreciate the importance of this task. Understanding a bit more about how to make decisions effectively is an essential life skill to learn and apply.

Deciding and Learning
Decision making, especially conscious, intentional decision making, is also intimately related to our learning life. People stay in the same stuck place for several simple reasons. They do not see opportunities to choose, choice points, all throughout the day. They do not know they can choose. They do not elect to make a choice. They just see the cage, the same cage they have always been sitting in, for as long as they can remember. Change begins when we start to really pay attention to and notice the moments of choice. Because of habit those moments can be below the surface, less visible. Without even consciously choosing Anthony is now off task and heading to the fridge to get some food as his work assignment is distressing him. The main point, if Anthony was developing his decision making skills, including applying mindful awareness, he would have recognized that choice point, that moment of deciding, "Is it in my highest good to continue on this task or to take a break right now?" Sometimes taking the break is THE BEST ANSWER. Other times it is avoidance fueled by distress. This is where a conscious, intentional decision making strategy is a key to self-directed, empowering, liberating change, growth and success.

Why We Avoid Making Decisions

Not Recognizing Choice

The first reason people avoid making decisions is that they fail to recognize that they have a choice. It is like the dog in the cage endlessly getting zapped. Maybe the chain that kept the dog locked down was removed long ago, but the dog learned long ago that there was no choice, that its fate was sealed. In reality, however, choice is often there, even though we might deny, discount, or avoid it. Certainly there are times when things are set in stone, no real options, no choices. The train left the station early and you are stuck in this tiny little town one more night. Even then, however, choice appears, a chance to decide on how you will behave in light of the hand you have been dealt. ***One of the first steps to freedom is to recognize, that more often than not, there is indeed a choice.***

Habit

Habit is another reason people avoid making decisions. When actions are performed as a matter of habit they do not require much conscious deliberation, little in the way of active decision making. Habit bypasses deliberation. You just do it. The phone rings and you smoke a cigarette, no decision, just habitual response. Your partner comes home an hour late and you feel hurt. The math problems get harder and you walk to the refrigerator. Habit is conditioned mind, conditioned behavior. Is that bad? No, it can be very efficient. It is 5:30 so you go for a run. You ride the bus home after school and get in 15 minutes of reading. Dinner is over and you wash the dishes.

If the habit is a productive one then it will propel you into right action without having to think about it. That is very useful. A person with good work habits will not have to decide every ten minutes whether they should surf the internet or keep working, they just keep working. If the habit is efficient and effective, bringing positive results, then it is probably the right decision. It moves you closer to your goal. If, on the other hand, a particular habit is less constructive, then recognition and conscious decision making become more important.

Information Gap and Uncertainty

Another reason people avoid making decisions is that they lack sufficient information to make informed choices. In a perfect world you have all the information you need to make the most knowledgeable decision, the wisest choice. Truth is, that is often not the case. In reality, very often there is missing information, imperfect knowledge. In reality that can be a very valid reason for not making a choice. Consider the dreaded trip to the auto dealer. You see a car you like. The sales person says if you buy right now he will give you a killer price, but you have to decide now, you cannot come back later and get the same price. He has made it sound like a really great price, and you have to act now to get it. The problem, you do not really know what other dealers are offering on similar cars. In fact, you are not even one-hundred percent sure that this is the kind of car you want to buy. Do some people close the deal right there? Yes, of course they do. Do some of those people come to regret that decision? You bet, as soon as they see the same car for $1000 less, or realize they really wanted a hatchback not a sedan. Lack of information should not be an excuse for a bad decision or no decision. If there is information available then part of the task of effective decision making is to get it, to get the most authoritative, most reliable information available.

Fear of the Cost

Another reason for not making decisions is fear of making the wrong decision. People can worry about the "what if…" so much that they avoid deciding at all. Making a decision is making a commitment to a path. That commitment limits other options and ties up resources. When you marry a particular individual, buy a particular car, decide on a particular job, the door closes (at least temporarily) on alternatives. You are getting something, you are getting Mary Sue or Kenny Bob. Awesome! You are also giving up everyone else. That is one of the costs, which is one of the reasons people avoid decisions. A decision also means you are allocating resources to a specific path in the form time, money, energy, reputation, health, and that resource commitment can potentially be substantial.

The reality is that deciding to sit it out or deciding to take the plunge can both be extremely costly. We are making decisions all the time, even if we do not think so. Not making a decision, or postponing a decision, is a decision. Postponing a decision can be a very good choice if we use the down time to work on clarity. It can also be counterproductive if it just prolongs avoidance, or prolongs self-limiting habitual behaviors.

Foundations of Wise Decision Making

Contemporary cognitive and neuroscience research suggests that a lot of our decision making is quick and unconscious. It is based on heuristics (rules of thumb, customary ways of doing things, habit), intuition (gut sense), and body-brain reward mechanisms (Gigerenzer and Brighton, 2009; Gilovich et al., 2002; Kahneman and Frederick, 2005; Volkow et al., 2012). We are making lots of these unconscious/semi-conscious decisions all day long. That is efficient. Maybe the question is whether to buy navel oranges or Valencia oranges for the fruit salad. A matter of tasting one of each might provide sufficient gut response information to close the deal, or a squeeze reminds you of what a juicy orange feels like, or a quick chat with the green grocer, or best price. Given the low cost of the decision, if it is not the best decision, you can hardly go wrong. You are not getting married, just choosing an orange. But research shows that even with smaller decisions it can potentially improve outcomes if we are more intentional in our decision making process (Moxley et al., 2012).

By comparison, other decisions can be much harder – which major to select, where to live, which of two jobs to take, whether to have the surgery or not, if it makes sense to continue the long distance relationship. Big decisions can be very difficult, potentially quite painful. In some situations either choice can feel like a loss, and indeed that might be the case, giving up one valued reality for another. That is what makes big decisions big, the perceived cost. Those really do require some conscious and intentional processing if we hope to make the best choice.

It is what it is. Decision or not, life goes on. Learning to make decisions skillfully, as best one can, and living with the result, is one key to an effective life. In this first section we will look at a more intentional approach to decision making. That will be followed by ideas for improving the intuitive approach we also rely on throughout the day.

1. Remember That You Have a Choice - Be Honest

This is a key point, so remind yourself whenever necessary, "***I have a choice. I make informed decisions and I act on them accordingly.***" Simple self-talk can be very helpful in this regard. If the urge arises to stop studying because it is getting hard you can say to yourself, "I have a choice. Should I continue to study or should I go to the refrigerator now to get eat ice cream and watch TV? What is my priority goal right now? What is the most important thing for me to do right now?" ***Use your words!*** "I have a choice," is a statement of personal control. It is the quality of internal locus of control that the healthy executives displayed in the Kobasa studies on resilience. Internal locus of control is about taking personal responsibility for your own life journey.

You will be amazed how helpful self-talk can be in those moments. Have an adult conversation with self. Thinking about it in this way, as a choice, provides an opportunity to reflect on what you really want and the consequences of the different choices you could make or not make. That will put you back into a goal-oriented perspective, and that simple act engages the slower prefrontal cortex. "My goal this semester is to ace this class and I need to get this piece of work done now." Engaging the prefrontal cortex helps to put the brakes on the faster acting limbic system, our emotion center. The limbic system is sending the message, "I am bored/anxious and I need to eat something sweet to help me cope." Recognizing this mind-body process and the moment of choice is where new habits are born, where freedom and power begin. The day is filled with these small opportunities to make a more conscious choice. We can call these choice points. The moment where we come to a new fork in the road and have to decide if we will go left or right. Recognizing we have a choice, bringing intentionality into those moments, reflecting on our bigger goals, is a foundation for a more directed and powerful life.

It must also be said that sometimes the tides are strong and it can be hard to quiet the mind, the emotions, the body, hard to change our life situation, hard to find what we need. Choice may seem very far. It is always imperative that we practice patient with self and others, practice kindness, and do what works to get through the moments as we seek to find our way to the next level of the game. It is what it is.

2. Be Aware of Moments of Choice – Use Mindful Awareness

The simple practice of mindful awareness can help us to see our choices more clearly, helping us to make our decisions more wisely. What was previously a reactive, unconscious, habitual response can become a living response. "I see that I am getting angry," gives a person a lot more room for choosing skillful behavior than just reacting from anger in a habitual, unconscious fashion. Mindful awareness increases behavioral flexibility. We begin to see new decision points throughout the day. That awareness supports the gradual awakening and reshaping of conditioned mind and body. If old patterns are particularly strong, they will often be very automatic, unconscious, and guarded. They will be resistant to change. Bringing in conscious awareness and recognizing the possibility of choice, even if that choice is not acted on, is a powerful first step.

Once again, self-talk can be a very helpful strategy in this regard. Use labeling. You can make a note to self, "I am sad right now," or "I am angry at her for what she just said." Then you can tell yourself, "I have a choice in how I will be with this sadness...with this anger I am feeling right now...with my desire to eat sugar and avoid studying." Another self-talk strategy, at those moments of awareness of any choice point, is to write down or state clearly (out loud or in your mind), "*I am choosing between X and Y*." "Right now I am choosing between yelling at my kid or taking a breath and getting my composure back." Specifying one or more options makes the "I have a choice" more obvious, more real. "I am choosing between continuing to work on this essay or texting friends on my phone." Again, whether you act on that choice or not, or pick the right choice, is less important in the beginning. The first step is building awareness and priority. "***I have a choice. I am choosing between X and Y. Which decision will bring me the greatest happiness and sense of accomplishment in my life?***"

> **REFLECTION**
>
> Pick one or two patterns in your life where there is room for improvement. Once again you skated on starting a conversation with the man/woman at the bus stop. Once again you let someone take credit for your work. Once again you lost it in a meeting in front of everyone. We make decisions in all of those cases, but that decision making process is probably fairly subtle and there is a lot of other energy running through the system at that moment, a lot of history at work, conditioned mind and body. What you want to do is bring more planning and intentionality into some of those moments, especially if they are important for greater happiness and success in life. Stop criticizing or blaming, commit to self-acceptance and growth, start being mindful, notice the loops, the pattern, and decide on some small step to begin playing with the old pattern. That simple decision, that one small step, can be the beginning of a new way of being. It is what it is. "I don't know how to do that yet, but I will learn." So list one or two patterns where you could bring in some awareness of choice at the decision point. Write down the pattern and two or more choices you have at the decision point, such as the decision point of whether to procrastinate or not.

_____

_____

_____

3. Know Your Life Goals and Values

Knowing you life goals and values will facilitate better decision making. When goals are grounded, thoughtful, and clear they can help guide the process. One of the things that makes decision making challenging for many people is they have too many alternatives. However, if one of them more clearly supports attainment of one of your important goals then that is potentially a good choice. If your key goals are deeply rooted, internalized and committed, then they will naturally become guiding lights for decision making. Say you have a major life goal, "Get a good job to be able to support my family and give back to my community." That kind of goal will guide decisions about education, investing, and career choices. If you know your key goals, commit to them, remind yourself of them, and live them, they will inform many of your life decisions, large and small, in an ongoing fashion. That is powerful and efficient.

Having clear goals can also help you consciously make the 'wrong' choice when you need to, and being okay with that. Say there are two food choices on the menu. Your goal is to be healthy, but maybe it is a special event like your birthday, so you have the one that is less healthy. At least you have made a conscious choice with clear knowledge of your long term goals and the ability to live flexibly within that framework. When you know where you are going you can evaluate choices more clearly and live with less guilt.

If we do not know what we really want in life it can be harder to make skillful choices. A skillful choice gets us closer to the desired state. If we do not know what we want, then the choice does not matter as much, anything is fine, whatever feels good, whatever is easy. That is a path to nowhere in particular. If there is no goal, the choice becomes less important. That person might start to settle for mediocrity, the easiest path, the most convenient, whatever the world offers (which is often garbage, someone else getting rich feeding you trash, getting you high, ripping you off). That is one of the challenges of poverty. There is no bright future, there is not much hope. It matters less what one does right now, because there is nowhere better to go. That is a great disservice to human beings, to human potential, and the high price of poverty.

4. Appreciate That Decision Making is a Process

Making a decision is essentially a problem solving process. There is the current state (uncertainty, not knowing, not decided) and the desired state (clarity about something and confidence in it) and the gap in between. The desired state might be having clarity about whether to get a divorce or continue with counseling, to attend school in New Hampshire or in Oregon, to buy the sports car or the hybrid. When making decisions it helps to think about the desired state, what do you really want, what is in your highest good and the highest good of others. The challenge in making a big decision is that it can be hard to know if you would be better off divorced or not, in New Hampshire or Oregon, driving an eco conscious hybrid or a zippy roadster. There is often a cost and benefit to both sides of the decision, which is one of the things that makes deciding difficult. The competing choices, roadster or hybrid, can also reflect different, potentially competing values and beliefs that you hold, you want to have fun and you also want to be eco. It is a process.

If it is a big decision then it is a good idea to engage in a more serious problem solving process (refer back to the Learning Life Problem Solving Model in Chapter 8 on continual improvement). If it is a simpler issue then use simpler methods. In the decision making literature there are two related concepts – satisficing versus maximizing (Simon, 1956). Satisficing relates to using a simple decision making process, and being willing to accept an adequate rather than an optimal outcome. The goal is to reduce the cost of effort involved in the decision making process. This tends to result in suboptimal decisions. When the stakes are low that may be fine. Why waste a lot of time making a decision when it is not very important. There is only so much time in a day. That is when habit, custom, simple decision rules can be very useful. People can get stuck in analysis paralysis, analyzing decisions to death. Sometimes you just need to make a choice and move one. "Yes, just give me one of each color." Boom, done. Sometimes, however, you want to optimize, to get closer to an ideal, when the investment is significant. The main point, know that we use both, and consider maximizing if the decision is important.

5. Gather Sufficient Information and Refine Your Choice Criteria

Making the wrong choice is very often the result of insufficient information or wrong information. Good decision making is a critical thinking process, and gathering necessary information helps us to think clearly. It begins with self-knowledge, information about personal goals and needs, "What do I really want? What do I really need? What are my long term goals? What will give me the greatest sense of accomplishment?" This of course once again speaks to the importance of knowing your goals and values.

Why spend time gathering information? The process of information gathering can be extremely useful as it can actually help you know what you want. How? Because it informs you as to what is out there and also what you really want and need. In the Learning Life Problem Solving Model one of the key elements is clarification of the Desired State. One of the core reasons people have problems making decisions, quite surprisingly, is that they do not really know what they want. They know something is wrong, a feeling of discontent, nonalignment, unhappiness, but that can equate to a very vague awareness of what the preferred alternative is. Getting information can contribute significantly to clarifying the Desired State. If you do not know something exists you will not want it, you will not look for it, and you will probably not find it. *You don't know, that you don't know, what you don't know.* It is not on your map. The more information you gather about universities or career paths or places in the world to visit, the more detailed that map becomes, the more useful that map becomes, the more reliable the routes and distances. It is like having two maps of the earth, one from 1500 and one from today. Which one would you rather use to navigate your sailboat from Madagascar to Maine?

The more information you get the greater clarity you have about options and that can help to refine your choice criteria, your selection criteria (what is really important to you in your final choice). The research process helps inform you as to what is out there, what you want, what you need, and what would you accept. "I need one that can float, is light enough to carry, highly durable, and fire proof." Those are very clear choice criteria and will refine the search process. It they are based on things you have seen in your research (they exist) they can lead to a better match of what you want, need and will accept. For example, Cleopatra wants to buy a car. She does her research and learns more about options, what is available. There is lots of information on colors, sizes (mini to family), gas mileage, safety ratings, numbers of doors and passengers, user satisfaction, and more. She wants something sporty but being a student with limited income she also needs it to be less expensive. Three small cars seem to match her initial criteria, so it makes sense to just buy the cheapest of the three. As she continues her research, however, her choice criteria begins to increase and refine. She now decides that since it is a small car she wants it to have a decent safety record and low maintenance costs are also important. With these new choice criteria, safety and maintenance, and reading some consumer reviews, she realizes that the lowest priced vehicle she was initially selected actually has the highest repair costs, and it is not so great in crash tests either. Those choice criteria were not on her radar before her research. Her new information helped influence her final choice, and probably helped her to make a choice that will save her money and anxiety in the long run. That was a more informed and productive choice because her knowledge of choice criteria was thorough.

It does not take that much time to collect information, and that information can provide valuable insight into both what is out there (options) and what is really important (choice criteria). In the decision literature this is referred to as multi-criteria decision analysis (Zeleny, 1982). Knowing your choice criteria ultimately narrows the range of possible choices and increases the odds of finding a best fit. In other words, it ultimately makes for a simpler and more effective decision making process. When you have your criteria you can compare options against each other. The ones that do not match your criteria are quickly eliminated from competition. Example, entrants to Miss America pageant. "Here is an application from William Daventrosky???" Criteria mismatch, simple decision, into the reject pile. Clear criteria helps with the sort process and makes elimination of mismatches simple. As you get down to a few 'best fit' matches you may need to reassess and fine tune your criteria or pick one or two criteria that are the most important, like cost and portability, and then choose on that basis. In the decision making this last aspect is known as elimination by aspects (Tversky, 1972).

6. Manage Thoughts and Emotions

In the ideal world people make decisions that will maximize their gains, decisions that help them derive the most benefit from among the available choices. In reality, however, humans make many bad decisions due to the nature of the human decision making process. That is where mind-body management comes into play in decision making. Emotion and thought are a team. No doubt everyone has had the experience of making a big decision, such as whether to attend a particular university, buy a certain car, or marry that special someone. On Tuesday, red hot ready to go, no question, clear as a bell, "USC, awesome! Harvard, yuck!" On Wednesday doubt creeps in, "What was I thinking? Los Angeles? Am I crazy. I don't even drive." On Thursday, love returns, "Go Trojans! Go palm trees!" Friday, tired of thinking about it. Saturday not sure at all anymore, just want to watch cartoons, maybe get a job at the waffle hut and forget school.

Several structures of the brain are instrumental in decision making. These include the anterior cyngulate, the orbitofrontal cortex, and the ventromedial prefrontal cortex. They help to provide a mix of insight, motivation, memory and emotion that can inform and color the process. The lower aspect of the anterior cingulate has connections to the amygdala, nucleus acumbens, and hypothalamus, which bring emotional arousal and motivated behavior into the picture. The upper aspect has ties to the prefrontal and parietal cortex, which bring deliberation, planning and expectancy into play. In this way emotional and analytical components are built into the neurology of decision making. They both provide important information, serving somewhat complementary roles. We need both.

The challenge, the combination of thought and emotion, not well managed, can create more confusion than clarity. The emotional tone of the decision can shift from yearning to disdain in two minutes. The analytical brain can change the story from "costs too much" to "too good to pass up" in the same span. Research shows that in decision making people often make errors in judgment based on how the alternatives are framed or presented (Bies-Hernandez, 2012), what is most easily remembered, and what gets viewed as more important (referred to as the availability bias) (Tversky & Kahneman, 1974). Research also shows that people tend to be unduly optimistic (Brown & Cliff, 2005; Meinert, 1991), biased toward low probability, high reward outcomes versus low reward guaranteed outcomes (such as in gambling), and drawn toward salient cues that may provide inaccurate information on actual probability of an outcome (Zentall & Laude, 2013).

We have an emotional brain and an analytical brain. Both of them can work for us or against us. ***Learn to work with them*** for more effective decision making. Be mindful of what your head and heart are saying. Gather information, clarify and list your criteria, pay attention to what feels right, assess the costs and benefits. If things start to spin then breathe and release. Make your best decision. Ultimately, cultivating greater life equanimity will make you a better decision maker. You will be less pulled by the ever-changing tides of thoughts and feelings.

7. Take Your Time (if Possible)

Being deliberate in decision making has been shown to improve optimal decision outcomes (Moxley et al., 2012). If it is an important decision then taking time and being intentional in your strategy is a good idea. Sometimes it is useful to postpone making the decision for a while, especially if there is a lot of emotion and mental activation around the question. That dust storm can obscure the decision making process. We want our decisions serve us in the long run, to bring us closer to our goals. Sometimes it is useful to sit with it for a bit. You may want to get one last round of information or check in again with trusted others to get their opinions. Then when you are clear, within reason, that this is the way to go, then move forward with it.

I remember way back when I was finishing graduate school, selling an old junker car. A family came to see it. After showing them the car the father and mother said that they would have to go home and pray on the decision first, and that they would call me if they wanted the car. They never did. I presume the good Lord saved them from buying a piece of junk. I would never know for sure if "go home and pray" was their escape line or an actual practice, but as a practice it was a good idea, a way to get some space between the impulse and the final action (prefrontal cortex). Take a cooling off period before making a very big choice, even a quick one for small decisions that are deeply rooted in habit. Grocery stores put small, inexpensive items by the cash register to encourage last minute impulse purchases. Impulse implies no thought, no serious deliberation. They know we will rationalize, "It is only two bucks!?" If you take a moment to STOP (Stop, Breathe, Orient, Proceed), take a few deep breaths, consider your goals (like health or money), and mindfully check in, you can proceed and probably make wiser choices.

8. Take Some Risks (Smart Ones)

Nothing ventured, nothing gained, as they say. The great hockey player Wayne Gretzky once noted that, "You miss one-hundred percent of the shots you don't take." Taking some calculated risk in life increases the odds of bigger wins. That is what makes something a risk, there is a cost, something to loose. There are certainly some circumstances when decision making should absolutely seek to minimize risk, like when the costs of mistakes or failure are extremely high. At other times, some risk can be very beneficial. How much risk? Depends on the person. Some people may actually be compelled by the dopamine surge of high risk behaviors (Abler, 2009). Not everyone's cup of tea. It is good to acknowledge and honor one's risk tolerance. It can also be good to consider stretching that tolerance at times if risk averse. This may be especially true if the potential benefit outweighs the cost sufficiently, if there is a reasonable probability of success, and if your goals are in alignment.

In reality, when it comes to bigger decisions in life most people take an incremental approach. We typically raise an eyebrow when we hear about a couple who dated for a week and then ran off to Vegas to do a drive through wedding. "Let's see how long that one lasts!" To most observers that decision does not seem prudent, too much too fast. That is why people date, and possibly cohabitate for a while, to see if they can stand each other before having a child together or sharing a mortgage. We often make smaller decisions and increase our commitment to the bigger decision over time. It is an unconscious small steps approach that is common in human decision making. Consider taking incremental small risks, a small steps approach.

9. Streamline Your Decision Making Process

Develop an effective decision making process. Get in the habit of being present in the moment, recognize important decision points, remember that you have a choice, focus on life goals, get information, determine your choice criteria, maintain equanimity, and solve the problem, make the decision. A flow like that will make you a much better decision maker. Ultimately learning the skill of effective decision making will enhance life productivity, accomplishment, ease, and fun, contributing to a more streamlined journey. Coming to the perfect decision, however, if there is such a thing, can take a lot of work. There is an obvious trade off between how much energy we want to put into making a decision and the impact of that decision on our life. If the decision has long term implications it merits more time and energy, take a more thorough approach. If it does not, then a 'good enough' approach is more efficient and can be equally effective, sufficing rather than maximizing. There is a useful saying in this regard – Don't let the perfect get in the way of the good. Do not chase perfection needlessly. Use your precious life moments for the important decisions and actions.

10. Monitor Decisions

Once you have implemented a decision it is a good idea to monitor it. You will want to see the impact of that choice in your life. Does it make you happier? Does it make you healthier? Does it keep you running on the same wheel in the rat cage month after month, year after year? If what we are choosing, especially regularly, does not help us move forward on important life goals, then we need to reassess our goals or our choices. Something is out of alignment. If we are successful in our decisions we want to replicate them. If we make mistakes we want to learn from them. Paying attention to patterns, with eyes and mind wide open, will improve that process.

11. Evaluate

Decision making is a problem solving process, and some solutions are lousy. It is useful to consider the quality of the decision, the effect it brings into your life in the long run, the capacity it has to bring you closer to your goals. Once you have observed the effects of the decision over time, you can make a determination if that decision is a best fit. If it is not, then you need to reassess the options and try another solution (remembering that decision making is a problem solving process). If something is clearly not working then it is often better to cut your losses sooner than later, to avoid wasting more time and energy, more precious resources. Or, perhaps there is enough benefit from the current decision, but it needs some fine tuning. Do that. Do more research and get more information.

12. Act and Standardize

Decisions, like goals, are only as good as the results that emerge from them. Humans do not like uncertainty, and decisions often carry some degree of uncertainty. It is what it is. We do the best we can given our resources and current levels of knowledge and skill. We use our skill, make a decision, and act. With a commitment to continually improving, living a learning life, we will get better. Never forget, "I don't know how to do that yet, but I will learn."

Once you have made a decision and tested it, and find that the decision serves you, you may want to standardize it into your workflow, make it a habit. An extremely helpful strategy for reducing decision demand is to have routines in your life. You do your laundry on Saturday mornings, you exercise right after work every other night, Friday from 2pm until 5pm is review time, you make a list of what you need before you go shopping for groceries, you have a process for handling email efficiently, you have folders for all key documents and as soon as you get a bill you put it where it belongs. A systematized approach means no thinking required, essentially no decision making involved. You have an effective pattern, an effective process, a way of doing things that is built into your schedule, into your workflow, into your life. It is efficient. No time wasted thinking about it. It is a 6-milimeter diameter bolt. You know which can it goes into. Not having to make decisions because you have an effective process will save you a lot of time and energy over the course of a lifetime. Seek to reduce decision load by standardizing and simplifying processes.

Decision Making Methods

Analytical Decision Making

The steps outlined above in the previous sections describe a more analytical or linear approach to problem solving and decision making. It is a process of clarifying and focusing on life goals, recognizing decision opportunities or choice points throughout the day, remembering that we have a choice, getting information, determining and refining choice criteria, and making the decision. This is a very effective strategy for important decisions, a strategy for making choices that are more likely to serve your higher good in the long run. Ultimately when you find a consistent decision path that enhances your life it can be beneficial to standardize it, make that a habit so you longer need to make a choice, you just do it.

1. Remember That You Have a Choice – Be Honest
2. Be Aware of Moments of Choice – Use Mindful Awareness
3. Know Your Life Goals and Values
4. Appreciate That Decision Making is a Process
5. Gather Sufficient Information and Refine Your Choice Criteria
6. Manage Thoughts and Emotions
7. Take Your Time (if Possible)
8. Take Some Risks (Smart Ones)
9. Streamline Your Decision Making Process
10. Monitor Decisions
11. Evaluate
12. Act and Standardize

Creative Decision Making

Another approach we must consider engages our creative, non-linear, intuitive aspect of brain/mind/body. There are two halves to the brain, the left and right hemispheres. The left hemisphere is associated with logic, linear thinking, and language. The right hemisphere is associated with intuition, spatial sense, and creative non-linear understanding. Use of intuitive processes has been found to be common, results in satisfying decisions, and is a characteristic of expert decision making (Dane et al., 2012; Gigerenzer and Brighton, 2009; Gilovich et al., 2002; Kahneman and Frederick, 2005; Volkow et al., 2012). Applying intuitive methods more deliberatively is a powerful component of decision making, for even better outcomes. Intuitive decision making methods include non-conscious, quick, holistic associations, and utilization of affect or feeling (gut instinct) (Dane & Pratt, 2009).

So now we will take a short tour of some intuitive/creative decision making strategies. This is a productive counterbalance to logical analysis. It is especially important when there is limited information available, when you need to make quick decisions, or when you want to add another layer of reflection to an important decision. As mentioned in the beginning of this chapter, contemporary research suggests that a good deal of our ongoing decision making, which program to watch, what to grab from the refrigerator, whether or not to pack extra socks, is a fairly quick and unconscious process. That is efficient, and more often that not good enough to suffice. Here are some ways to start working more intentionally with this intuitive approach.

Checking In
This is a particularly useful method for getting quick, real-time feedback related to a decision you are considering. Let us say you are driving down the highway and you have no idea where you are. You are coming to an intersection, poorly marked, and you have to make a choice in about one minute. There is nowhere to stop and pull over to look at a map. "Holy turnpike Batman!" What to do? Say you are shopping and need to decide if you should buy carrots or broccoli, or you need to decide if it would be all right to go out with friends or better to stay home and work on that paper.

For many decisions in life it is helpful to have a way to make more intuitive decisions on the fly and to do so in a way that serves your highest good. There is no time to pull out a piece of paper and do a cost-benefit analysis. Although the ***Checking In*** approach may seem a bit limited at first, as you become more comfortable with the technique it can be used to work with very challenging decisions. Why bother? Because it is an intentional way to work with the more holistic, non-verbal, intuitive aspect of our human nature as well as the more linear, logical capacity. It helps us to run on two legs instead of just one, more holistic, integrated, and efficient, using input from the emotional and logical aspects of mind and body. The way nature built us. There are several ways to do this method. Here is one good approach.

Background
- Think of something that you want to make a decision on.
- Select a question that has a "Yes/No" answer, not a 'What is the meaning of life' item.
- If you ask the question and it cannot be answered with a "Yes" or "No" try another method.
- Remember that the focus is on you, not for getting information for someone else.
- The answer you are seeking is intended to serve your highest good.
- The best timeframe is near term, more immediate future, not long term.

> ⭐ **DO THIS: THE METHOD**
>
> 1. First think of your question.
>
> 2. Then get into a quiet, focused state of mind and body. That can be as simple as closing your eyes and going internal for a moment, taking a few deep breaths, relaxing the muscles, telling yourself that your body is relaxed, your mind is quiet, and your heart is happy. Or just take a few deep breaths and tell yourself that you are relaxed.
>
> 3. Then ask yourself your question, and ask it in terms of whether the outcome is in your highest good. "Is it in my highest good to eat ice cream for dinner?" "Is it in my highest good to stop studying and watch television for a bit?" "Is it in my highest good to apply to this graduate school?" "Is it in my highest good to change my place of employment?"
>
> 4. Once you have your question then you want the answer to come to you, preferably not in words. The idea is to bypass the typical internal narrative. We want to move from our more linear verbal left hemisphere 'thinking about the issue' into our more intuitive, non-verbal right hemisphere approach. There are several ways to play with this. One of the better ways to do this is to get out of thoughts completely and into the body. Our thoughts and inner narratives often whirl about, driven by the winds of emotion, and that can significantly reduce visibility. If we can bypass thinking in words that can provide a productive alternative means to insight and decisions.

Using the Body

There are several ways to use the body as the vehicle for getting decision input. It may take a bit of experimenting. Here is what works well for me. It involves the use of head movements. In the West we use our head as a way to express agreement and disagreement, by moving it forward and backward for 'Yes' and side to side for 'No'. You can use head movement in the very same way for non-verbal decision making. The method is simple. Ask the question and allow the head to move by itself, Yes or No. When you do this method, especially in the beginning, the movements can be very subtle, micromovements, just discernible to you on a subtle sensation level. They can also be quite distinct and clear. This type of method of communicating through the body is call ideomotor movement, or the idea (ideo) becoming a movement (motor).

With practice you will recognize the movements, both subtle and more pronounced. The value of letting them be subtle is that you can actually use the method to check in while you are talking to someone or doing something else where you want an unobtrusive way to check in, "Is this a good deal or should I leave now?" It is actually a good idea to work on using this in a subtle fashion. If you are standing in the frozen foods section, shaking your head wildly deciding which brand of ice cream to purchase, someone might call a paramedic. If done subtly the person next to you picking up a bag of frozen broccoli will not be able to see what you are doing.

Once you get your answer it can be helpful to repeat the process a few times to confirm the answer, especially in the beginning. Remember to take a few deep breaths between each re-questioning. This allows you to clear the slate. If you repeat the process several times, and you get the same response (which you probably will), that is useful information. The main thing is to get out of your way and let the answer come. This is not a conversation in your head, it is the body providing information from a more intuitive level, to answer the question, "What is in my highest good?"

O-Ring

Another ideomotor movement approach is the O-ring method. This is similar to the muscle testing approach used by some somatic therapy providers. To do it you make a circle with the thumb and index finger, the tips touching lightly. It is probably best to use your non-dominant hand for this process. With the other hand pinch the same two fingers together lightly, like you were picking up a grain of rice. Place those two pinched fingers inside the finger circle of the other hand. Then ask your question. Gently open the pinched fingers and try to break the finger circle. If the circle breaks easily then there is not much integrity or strength in that particular choice. Try various choices and see which holds up more to pressure, which has more integrity or strength. If the finger circle remains strong for a particular option then that provides information about the utility or strength of that decision for you.

Proprioceptive Signals

The final body method, is to just read your own inner proprioceptive signals, the inner body sensations, the same ones you might pay attention to in your mindfulness meditation practice. If you practice this on a regular basis you will start to recognize what your body is telling you, what it needs, or what it is suggesting would be good for you. If you are walking down the street and a stranger comes up to ask the time you may get a 'strange vibe'. That is probably a feeling in your body, a gut reaction. It is useful information to pay attention to. It does not necessarily mean that this is a dishonest person. It just means that it is prudent to be vigilant and not foolishly trusting of all strangers. Like all decision making resources, this method is just providing additional information for you to use for your final decision and response.

Non-Body Feedback

There are a number of other ways to check in that do not rely on the body. They use the imagination for answers. In these approaches you work with your imagination as a source of decision feedback. For example, you can think of a sound that represents your 'Yes', and one that represents your 'No'. That might be a bell-like 'ting' and a 'shplattt'. If you wanted to work with an image you could come up with a representative yes and no image, like a green light and red light or a thumbs up and down. It could even be a 'Yes' or 'No' image. Once you have that sound or image you ask your question, eyes closed, and then pay attention to what you get. The method may seem unusual, but in time, with a little practice, you will develop confidence with it and the ability to use it for decision making at all levels, real time, to help you steer your boat to the other shore.

Other Strategies

The following are not necessarily intuition methods, but ways to stimulate creative thinking around an issue.

Unconscious Input
In this method you just hold the question and let one or more answers come to you. It can be quite interesting to see what arises, often very creative insights. If you are working on an important question then write down the answers. Repeat the process a few days in a row to see if the same answers come again. You may also want to work with historic divination tools. These can be excellent sources of creative insight. Methods like the Tarot or I Ching can be ways to get additional ideas related to your question. Use the answer from these sources as additional pieces of information to help stimulate insight into the final answer. It is all grist for the decision making mill.

As an example, to use Tarot as a method for decision making ideas you ask the question while shuffling the deck. You spread out the cards and pick one or more depending on what you are asking. If you are comparing two or three choices you might pick three cards. If you are looking for ideas about one decision you might pick one card, or two representing the cost and benefit. No matter what cards you draw you will get some food for thought that can be quite useful. Use it as a vehicle to think about parameters of the question, not necessarily as the answer. Let it be an additional source of information. Also, if you are going to use a method like the Tarot you need a book for interpreting the cards. Get one with a more contemporary, psychological spin. The older books often tend to interpret the cards more literally and can be rather limiting for idea generation. Another approach would be to just go into a library or book store, holding your question in mind, and opening a random page. You might get lucky and get a useful idea. If you get a 'message' that is called synchronicity, where the universe becomes an ally. You can also pray for the answer. You can even ask the question and then go for a jog, swim or take a long walk. Let the question 'be' in the body, do not think about it. When you are done and have rested for a bit close your eyes and see what answers come to mind when you ask the question. The path to these insights cannot be effortful, that is counterproductive with this approach. You just need to inquire and see what comes to you.

Imagery
Another approach is to incorporate imagination and imagery into your process. Work with your inner coach, inner wise person, inner power animal, your favorite saint, whatever speaks to you. They can offer advice, provide sound council when you are out of alignment, or just be present. In addition to doing this in your head you can also do it out loud (just keep an eye open for the mental health workers). You can get your own one-inch Buddha or plastic Jesus at some novelty store. Then have a conversation with your wise friend. Instead of a little statue you can get a picture of someone you admire and ask that person his or her opinion, or just let them advise you. Listen and you will hear. Let them be a coach, an ally, a true supporter. Just remember, if they are talking trash, then that is old conditioned mind overriding. Discount that. If they talk kindness and support, listen. If you listen they will have something to say. You may be surprised at the value of the information you get.

Dreams
If you are someone who remembers dreams then use dreamtime to get answers to important questions you are working on. You can use dreams to get ideas for major papers or special projects in addition to helpful information for making decisions. I do this all the time and find it exceedingly

helpful given the profoundly creative power of dreams. Talk about non-linear access, dreams are exactly that, no limit of time, space, or logic. They are energy and symbol, a dynamic 'lived' experience in the subtle inner world.

If you want to try dream/sleep problem solving the method is quite simple. As you are preparing to sleep just think of what you need an answer to, ponder that question or issue for a moment. Once you have done that then allow yourself to relax as deeply as possible as you fall asleep. While relaxing hold an image in your mind where you see yourself as having great clarity the next day. Prime that outcome. Mentally tell yourself that you will awaken tomorrow with an insight to the problem. That is an important step. Tell yourself that when you wake up in the morning you will have an insight into how to solve this problem, how to write the paper, what steps to take next in the process. Then let it go and fall asleep. When you awaken the last dream of the night is the answer to your question. If the content is hard to interpret, then start with the feeling, the emotional tenor of the dream. If you do not remember the dream, not important, know that the unconscious problem solving mind (that integrates information during sleep) has been working on your question. At some point during the day you will have greater insight into what to do next. Try it, trust the incredible problem solving brain that nature has given you, and see what happens.

Follow Your Bliss
Another source of energy, enthusiasm, and insight comes from being plugged in to your life current, doing your dharma, doing what you were born to do. Joseph Campbell, a wonderful teacher of world mythology, encouraged students to follow their bliss, to do what they loved. Let's say you bought yourself a new coat, ordered from some online merchant. It arrives and the color and fit are different than what you expected. You can do three things: First, you can return it. Second, you can keep it and let it be perfect the way it is. Third, you can keep it, and although unsatisfied, you continue to remind yourself of its ok-ness. The last of these three is the least productive. If you can send it back, then send it back and get what you want. Follow your bliss, trust your gut, go with the feeling. Following your bliss is paying attention to an internal, non-verbal message, a feeling, something in your heart, a signal. If you cannot send it back, then make it so, let it be the perfect thing for the rest of the season and then give it to some poor person who might really enjoy getting a 'new' warm coat.

In your life if you have an inner sense, a calling, a feeling that *you are on a mission*, then trust that. You do not have to abandon practicality. You can make an impractical mission an avocation, a delightful piece of a full life. If it is your true calling it will never be quiet. It will continue to call to you for the rest of your life. Listen to it. Do not neglect it. Do not put it off with the thought that you will get to it some day. Some day may never come. Give it some space in your life, even a few minutes a month. Many years from now you will be very, very thankful you did. ***You are sincerely encouraged to consider this***. Many years from now you will be thankful you did.

Final Thought

Effective decision making is a path to freedom. It is also a process. Casting a wide net increases the chance of catching the big fish. Our tool kit should include a variety of strategies, from logical analysis and research to working with inner knowing and creative insight. It all starts with the recognition that we have a choice. With that recognition comes a greater opportunity for change, growth and success. If someone wants to work on changing some old pattern, then the next step is to make the choice points more visible. That takes a commitment to see those moments and to STOP and start pulling in a new direction whenever that fork in the road becomes visible. The old habitual track will be deeper. There will be a natural tendency to go down the familiar path, less effort, reinforced over time, shiny reward visible not far down the way. If you take a breath, remember your goals, and decide to take the new path, you will see that it is not well trodden yet, not as clear, no obvious shiny reward down that way. "Why would I want to go there?" Exactly, why go there? That is going to take some motivation, commitment to a new way, a clear goal, applied regulation of mind and body, conscious choosing and choosing and choosing until the new path becomes clear and well worn. In time the old path will start to grow over with weeds and underbrush because of disuse. That will take some time, but eventually you will no longer need to think about it when you come to that fork in the road, you will know which way to go, and the shiny reward will now be illuminating the new way.

SUMMARY

In this chapter we looked at the process of making informed life decisions. The methods considered included analytical approaches such as remembering key life goals and refining choice criteria to be used for making decisions. It also included intuitive methods such as ideomotor movement and methods to tap into our inner creative resources, such as getting ideas from dreams. One of the key messages of the chapter was the awareness that more often than not we do have a choice. Because of habit, conditioned mind and body, we lose touch with our power to choose, our ability to choose. Reawakening to that choice is a foundation of a successful learning life.

MIND-BODY PRACTICE

Sitting Meditation

This week focus on the object of your choice body, breath, sensory input, and thoughts/feelings. If working with thoughts and feelings, then work on labeling them.

Mindful Awareness

This week pay particular attention to places where responses are habitual and informed choices are not made, such as not exercising, eating low quality foods, procrastinating instead of getting work done. Be very aware of what is going on in Person, Behavior and Environment. What is the thinking that supports the old habit. Remind yourself at those moments that you have a choice. Practice making a choice on one of these patterns, thinking in terms of your long term goals.

Priming

Think of your goals for the week. Use priming mental imagery to see the most incredible week/semester of your life so far. Notice if there is any habitual thought/feeling that does not serve your highest good. What does that aspect of self need to be complete. Using Priming imagery to see that whole self as if already complete, happy and successful.

REFERENCES

Abler B, Hahlbrock R, Unrath A, Gron G, Kassubek J. At-risk for pathological gambling: imaging neural reward processing under chronic dopamine agonists. *Brain*. 2009:132;2396-2402.

Bies-Hernandez NJ. The effects of framing grades on student learning and preferences. *Teaching of Psychology*. 2012;39(3):176-180.

Bordalo P, Gennaioli N, Shleifer A. Salience theory of choice under risk. *The Quarterly Journal of Economics*. 2012;127(3):1243-1285.

Brown G, Cliff M. Investor sentiment and asset valuation. *The Journal of Business*. 2005;78(2):405-436.

Dane E, Pratt MG. Conceptualizing and measuring intuition: a review of recent trends. In: Hodgkinson GP, Ford JK. *International Review of Industrial and Organizational Psychology – Volume 27*. Hoboken, NJ: John Wiley and Sons; 2009:1-40.

Dane E, Rockmann KW, Pratt MG. When should I trust my gut? linking domain expertise to intuitive decision-making effectiveness. *Organizational Behavior and Human Decision Processes*. 2012;119(2):187-194.

Gigerenzer G, Brighton H. Homo heuristicus: why biased minds make better inferences. *Topics in Cognitive Science*. 2009;1;107-143

Gilovich T, Griffin D, Kahneman D. Heuristics and Biases: the psychology of intuitive judgment. New York: Cambridge University Press; 2002.

Kahneman D, Frederick S. A model of heuristic judgment. In: Holyoak K, Morrison RG, editors. *Thinking and Reasoning*. New York: Cambridge University Press; 2005:267-293.

Meinert J. Financial advice from a business veteran. *Journal of Accountancy*. 1991;171(6):134-140.

Moxley JH, Ericsson KA, Charness N, Krampe RT. The role of intuition and deliberative thinking in experts' superior tactical decision-making. *Cognition*. 2012;124(1),72-78.

Simon HA. Rational choice and the structure of the environment. *Psychological Review*. 1956;63(2):129-138.

Tversky A. Elimination by aspects: a theory of choice. *Psychological Review*. 1972;79(4):281-299.

Tversky A, Kahneman D. *Judgment under Uncertainty: heuristics and biases*. 1974;185(4157):1124-1131.

Volkow ND, Wang GJ, Fowler JS, Tomasi D, Baler R. Food and drug reward: overlapping circuits in human obesity and addiction. *Current Topics in Behavioral Neurosciences*. 2012;11:1-24.

Zeleny M. *Multiple Criteria Decision Making*. New York: McGraw-Hill; 1982.

Zentall TR, Laude JR. Do pigeons gamble? I wouldn't bet against it. *Current Directions in Psychological Science*. 2013;22(4):271-277.

Changing Habits 13

> *Everyday I make progress on my most important life goals.*

CHAPTER THEMES
- Habit and the Brain
  - Reward Mechanisms
- Habit Modification
  - What – The Goal
  - Why – The Motive
  - How – The Approach

Some behaviors beg for change – smoking cigarettes, not exercising, putting off homework, avoiding asking that special person out for a date. Those are behaviors that create problems. There is often a clear desire to change them. There are also behaviors that may be very useful, contributing to our success and happiness. There might be a strong desire to do those even better. In this chapter we will explore how to work with both types of habits, reducing the patterns that no longer serve us and enhancing the ones that do. Whether adding or eliminating, the strategies offered in this chapter will provide very useful ideas for managing the dynamic and profoundly interesting process of personal change and growth.

Habits and the Brain – The Conditioned Mind/Body

Having some knowledge of the neurophysiology underlying behavior can significantly help us in our efforts to strengthen or eliminate specific habits. One key contributor to the creation of new habits, both productive and unproductive, is the brain's reward system. The reward system influences behavior by producing a positive state, a good feeling. This subjective positive feeling, this reward, is associated with the release of the neurotransmitter dopamine. The ventral tegmental area, located in the midbrain, innervates the nucleus accumbens, the main site for release of dopamine. When a particular stimulus, like a piece of candy, activates the release of dopamine, that candy stimulus becomes associated with a subjective positive feeling, a good feeling, a sense of reward. That good feeling strengthens the association and the formation of habits. That sense of reward reinforces and thereby increases the likelihood of repetition of the behavior, such as eating candy.

Related research shows that when a rat is introduced to a new reward food, like a raisin, it gets a dopamine spike after it eats the food for the first time. That first encounter with the food registers in the rat's brain, "Yum, that raisin was good! (translated from rat talk)." The next time the rat sees the raisin it gets a dopamine spike *before* eating. That makes sense. The brain sends a message, unconsciously informing the rat about a possible reward, so go there and get it. When the rat goes over and eats the food it gets a second, smaller spike. ***Very important point*** – the *anticipation* of the thing gives the bigger spike, the bigger happy hit. The brain (nature) wants you to go over to eat the food and survive. Because nature wants to motivate you (move you) it would be logical to make the anticipation an even bigger happiness hit (dopamine spike) than the actual behavior. I suspect most of us have had the experience of a big anticipation for something, like a birthday present, only to get a rather mild sense of happiness when the gift is finally opened. The anticipation is often bigger than the experience itself. Indeed the actual experience can be rather disappointing.

The Pre-frontal Cortex and Reward Override

One of the reasons that this reward mechanism works so well is that it ties together various brain processes involved in reward detection, decision making and planning, motivation, previous learning (memory), and behavioral responding. Once a potential reward is detected, often initially out of conscious awareness, a signal is sent through to the nucleus accumbens and on to the executive system of the prefrontal cortex (related to decision making). These various areas of the brain interact to inform the organism as to the quality, quantity and perceived value of the reward (Schultz, 2001). The nature of the reward determines the strength of the gong that you hear, one little piece of boring hard candy will get a ping, versus a box full of perfect chocolates sets off the fire alarm. The louder the bell the greater the subjective expectation of reward, and thus the higher the motivation to act.

When there is a potential reward the brain does a calculation regarding the value of the reward versus the cost of taking action. If a monkey sees a beautiful piece of fruit on a tree that will be a clear "ding!" On closer examination the monkey also sees a python wrapped around the trunk of that tree, a hungry python. The executive system of the prefrontal cortex considers the costs of action versus the benefit. The hippocampus and amygdala bring back memories of snakes and a sense of fear kicks in (perceived threat, fight-or-flight survival response). Everything gets weighed – the good feeling, the perceived reward and pleasure, memories of snakes, fear, perceived risk of approaching a snake – and a decision is made (often without any conscious awareness). In this same way our body-mind helps us make quick, often unconscious decisions about whether or not to act on potential perceived rewards (Bijleveld et al., 2012).

Has this ever happened to you? You are walking down the street and you spot a green rectangular piece of paper up ahead on the sidewalk, same size as a dollar bill. That could be free money!! Potential reward – the dopamine neurons fire. The ensuing surge of dopamine gives the person information about the presence of an opportunity, positive feeling, that might be something good. There is a sense of anticipation, a motivation to speed up a bit so the wind does not whisk the bill away, or so someone else does not grab it first (like just missing that perfect parking spot). Memory and imagination kick in. Maybe it is $10, maybe a $100, how cool would that be! When you get close enough to pick it up you can clearly see it is a fake $100 with some advertising printed on it.

No inherent value, just dirty paper on the street, anticipation quickly turns to mild disgust. The dopamine circuit quiets down, the executive function makes a decision to pass, and you step over the green paper without missing a beat.

The reward system helps us take advantage of opportunities in the environment. It is an inner alarm bell – you snooze you lose. That alarm bell wakes us up so we can act on opportunities that could improve the odds of individual and genetic survival. It drives the organism to act. It is a root of habitual behavior, of conditioned mind and body patterns.

Habit Modification

Some habits are useful, like getting work done on time, or effectively managing our emotions in difficult situations. On the flip side, some habits of conditioned mind and body are less useful – procrastinating and avoiding study time or important work, being overly self-critical, drinking too much beer or smoking too much dope, not exercising enough, eating foods that taste good but lack nutritional value. So if we want to work on increasing or decreasing a particular habit, what is the best way to do that? First and foremost is to *start*, to do something. We need to move from ignoring it, to thinking about it, to acting on it, to being in a new relationship with it. It may take time, well yes, it will take time, if it is a big habit, probably at least a year or two. Getting ones life on track, however, in the direction of the desired destination, the desired state, is remarkably rewarding.

We can think of habit change, reducing old habits or building new ones, as a problem solving process (see Learning Life Problem Solving Model in Chapter 8 on Continual Improvement). In that Learning Life model we recognize problems, the gap between current and desired states. We explore causes, roots, consider solutions, pick the best and do a pilot test. If it proves to work well, more of the same, and if not, back to the drawing board. In this chapter we will work with these same ideas. As a way to organize all of the possible strategies that can be brought to bear on habit change we will consider three simple questions – What, Why, How?

1. What?	The Goal	What is my goal?
2. Why?	The Motive	Why is this important to me?
3. How?	The Approach	What is my plan? Am I on task? How did it go?

1. What - The Goal

What is my goal? This is the first essential step in the change process. It is both a foundation to change and a guiding question – What is my goal? From the Problem Solving Model this relates to having recognition of the problem, insight into root causes, and a sense of the current and desired state. The ultimate 'what' is the desired state, what do I want/need, what is my goal.

Have A Clear Goal

The ideal is a clear, well-formed goal (revisit Chapter 2 on Goals for specifics). This is important. Get clear on the goal. Have a sense of the desired state, where you want to go. If you want to change some pattern, then you need to be clear on what your goal is, what that change will look like. Be able to describe the desired state in specific terms. To say, "I will be healthier," is not meaningful. When making any significant life change it is important to know what you want. Specifying important criteria can also be useful (see Chapter 12 on decision making for ideas on criteria). Also know that the goal you are working on may be comprised of a number of related elements, like the goal of maintaining weight can be related to changes in diet, exercise and time management. ***Consider writing down your working goal, motivation, and key solution, and carrying that in your wallet as a reminder for those times when your plan is being challenged by the desire to do the old habit.***

Clear goals help with habit change on a neurological level. The limbic response and dopamine reward circuit are fast acting. They are important neurological drivers that activate the individual to unconsciously run toward the candy, the sex, drugs, new shoes. Those neurological forces are counterbalanced by the slower acting executive function of the frontal cortex. The frontal cortex is the discriminating mental function involved in the consideration of consequences of actions, long term goals, and personal values. Clear, compelling goals, which involve the planning function of the frontal cortex, can counterbalance the fast acting emotion/reward-based drive of the limbic and dopamine responses. The immediate flash of the limbic system is to stop and pick up the piece of candy on the sidewalk. The frontal cortex interjects, "Gross, are you kidding me?" That particular choice, to pick up candy off the sidewalk, would be easy for most of us. When the habit is strongly driven, however, as in the case of addiction, the cortex may be too slow, or its argument too weak, to override the reward system drive. The stronger the reward drive the more other resources need to be integrated into the solution, including clear goals, social support, stress management techniques, reframing and positive self-talk, values and reflection on motivation, and whatever else is needed.

> **REFLECTION**
>
> Pick one habit to work on. What is the goal? (See Chapter 3 for ideas on goals.)

2. Why – The Motive

The next essential step is to get clear on motivation. Why is this important for me, important for my success and happiness? Why am I embarking on this change process? What is my motivation to do this? Without a sense of purpose, a sense of meaning, it can be hard to persist with change, especially when it comes to shifting a well established, strongly rewarded habit, or when the road gets rough. The 'what' and the 'why' are both part of the first step of the five step Problem Solving Model, the step related to problem identification. 'What' seeks to clarify the goal and 'Why' clarifies its importance. The 'How' has to do with the next four steps in the Problem Solving Model, how do I solve the problem. The fact that both the 'what' and 'why' are in the very first step speaks to the importance of getting clear about what your really want, what you really need, and *why it is important*. Without a clear what and why the how becomes less meaningful. Indeed, without seriously reflection on those first two elements it can be hard to pick a solution, implement it, or maintain it over time. Here are some ways to work with the 'Why'.

Remember Your Motivation for Change

One of the big reasons people do not change is because they lack a clear sense of why they should change. When people know the reason for doing something, and that reason is compelling and clear, they are much more likely to act. Clarity leads to conviction and conviction leads to action. The motive, the reason for change, can be anything – making more money, being healthier, feeling happy, being successful, finding a good relationship, giving something of value to the world, taking off the collar and being free. The point is to get clear about what will move you to change, to find your MOST IMPORTANT reason.

This is an important step. If the goal you are working toward is to have a better diet, then ask yourself, "Why? What is the benefit of a better diet?" Better diet for the sake of a better diet can be hard to swallow. Better diet to look attractive to the right person can be a strong motive, better diet to not have a heart attack can be a strong motive, better diet to have more energy and feel healthy again is powerful. Tie the desired state goal into deep, compelling motives. Think in terms of potential rewards, what will be the biggest reward, the most compelling benefit. What is the hook. Why would someone waste energy on a goal if there was no perceived benefit. Humans are rational energy conservers. We need to see the value in change, the reward. ***Write out the motives for making the change, why it is important to you***. "I am changing this pattern because I am going to be healthy and strong, because I love my partner, because I want to be financially successful, because I deserve happiness and respect..." The motives can range from grand to mundane. "My motive for working on this goal is that it will build my sense of self-worth and personal value." "My motivation for completing this goal is that I will get a new pair of socks as a goal completion reward." Both excellent if they will compel you to action and success. The main thing is the power of the motive to move you, to help you to act, maintain, and succeed. It is the psychic fuel.

> **REFLECTION**
>
> For the habit listed above, what is the motivation for change?

Acknowledge Choice

You have a choice. Remind yourself. "I have a choice." What to eat, whether or not to stay on task with an assignment, what to say or not say, what to think, how we respond to emotions that come up. We have a great deal of choice over so many things once we begin to recognize and acknowledge it. "I have a choice." We looked at the process of decision making in Chapter 12, strategies and tools for making the best choices. That process begins with accepting our responsibility, accepting choice. Whenever we recognize that the switch has been flipped and an old habit is starting to roll, that is a good time to remind self, "I have a choice." That can be a very, very powerful small step. Just acknowledging to self, "I have a choice." It does not mean we make the 'right' choice. It just means we are starting to insert awareness and acknowledge our agency, our power.

A related strategy when old habits are trying to reassert themselves is to ask yourself, "Is this in my highest good? Will this take me closer to my key life goals? Is this the most important thing for me to do right now?" Is skipping class and hanging out with friends in my highest good right now, having another beer, getting angry at my partner? Ask and then allow yourself to receive an honest answer. It is a way to begin seeking evaluative information regarding our choices, self-informed, not someone else telling us what to do, but asking our highest self, our discriminative mind. It can be another helpful way to gain more insight. "Is this in my highest good and the highest good of people I care about?"

Reflect on Your Learning Life / Consider Root Causes

The endpoint of much of our learning, in school and out, is about greater agency, greater autonomy, an increased capacity to effectively live in a wider circle, to have a wider scope of being. Removing limiting old habits is one step. Building positive new habits is another. Where did the old habits come from? Many are probably old coping strategies for dealing with some perceived threat. Something in our family, environment, the larger world evoked a coping response, a potentially less skillful coping response.

In all my years working with people I have noted three major threats that can evoke less productive coping patterns: a threat to safety; a sense of not being loved or lovable; and a loss of meaning, no place, no role, no room. If people cannot solve the problem directly then they often turn to things to soothe or distract, using whatever works. Ice cream works, drugs work, sex works, video games work, working all the time works. These are indeed solutions to the problem on one level, and as such they can persist for a lifetime, even long after the threat has been removed. The response becomes a habit, an invisible collar, conditioned mind and body. Ultimately (longer term plan) what we want to do is to build capacity to cope with life challenges in a more proactive, skillful fashion, both in terms of addressing problems directly, and in terms of managing our internal mind-body responses (anxiety, anger, low energy, and the rest).

Consider the Costs of the Habit and the Benefits of Change

A related strategy for understanding motives is to consider the costs and benefits of the old habit and the new habit. Even though we may not like a particular habit it can persist for a long time, potentially for many, many years. We are obviously getting something out of it. So take a look and honestly assess the costs and benefits of habits. People will continue to do something that may no longer be useful, may even be harmful, because of some perceived benefit it brings (or used to bring), and that benefit can be a pretty shabby upon closer inspection.

Doing a cost-benefit analysis can help clarify the decision and increase the motivation for change. Just take a sheet of paper, divide it down the middle, and write down the costs on one side and benefits on the other. Do this for both the old habit and the new habit. Procrastination provides a good example. Benefits – it saves energy (we are not working), it buffers us from the feeling of discomfort associated with working on the task, we can hang out with friends or engage in other fun distractions, and we are still able to get the work done at an okay level at the last minute. Costs – lower quality work, feeling stressed by having to do last minute work, and recognizing that we have probably been wasting time on unrelated activities instead of doing our work (a reduced sense of accomplishment and an awareness of how we are unwilling to commit to personal goals, which can affect self-worth). How about stopping procrastination. Cost – facing the unpleasant assignment, disciplining self to sit and work, deferring fun and distraction. Benefits – better quality work, less stress in the long run, a sense of being in control of our lives, a greater feeling of accomplishment. ***Spending a few minutes and writing down the costs and benefits of the old and new habit can help to make the choice clearer.*** Consider including some of these thoughts on costs and benefits in your goal statement and put it where you can see it as a reminder (recommitment) to the new way.

Consider Secondary Gains

A concept related to costs and benefit analysis is to consider secondary gains. People can become committed to their problems. The problem, although it limits success and happiness, also provides some benefits, which provides a motive for consciously or unconsciously maintaining the old habit. The classic case is the person who is committed to their chronic pain condition because it provides them with access to narcotics. This is a big problem and one of the reasons that healthcare providers try to reduce reliance of addictive substances for pain management and work on lifestyle modification as an alternative, including psychotherapy, yoga and massage. Holding on to the chronic pain can also be a way to get a disability parking sticker, monthly workmen's compensation checks, and sympathy from family members. Many limiting habits have this same potential challenge, this secondary gain. If our old habit leads to self-soothing behaviors, like drug use, that are intrinsically rewarding (dopamine), there will be some desire to sustain them. That needs to be looked at honestly, how that brain biochemistry and 'good' feeling is keeping us in an old loop. It can make the change process much slower if not recognized and addressed. Look at the benefits derived from the habit. There is often a payout. Your family taught you to hold back so your brother could shine. As a reward for holding back you got to eat ice cream. What is the antidote, the medicine, that the body-mind needs to unlock or override that perceived benefit?

3. How - The Approach

The final step in changing patterns relates to the 'How'. In the Learning Life Problem Solving Model the 'How' relates to step 2-5 (consider solutions, pick one, test it, evaluate effects). The 'How' is the solution path, the map home, the way to happiness, the approach you will use to get from here to there, from current to desired. There are three elements to this final step that will guide the journey. Those elements are: (a) How do I get there? (b) How am I doing? (c) How did it go?

3a. How Do I Get There – The Action Plan

What's the plan Stan? How do I get from here to there? What is my plan? This first 'How' question considers strategies for getting to the desired state, elements of the Action Plan for reaching the goal. What is my plan? Without a plan the approach one takes will be random. A random walk in the forest can be nice, but it is also a way to get lost, or at least to make slower progress to the next destination. Most of the time we want to keep the action plan simple. Coming up with your plan can often be accomplished with a few minutes of thinking before you begin your homework, your soccer practice, your guitar lesson, your presentation, your day without smoking a cigarette or eating junk food. It can be a time-based closed to-do list. It can be pulling out your writing checklist before starting on a new research paper. This section presents ideas that can be used for building a simple, direct action plan to get to the solution.

Plan / Schedule

To be successful in life we need to understand and work more efficiently with time and space, with change. It is important to make a plan. How do I get from here to there? Think it out. Write it down on paper. If it is important then absolutely set aside some time and list the key elements down on paper – what is the goal, the motive for change, the deficiency (what is missing), the action plan (what solution strategies), how will I monitor the process and evaluate outcomes.

Once you have a plan, book it. Calendars and schedules are potent tools for managing change. Planning engages the prefrontal cortex, the executive function. It makes us look at our life in terms of *where we need to be* and *where we want to be*. It makes us intentional and more self-directed. Taking some time every day, week, month, quarter, year to reflect on life goals is a tremendously good use of time. Get in the habit of planning, of using schedules, of making to-do lists. If you are working on a specific habit change then include your new habit on your to-do list, make it one of your goals for the day. See Chapter 9 for more ideas on scheduling. A final thought, planning can also help reduce stress by making life a bit more predictable. Good use of calendars and schedules will reduce stress – no question.

Adopt an Improvement Attitude

The goal of habit change becomes real when we act on it, when we finally do something about it. Thinking about it is great. Acting on it is real. When we do start it is not uncommon to have setbacks, to fail in our initial attempts. "I don't know how to do that yet but I will learn," acknowledges that learning is a process. It also implies a commitment to improvement. Ultimate success requires commitment to the desired state, and recommitment and recommitment, until we are there. Ambivalence is fine in the early stage. When you wean a baby off the bottle there is frequently a period of great discontent. You have to encourage the younglet for a week or more, that drinking from a cup is what big boys and girls do. Being a big boy or girl is motivating for youngsters. They have a natural desire to be more independent. It is still hard though, as the bottle has been a source of comfort for their whole little life. Once they are over it, however, they know that bottles are for babies, not them (unless there is a crisis and then there might be a moment of regressing back to the old comforting behavior; adults do the same thing, not with baby bottle of course, but other bottles and related comforts; it is human nature).

Commit to improving, small step by small step (for more ideas on this refer back to Chapter 8 on quality). Key point – thinking is good, doing is better, improving is best. We do the behavior, we make mistakes, we get feedback, evaluate and modify, we learn and improve. So practicing, rehearsing, doing, with the emphasis on improving, are essential steps for any learning, including dropping old habits and developing new ones. If we commit to improvement and quality in our lives it is possible that old habits, no longer in line with our growing self-respect and agency, will begin to wither on the vine. A quality focus in our personal life leads to dignity.

Get Information / Knowledge

Know thy self. Use available resources to get more information on the problem/challenge. Get information online, join a support group, talk to an expert (professor, counselor, therapist, journeyman plumber, golf pro), get a book, search public or university databases like PubMed or Google Scholar to find the latest research on the topic. People who are quite ill, especially with more challenging or unusual health problems, will often know more about treatment options than most physicians. They WANT to stay alive, reduce pain and suffering – that is motivating (talk about being clear, knowing your mission). There are many smart people who have spent their entire career exploring whatever it is you are working on. If you really want to get traction around an issue go out and see what you can find. You may be surprised. Raise your hand if something you have read or scene on the web has changed your life. Sometimes just one bit of information will do that, the same way it did for the ugly duckling. Once you know the truth you cannot un-know it, you have taken the red pill. Truth changes us. Information and knowledge increase our sense of control, knowledge is power. Getting information is a productive coping strategy, a proactive element of the success journey. It shows agency. Do some background research on the habit in question and on related methods for change.

Avoid Triggers

Take the cookies out of the cupboard. Remove the cigarette lighter from the coffee table. Turn off the cell phone. Do not study while lying on your bed. A great way to fail is to have the tools of your old habit right there where you can grab them. That is tempting fate, asking for trouble, a set up for failure. It is like the person quitting smoking who says, "I will smoke just one cigarette to prove to myself I have control." Yah, right. Not a good plan. Clear the decks. Out of sight, out of mind, in sight, in the mind (and when in mind the wheels start rolling). Conditioned mind and body are a lock waiting to be opened, a switch waiting to be flipped. You flip the switch, it wants to roll. Once it starts you have to deal with that energy, that weight. If it is a big habit, and you flip the switch, and it can come on hard and heavy. "Don't tease the rhino, Billy." Control your environment, remove or reduce triggers. I remember once living in a small apartment complex. One of the neighbors, nice enough chap, was clearly addicted to porn and quite proud of his collection, everyone knew about it. He had no friends, no job, no life, just his magazines and his fantasy world. He was lost, endlessly swimming in an ocean with no shore in site. The Person, Behavior and Environment engage each other. You can intervene at any of those levels, and Environment is often a good one. *Clear out the triggers*. Remove the triggers from your life that no longer serve your highest good. Will you miss them for a while? Probably yes. Will you get over it? Most likely. Will you have more freedom in your life when you do? Absolutely.

Use Mental Imagery / Prime the Day

Use mental imagery to see yourself actively and positively engaged in the new pattern. See the desired outcome clearly, full-sized, real life, powerful and accomplished. You can use Priming to vicariously see your successful self and build self-efficacy in this fashion. Refer back to Chapter 3 on Priming for more information on this method. Prime the new habit every morning. See and feel the new pattern. Make it an intentional part of an intentional day. Sit down, close your eyes, relax, see yourself at the end of an epic day. Let it be awesome, let it inspire you, breathe that in, then start your day. Do this regularly until the new habit becomes natural.

Practice Mindful Awareness - Observe the Problem/Challenge

There is a great phrase, which states that, "nothing is obvious to the uniformed." Our habits are not obvious until they become obvious, and that is a problem because unconscious habits are hard to change. We need to start paying attention in order to see how such habits live in us. The simple act of applying mindful awareness can begin to change old tendencies – a watched thief does not steal. The first thing is to *look for* the pattern. If you know what that habit is, the next action is to *look at* the pattern, just start observing. Engaged mindfulness during the course of the day, week, month, year is one of the best ways to recognize the triggers, the downward slope, the negative loops, the elements of success, the incremental changes, the strong and weak links. Even if it is not possible to stop the habit at first, just being mindful of it will provide greater understanding over time. Albert Einstein once said, "Peace cannot be attain by force, but only through understanding." That is a brilliant idea. It changed my life.

Applying mindful awareness does not require us to change anything. The goal here is to be mindful of the process, to be mindful of the habit, of the interplay of person, behavior and environment. When you get angry or smoke pot or stop working on an assignment and surf the internet, just take a moment and notice. What is the trigger? What is going on in mind and body? Are others involved, is there something about the social environment, or physical space? What is the story, how is that choice rationalized? Notice how it starts, unfolds, and concludes. Observe without judgment. If you really want to explore observe and jot down the sequence of events (create a process flow chart, see Chapter 8). Try this. *Every time the habit loop starts to run be mindful of as much of the process as possible, without judgment, like you were watching a movie.* It actually is a movie, a segment of the great story of your life. (See Chapter 4 for more ideas on mindful awareness).

Practice Sitting Mindfulness Meditation or Concentration Meditation

In addition to ongoing mindful awareness during the day it can also be quite helpful to develop a regular practice of meditation, either mindfulness or concentration style. A simple daily meditation practice can reduce ruminative thoughts, anxiety, increase well-being and produce other positive benefits. It can be particularly useful for habits that are stress related to coping, such as use of drugs and alcohol. Refer back to Chapter 2 on Mindfulness or Chapter 10 on Coping for more information on concentration meditation. Meditation helps to build a broader base of equanimity in life. "If there is a problem I will do my best to manage it and resolve it." Any method you can use to develop more equanimity in your life, whether that is prayer, optimism, or developing your problem solving skills and self-confidence, will reduce anxiety and avoidance.

Solve Problems / Reduce Stressors

You remember in Chapter 10 we explored the topics of stress and coping. We considered two major types of coping, problem-focused coping where you address the problem and state-focused coping where you address the inner body-mind stress response state. One of the keys to rooting out certain types of old habits is to develop better skills at effectively managing problems in life. A 20-page paper does not go away because we avoid it and surf the web. Everyone has their limits on how far they are willing to go to confront problems directly. Peasant uprisings get crushed. Peasant uprisings also become successful revolutions and the oppressors are removed from power. So is the story of humanity. It is a process. The main thing to remember – we are born problem solvers. *Use the Problem Solving Model (Chapter 8). Map out your strategy and do it.*

Be Prepared

The old Boy Scout motto "Be Prepared" is a pretty good life strategy. Obviously we cannot be prepared for all scenarios. That is why we have a brain, to solve problems in those moments, to use our creativity and ingenuity to get out of jams. Being prepared for probable challenges to our change process, however, is a good plan. Say you were quitting smoking cigarettes. You are going to a party and you know one of your friends will be there who is a heavy smoker. You will have to deal with that, not asking for cigarettes, not taking one when offered, having alternatives in mind. You will be prepared to say "no thanks," and tell people you have quit smoking and that you appreciate their support. Pre-planning can include intentionally avoiding triggers, having a few encouraging phrases ready to keep you on track (positive self-talk), having techniques for changing body states when urges come up (deep breathing, drinking a glass of water). A big value of pre-planning, thinking ahead, is that it preloads the frontal cortex, the part of the brain that helps us make more informed decisions. It is like knowing where the exits are on an airplane before it takes off. If there was an emergency and the cabin suddenly filled with smoke you would not want to be figuring out where the doors were. Having a predetermined plan of action can make the difference between success or failure, even life or death in some circumstances. *Think of relevant alternatives ahead of time*.

Use Positive Reminders

One of the ways to stay on track is to remember where you are going. Use reminders to keep goals, action plans, and motives in mind, to encourage success. Consider putting up your goals in places you will see them. Carry them in your wallet. Memorize Dr. Burke's 18 Principles (see Resources Section at end of book).

Enlist Positive Social Support/Resources

Get help from your friends and community. People close to us are often more than happy to help us succeed. It is part of human nature to help the people we care about. There are also many individuals committed to helping because they have been through related challenges, and they now want to provide support to others making that transition. Groups like Alcoholics Anonymous are built on that model. Finally, there are many professional resources available in person and online. If on a college campuses there are typically social support resources available, from campus clubs to professional services. Taking advantage of these can significantly improve the chance for successful change.

Conversely, it may also be necessary at times to create some space, moving away from certain social connections if they no longer serve your highest good. There may be unwritten contracts in the family system or community or friendship groups about how we are supposed to be. The contract states – "If you want us to accept you then you need to be a certain way. If you change you will disrupt our social order. So do not change. You will upset the harmony in our little universe. No one wants that. So just be good, stay the same, never change." That type of message is typically unconscious and invisible, but it can be oh so real. Are families, communities, friends sometimes a bit crazy? Yes, they are. Do we still love them and work to make things better in the long run? Yes, hopefully we do. The point, consider the social environment to see if it serves your highest good and the greater good of our world. If a person or group is keeping you locked in the same unproductive loop then maybe it is time for some new friends.

Observe Effective Role Models

We learn by doing. We also learn by observing others doing the thing we want to do, especially if they are somehow like us and better at that behavior than we are. Observing a similar other do the behavior gives us a sense of confidence that we can do it as well. Observing role models also helps develop capacity by virtue of the neurology of learning. When we watch someone doing an action, then mirror neurons in our brains fire as if we were doing the action (Cozolino, 2006; Grezes et al., 2003). Once again nature is brilliant. It is a very powerful way for us to learn, very parsimonious, as we do not have to do the action ourselves to learn. *Find people who are good at what you want to learn and associate with them.* That will lead to natural changes in your behaviors and attitudes.

Also, observing does not mean you have to be with the actual person. *You can also associate with positives role models via books or media or vicariously in your mind.* You can read about someone doing it or watch them on video, like playing a computer chess game that shows you moves a chess master would make. You can also see your virtual self doing the action with the use of mental imagery (Priming, Chapter 3). When you see yourself doing the behavior successfully in your mind you are learning and building confidence. Mental imagery is a simple, yet powerful way to observe and learn.

Do the New Behavior / Avoid the Old Behavior

If you want to learn something new you need to work on it. A goal is only as good as the action that comes from it. We learn by doing, whether that is doing more math problems, hitting more baseballs, or giving more speeches. If a person is quitting smoking they practice not smoking at parties, not smoking after meals, not smoking with their first coffee in the morning (wow does that sound gross, and I used to smoke a bit – in time some old habits become so foreign you could never imagine doing them again, they no longer fit, you have seriously outgrown them). Practicing the new habit, some small step, is what builds new skill and self-efficacy. People can contemplate changing for years but never really get traction because they never really do anything about it. Contemplating change is a start and that is good. Until a new habit is established, however, the job is not done.

> Kaizen Hint: start small, take small steps, just do a tiny piece at first, but do something. Start to build comfort and self-efficacy with a small step, as ridiculously small as needed. In time that small step will become easy and you can then move on to the next step. Breaking things into smaller elements is a fundamental Continual Improvement strategy (see Chapter 8). We are more likely to succeed with small steps, and those successes will lead to a sense of accomplishment and growing self-efficacy. Focus on doing the things that lead you closer to where you want to be, the desired state. The main point is to stop waiting and to start doing (as soon as you are able).

3b. How Am I Doing – Implementation and Monitoring

The second 'How' question is, "How am I doing?" The first stage was coming up with an action plan, the "How do I get from here to there?" Stage two is the action plan implemented, taking action toward the new behavior. Once implemented an important element in this stage is monitoring to know, "How am I doing?" This question inquires about the path and seeks feedback to make corrections as needed. Starting is easy, persisting can be much more challenging. This section offers strategies for maintaining correct direction and efficient progress, staying on task.

Implement and Monitor

You put your plan into action. Now you need to track or monitor two elements – your implementation and your progress. Implementation: are you actually running 3 times per week as planned? Progress: what is your time for each of those runs, how many minutes per mile? If you do not keep some type of record, even a very simple record, it is easy to lull oneself into thinking all is well. You implement your action plan to achieve your goal, your desired state. The desired state is to go from getting B's to A's in your writing classes. You implement an action plan which includes weekly meetings with the writing tutor in the learning center, completing all assignments with sufficient time to edit at least once, and discussing returned papers with the teaching assistant. You keep track of whether you are doing those things.

In terms of monitoring progress, you could monitor improvements related to comments on your papers, grades on those papers, improved understanding of grammar, and your overall class grade. There are of course an infinite number of things one could track. Pick the ones that are simple to collect and that provide information useful to you. The ideal approach provides simple, accessible, visible feedback over time. The writing student could check off on a calendar when she met with the tutor and when she got assignments done early. She could also put grades for each paper on the same calendar. Simple, accessible, visible feedback over time. She can easily see how if she is doing her plan and if it is working.

Recognize the Reward System in Action

We have considered the brain's pleasure center, the innate reward mechanisms. They have done studies in which rats could press a lever and stimulate electrodes inserted into that section of their brains. They found that the rat would press the lever endlessly, not eating, no longer mating, just endlessly self-stimulating their reward center (Rossi & Stutz, 1978). A common root to many habitual responses is the unconscious mind-body dopamine reward surge. It is interesting to reflect on this. On some level, what we are getting out of any rewarding action, whether it is eating ice cream, buying shoes, or looking at porn, is the same thing that the rat got, pressing the bar until it starved to death. The common ingredient is the hit of dopamine, the reward elixir, the activated pleasure center, a root driver of motivated action. What we strive for, the food, sex, booze, is the experience associated with that pleasure center. The common denominator is that little dopamine surge, moving us to action, hidden from view like the Wizard behind the curtain. It is helpful to understand this underlying mechanism. It is not really the shoes, porn, or lottery ticket. It is the pleasure they bring, conditioned in mind and body over time. If you give those same shoes, porn, or lottery ticket to an orangutan do not expect a big, "Thank you Cornelius." (Does anyone know why orangutans like to call strangers Cornelius? Digressing...) That knowledge can lead to more insight into our own patterns. When an old habit starts to rev up, stop to reflect on this basic biological reward mechanism in action. Label it, "Dopamine surge motivating action." *Whether you choose to act on the urge or not, take a moment, close your eyes and get in touch with this ancient biological driver of human action. What we want is not what we think we want...*

Be With It

It can be very useful to see our challenges as learning experiences, opportunities for growth. That is a productive reframe (taking a negative and finding the positive in it). You may remember the work of Susan Kobasa, as described in Chapter 2. She studied business executives working in stressful environments. Her goal was see who got sick and who stayed healthy based on personality characteristics. Kobasa noticed that the individuals who stayed healthy had several things in common. First, they were committed to their goals. Second, they believed that they had control over their destiny. Finally, the main point here, they saw problems as challenges, opportunities for growth.

Joseph Campbell, the scholar of world mythology spoke of our tendency to psychologically concretize problems. We make the problem a thick wall that obstructs progress. He suggested, that if we can learn to work with life challenges more psychologically, more metaphorically, more energetically, then they actually become the way, the path. If the problem is the thing that keeps us from being complete, from being happy, from being successful, then passing through that problem is the obvious way to the next level. It is a key in the hero's journey. One of my colleagues used to say that if there is a bump on the wheel then that is where you need to go and do the work. If shyness keeps a person from meeting someone special, then one's shyness is the energy field that needs to be embraced and entered, not run away from.

A key to being with the problem, when the urge is strong, when the reward bell is at fire alarm level, is to *learn to be ok with not being ok*. To learn to be a witness to it. That is not necessarily easy to do, it can actually be quite hard, but *being able to sit with it, to be mindfully aware of what is going on in mind and body and be with it, can be deeply transformative*. This too shall pass. If we can sit with it long enough then the alarm bell will eventually stop ringing. We have made it through that wave. We are learning a new pattern. That is a big step, probably resulting from a series of small steps over time. In Chapter 11 on emotional literacy we looked at how to use this approach. The basic strategy, remind yourself in those moments of discomfort, "That is a feeling.

I am not my feelings." "That is just a thought. I am not my thoughts. I no longer support that thought. I no longer need that thought." Then bring in antidote positive self-talk.

Manage Your State

You remember from Chapter 10 on coping and equanimity that there are two basic types of coping. One is problem or *stressor* focused and the other is STATE or *stress* focused coping. In state focused coping we are trying to manage the internal thoughts, emotions and physical feelings that are associated with being stressed. One of the reasons many people hold on to less productive habits is because those very habits help them manage their aversive internal states. Someone drinks too much because he is anxious, shops too much because she is lonely. If we want to be successful in our change process we need to adopt effective strategies to cope with less pleasant internal states associated with life's ups and downs of life. Here are some simple ideas.

Breathe

Body chemistry can be manipulated with water and breath. Stop breathing, you die. Drink extreme quantities of water, you die. Or, do either of these appropriately and they will help you feel better. When feeling anxious take long, deep inhales and slow exhales, with the exhale being about twice as long as the inhale. So, for example, inhale to a count of four and then exhale to a count of eight. Another useful strategy is to exhale like you were fogging a mirror, a heavy breath exhale with the throat slightly constricted. This has a noticeably quieting effect on mind and body. Another predictably quieting breathing pattern is to breathe at a rate of six breaths per minute, five-count in and five-count out. Research has found this pattern to be very relaxing (Bernardi et al., 2001). Other breath modifying methods include laughing out loud (a benefit of feeling deranged, which only adds to the humor), or singing boisterously (also a potential cause of mirth and merriment, and who does not like mirth and merriment?). If you are anxious or depressed drink a tall glass of warm water, maybe with lemon for taste, not cold (less ideal for internal biochemistry). It is important that you drink water, not juice, sugared beverages, energy drinks, caffeinated beverages, or soda. Drinking water increases fluid volume in the body, which affects blood biochemistry. In about twenty minutes there is a very good chance that your blood chemistry will change and that your mood may change noticeably as well. Research suggests the benefits of water and warm beverages (Edmonds & Jeffes, 2009; Quinlan et al., 1997).

STOP

If you are starting to spin you want to start tapping the brakes and slow things do as soon as you recognize it. Remember to **STOP** – ***Stop, Take*** a few deep breaths, ***Orient*** "What am I thinking/feeling? What is the presumed threat? What small step can I do to reel it in? What is the next most important thing to do?", and the ***Proceed***. "What is the threat here?" Sit with that for a moment and think about it. Re-evaluate the challenge. Often you will realize it is not really very big, what is happening is just an old, unconscious, reactive habit. NO DRAMA, just do it. You are now re-learning and shifting an old pattern. "What is the next most important thing to do?" That might be to sit and meditate for a moment, talk to a friend, drink a large glass of water, laugh, go for a walk, pray, talk to your plastic Jesus, jump up and down, give yourself a pep talk, respect yourself, hug a monkey, take a cold shower, take a hot shower, remember that this too shall pass, also definitely remember that "I don't know how to do that yet, but I WILL LEARN!" Do what you can to move the needle back toward the center, move back toward homeostasis. *Use whatever dignified, healthy, effective methods work for you to bring the mind and body back into balance.*

Use Positive Self-Talk

Transform the inner voice. If it is not supportive then remind yourself, "That is a thought, I am not my thoughts, I no longer support that thought, I no longer need that thought (or feeling)." Get in the habit of using positive self-talk to encourage and inspire. It is free, effective, and available any time we need it. You can talk to yourself or you can imagine the voice of a mentor talking to you, like having your own coach or personal trainer in your head. The quality of that self-talk should always be encouraging, positive, and helpful for maintaining equanimity. The messages should remind you that you are good, capable, strong, deserving, and that you will succeed. You can remind yourself, "I can do this", "I feel incredible," "I am having fun," "I am strong and capable."

Another very good strategy is write out specific phrases related to your habit change process. This can include your motives for change, encouraging phrases, and prepared responses to use when the internal story is trying to talk you into doing the old habit. Carry these notes with you or post them where you can see them. When the loop begins to emerge you can refer to them. One of my students carries small cards in her purse, positive reminders of why she wants to stay on track. When the old habit voice comes up she takes out her cards to remind her of the goal. On one card you can write your key motive for change, "I want to be free from fear". On another an encouraging phrases, "I don't know how to do this yet, but I will learn." On a third, responses to old habit mind when it says, "You are stressed, you deserve another beer." Anticipating this pattern the card would have the reminder phrase, "Having a second beer will not help me learn how to deal with the root of this old pattern and it is time to change. It is time to accept myself and heal."

A final self-talk strategy that can be useful is to recognize internal states, such as the sensations of butterflies in the stomach and a racing heart, and reframe them via self-talk. They can be changed into qualities of excitement, readiness, power. Instead of, "I am freaked," it becomes, "I am psyched! I embrace this vital energy and it will take me to the finish line."

Practice Acceptance & Kindness

Acceptance and patience are important elements of successful habit change. The current state is what it is. Judgment and self-criticism about it does not help. Indeed, self-criticism can contribute to feelings of unworthiness and despair which can lead to medicating away the unhappiness with food, drugs, videogames, more clothes. It becomes a vicious cycle. What we want to do is introduce the medicine of self-acceptance in place of judgment. Self-acceptance is an important element of a successful change process. We just need to remember. It is what it is. I am who I am. Now here we go.

Self-respect and self-love may be the best medicine to treat the root of many self-limiting habits. It may seem odd to love self where we may feel our weakest or worst, but self-respect is a root antidote. Love is healing. Think of the people in your life who have helped you feel capable and worthy. I would bet good money they loved you and that their love made you recognize your goodness and your sense of capacity. Be patient, be kind, respect self and others.

Apply Self-Discipline

One of my teachers used to say that without discipline nothing was possible. He was a very disciplined person. In a famous Greek myth king Odysseus had to sail past the island of Sirens. It was a dangerous passage, with many shipwrecks because the crew became so distracted by the beautiful songs the Sirens would sing. Odysseus had all the other men of the ship fill their ears with wax so they would not hear the song. He then had them tie him to the mast so he could listen but not act on the blind impulse to sail straight toward the rocky shore. When the urge is strong we have to apply discipline. We must remember that we are working with the powerful engine of the biological reward mechanism, the survival drive of the stress response system, conditioned mind and body, and the inertia of years of old learning. It is a process. It will take time. It requires discipline. If you want to make it real there comes a point where you just have to say, "Enough. It is time." When the old urges, driven by fear (limbic system) or craving for the distraction of pleasure (dopamine reward system) come up behind you unexpectedly and start pushing, pull your shoulders back, stand up straighter, plant your heels, and in a quiet but very serious voice inform them, "Don't push me." Old patterns can be bullies. They may continue to win for a while, but if you persist you will be able to turn around and look them in the eyes. Once you do that they will think twice before messing with you again. Stay motivated, stay in the game.

3c. How Did It Go - Evaluation

The final 'How' is, "How did it go?" This step has to do with evaluating the outcome – excellent, close enough, back to the drawing board. All fine. Once you have implemented the plan you evaluate. With that information you can recalibrate or swap out any parts that need adjustment.

Build Self-efficacy for the New Behavior

Building self-efficacy, a sense of capacity for a new behavior, is a very important aspect of successful habit change. The stronger our self-efficacy the more likely we are to do the behavior. When we doubt our ability we do not put as much investment of time and energy into a goal. It withers on the vine. Albert Bandura, professor emeritus of psychology at Stanford University, spent a good deal of his career exploring this notion of self-efficacy. He consistently found evidence of the relationship between self-efficacy, task persistence and completion. Individuals with higher self-efficacy for a task were more likely to persist and get it done (Bandura, 1997; Schunk, 1991).

Persist

One of my teachers used to say that it takes about two years for a new behavior to become second nature. Dissolving old patterns and building new ones takes time. We live in the field of time and space. Change requires the application of strategic and skillful action in space over some period of time. When a productive change path has been found it is important to continue walking down that path until you are past the finish line. If the house is burning down it is possible that the entire house could collapse. You need to get far enough away from the fire to not get burned.

Recover From Crashes

Recidivism, or backsliding, provides a great opportunity to reflect. Insurance investigators go back to the car accident so they can understand what happened. We can do the same with crashes. Once the dust has settled, sit down, and with patience and acceptance, and consider what was going on in Person, Behavior and Environment. What led to the spiral. A self-reflection process can help to shed light on that sequence. With more knowledge it will be possible to notice when things are heading toward a crash and potentially put the brakes on before that happens. The longer it takes before we start tapping those breaks the greater the velocity and the bigger the crash. As soon as it becomes apparent that things are heading in the wrong direction that is the supreme time for positive self-talk, reflection on motivations, recommitment to deeper goals, changing states of mind and body, and using any and all coping techniques.

Maintain Optimism

Optimists believe that they will eventually find a way. It is a belief in one's own capacity and a recognition that tomorrow is another day. Thomas Hanna, a pioneer in somatic therapy, used to joke about suffering from reverse paranoia, claiming that the world was out to help him. Find a way that works for you to build optimism in your life. Priming builds positive expectancy and optimism, which is one of the reasons that it is encouraged as a practice (Chapter 3). Revisit Chapter 11 on Emotional Literacy for more ideas on optimism and other positive mind states as well.

Use Rewards

The brain has a powerful natural reward mechanism that helps to move us into action for the sake of survival. Indeed, many of our daily actions are driven by the potential for reward. We do things that bring us pleasure, pride, comfort, and physical resources, many types of rewards. We can use that innate drive for rewards as a tool for successful habit change. To do this think of goals and select a suitable reward for the accomplishment of that goal. Find rewards that are suitable and available. Small rewards are perfect for small steps, and a bigger rewards make sense for bigger outcomes, like reaching the final desired state, or important benchmarks along the way.

Kaizen suggests small rewards so that the emphasis is on the joy of problem solving (intrinsic) versus the joy of getting a reward (extrinsic). Big or small reward, your choice. The main thing is that the reward be realistic, something that you actually can give to yourself, and one that matches the accomplishment. Positive self-talk can be a reward as well, "Good dog." Sometimes a bit of praise (from self or other) is all we need to hear, just like hearing from a respected mentor that they are proud of us. Eventually, the pleasure of our new habit and of our increased sense of agency, accomplishment, and capacity will become their own rewards. We will no longer need badges and candy.

Note Your Accomplishments

Another simple and encouraging way to reward yourself is to keep tabs of your accomplishments. The Taoist sages suggest that self-respect is a central foundation of equanimity and happiness. It is good to be proud of one's self, to have a sense of self-respect and to build self-worth. One way to do that is to keep a running record of your accomplishments. Keeping track of accomplishments provides evidence of progress, data on your growing self. That can be inspiring and stoke the motivation to continue working. As an example, one of my students bought a small notebook. She used it to record her ongoing successes. She said it gave her a sense of progress, pride in her successes, and the desire to keep working on her goals. The Learning Life strategy is to **keep an Accomplishments page and regularly enter accomplishments for the day, week, or month as they emerge**. Be proud of yourself, that alone is healing and empowering.

Daily Review and Journaling

As in any problem solving or change process it is important to evaluate the outcomes. One simple strategy is to do a quick review at the end of the day. Reflect back on how things went, what worked, where there is room for improvement, and what you might do differently next time. Important – this is not a time for self-criticism and judgment. This is a time for reflection and learning. Abuse and punishment is not a great learning strategy. It is more likely to be counterproductive. Similarly, after specific activities, it is very useful to do a quick review. Take a few minutes after a block of writing or reading, after the exam, after classes, after the meeting, after eating a meal, after realizing you had been procrastinating for forty minutes. Again, this is not a time for judgment. It is a time for reflection and learning – what is my goal, why is it important, how do I get there.

A related idea is to keep a journal of your process. Note insights, jot down things you notice about habits, positive and negative, observe triggers, sequences. Think about things that hang you up, waste your time. Meditate on how you can streamline, make things more efficient, make your life more positive or productive. The main value of a journal is to have a place to get things off your chest, out of your head, and onto paper. That can be quite liberating. You will not appreciate it until you do it. You can also use the journal to keep tabs on solutions you have implemented, keep data, make notes on how it is going, what is working or not. The quality of writing is less important than just getting ideas out there. Suggestion, when you do enter something include the date and possible give the entry a title.

Have Fun

Another way to deal with life challenges is to make the change process fun, however you do that. If you want to lose weight, find an exercise program that is fun, like some crazy dance class. In essence, one of the ways to make any task lighter is to make it fun. Life is short. Have fun. Good rule of thumb. Use self-talk for this purpose. Tell yourself, "I love this. I am having fun. I am living my goals." If the stress response is rolling and body and mind are overly amped you can turn that nervous energy into encouraging energy, just reframe it, "I am pumped, this is awesome, bring it on!" Whatever works.

Standardize

If something works for you, seems to be effective, then it can be a good idea to stabilize, maintain, and then internalize that piece over time. Turn it into a habit, a new habit. That is an excellent feeling when the new pattern begins to appear naturally, without thought or effort. It is moving into habit territory, and a standardized good habit is a good thing. That probably takes at least 1 to 2 years for bigger patterns to shift and become more deeply rooted.

> **REFLECTION**
>
> What are some strategies you will use to reach your goal?
>
> _____
> _____
> _____
> _____

Stages of Change (SOC)

A final topic to include in any habit change process is a reflection on where we are in that process. A nice depiction of this is in the *Stages of Change* model developed by Prochaska and DiClemente (1984). The model looks at habit change as a process that occurs in stages. They describe five stages, with different characteristics at each stage, and ideas for navigating each stage to facilitate movement to the next level.

1. Precontemplation

This stage is characterized by a lack of insight or interest in change. This can be the case when a person does not know that they have an issue to deal with, such as a subclinical or asymptomatic health problem. A person can be diabetic and not know it for some time. A family member may be encouraging them to start eating a healthier diet, but they see no reason to do so. Conversely, a person may be clearly aware that they are addicted to methamphetamine, but have no interest in stopping. They are enjoying the ride. It feels too good to consider stopping. Both of these can be challenging, but the later potentially even more so as the person may be in a great deal of denial, not just ignorant, but actively resisting any contrary information or offers of help.

At this first stage it is useful to acknowledge the current reality – not motivated, not ready yet. It is also useful to contemplate the costs and benefits of change. How does the choice of one path versus the other affect the current quality of life and future possibilities. Some schools of thought believe it important for each person to make his or her own decision to change based on insights into how the old habit may be holding them back. This stage is a perfect time for reflection on what life is about, what is truly important, and what the future will bring.

2. Contemplation

The second stage, contemplation, is characterized by reflection on the possibility of change. At this point the individual is contemplating change, but still ambivalent about taking action in the immediate future. What is promising at this stage is that the person in engaged in an active consideration of changing an old pattern (at some point). Transformation and growth are no longer out of the picture, out of the realm of the possible. Change is being considered. The SOC model puts that contemplation to change with the next month. Personally, I think if someone is open to the idea of change and considering it, they are in the contemplation phase.

The EXTREMELY IMPORTANT thing to recognize is that, in reality, a person can be in the contemplation phase for years – "How much of life is lost in waiting." It is a way to feel good about the loop we are still stuck in, by thinking about quitting in a while. That "in a while" may never come, however. People will turn 30, 40, 60 and still be dealing with the same pattern. If the goal is to get some traction, to make it real, then things to do during the contemplation phase include developing clear goals related to the desired state, seriously considering the pros and cons of the old behavior, formalizing some strong motives for change (the Why), working on positive self-talk phrases, and building optimism and positive expectation for success.

3. Preparation

The next stage is preparation. In this stage the individual is gearing up to make the change. They are now taking active steps. Let's say a person wants to quit smoking pot. In the Preparation phase they are thinking about unloading their paraphernalia, selling the vaporizer, joining a campus support group, thinking about how they will use the money they save once they stop purchasing pot, including deciding what rewards they will use for each successful non-smoking day, and considering how they will deal with urges, friends, parties.

This is the perfect place to use the Learning Life Problem Solving Model. Turn this into an Integrative Learning Project. The point of the ILP is not a one-off class exercise, it is a strategy for a life of ongoing improvement. Get in the habit of using the model and the idea of successive 'learning projects'. Go into problem solving mode. A problem solving mind engages curiosity, creativity, exploration, and insight. Engage the frontal cortex. Clearly describe the desired state. Write out specific, taskable goals. Think of the solution space, what sequence of small steps you can take to get to the desired state. Do background research to understand the challenges and options. The more you know the more power you have. Think of your escape routes, the contingency plan, what you will do if things get dicey, what to do when triggers get activated, when things start to spiral down, when urges are strong, when backsliding occurs and there is a temporary fall from the wagon. Have a plan, a thoughtful plan.

4. Action

This is the phase where the person has implemented the change process. In the SOC model this phase is characterized by practicing the new behavior for 3-6 months. Doing something for a day or a week is often easy. Persisting with a new habit for several months is a sign of some serious progress. Starting, stopping and restarting may be part of this training period. At this stage it is important to continue working on recognizing and managing triggers and old patterns. Self-efficacy is growing but can still be somewhat fragile. This is a good time to use social resources, social support, positive self-talk, recognition of successes, rewards, and recommitment to goals as means of encouragement and support. Keep the focus on short and long-term benefits, motives for change, and overarching life goals. "What do I want? Why is it important? How am I going to get there?"

5. Maintenance and Relapse

This is the stage of continued practice of the new behavior for 6 months and beyond. One of my teachers used to say that it takes two years for something to become a new habit. This is about right in my mind, certainly at least one year. Especially during the first year or two it is important to recognize the risk of relapse and to create contingency plans for dealing with unexpected urges. Urges can persist well into the future, when you go to old haunts, see old friends, have a bad day, urges can jump right up behind you pushing you in the wrong direction. Continue to reinforce the new behavior with reward and positive self-talk and continue to note and record progress. This is why 12 Step folks say, "My name is Taylor and I have been sober for 8 years." Taylor is proud of that. He should be, and by being public about it there is some increased accountability, some incentive to keep going. There is an old East Indian saying that a person who wears white clothes does not sit in the dirt. Someone who has committed to a long period of sobriety would have to think twice about falling off the wagon, that would be painful, costly. Same with any change process. As you get more mileage from the old and into the new it becomes more painful to go back. It often becomes much clearer how the old is a collar, a limiting belief, a place of absence being artificially filled with some distraction. When the truth is known it is hard to go back.

That said, relapse happens. Relapse is when the old habit resurfaces and the person backslides. It may be a momentary slip or a serious reversal into the old pattern, full-fledged. Such reversals can happen as a result of emotional loss, serious frustration, mind-body imbalance, or something else increasing the sense of vulnerability or threat. Take heart. This too shall pass. Regroup and make a plan to get back on the path as soon as possible. Never give up.

Final Thought

One of my folk heroes, Fred Rogers, yes, the old television Mr. Rogers, was a fairly wise chap. He once said that all things human are manageable, and all things manageable are mentionable. We are all human. We are imperfect creatures. Yet most of the great wisdom traditions recognize that perfection is our essence. Getting stuck – it is what it is. Liberation from the habitual world can be the greatest act of self-love. Small steps toward the light. One day at a time. Never give up.

Restrain
Restrain unwholesome from arising

Abandon
If it arises let it go

Cultivate
Build the wholesome

Maintain
When you have it, maintain it

~ the Buddha

SUMMARY

In this chapter we looked at the process of creating new habits, either by removing long-standing, no longer useful habits, or by adding constructive new ones. Many of the elements are the same for both. One of the things that strengthens habits is when they become associated with reward. The brain's reward mechanisms, particularly the dopamine reward system, is a powerful biological driving force. Not recognizing or understanding what it is and how it works can make any habit change process much harder. By learning how to constructively work with it and use strategies for strengthening new patterns of thought and action, we can build the foundation for a very successful life, step-by-step, day by day. The keys involve knowing the what, why and how. The what is the goal, what we really want. As obvious as that sounds people often fail to change as they do not have a clear sense of the desired state. Second comes the why. Again, seems obvious, but many people lack a clear and motivating understanding of why they need to change. Without roots, a committed 'why', any strong wind is likely to blow that change process away in minutes. Finally, the how, the strategies to make change real. A wide list of ideas are provided, as different challenges will benefit from different approaches. The chapter concludes with a presentation of the Stages of Change model.

MIND-BODY PRACTICE

Sitting Meditation

This week focus on body sensations. Allow the attention to move through the body and take notice of sensations in the body, positive and negative. Find one and stay with it for a bit. Notice how it evolves over time as you sit with it. Breathe deeply into it and see what happens. Find a positive sensation in the body, some sense of relaxation or a place of comfort. Allow the mind to explore that sensation as well.

Mindful Awareness

This week pay particular attention to places where responses are habitual and less constructive. Pick one that you would like to work with a bit. Be very aware of what is going on in Person, Behavior and Environment when the habit appears. What is the thinking that supports the old habit, the environment, the behaviors. Remind yourself at those moments that you have a choice. Remind yourself of your goal, the what. Remind yourself of your motivation, the why. Pick one or two strategies from the chapter and practice working with them and the old habit. This is not necessarily the time for change at this point, it is just time to explore and learn new ways of working with habit. See what works for you.

Priming

Think of your goals for the week. Use priming mental imagery to see the most incredible week/semester of your life so far. If you are working on habit change then get clear on the desired state and see it, feel it, let it be real. This process can also help you to work on goal clarity. If you cannot see it then there is a good chance the goal is not clear yet. If the destination is not clear, the path will not be either. If hard to know then Prime clarity and motivation. See yourself as being very clear about what is in your highest good and the highest good of others.

REFERENCES

Bandura A. *Self-Efficacy: the exercise of control*. New York: Freeman; 1997.

Luciano B, Sleight P, Bandinelli G, Cencetti S, Fattorini L, Wdowczyc-Szulc J, Lagi A. Effect of rosary prayer and yoga mantras on autonomic cardiovascular rhythms: comparative study. *BMJ*. 2001;323(7327):1446-1449.

Bijleveld E, Custers R, Aarts H. Adaptive reward pursuit: how effort requirements affect unconscious reward responses and conscious reward decisions. *Journal of Experimental Psychology: General*. 2012;141(4):728-42.

Cozolino L. *The Neuroscience Of Human Relationships: attachment and the developing social brain*. New York: WW Norton & Co; 2006.

Edmonds CJ, Jeffes B. Does having a drink help you think? 6-7-Year-old children show improvements in cognitive performance from baseline to test after having a drink of water. *Appetite*. 2009;53(3):469-472.

Grèzes J. Armony JL, Rowe J, Passingham RE. Activations related to "mirror" and "canonical" neurones in the human brain: an fMRI study. *NeuroImage*. 2003;18(4):928-937.

Prochaska, JO; DiClemente, CC. The transtheoretical approach: crossing traditional boundaries of therapy. Homewood, IL: Dow Jones-Irwin; 1984.

Quinlan P, Lane J, Aspinall L. Effects of hot tea, coffee and water ingestion on physiological responses and mood: the role of caffeine, water and beverage type. *Psychopharmacology*. 1997;134(2):164-173.

Rossi RR, Stutz RM. The self-deprivation phenomenon: competition between appetitive rewards and electrical stimulation of the brain. *Physiological Psychology*. 1978;6(2):204-208

Schultz W. Reward signaling by dopamine neurons. *Neuroscientist*. 2001;7(4):293-302.

Schunk DH. Self-efficacy and academic motivation. *Educational Psychologist*. 1991;26(3-4):207-231.

SECTION IV

APPLICATIONS

14 A Healthy Lifestyle

15 Social Support – Friends, Family & the World

16 Life Purpose & Career Clarity

17 Personal Finances & Abundance

18 You and the World

A Healthy Lifestyle 14

I feel awesome!

CHAPTER THEMES
- Alameda Study
- Healthy Aging
- Nutrition
  - Sugars, Fat, Protein, Fiber, Water
  - Cooking
- Exercise
- Sex, Drugs, Rock and Roll

We are of this earth, designed by nature. Nature has certain requirements to keep things running smoothly. We need food, we need water, we need to move, we need to breathe. The requirements are simple, but essential, and it is important to have them in the right balance. Too much of this or too little of that can throw things out of alignment, disrupt the inner ecology. You give a plant too little water or too much water and you end up with a dead plant. Knowing what it takes to stay healthy is not rocket science, but it is not necessarily obvious either. This chapter provides ideas on a healthy lifestyle, the kind of lifestyle that will support a happy and successful journey now and long into the future. It feels good to feel vital. Here are some ways to make vitality a reality.

The Simple Seven

The Alameda Study was one of the early investigations that provided information on the relationship between lifestyle choices and health. The study began in 1965. It was conducted in (guess where?) Alameda County, California. Dr. Lester Breslow from UCLA was one of the principle investigators. The study involved a group of 6,928 people randomly selected from the community. The participants completed surveys asking a list of questions including items on activity level and lifestyle practices. The participants were contacted a number of times over the next 30 years to update information on lifestyle, health status, and mortality outcomes.

The goal was to see if certain health practices would affect health status and lifespan. In the end Breslow and his colleagues found seven habits significantly related to better health and a longer life. Can you guess what they were? Times up! Here is the answer, and these are not in order of importance: (1) not smoking, (2) regular exercise, (3) maintaining proper body weight, (4) not snacking, (5) eating breakfast, (6) limited use of alcohol, and (7) 7-8 hours of sleep a night. Follow-up studies narrowed these down to five. The two items that were dropped were eating breakfast and not snacking between meals (Belloc et al., 1971; Housman & Dorman, 2005).

So how much longer did the individuals who practiced these habits live? If a person did six of seven of them they lived 11 years longer if male and 7 years longer if female. Think of how many *Batman* reruns you could watch in that period of time, how many sunsets at the beach, how many more songs you could sing, how much closer you could get to understanding the great mysteries of life. That is a huge chunk of time. Plus, in addition to living longer, those same individuals lived better. They had a better quality of life. It is one thing to keep someone alive another 3 years with some new technology or medication, but if that person's life is wretched for most of those 3 years is it worth it? So the goal is not just to live for as long as you can, but to stay healthy and live as long and full a life as you can.

What about stress or things like organic foods? Those are things we think about today as contributors to health and disease. In the original study they did not look at those factors as they were not quite on the radar yet. It was 1965. In subsequent work done by Strawbridge and others, social support was examined and found to be quite important as well (Strawbridge et al., 2001). Research found that individuals who were more socially integrated, such as belonging to a church group, were healthier and lived longer. We will consider the role of social support more in Chapter 15 on Social Intelligence. We looked at stress in Chapter 10, and it clearly plays a role as well. Taken as a whole, the Alameda Study found that someone who exercises, has an appropriate body weight (which usually means they have a healthier diet), does not drink too much, is a non-smoker, and has positive social support, is more likely to be in good health and live longer, more likely to be vital.

Healthy Aging

The Three Ideals

In traditional Chinese culture a good life is characterized by abundance, happiness and longevity. Good health is clearly a root of all three. Good health provides the energy to make money and have fun with it, the time to build deep intimacy and lasting friendships, and the vitality that supports longevity. So what characterizes good health? The first answer is – to live a long life, to delay mortality, to put off death for as long as possible. I had friends and colleagues who died in grade school, high school, college, early 20's, and on and on. Some from illnesses, some from accidents, some from violence, and others from self-inflicted trauma. Life can indeed be random, disease and death just happen, little the individual can do about it. The majority of times, however, there is a lot we can do about what happens, steps we can take to be healthier and live longer. This life is precious and we never know when our card will be called. That is why it is so important to live with passion and purpose every single day. So that is the first characteristic of good health – long life.

The second characteristic of good health is – reduced morbidity. We want to minimize how often we get sick, and when sick, to compress it. In other words, to avoid getting sick, and if sick, to minimize its effect (to make the duration as short as possible or to limit the long term negative consequences as much as possible). This is a serious issue today as the number of individuals with chronic illnesses, such as type 2 diabetes in increasing. The sad thing is that many of these disabilities could be prevented if better lifestyle choices are put to work.

The final characteristic of good health is the maintenance of high level well-being during the lifespan, not just avoiding sickness, but achieving vitality, abundance, and happiness.

Senescence

To embody all three of these qualities – delayed mortality, reduced morbidity, and high vitality – it is necessary to understand the concept of healthy aging. So what is aging? Aging is a biological process, and like many natural processes it is a continuum. There are a very few points in the continuum of the human lifespan that are marked by obvious and specific biological changes. Puberty and menopause are examples of transition points in which distinct changes in form and function are more obvious. Other than that, the process of biological change over time tends to be more subtle, gradual.

Every day that passes we become another day older, every birthday another year older. That is chronological aging – birthday candle years. It is part of each person's story, meaningful indeed, another year older, another year wiser (we can at least hope). From the perspective of healthy aging, however, we are less interested in chronology and more interested in something called senescence. Senescence refers to biological age, how the biological organism is aging in time. Hours, days, weeks and years passing by is chronological time and chronological aging, birthday candle aging. Biological change over time, by comparison, is called senescence.

I am sure everyone has met two people, maybe siblings, about the same age. One of them looks like dog meat, and the other looks like a spring chicken. The one who looks weathered was the heavy smoker, maybe a heavy drinker, possibly afflicted with serious drug abuse issues. The spring chicken on the other hand ate well, exercised, had a good attitude, and hung out with nice people who could show appreciation and respect. Both are the same chronological age, but they are very different biological ages. One is them is biologically younger. That one will, with some higher probability, have fewer illnesses, live longer, and be more vital. The 'older' one burned the candle at both ends, so there is not much wick left. Healthy aging has to do with the wise use of chronological time in order to slow biological time, to maintain our biological vitality or robustness for as long as humanly possible. Capish?

The State of Affairs

So how are we doing as a society in terms of healthy aging? We have certainly made progress over the past few millennia in both morbidity and mortality. During the Bronze Age in the Near East, about 3300-1200 BCE, people lived to an average age of about 25. A big part of that was due to high infant mortality (the very young, like the very old, are much more vulnerable to diseases and other traumas, and thus have a higher mortality rate). From the Bronze Age to 1900 (about 3100 years) life expectancy increased 27 years. In the developed world from 1900 to the present (about 100 years) it increased another 27 years. It took thirty-one centuries for the first 27 year jump and then one century for the second 27 year increase. That second jump of another 27 years in just one century was largely due to improvements in sanitation, nutrition, and medical care resulting in reduced infant mortality and fewer deaths during mid-life. In 1900 4% of the US population was over 65, today it is 13%. This is one of the reasons that Medicare and Social Security are going broke, simple math, the money is not keeping up with the increasing number of people who are living longer. When Social Security was first created the average American died at age about 60 (and retirement began at 65!). Today the average lifespan is 79 years. A lot more people are living longer, sometimes a lot longer, which is a sign that we are doing some things right.

Can we do better? Heck ya. In the book, *Between Zeus and the Salmon: The Biodemography of Longevity*, the authors provide a model for calculating the typical lifespan of an organism (1997). To get an estimate you simply multiplying age of maturity times 6. A mouse matures in 5 weeks, an elephant in 9 years. Since humans mature at around 20, multiplying that by 6 would get you a lifespan of 120 years. In the ancient Indian Ayurveda medical system the span of a human life was said to be 120 years. Indeed, some of the oldest adults for whom we have well documented records are about 120 years old. Jeanne Calment, for example, was a 122 year-old French woman. Lucy Hannah of the United States was 117. These are obviously exceptional people on some level, very good genes, but it does show what is possible.

Today in the US the average life expectancy for all races is about 79 years old. It does not take much math skill to see that we are not even close to 120, so lots of room for improvement. In fact the US ranks 26th internationally in life expectancy of the 36 member countries of the Organization for Economic Cooperation and Development (OECD, 2013). Amazingly or paradoxically, we spend more per capita (per person) on healthcare than any other country on earth. Does that seem like a pathetic result to you? Something is clearly wrong with the equation. Japan is ahead of us, France, Spain, Canada, Cypress, Malta, Cuba. Think about it, Cuba. Cuba is dirt poor (which is one reason they may be healthier). The underpowered Cuban economy means more people riding bikes instead of driving cars, more of them probably have gardens, cook unprocessed foods rather than eat high fat, high sugar, high salt convenience foods. In Cuba they cannot afford expensive medical care so they put an emphasis on prevention. You do not need a barrel full of medications if the main treatments include walking, spending time with family and friends, going to work, dancing, and eating healthy home cooked meals. If a healthcare system becomes overly focused on making profits then simple, less profitable preventive lifestyle habits like these will not be as relevant.

What kills people in the US? For many decades the major killers have been coronary heart disease, stroke, and cancer, approximately 75% of all deaths. These diseases are all associated with preventable lifestyle choices. What simple lifestyle choices would make a serious dent in all of them – not smoking, eating healthier food, regular exercise, having friends and doing fun stuff, getting toxins out of food, water and air, contributing to the greater good and finding meaning, promoting opportunity and social equity, developing equanimity. It can really be quite simple, and like Kaizen suggests, simple is good. So let us take a look at some key factors that contribute to a much longer, healthier, more energetic, fun, productive life.

Food and Nutrition

Sugars/Carbohydrates

Your body needs carbohydrates (sugars) from foods in order to fuel its systems and processes. Your brain, for example, primarily burns glucose, a simple sugar. There are two types of carbohydrates, simple (sugars) and complex (starches and fibers). Examples of simple carbohydrates include glucose and fructose. Sucrose, common white table sugar, is another simple sugars. It is a disaccharide (di- two saccharide-sugar) molecule made from the combination of two monosaccharide sugars (glucose and fructose). It is found quite abundantly in a number of foods such as sugar beets and sugar cane. Complex carbohydrates, by comparison, are composed of longer chains of sugars strung together. The starch found in potato chips and bread is an example of a complex carbohydrate.

We get sugars from a wide variety of foods, including fruits, grains, and legumes. In the US we also add a considerable amount of sugar to our foods. The US Department of Agriculture (USDA) estimates that the average American consumes 150 pounds of sugar a year, a bit less than a cup a day (USDA, 2003). How is that possible you might ask, seems crazy high. Well ponder this sweet fact. One 12 ounce cola has about 50 grams of sugar. There are 454 grams of sugar in a pound. So 9 colas, one per day and two on the weekend, is a pound of sugar added per week. That is two cups of sugar a week just from that single item. Add to that candies, cakes, cookies, breakfast cereals, power bars, flavored yogurts, sports drinks, protein shakes, sugar added to fast foods and many packaged foods, and you are getting a lot of added sugar per week. Between 1950 and 2000 sugar consumption in the US has gone up about 39 percent, mostly from additional high fructose corn sweeteners. If you read any food label you will often find added sugars, in surprising places, even many baby foods. Some scientific research suggests that all of this added sugar is having serious negative effects on our health and well being, contributing to problems such as diabetes, coronary heart disease, musculoskeletal disorders, mental health and more.

Glycemic Index

One of the helpful ways to start thinking about and managing sugar is to think about it in terms of the concepts of glycemic index and glycemic load. It was believed at one time, not that long ago, that complex carbohydrates would break down more slowly in the body, and as a results would produce a slower rise in blood sugar compared to simple carbohydrates like table sugar. Eventually it was discovered that the blood glucose levels resulting from different complex sugar sources varies. To compare this blood sugar response, or glycemic response, a glycemic index was developed. The purpose of the glycemic index was to provide information on how the body responded to foods commonly eaten.

The index works by having a person drink 50 grams of pure sugar water. Blood sugar is then tested at regular intervals over a 2-hour period to determine changes in blood glucose levels. The data is plotted producing a curve representing dropping sugar levels over time, highest at first and lowest 2 hours later. This is the bodies response to pure sugar. The next day 50 grams of a comparison food are consumed, like white bread, or brown rice. Blood sugar is similarly measured at regular intervals over a 2-hour period. This results in a similar curve from highest blood sugar to lowest 2 hours later. These two curves, pure sugar water and test carbohydrate food, are compared with each other. The average area under the curve for the target food, the bread or rice, is divided by the area for pure glucose and multiplied by 100 to provide a percentage. The result is an index of how much a specific food affects blood sugar levels compared to drinking pure sugar water. As an example, a piece of white bread has a glycemic index of 71% and brown rice 50% compared with the pure sugar water standard (100%). Although both the bread and the rice are high in complex carbohydrates, the brown rice will have a less dramatic effect on blood sugar. Why? Because it is not refined, so it does not break down as quickly in the body, producing less of a sugar surge. Being unrefined it delivers a slower, steadier supply of carbohydrate over time. By contrast, because the flour in the white bread is highly refined its sugars or carbohydrates are broken down very quickly by the body, thereby producing a faster, larger surge of sugar, which gives white bread its higher glycemic index.

Glycemic Load

As we will see shortly, high blood sugar levels are not so good for the body. Considering that fact perhaps it is better to only eat foods with a lower glycemic index, like brown rice versus baked potatoes. But what if you have Irish, Indian or Swiss genes? You have to eat potatoes. How could you possibly live without them? So what is the solution? Limit the quantity. Sugar levels are not just about the specific food, they are also about the amount, which relates to something called glycemic load. Higher glycemic index foods, like baked potatoes, rapidly increase the amount of sugar in the bloodstream. The body needs to adjust this excess of sugar to return to homeostasis. To do that the body releases a higher dose of insulin, which helps the body absorb sugars into the cells. Spiking insulin levels on a regular basis, however, is not so good for the body, contributing to diabetes and other serious health problems. One of the ways to compensate when eating high glycemic index foods is to adjust the quantity, the amount of those carbohydrates eaten at a meal. As an example, figs are very high glycemic index foods, but people as a rule do not eat a pound of figs at one sitting. The amount of a food consumed with a specific glycemic index will determine it glycemic load. So for figs, they would have a high glycemic index, but typically a lower glycemic load, because people generally only eat a few at a time. If someone wanted to calculate the glycemic load value of a food eaten they would take the glycemic index and multiply by the grams of carbohydrates in the food and divide by 100. It is easy to find glycemic index and glycemic load tables online. Since the number of grams of carbohydrates is listed on most food packages it is easy to figure out glycemic load. Simplest thing to do, do some quick online searches of sugar content of foods you commonly eat. Also read nutrition information labels on foods. Compare two boxes of cereals and take the one with less sugars (good way to start), same with any foods you purchase.

Diabetes

There is a clear association between high-glycemic foods and type II diabetes. Type I diabetes (versus Type II) is believed to be an autoimmune disorder that typically affects people when they are quite young. In those individuals the pancreas stops producing insulin. As a result their cells cannot get the glucose needed to function and survive. Type II diabetes, by comparison, develops slowly over time and is related to lifestyle habits including limited exercise, poor diet, and excess fat around the waste. Diabetes affects an estimated 25 million Americans, with the majority suffering from type II, about 90% to 95% of all diagnosed cases. Data from the Framingham Study, a historically and medically important ongoing community-based health outcomes study, has noted a doubling, 100% increase, in the number of individuals with type 2 diabetes over a 30 year period (1970-2000) (Fox et al., 2006). Other studies note a steady increase in incidence and anticipate significantly higher numbers in the future (Narayan et al., 2006). Also, notably, mortality rates from diabetes have increased significantly since 1987 (Jemal et al., 2005). Until recently type II diabetes was referred to as adult-onset. Within the past several decades, however, it has become increasingly common in children (Koopman, 2005). Why??? Certainly a big culprit has to be increased sugar consumption. During the past several decades as Type II diabetes has been increasing so has consumption of high fructose corn sweetener. Data from large national studies also support this finding. The Nurses' Health Study (NHS) found that women with the highest glycemic loads in their diets were 40% more likely to develop Type II diabetes, 40% more likely (Colditz, 1992; Salmeron, 1997).

High Fructose Corn Sweetener
So what is a high fructose corn sweetener (HFCS)? As the name implies, HFCS is made from corn, corn syrup specifically. Also, as the name suggests, it is high in fructose, fructose has been added to it. High fructose corn sweetener has become a ubiquitous sweetening agent and also serves as a food preservative as well. It is the sweetener used in many soft drinks and prepared foods, including ketchup!!! Why? Because it is cheaper than regular table sugar which typically comes from sugar cane or sugar beets. Growing and harvesting corn is cheaper that growing cane or beets, making the production of HFCS a cheaper product. It also tastes sweeter than regular table sugar, sucrose, so you need less of it, and it helps to increase shelf life of products. All of this is good for producers of products.

To make HFCS a base of corn syrup is used. Corn syrup is like maple syrup or molasses. It is the extracted sugar juice from the food source, like maple syrup from a maple tree, in this case, sugar juice from corn kernels. This syrup is fortified with pure fructose, increasing the relative percentage of fructose. One reason for adding the fructose is that it makes the syrup considerably sweeter to human taste, pound for pound. The problem with fructose, however, is the way it is processed in the body. When glucose enters the blood stream it causes a rise in insulin. This hormone helps to move the sugar into the cells of the body to be metabolized and used as energy to power their activities. Fructose, by contrast, does not stimulate insulin secretion. Ironically, because of this difference in the not distant past it was believed that fructose was going to be a wonder sweetener for diabetics. Unfortunately the opposite was true. Fructose tends to be metabolized in the liver, and this hepatic metabolism favors lipogenesis, or turning the sugar into a fat for storage and use later during times of greater need, like during prolonged stress. As a result fructose has been found to actually be worse than regular sucrose (table sugar) for diabetics because it is turned to abdominal fat, brown fat, which ironically is related to Type II diabetes and other chronic diseases. Indeed, many studies have also shown a strong relationship between consumption of high-fructose corn syrup and the obesity epidemic in the US (Bray et al., 2004). The challenge with high fructose corn sweetener it that it is everywhere. The solution – simple. Read the label. If it says high fructose corn sweetener, or any variation on that theme, put it down and walk away, no, run away.

NOTE: Actually, to be fair, refined sugar is a root cause. Some companies will seek to appear to be more holistic and use organic cane sugar to try to appease worries about added sugar. It is refined sugar that causes the system to spike in an unhealthy way, organic does not make it any better. The best solution is to reduce sugar consumption, significantly, period. Read the label. Purchase the item with less sugar. Sugar triggers a strong reward signal in the brain. It can take a while to make the change. It will certainly require clear goals, motivation, positive self-talk and self-discipline.

What Sweet to Eat
Cutting down on sugar consumption is a self-caring and patriotic thing to do. It will improve your health and reduced the national debt related to escalating healthcare costs from preventable diseases. Two simple strategies - avoid HFCS and eat fewer refined carbohydrates. When it comes to sugars, or carbohydrates, the key is to reduce the amount of refined carbohydrates of any sort. High fructose corn sweetener is a problem, and refined white sugar is not much better. The more processed, or refined it is, the more quickly it enters the bloodstream. That spikes blood sugar and jacks up insulin, not so great. Here is an example to make that clearer. Take two versions of the same food, oatmeal. One is very refined, like instant oatmeal, and the other less refined, like five-minute oatmeal. The instant oatmeal is called instant because it has been processed, broken down. You add boiling water and it is ready to go, no cooking required (cooking helps to break foods down to makes them more edible, like cooked versus uncooked potatoes). The same thing is happening in your body. Digestion is like cooking, it is adding fire and breaking down the food products for assimilation by the cells. In the case of instant oatmeal, it has already quite broken down, so the body does not have to do much work to access its sugars. As a result that instant oatmeal carbohydrate (sugar) gets into the bloodstream faster. It has a higher glycemic index. By contrast the five-minute oatmeal carbohydrate (sugar) is less refined, takes more time to break down, and as a result releases its sugar into the bloodstream more slowly.

As an analogy, let's say you have two logs that you are going to throw on the embers to restart the fire. Like the food we eat those logs are fuel. What if one of those logs was buzzed down to a pile of sawdust (it is now highly refined, like the instant oatmeal). The other one is still a normal log. If you now put them on the fire, first the sawdust then the log, what would happen? The sawdust would create a big, fast, flash of heat and light, then darkness again, lights out. The second log? Steady burn, steady light and warmth for a much longer time. The moral of the story, if you want sustainable energy, no flash and burnout, then eat less refined carbohydrates, less white flour, less instant, less quick cook, less out of the wrapper and into your mouth, less sugars added, any kinds of sugars (sucrose, glucose, fructose, high fructose corn sweetener, honey, molasses, maple syrup, rice syrup, agave, maltose, dextrose). Use whole ingredients or at least ones that are less prepared, less processed.

Fat

Trans fats
Another serious culprit on store shelves, sneering at us with greasy lips, is trans fat. Like HFCS trans fat is a substance that is used for the benefit of the manufacturer, not the consumer. It actually harms consumers. It is used as a shortening substitute because it is cheaper than butter, works like butter in baking and cooking, and provides a product with a much longer shelf life. So what is it? Back in the 1970s there was growing concern about heart disease, the country's number one killer. We knew that smoking was clearly related to heart disease and we were beginning to get suspicious

about fats and cholesterol, such as fats found in meat, eggs and butter. As people moved away from butter there was a need for a substitute. You could use oils, like soybean oil. They were low in the types of saturated fats found in meat, eggs and dairy products. The idea of putting soy oil on your waffles, however, was not going to cut it. The solution? Make the oil solid like butter with a process known as hydrogenation.

In the 1800s researchers found that if hydrogen was pumped through hot vegetable oil the hydrogen molecules would bind with the atoms in the oil. After hydrogenating the oil in this fashion, when cooled, it had a consistency similar to butter at room temperature. Using this process of hydrogenation liquid vegetable oils could be turned into sticks of margarine and used like butter on toast and waffles, or in baking for cakes and cookies. It had the right consistency, right taste, was cheaper than butter, and gave products longer shelf life. How could you go wrong with that? Well as fate would have it, tinkering with mother nature often backfires, and so it did in this case. Ironically, trans fats, those partially hydrogenated oils, have been found to actually increase the risk for coronary heart disease (Sun et al., 2007). Unfortunately, by the time this was understood the product had caught on as a core ingredient in industrial foods and as the cooking oil in a lot of commercially prepared fried foods. Recognition of its harm to human health, however, is now leading toward a ban on its use in food products in the United States (FDA, 2013).

Phat Research
Trans fats are also significantly more harmful for the cardiovascular system compared with regular fats. There are two types of cholesterol in the body, LDL and HDL, or low and high density lipoprotein. Trans fats raise the harmful LDL and lower the beneficial HDL, as well as raising insulin and triglyceride levels. Trans fat is also oxidative (easily loses hydrogen atoms) which is damaging to arterial walls. Two large nursing studies of over 80,000 participants found that a 2% increase in trans fats in the diet was associated with a 33% increased risk for coronary heart diseases (Kyungwon et al., 2005). Trans fats are everywhere. The solution is simple, the same as for HFCS. Read the labels. If the ingredients include the terms "trans fats, hydrogenated oils, or partially hydrogenated oil," put it down and walk away. Maybe even grease the bottoms of your shoes with the stuff and skate away as fast as you can, like greased lightening, as my father used to say. Grease on America!

Good Fat
Fatliness is next to godliness (or something like that). We need fat to survive. There are three types of fat: saturated, unsaturated, and trans fats. Saturated fats are the fats from animal products, basically meat, eggs, and dairy. These foods tend to increase cholesterol and it is suggested that you limit intake to less than 7 percent of their total daily calories (which varies per person) (Renata & Mozaffarian, 2010). If a person consumed about 2000 calories a day that would be around 140 calories. A large egg is about 65 calories. Two eggs and you are there. Unsaturated fats include polyunsaturated and monounsaturated. Unsaturated fats in the diet come mainly from nuts, fish and vegetable oils, like olive or canola oil. The recommendation is that these fats constitute about 20-30 percent of total daily calories. Trans fat is a commercially produced industrial food product, like high fructose corn sweetener. It is not a natural product. It is not something the human body needs. It is recommended that it be avoided completely.

Naturally occurring fats play a vital role in hormone production, vitamin metabolism, brain function, daily energy needs, and more. One of the reasons they need to be part of a diet is because they contain essential fatty acids (EFAs). They are called essential because they are molecules that are required for the cells to function but the body does produce them. It is therefore essential that you get them from your diet. There are two EFAs the human body needs from food sources. These are alpha-linolenic acid, also known as omega-3 fatty acid, and linoleic acid, or omega-6 fatty acid. Historically the ratio of omega-6 to omega-3 in the human diet was about 1-to-1. Today that ratio has become seriously skewed toward omega-6, with ratios in Western diets of about 16-to-1, much less ideal. EFAs are plentiful in specific foods including fish and fish oil, hemp seed and canola oil, walnuts, spinach and other sources.

Protein

Protein provides the building blocks for every cell in your body. Protein helps to build hair, bones, blood, muscle, organs, and the immune system. It is an essential nutrient that the body needs to function properly, to function at all for that matter. Protein in foods primarily comes from animal products, such as meat, fish, eggs and dairy, as well as from nuts, beans and grains. Proteins are composed of amino acids (amino relates to the nitrogen bearing aspect of protein molecules). These molecules bind together to form long protein chains. There are 22 amino acids that we need. Your body can produce 13 of them, the other 9 have to be obtained from food. Those 9 are called the essential amino acids. Like the essential fatty acids, the body cannot produce them, they have to come from food.

Foods that contain all of these 9 essential amino acids are called complete proteins or high quality proteins. They optimally support biological needs. Getting all 9 in your diet is the goal. This is not a problem if you consume animal products as they contain the full set that we need. If you are vegan or vegetarian with limited use of dairy, fish or eggs, then you need to pay a bit more attention to make sure you are getting the complete set of essential amino acids in your diet. Most non-animal sources tend to be lower in one or two amino acids (grains are lower in lysine and legumes are lower in methionine, for example). One solution is to combine the foods that are lower in one or more amino acids to make a complete set, these are referred to as complementary proteins. So combining grains and beans (both of which are lower in one), creates a complete set. This is common around the globe, a combination of a grain with a legume to make a complete protein. Some examples include the following grain and legume combinations:

India – dahl made from rice (grain) and lentils (legume)
Mexico – a burrito made with flour tortillas (grain) and beans (legume)
United States – bread (grain) with peanut butter (a legume)
Middle East – pita bread (grain) with chickpea hummus (legume)

I am getting hungry! Another simple way to make a complete set is to make sure you eat a variety of protein sources throughout the day (a varied diet of whole grains, nuts, seeds, legumes and leafy green vegetables). Even if you eat a food with limited amino acids at one meal, if you have any complementary food within a few hours the body uses them together efficiently. If you are vegetarian and consume dairy or eggs you are covered, both of those have complete proteins. Granola and milk, macaroni and cheese, an egg for breakfast, all good. If you are vegan you can consider a number of non-animal high quality proteins, including soy, amaranth and quinoa. Variety truly is the spice of life, (oh, use spices too, other benefits as well).

Protein Supplements

Protein supplements, do we need them? The average adult gets plenty of protein from a healthy diet, no supplementation necessary. The recommended dietary allowance (RDA) for protein is 46 grams per day for women and 56 grams for men. A glass of milk has 8 grams, an egg has 5, and a cup of yogurt 11. So for breakfast you just got 24 grams. For heavy physical workouts what your muscles really need immediately is energy from carbohydrates, not protein. A glass of chocolate milk before or after a workout is one of the simpler ways to get a fast recharge, protein and plenty of carbohydrates. Be sure to drink plenty of water too, muscle is about 20% protein and 70% water. One final thought, my humble opinion, nature did not invent protein powder. It is an industrial food. There is a ton of hype as manufacturers are making a lot of money on it, mucho. The 2003 USDA Agricultural Marketing Service report listed the price for a pound of whey at $0.17. The whey protein sold for weight lifting and related activities is easily selling for $10-$20 a pound. Sure they doctor it up, but still. The base ingredient probably costs the manufacturer pennies to the many dollars in profits. Most importantly, talk about refined, easy access for the body. There is very little research on these things. Anyone using them is basically participating in a big science project. My hunch is that in time we will find they are not so good for us. Remember it took several decades to realize how unhelpful HFCS and trans fats were, just something to consider. If you must use them, consider moderation, even better, create your own healthy alternatives.

Fiber and Micronutrients

Complex carbohydrates include starches and dietary fiber. Fiber is a very important component of dietary health. It is found primarily in fruits, vegetables, and whole grain cereals. It contains important phytochemicals, antioxidants, vitamins and minerals. It affects digestion, elimination, nutrient absorption, metabolism of sugar and fat, and other critical biological functions. Research studies have show women who consumed lower amounts of cereal fiber had a significantly higher risk of developing Type II diabetes (Salmeron et al., 1997). Low fiber diets have also been associated with colon cancer, diabetes, heart disease and other serious health problems (Otles, 2014). Foods contain both soluble (dissolves in water) and insoluble fibers. A general recommendation is about 30 grams of fiber a day. Most Americans get far less than that because they eat sawdust in the form of junk food, highly refined, heavily processed, manufactured foods. Grains that have been refined remove some of the fiber and other vital nutrients. As a result they need to be fortified with essential vitamins and minerals because the natural vitamins and minerals were removed in processing, what is left is the filler. No wonder certain breads have to be refortified. There is little food value left in them. Why remove what nature built. Humans and foods co-evolved. They have what we need to survive. Why take that nutrition out of the food? Manufacturers do it because the refined product generally has a longer shelf life and is cheaper to produce. The components that have been removed can then be sold separately. Great for the manufacturer, increased profit to the company. Not so great for you and me, reduced nutritional value. If you are smart you will find foods that make YOU rich (in energy, health, capacity to work), not some stranger cashing in on your poor food choices. Find foods that have not been adulterated, foods that retain as much of their nutritional value as possible. Use food the way nature intended, in an interdependent relationship between human body, earth and sky.

One great source of fiber is vegetables, green leafy vegetables specifically. The other benefit of eating greens, and any other colorful vegetable or fruit, is that they provide micronutrients. Plants are rich in phytochemicals. These are substances produced by plants that give them their color, taste, and aroma. There are no minimum daily requirements for these substance in the human diet, but there is clear evidence that many of them are beneficial to our health.

Water

Your body is about 60% water, your brain 70% water. You cannot live more than a week or two without water. On the flip side, you can also kill yourself by drinking too much water by diluting your body's electrolytes (that takes a lot of water). Your body needs a certain amount of water to maintain its inner equilibrium or homeostasis. Water helps to maintain balance (not too much or too little) and harmony (effective interrelationship of all the constituents). Water helps the body eliminate waste, lubricate joints, regulate temperature, and replenish the cells. Water moves things. It allows for a more efficient flow of molecules throughout the body, facilitating the subtle adjustments needed for effective function. Water is a major ingredient in the formula of life. Even your neurons fire faster when there is sufficient water in the body (water volume affects the size of neurons and that affects the rate of transmission, so your hydrated brain is smarter). Water contributes to form, functionality and stamina. Think of a plant that has not been watered in a few weeks. It is drooping, hanging slack. No water pressure to keep it upright. Give the plant enough water and in a few hours it will be standing straight up.

You get some of the water you need through foods, such as fruits, but the majority of it has to come through drinking water and beverages. Carry water with you (use your own bottle, to spare your neighborhood and the planet from useless plastic trash, plus you can use a non-toxic, BPA-free bottle and protect your health – a win-win). Avoid sweetened beverages that just decay your teeth, add unnecessary weight to the body, and potentially contributes to diabetes, heart disease and cancer. Drink water, or tea, or other non-sugared beverages. Although there is a common idea that you should drink 8 glasses a day, there is actually no scientific evidence to support that. Drink the amount that makes you feel your best. If you are thirsty it means the tank is running low. You need to refill before that point. Drinking a cup of warm water about 30 minutes before a meal can also help reduce appetite and therefore reduce weight gain and can be a good substitute for sugared beverages (Davy et al., 2008).

Pro-inflammatory Diets

If you pay attention to trends in health you will notice that there is more buzz about the negative effects of inflammation in the body these days, low grade, chronic inflammation. Some pro-inflammatory sources, such as pollutants in the air, can be hard to avoid. One area where we can reduce the impact is by cutting down on pro-inflammatory foods. Sugar (of any sort) has been implicated as a pro-inflammatory substance. To reduce sugar intake avoid refined carbohydrates, white sugar, white flour, cakes, candies, sugared soft drinks, and sugar sweetened breakfast cereals. These foods have a high glycemic index, they spike insulin and promote the release of cytokines, body chemicals involved in the inflammation process. Foods with a lower glycemic index, are digested more slowly, releasing less sugar into the blood stream which results in lower insulin and cytokine production. Avoid trans fats as well as foods made with or cooked in corn oil, cottonseed, soy or other oils high in omega-6 fatty acids. This would certainly include most commercially prepared fried foods, and most junk food. Diets high in omega-6 fatty acids are pro-inflammatory and have been linked to poorer health outcomes (Noori et al., 2011). Saturated fat, found in animal products, like meat and cheese, have also been linked to inflammation in the body (Gupta et al., 2012). Good substitutes include unsaturated fats from olive and canola oil, almonds, salmon, avocados and other good alternatives (Djuric, 2012).

Supplements and Botanicals

Many people believe that it is a good idea to supplement ones diet with vitamins and minerals and possibly other botanical products for specific issues, like St. Johns Wort for mild depression. Given busy lifestyles, and the uncertainty of whether we are receiving all the nutrients our bodies require from the foods we eat, one solution could include taking a multiple vitamin now and then. Any good quality vitamin/mineral supplement will do. If you want to explore botanicals and nutriceuticals you need to do more homework on that. They are medicine. Because they are marketed as natural products people often incorrectly think that they are safe to use indiscriminately. Many pharmaceutical drugs come from these same natural products, aspirin being a good example, derived originally from willow bark. Similarly, digitalis used for heart conditions is derived from the foxglove plant. It is important to recognize this fact when taking botanical products, and to realize that like western drugs, herbal products can have side effects. They can potentially interact with other drugs and foods (like St. John's Wort making birth control pills less effective – not so good). They need to be used properly. More is not better. Do not just listen to the clerk at the herb store. Do some research first, books, online. Be knowledgeable. If you go to the website of an herb company remember that they are selling products. So they may be biased. If you search for "herbal product information" you will find numerous sites, affiliated with the government and well-respected medical centers that can be sources of evidence-based information. If you do use these products remember to take them as directed and for their intended purpose. When used properly they may be a good addition to support health and well-being.

Foods and Moods

Food can be a psychoactive substance. We clearly eat to affect how we feel, emotionally. What kinds of foods do people seek out when they are depressed? Fats and sweets. A bummed out person will go for ice cream, chocolate, cookies or cake, never broccoli. We crave fats and sugars because they make us feel better. Carbohydrates (sugars), found in abundance in cakes and cookies, are high in the amino acid tryptophan, which converts to serotonin. Serotonin is a neurotransmitter that helps us to feel positive, happier. Tryptophan is also obtained from high quality carbohydrates, like whole grain cereals, whole wheat breads and starchy root vegetables like carrots. Foods that are high in fat, like ice cream, increase dopamine, associated with pleasure. Other foods that increase dopamine include pumpkin seeds, bananas, almonds, avocados, and lima beans.

Healthy Diet Essentials

There is no one perfect food or one most evil food. If you eat junk food, just eat less, and work toward building a healthier diet over time. If you eat healthy food you may find that what works for you today may not work as well tomorrow, or what is good for your friend is not good for you.

Bring mindful awareness to your diet and eating. Notice how foods make you feel, especially about an hour after you have eaten them. That is when they are in your system and affecting you more clearly. Check in an hour after your meal to see if you are tired, cranked, energetic or focused. That is important information, very useful Kaizen data. Be open to explore and modify as needed.

Special Diets
Food is a most remarkable adventure, a great way to discover the world, to help the planet, and to live a strong and healthy life. One diet that has gotten a lot of positive press in recent years is the Mediterranean diet. The diet is often represented as a pyramid with the base built on grains, above that vegetables, beans, fruits, nuts, then olive oil, cheeses and yoghurt, then stepping up one level each is fish, poultry, eggs, sweets, and at the very the top, the smallest segment, would be other meats. The Paleo Diet is also popular these days. When you have been around a few years you will see diets come and go. The ultimate reality test for your body and biochemistry is how specific foods and specific diets make you feel. If you eat and an hour later you have energy, a clear mind, and the ability to do productive work, that is a good sign. That is potentially a good food or a good diet for you. In general, it is probably a good idea to pay attention to your eating pattern, the whole plate, rather than any specific nutrient or food (Djuric, 2011)

Additives
Another thing to avoid if possible (and it usually is) is additives in your foods. Manufacturers will add artificial colors, flavors, stabilizers, extra salt and sugars. Some of these may be linked to negative health outcomes, like certain artificial colors (Stevens, 2013). One good example is recombinant growth hormone (RGB) given to cows to increase milk production. The United States is the only developed country that has allowed the continued use of this product. It is a growth hormone. One of the theories for earlier menses in girls is because of these types of additives in foods, some of which mimic natural body hormones. These are known as endocrine disruptors. Bisphenol A (BPA) used to harden plastics is another example of an endocrine disruptor. If you have a hard plastic container for your water make sure it is BPA-free. It gets better!

Eat for the Earth
Finally, consider the impact of your food choices on the planet. The simpler your diet the less harmful impact it is likely to have on the earth. Eat organic, eat local, eat in season if possible. These practices reduce the carbon footprint associated with shipping foods. It also supports local farmers and reduce the application of pesticides and other potentially harmful products into the environment. Eating less meat reduces deforestation globally by reducing production of animal feed crops. Learn more, vote with your wallet. You can make a difference. Remember RGB? One of the reasons many large supermarkets stopped carrying RGB milk was because mothers said they were not going to buy this milk for their children anymore. That simple act got many stores to stop carrying RGB milk because it was not selling as well, which shifted dairy farmer production practices (at least a bit). When they stopped using RGB they had to give the cows less antibiotics. (RGB contributes to utter infections requiring greater antibiotic use). There is a growing international problem with antibiotic resistant bacteria resulting from the overuse of antibiotics in humans and especially in animals. Two big changes from one small choice. Together we can make a big difference with the small choices we make every day.

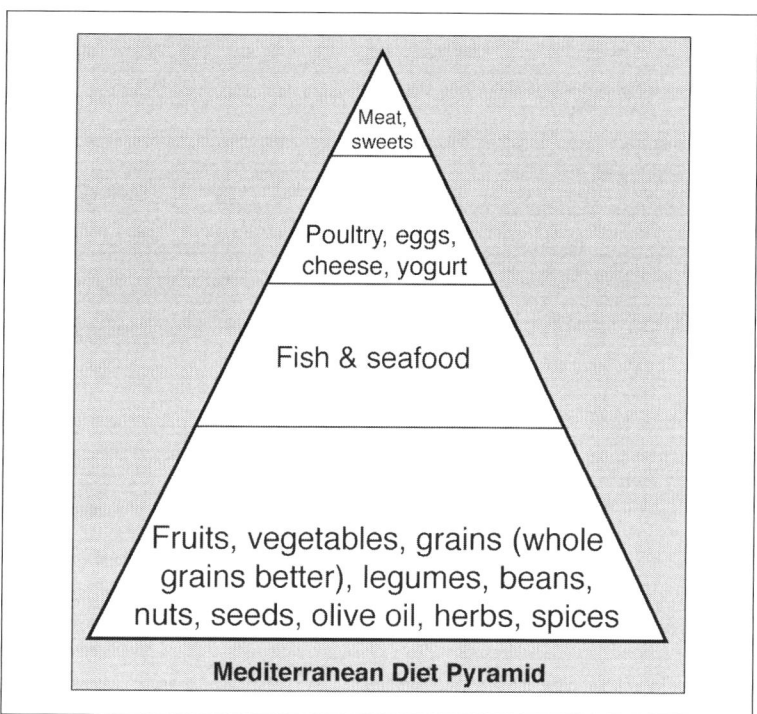

Mediterranean Diet Pyramid

Cooking

One excellent way to improve your health is to cook your own food. There are innumerable benefits to cooking for yourself. One of them is that you will save money. If you buy a loaf of bread you can make 10 sandwiches. If you made peanut butter and jelly sandwiches from that load it would cost about $3 for bread, $4 for peanut butter and $3 for jelly, or $10 for 10 sandwiches, $1 per sandwich. If you bought a premade sandwich at the cafe it would be about $4.50, or $45 for 10 sandwiches. That is a $35 difference. How long does it take to make a peanut butter and jelly sandwich? Maybe 7 minutes if you are really love the process and take your time. How long does it take to go to the store, pick out your sandwich, wait in line and pay for it? Probably about 15 minutes. You now have something you made (has some love in it), was faster to prepare, was more convenient than waiting in line, and you saved $35 which you can use toward a major trip by the end of the year (20 sandwiches per month = $70 savings/month x 12 months = $840, and that is just on sandwiches).

In addition to saving money it will be healthier. Consider again the sandwich purchased at the cafe. When you make something at home you have greater control over the quality of the ingredients. How do restaurants, stores, cafes make money? Very often by cheaping out on ingredients. In order to make lower quality ingredients taste better what do you do??? You add fat and salt and sugar, often HFCS or trans fats, and flavorings. Lower quality ingredients enhanced with artificial flavors, colors and salt and fat. All that equals donkey quack and a great, "Boo-bad!" It is also fun to cook with other people. If you live in a house with other folks or have a relationship with someone it can be a very nice way to spend a Friday night. No parking to deal with, better quality ingredients, your choice of music. You could even cook naked (but that could be a bit dangerous if you were making French fries). Finally, you can save time by preparing one dish that will last for several days, like casseroles, soups, or a roasted chicken. These are all easy to make and can keep you fed for a while. In the Resources section you will a few recipes, ideas for a few fun, simple, healthy meals.

Exercise

Exercise is an essential part of a balanced lifestyle. Exercise increases a sense of wellbeing, improves energy levels, makes the body stronger, improves muscle tone, and fortifies the immune system. Numerous large scale epidemiological studies have consistently shown the relationship between exercise and positive outcomes including reduced mortality, reduced morbidity, and improved quality of life, including better sexual health (Kruk, 2007; Capalbo et al., 2008). A classic exercise study looked at bus conductors in England and coronary heart disease. It studied the men working on buses, comparing the drivers with the ticket collectors, to see if there might be differences in heart disease over time. The study found that the ticket collectors, who walked all day on the bus taking fares and thus more physically active, had significantly fewer heart attacks. Another creative study was conducted with San Francisco longshoremen between 1951 and 1971. They found that the 4,000 men in the study who were cargo handlers, doing heavy physical work all day, had a death rate from coronary heart disease about half compared with those in sedentary desk jobs (Paffenbarger et al., 1977; Paffenbarger et al., 2001).

One common question is how much exercise and what type. In terms of amount, the American College of Sports Medicine suggests that 150 minutes of *moderate* exercise per week is a good amount for maintaining fitness and weight. They suggest 150-250 minutes per week if the goal is weight loss. By moderate they mean working up a sweat, some heavy breathing, and a sense that you worked out when finished. In terms of type of exercise it is probably a good idea to have some variety, a combination of aerobic, strengthening, and flexibility workouts throughout the week. Another good rule of thumb is to do something that you enjoy. If you hate swimming then getting a pool pass will be of limited value. I was once shopping for a new bike. A friend, who is an avid rider, gave me one bit of advice when I was doing research on various models and options. He said to get the one that I wanted to ride. That was a core criteria and it has paid off. I love to ride my bike and I do it whenever I can.

Stress Management, Social Support, and Positive Attitude

Stress management is a key to health and a big contributor to well-being. See Chapter 10 on stress, coping and equanimity for more detailed information. Emotional balance and social support also contribute significantly to well-being. See Chapter 11 on emotional literacy and Chapter 15 on love and social support.

Sleep Hygiene

Sleep hygiene is an important ingredient for health, happiness and well-being, both the quantity and quality of sleep. As mentioned in the beginning of this section, the people who lived the longest in the Alameda study slept about 7-8 hours a night. Different people need different amounts, but research has found that people who sleep much less or significantly more than the average did not live as long. Of course these are just averages and everyone is different. A very important consideration besides amount of sleep is the quality. You can sleep for 7 hours, but not sleep well, and as a result you wake up tired and not well rested. There are four stages of sleep during the night, one REM stages (associated with dreaming), and three non-REM stages. The third non-REM stage is the deepest level of sleep.

The goal of sleep is to wake feeling refreshed and ready to go. For that you probably want to sleep in a quiet space on a good bed. Do not eat too close to bedtime, preferably at least 2 hours before sleeping. If you do eat late then eat less. Do not work too near bedtime either if you can help it. You want to disengage from activities that set off the stress response, such as watching disturbing movies, ready action novels, or struggling with chemistry homework. Get ready for sleep by slowing down, the way nature does it, then drift into sleep easily and naturally. If you need help with sleep you can try hot milk, chamomile herb tea, a bit of carbohydrate rich food. Carbohydrates are good as they increase serotonin, which facilitates a sense of calm and sleep. A piece of toast will help in that regard. Hot milk provides the amino acid tryptophan, which also supports sleep. If you need more help falling to sleep you might also want to try melatonin, valerian root, or other herbal approaches. A hot bath and quiet music can help. When you are in bed if you cannot fall asleep then just lie there and meditate. If you do not fall asleep at least you are meditating. If you are meditating, the relaxing and monotonous activity of meditation will eventually put most people to sleep. You can also try a bit of Priming as you are getting ready to sleep. See yourself falling asleep easily and getting up feeling refreshed and alert. Another nice thing to do, especially if you sleep with someone, is to ask each other (or ask yourself), "What was the nicest thing that happened to you(me) today?" This produces a reflection on the day, and a search for positive experiences. It provides an opportunity to fall asleep thinking about the positive things in your life. That is a much more peaceful space to be in, good for sleep.

Drugs and Alcohol

What can I say. Too much of a good thing is not a good thing. If a person has any problematic addictive tendencies then it is best to avoid drugs and alcohol or at least seriously constrain their use. Drugs and alcohol can dramatically reduce productivity in school and life. Some research evidence suggests that moderate alcohol use may have some benefit for health, but the jury is out on that, and moderate means not much. The bottom line is to enjoy life in ways that are healthy, keep things constructive, and prevent you from killing self or others. Binge drinking in college, especially the first year, is not uncommon. It can be the root of a bucket of troubles. If there is an issue with drinking, then cut down. Go back to Chapter 13 on Behavior Change and make a plan for action.

Every semester I have at least one student, sometimes more, who choose cutting down or cutting out drugs or alcohol as their Integrative Learning Project. A common goal in this regard seems to be curtailing or eliminating pot smoking. People who say pot is not addictive do not smoke, are selling pot, or are addicted to pot. For some people it is very addictive. It reduces productive activity. It is expensive. It fosters criminal behavior in the US and other countries, unfortunately (as in serious illegal activity in other countries). When students cut down on drinking, smoking, or related, they report at the end of the semester how surprised they were by the results. When they cut down or quit they were less depressed, did better in school, and felt better about life. I am not surprised, but happy to see they figured that out. People do what they do, no judgment. If we can handle it, however, feeling life as it is, meeting life where it is, no cloud, no cover, more of the time, can make for a very rich journey. It is what it is. We all make choices. We learn and grow.

Sex

Good sex is good, bad sex is bad. What is good sex? That evolves as you evolve. In the beginning it can be finding a connection, with anyone. It can be figuring out how all the naughty bits work together. It can be picking up a few creative positions from the Kama Sutra, "Really? Someone can do that?" Once you get past the basics (and lots of folks are happy at that level) comes the long journey of learning to love another person, with sexual connection being part of that experience. The Taoist sages suggested that it takes 7 years to know your partner physically, 7 more to know them emotionally, and 7 more to know them spiritually. That is a lot of uncovering. As for the basics, be safe, with both your heart and your body. There is a lot of bad, transmittable sexual juju out there. You want to avoid that. It is one thing to pick up something nasty that you can treat with penicillin. It is another to pick up something that does not have a cure or takes a lifetime of treatment to manage. Then there is the whole issue of a surprise pregnancy, not cool if not something you are seeking or ready to handle. Know who you are with, communicate, be respectful, do not be stupid, be safe, seek to do no harm, even better, seek to do good. If you are on campus there is probably at least one student group doing sexual health education. The student health center probably also offers counseling, preventive services and products, and treatment for sexually transmitted diseases. Your public health department does the same, and in many cities, anonymous non-profit service organizations as well. A quick internet search for "safe sex, sexual health, sexually transmitted diseases" will give you a number of links to consider. Like all things, learning is good.

Rock and Roll

What goes with sex and drugs? Rock and roll of course. Protect your ears.

Simple Keys to Good Health

Exercise several times a week - 150 minutes
Eat better
    No transfats, no HFCS, less sugar, no artificial flavorings
    Eat more vegetables, fruits, beans and seeds, grains, olive oil, sustainable fish
    Get your phytonutrients, natural compounds that give plants their deep, rich colors
    Eat more fiber - whole grains, fruits and vegetables
Drink enough water
Breathe
Spend time in the fresh air and sunlight every day
Be happy
Get enough rest
Do your work
Make friends, be a friend
Do not smoke
Be happy
Limit alcohol/drug use - none or moderate
Recognize your limits

Never give up
Try alternative health methods
    Meditation, herbs, massage
Avoid too much time with television, computers, and other screen devices
Keep your cell phone away from your head
If sexually active - be safe, healthy and happy
Eat moderately
Be happy
Have fun
Do something useful with your life, give back

DO THIS

Go to the Resources section at the back of the book and fill out the Week Lifestyle Log. Keep track of some health habits and see where there is room for improvement.

SUMMARY

In this chapter we looked at the importance of good heatlh in providing the basis for a life of success and happiness. Often the keys are based on simple lifestyle habits, like sufficient sleep, not smoking, and getting enough exercise. The Alameda Study showed how following some basic health practices significantly improved lifespan. Information was provided in the chapter on diet essentials, including ideas on sugars, fats, proteins, micronutrients, fiber, water and more. Ideas on sleep, exercise, drug and alcohol use, and healthy sexual practices were also presented. A healthy lifestyle can be a rewarding way to benefit yourself and the planet. A little knowledge can go a long way in this regard.

MIND-BODY PRACTICE

Sitting Meditation

This week practice concentration meditation, Hum Sah (Chapter 10) or mindfulness as you wish. Also work with some of the breathing methods, such as the 6 breaths per minute approach (Chapter 10). Work on relaxation and equanimity.

Mindful Awareness

Be aware of health habits this week. Notice how you eat, what you eat, when you eat, how it makes you feel, immediately and about an hour afterwards. Do the same with other health habits, both positive and less constructive. If you use drugs or alcohol, notice how you feel the next morning, levels of productivity, impact on mind and body.

Priming

Think of your goals for the week. Use priming mental imagery to see the most incredible week/semester of your life so far. If you are working on changing health habits then see the desired state. Use that image to help motivate you in your change process. Think of one small step you can take this week to improve your diet or some other aspect of your health habits. Small steps lead to large changes over time.

REFERENCES

Belloc B, Breslow L, Hochstim JR. Measurement of physical health in a general population survey. *American Journal of Epidemiology*. 1971;92(5):328-336.

Bray GA, Nielsen SJ, Popkin BM. Consumption of high-fructose corn syrup in beverages may play a role in the epidemic of obesity. *American Journal of Clinical Nutrition*. 2004;79(4):537-543.

Capalbo S, Cesari F, Abbate R, Gensini GF. Physical activity during leisure time and primary prevention of coronary heart disease: an updated meta-analysis of cohort studies. *European Journal of Cardiovascular Prevention and Rehabilitation*. 2008;15:247-257.

Colditz GA, Manson JE, Stampfer MJ, Rosner B, Willett WC, Speizer FE. Diet and risk of clinical diabetes in women. *American Journal of Clinical Nutrition*. 1992;55:1018-1023.

Davy BM, Dennis EA, Dengo AL, Wilson KL, Davy KP. Water consumption reduces energy intake at a breakfast meal in obese older adults. *Journal of the American Dietetic Association*. 2008;108(7):1236-1239.

Djuric A. The Mediterranean diet: effects on proteins that mediate fatty acid metabolism in the colon. *Nutrion Review*. 2011;69(12):730-744.

FDA. FDA targets trans fats in processed foods. FDA Consumer Health Information, Consumer Updates. November 2013. Available at: http://www.fda.gov/ForConsumers/ConsumerUpdates/ucm372915.htm. Accessed May 23, 2014.

Fox CS, Pencina MJ, Meigs JB, Vasan RS, Levitzky YS, D'Agostino RB. Trends in the incidence of type 2 diabetes mellitus from the 1970s to the 1990s. The Framingham Heart Study. *Circulation*. 2006;113:2914-2918.

Gupta S, Knight AG, Gupta S, Keller JN, Bruce-Keller AJ. Saturated long chain fatty acids activate inflammatory signaling in astrocytes. *Journal of Neurochemistry*. 2012;120(6):1060-1071.

Housman, Jeff; Dorman, Steve. The Alameda County Study: a systematic, chronological review. *American Journal of Health Education*. 20065;36(5):302-308.

Jemal A, Ward E, Hao Y, Thun M. Trends in the leading causes of death in the United States, 1970-2002. *JAMA*. 2005;294(10):1255-1259.

Koopman RJ, Mainous AG, Diaz VA, Geesey ME. Changes in age at diagnosis of type 2 diabetes mellitus in the United States, 1988 to 2000. *Annals of Family Medicine*. 2005;3(1):60-63.

Kruk J. Physical activity in the prevention of the most frequent chronic diseases: an analysis of the recent evidence. *Asian Pacific Journal of Cancer Prevention*. 2007;8(3):325-338.

Micha R, Mozaffarian D. Saturated fat and cardiometabolic risk factors, coronary heart disease, stroke, and diabetes: a fresh look at the evidence. *Lipids*. 2010;45(10):893-905.

Narayan KM, Venkat MD, Boyle JP, Geiss LS, Saaddine JB, Thompson TJ. Impact of recent increase in incidence on future diabetes burden U.S., 2005-2050. *Diabetes Care*. 2006;29(9):2114-2116.

National Research Council (US) Committee on Population; Wachter KW, Finch CE, editors. *Between Zeus and the Salmon: The Biodemography of Longevity*. Washington: National Academies Press; 1997.

Noori N, Dukkipati R, Kovesdy CP, Sim JJ, Feroze U, Murali SB, Bross R, Benner D, Kopple JD, Kalantar-Zadeh K. Dietary omega-3 fatty acid, ratio of omega-6 to omega-3 intake, inflammation, and survival in long-term hemodialysis patients. *American Journal of Kidney Disease*. 2011;58(2):248-256.

OECD. OECD Indicators. Health at a Glance 2013. OECD 2013

Oh K, Hu FB, Manson JE, Stampfer MF, Willett WC. Dietary fat intake and risk of coronary heart disease in women: 20 years of follow-up of the Nurses' Health Study. *American Journal of Epidemiology*. 2005;161(7):672-679.

Otles S, Ozgoz S. Health effects of dietary fiber. *ACTA Scientiarum Polonorum Technologia Alimentaria*. 2014;13(2):191-202.

Paffenbarger RS, Blair SN, I-Min L. A history of physical activity, cardiovascular health and longevity: the scientific contributions of Jeremy N Morris, DSc, DPH, FRCP. *International Journal of Epidemiology*. 2001;30(5):1184-1192.

Paffenbarger RS, Hale WE, Brand RJ, Hyde RT. Work-energy level, personal characteristics, and fatal heart attack: a birth-cohort effect. *American Journal of Epidemiology*. 1977;105(3):200-213.

Salmeron J, Manson JE, Stampfer MJ, Colditz GA, Wing AL, Willett WC. Dietary fiber, glycemic load, and risk of non-insulin-dependent diabetes mellitus in women. *JAMA*. 1997;277:472-477.

Strawbridge WJ, Shema SJ, Cohen RD, Kaplan GA. Religious attendance increases survival by improving and maintaining good health behaviors, mental health, and social relationships. *Annals of Behavioral Medicine*. 2001;23(1):68-74.

Stevens LJ, Kuczek T, Burgess JR, Stochelski MA, Arnold LE, Galland L. Mechanisms of behavioral, atopic, and other reactions to artificial food colors in children. *Nutrition Reviews*. 2013;71(5):268-281.

Sun Q, Ma J, Campos H, Hankinson S, Manson J, Stampfer M, Rexrode KM, Willett W, Hu F. A prospective study of trans fatty acids in erythrocytes and risk of coronary heart disease. *Circulation*. 2007;115:1858-1865.

Social Support
Friends, Family & the World

15

I respect myself. I treat others with respect.

CHAPTER THEMES
- Expectation and Outcome
- Social Support
- Making Friends
- Transforming Shyness

If something is fundamental to our sense of self, our experience of self, it can be challenging to know ourselves as distinct from it. "We don't know who discovered water, but we're pretty sure it wasn't a fish" (McLuhan & Staines, 2005). That quote implies how hard it can be to question or even recognize a reality that we are embedded in, something that significantly identifies who we are, like water for a fish. Our socially constructed self is like that. Our sense of being is forged in an immersive social context. That context shapes our beliefs, the way we dress, where we choose to live and work, how we speak. Once formed the world around us reinforces and maintains those beliefs and behaviors. There is pressure to comply, sometimes subtle, sometimes not. About 400 years ago most Europeans believed that the earth was the center of the universe. Galileo had collected new information and realized that was not true. He almost lost his life for challenging the dominant belief about the cosmos and our place in it. The fish lives in water, not out of water. Without the water, there is no fish. Let us consider the importance of the social self.

Expectation and Outcome

An interesting body of knowledge on the power of social influence comes from the social psychological research of Richard Rosenthal. It came to be known as the Pygmalion Effect (Rosenthal & Jacobsen, 1968). In Ovid's poem *Metamorphoses*, written at the dawn of the first millennium, Pygmalion was a sculptor in Cyprus. To test his skill he challenged himself to create a statue of a beautiful woman out of ivory. He succeeded and indeed became so enamored with the statue that he fell in love with it. He became obsessed with the statue and yearned for a wife just like it. The goddess Aphrodite responded, granting his wish, and the statue came to life. What he wished for became reality.

Rosenthal's research mirrors that same concept. He did his work with school children. The teachers in the study were told it was a research project on academically gifted children. It was actually a research project about teacher expectation. He told the teachers at the beginning of the school year that certain children were intellectually gifted and the rest of the children were of normal intelligence. The selection of the so-called gifted students was actually random. The students were all tested on a variety of measures at the beginning of the school year, including aptitude, social adjustment, and other factors. Although these were valid tests and real data was collected, the teachers were given false intelligence scores and informed which children (randomly assigned) were particularly gifted, with high aptitudes and other positive qualities. The researchers left and let the teacher run his or her classroom as usual.

Rosenthal and his team returned at the end of the school year and re-evaluated the same group of children on the same measures. Well guess what happened? The students who were randomly designated as gifted were doing better on all the measures at the end of the school year compared with those who had been labeled as normal. They achieved the greatest growth by the end of the school year, including positive changes in IQ, which is rather impressive, not something easy to move. At the beginning of the year there was nothing particularly special about the so-called gifted students. Assignment to gifted and normal was random. Yet nine months later those students had changed. They had indeed become what the teachers expected. Like Pygmalion, their attention and intention had brought them to life. Rosenthal found, as hypothesized, that the teachers had higher expectations for the gifted students. The teacher expected more from them, possibly gave them more attention, maybe provided more positive feedback and encouraged their efforts, and as a result they blossomed. The study is a powerful example of how the social environment, in this case teacher expectation, can strongly impact reality, how our beliefs about self and others affects life outcomes.

Social Support – Why We Need Each Other

Humans are social beings. We depend on other humans from the moment of our birth to the time of our death. That connectedness is part of what defines us as humans. Some creatures on earth merely attach their fertilized eggs to a food source, like a leaf or a ball of dung (thanks mom!), and depart. The young are born into the world, alone, untutored, guided by instinct from day one. Humans are also born with a few instinctual capacities, but for the most part our abilities grow through years of relationship with caretakers and community. This is how the growing child develops a working understanding of the complex symbol systems and social patterns characteristic of human community. It is actually hypothesized that one of the reasons for our larger brain is to manage the subtle complexity of human social interaction (Cozolino, 2006; Hari & Kujala, 2009; Sherwood et al., 2008). At the end of it all we die, and yet our inanimate bodies are not just left where they drop, to the elements and nature. The body is buried or cremated in a culturally appropriate ceremonial manner, family and community often present for this final farewell.

The Cost of Isolation

Some of the early insights into the importance of social support came from the work of the French sociologist Emile Durkheim. He was exploring how social isolation affected human well-being. In 1897 he published a study on suicide and anomie (alienation) (Durkheim, 1897). In his observations he noted marked difference in suicide rates within different populations. One distinct difference was between Protestants and Catholics, with Catholics posting a significantly lower rate of suicide than Protestants. He speculated that this was related to the greater degree of social integration of individuals in the Catholic community compared with the Protestants. The Catholics allowed dancing, had larger families, and were more likely to live in extended families. They had community. They belonged to a group that provided support and protection.

The second difference he observed was between married and unmarried individuals. Durkeim found that unmarried individuals were more likely to commit suicide than their married counterparts. Contemporary research similarly shows that married individuals are healthier and live longer, and that marriage is particularly protective for males (Harvard, 2010; Holt-Lunstad et al., 2010; Molloy et al., 2009). One of the theories behind the protective value of marriage is that the person is not alone, which helps counter isolation, loneliness and depression. Isolation can also lead to drinking, drug use, and other behavioral issues that can exacerbate thoughts of hopelessness and suicide, in addition to contributing to poorer health outcomes. Marriage also means that someone is there who can provide emotional and practical support, helping each other deal with life challenges that may be a cause of despair.

The third factor that Durkheim observed was that soldiers were more likely to commit suicide than civilians. This is also something we see today in the era of the Iraq and Afghanistan wars. In 2012 the rate of suicide among active duty military personnel reached a record high, about one suicide per day, since it started collecting data in 2001 (Burns, 2013; VA, 2013). When individuals are deployed for war they are separated from family and community, and they find themselves in hostile environments. Given the nature of our contemporary all volunteer military, individuals are doing multiple rotations, longer periods away from family and friends. In addition, the deep social bonding that occurs between individuals in a military unit can be shattered by the death or serious injury of a comrade. Such factors run counter to the soldiers' needs as social beings. Perceived or real threat coupled with loss of social support can contribute to serious psychological stress. Many return depressed or dealing with post traumatic stress contributing to drug addiction, spousal abuse, and suicide. It is estimated that a significant portion of the homeless in large cities, like San Francisco, are veterans, individuals who may have never fully recovered from the psychological wounds of war.

What Durkheim concluded from his observations was the presence a common theme – social isolation. People did better if they belonged to intact social systems that provided the benefits of nurturance, intimacy, and emotional support. John Cassell, a pioneer in social epidemiology, similarly found that social isolation was associated with increased risks for alcoholism, suicide, accidents, cancer, and coronary heart disease. These health effects were found to be related to a wide variety of social factors including family disorganization, rapid social change, and urban crowding. The results were observed in diverse populations, from Japanese-Americans and poor rural blacks, to successful executives (Cassel, 1976). One of the more touching examples of the power of human connectedness involves the first Chancellor of UC Santa Cruz. His name was Page Smith, a notable historian and honorable man. He and his wife Eloise had been married, obviously quite lovingly, for many years. She died before him and in giving the eulogy he described her death as losing half of himself. He died a few months later. This is probably an example of bereavement death, death from a broken heart, from the loss of a very significant other. Indeed, studies on stress find that some of the highest sources of stress for humans are related to social isolation, including death of a spouse, divorce, and going to jail (Brunner & Marmot, 2005; Cacioppo & Hawkley, 2003; Grant et al., 2009).

Types of Social Support

Two important factors affecting the value of social support are the quantity and quality of that support. Quantity relates to the number of contacts we have, our social connections. Having more social contacts increases the chance of support. However, someone can know many people, but not know them well or get much quality support from them. Quality of social support has to do with the depth and value of the association, whether that association is intimate or superficial, helpful or not helpful, dependable, reliable, useful. A quality social connection is one you know you can count on. In the long run it is probably better to have one or more important, intimate connections that a laundry list of superficial ones. In difficult times you will know who your real friends are. We also provide each other different types of social support. The four basic types of support are instrumental, informational, appraisal and emotional

Instrumental Support

Instrumental support is the practical support of someone helping you with a task, they are an instrument of your activity or success. You need to lift a heavy object. Several other members of the work crew see you and come over to help. That is instrumental support. It would have been hard or impossible to lift alone. Three people come over and together you can lift it and easily move it to another room. That is the power and benefit of teamwork, the reason why organizations from corporate enterprises to the military put so much emphasis on it.

Instrumental support can be more or less intimate. A moving company provides instrumental social support, and you pay for it. They are not part of your intimate social network, they are part of the larger societal network. Your best friends come over and help you move your furniture. They do it for free, and hopefully you give them lunch. They are part of your personal social network. They would not expect money.

Informational Support

Informational support is when someone provides assistance in the form of information. A stranger points at the sign to show you that your car is heading into oncoming traffic on a one-way street. You are at a dinner party and your friend lets you know that you have a small bit of salad on your front tooth. I remember once being lost in Chengdu, a very large city in Sichuan China. I had taken the bus to get to a particular historic site, but had gotten off a bit too early. It was not obvious from my Chinese language map how to get to my destination. I asked a stranger, pointing at my map. He had been walking toward me. He turned around and starting walking in the opposite direction and signaled to follow him. I did and we walked for 5-10 minutes in the direction he had come from, obviously the wrong direction for him. It was quite kind of him to go out of his way to show me where I needed to go. If it were not for the kindness of strangers our lives would be much harder.

Appraisal Support

The third type of support is appraisal support. This type of support also involves providing information, but this information is of a more evaluative nature. For example, someone is buying a new hat, and you provide information as to whether it looks good on them or not. It is more than just information, such as the clerk telling the person that this hat is a size 8. It is information evaluating the attractiveness of that particular hat on that particular person's head. It is information that contributes to the person's success, happiness, survival. "I see you have been drinking. You definitely should not be driving. Let's get you a cab." That support is based on an appraisal of the person's capacity to drive safely. Appraisal advice is the kind of feedback you might get from a good friend, a parent, a paid advisor. Of course it can also come from anyone who feels like they need to give you their opinion. I love to give my opinion to strangers, "Wow, your cat is really ugly," then I run and hide. If you care about someone then offering appraisal support can be a very important service. If your friend cannot give you feedback, who will?

Emotional Support

The final type of support is emotional support. This is very important for human well-being and happiness. Emotional support can come in any form, helping, informing, appraising, being. One of the important outcomes of whatever emotional support is that is helps the other person feel loved, helps her know that she belongs, has meaning, is heard and seen, will be safe. It is support that creates a sense of emotional connectedness, being there for others when they feel lonely, scared, sad, angry, jealous, need a friend. There have been a number of studies showing the very serious effects of depriving young children of sufficient love and attention. One tragic example is seen in the effects of Romanian orphanages operated during the repressive dictatorship of Nicolae Ceaușescu. Infants in those institutions were not touched or spoken too. They were basically warehoused in very substandard conditions, abandoned by parents and society. As a result many of the children developed severe physical, mental, and emotional disabilities, including notable reduction in the size of their brains. Fortunately, if adopted in a timely manner, some of these deficits could be improved (Sheridan et al., 2012) Many adults, based on personality characteristics, are quite fine with very limited social contact. Even for adults, however, most humans tend to do better when they have someone around, someone to tell jokes to, someone to eat dinner with once and a while.

Making Friends and Building Community

Making new friends is much easier than some people might have you think. First of all, you just need to believe that it is easier to do than some people might have you think (Priming can help with that). Second you need to recognize that we are all different and we are all the same. Everyone wants friends (all the same), but not everyone wants to be our friend (all different). Finally, having friends requires getting out there and being a friend. I remember once attending a large alternative community event called Burning Man out in the Nevada dessert. I am not a massive event person, so had always avoided attending, but as a social psychologist was curious. It was an eco theme that year, so I thought that maybe it was time to finally do it. I went with some friends, we got in late, muddled our way through the sand storm, and set up camp in the dark. The next day we rode bikes out on the Playa, the massive flat expanse of dessert. There was a random woman with a large wicker basket looking for someone to give her fortune cookies to (if that was you by the way, please contact me). I went up and took one. She thanked me, I thanked her. I opened it up and read my fortune. It said, " Your task is not to seek for love, but merely to seek and find all the barriers within yourself that you have built against it." This is an old Rumi quote, the 13th century Persian poet. I knew I had found what I had come for. I left the next day. So here are some ideas for developing friendships and creating a meaningful community.

Get Out There

If a person is always buried in the books, surfing the web, drinking alone at home, it is going to be hard for them to meet many people. It is important to be social if you want to have productive connections with other human beings, friendships and intimacy. That requires initial meeting and subsequent time together. The initial meeting can be random or arranged, casual or formal, a flop or a hit. It is what it is. No problem, no judgment, no drama. It is what it is. Self-acceptance is a critical ingredient in the process. The very insightful therapist Carl Rogers once wrote, "The curious paradox is that when I accept myself just as I am, then I can change." Accepting other as well is the other half of that equation. We do not have to like everyone, but we can respect them.

There are lots of places to meet people. We are more likely to meet people like us in places of shared interests and values. There is already a connection, based on a shared interest. It could a political event, a group hike, food scenes, lectures on physics or art, a chess club, a theme specific meet-up group. Going to places and events that are personally interesting increase the chances of finding someone of similar interest (and that is a basis for communication and future interaction). There are also various organizations that sponsor events that bring people of like minds together. Search the web for ideas on "how to meet people in My City." When you are out there in the world the next thing is to check in (intuitive decision making process) when you see someone who might be a candidate. Get a sense of whether it feels right. If yes, then proceed by saying "Hello." Keep in mind that you would like to be of help to this person. That person, like all other humans, needs social support too.

Smile, Use Appropriate Body Language, Nonverbal Cues, and Self-Presentation

When speaking with someone it is good to make eye contact at times. You do not have to constantly stare them in their eyes. That would scare most people, bring out their cornered dog. If you are looking into the other person's eyes and they growl then you are probably staring (or they like you, should be obvious which one). Smiling also goes a long way as well. I once had a friend who was a very successful regional sales manager for a large Canadian firm. She smiled a lot. She acknowledged that it was one of her sales tools. Smiling immediately makes the other person feel less threatened, while making the smiling person appear to be friendly (who wants a new friend who is unfriendly? Friend, friendly, unfriend, unfriendly).

Remember posture. Do not stand in the corner of the room with arms and legs crossed staring with a frowning face waiting for something to happen. People will think you are cuckoo, waiting to go off. Go sit at the counter and talk to someone. If they do not talk back then pick up your mug of coffee and sing a Russian folk song very loudly. Someone will probably join you for that. Also, sit up or stand up straight, do not hide yourself, be present. Look confident, even if you do not feel that way in the moment, remember "I don't know how to do that yet, but...." Also remember that first impressions do count, at first. Some clothes make you look friendly, some outfits make you look serious, others scary (depending on who you are talking to of course). All are fine depending on the effect you want to have, just as long as you know you are having an effect. Hair, makeup, posture, brushed teeth, quality of breath, length of ear and nose hairs, all of it is part of the image you present. Be mindful of what you are saying to the world. Think of how you want to be perceived. Be that, but be real. It is hard to maintain a false image forever. If someone does not accept you for who you are, no problem. They are not bad, you are not bad, you are just not each others people. On to the next bus stop!

Appreciate Difference

One of the root causes that holds people back socially is that they think they need to be different from who they are. They think they need to be like other people. What does that even mean, to be like other people? There is a fascinating body of literature on attachment theory that looks at the effect of mother-infant bonding on the child's ultimate social style. Research shows how this critical developmental relationship, in the first few months of life, even shapes the infants neurology. Attachment theory posits that infants develop styles of attachment with the mother based on the mother's caretaking behaviors. The four types of attachment are: (1) secure attachment, in which the mother and infant have a secure bond based on the mother's appropriate and timely care responses to the child; (2) avoidant attachment in which the child displays less attachment to the mother as a consequence of the mother showing little response when the child is distressed; (3) ambivalent/resistant attachment in which the infant seeks proximity but resists closeness to the mother. This is the result of responses from the mother that are unpredictably appropriate or neglectful; and (4) disorganized attachment in which the child's responses include freeze postures and rocking. This is in response to abusive behavior, negativity, and frightening maternal behavior (Ainsworth et al., 1978; Bowlby, 1982).

Research suggests that these patterns, imprinted in the first few years of life, can persist and affect adult behaviors and relationships. For example, an avoidant attachment pattern in adults would be represented in a pattern in which the adult individual tends to be less social, is happy being alone, and does not find great comfort in interpersonal relationships. They can be in relationships and love people, but not necessarily need people as much as other personality types. Not good or bad. It is what it is. We are who we are. The point is that we are all different, that very early experiences shape our responses to life, and that we need to recognize our tendencies and preferences and work with them. It is a lot like considering personality factors when contemplating a career path. If you have two people, one inclined toward introversion and the other toward extroversion, they will probably be happier in different careers. Same in relationships. Recognizing who we are, owning that, loving that, and working with that, is a key to a happy social life. Trying to be like someone else is not a path to happiness, and certainly not a path to an authentic life.

Listen and Communicate Effectively

Listening to the person speaking to you is a foundation for productive interpersonal connection. Sounds obvious, but often not practiced. Effective listening is a key social skill, a fundamental aspect of social intelligence. There are many ways to listen – ranging from not at all to exceedingly well. Poor listening comes in a variety of forms. The most blatant is simply not listening, ignoring the other. The next level is distracted listening, listening partially but actually being more interested in your own thoughts, or worse, in the conversation someone else is having (very disrespectful and clearly ineffective). After that comes listening but not seeking to understand what the person is saying. That is followed by listening and understanding, but not conveying that understanding to the speaker. The highest level of listening involves both parties working toward understanding each other and being understood by each other. That is referred to as active listening. In active listening you listen and reflect back what you hear to make sure you are understanding the other person. If you were talking about something very important and wanted to confirm receipt you would also inquire about the other person's understanding, to make sure that you are understanding the other person and that they are understanding you.

Conversation

Creating friendships also generally involves talking with people, making a connection. Learning to make small talk is a very handy skill in this regard. I remember meeting a chap once who did fundraising for a large nonprofit organization. He had travelled quite a bit in his life. He said that whenever he needed to make small talk with a potential donor he would talk about travel. Even if the two of them had not been to the same places, he said it got the other person talking about something they were interested in. That was a useful strategy.

In general, when you meet new people it is best to keep the conversation positive. People who are negative in a conversation with a stranger may appear to be angry, critical, or harsh, and that is a good reason for a non-angry, non-critical person to run away (who wants a new friend who is angry, critical and harsh?). Complimenting someone, sincerely, can be a way to break the ice. Find out something about the other person, be curious about them. You can ask people how they feel about the weather, the coffee, the art on the walls. Having the person talk about himself or herself rather than focusing on you is another simple way to keep the conversation going, but just try not to come across like a private eye doing an investigation. Unidirectional questions can become imbalanced and make the other person uncomfortable, unless they are a narcissist, then they will love it (and who wants a new friend who is a narcissist?). As the joke goes, "We have talked about me long enough, now let's talk about you. So, what do you think about me?" Bye, bye!

Forgive

Forgiving someone who hurt us can be a very hard thing to do. It seems that the closer someone is to us the harder it can be to forgive them. The poet William Blake said that, "It is easier to forgive an enemy than to forgive a friend." Maybe that is because the betrayal feels bigger coming from a friend, compared with someone we do not know as well. If someone is close we have a higher expectation, a sense that we should be able to trust them. When that trust is broken it can be hard to trust again. Perhaps the act of not forgiving, holding a grudge, has some evolutionary benefit. If someone has been hurtful we learn not to trust them, to be careful, so they cannot hurt us again.

It is a way of keeping ourselves safe, separating our allies from our enemies. Holding a grudge provides quick emotional assessment, "That person is bad."

In reality there are often two sides to any story. When you ask both parties about what happened you will frequently get two different versions of the same experience. The root of the problem can be one of interpretation, perception, or miscommunication. The other thing to consider, if it is an old grudge, is that people can change. Ultimately, holding on to a grudge is generally not healthy for the one who holds it. Research has shown the positive benefits to health related to forgiveness (Harris & Thoresen, 2005; Witvliet et al., 2007). Holding on to the past can be the root of anger and unhappiness. It can keep a relationship in a toxic place for a very long time, perpetuating negative thinking and emotions. There is a Buddhist practice, similar to the Christian ideal of loving the enemy. It is a powerful technique for learning how to forgive and how to love others. The essence of it is to recognize that everyone suffers and to wish that all beings find happiness and freedom from suffering, even those who have hurt us. This practice is called Metta.

Keep Growing

Looking for someone special? One of the best ways to find a good person is to be a good person. Keep working on continual improvement. Develop skills and appreciate the fact that we are all a work in progress. When you talk to people who have been happily married for a long time they always say the same thing, that they married their best friend. What does that mean, to marry your best friend? It means to find someone who knows you, accepts you for who you are (actually likes who you are), wants you to be happy and successful (as you interpret that concept), and cares about you. A friend is someone you can count on to be there if something goes wrong, no, to be there **when** things go wrong, because they will. If you keep growing, and practice being a good friend, then you will be more likely to attract someone who is respectful of self and others (you), and who will help you to become an even better person. Also, be clear about what you really want and go for that. Super model, rock star, sure what the heck, just remember that it is the human, not the image, that you will be living with.

Transform Shyness

Shyness and social anxiety can seriously limit our quest for happiness. Those qualities can be rooted in anxiety, ruminative thinking, and negative expectations for how others might perceive us and respond to us. Like many things in life, those qualities can be assessed and worked on over time. Ultimately the basic goals are to meet people and to talk to them. Ironically, those are the things the socially shy person is self-conscious about. For general ideas on pattern transformation refer back to Chapter 13. For some specific ideas on shyness read on.

Assert

Assertiveness is a very important quality for developing positive social connections. Assertiveness is not aggression. The assertive person is not intimidating or angry, seeking to dominate or control. Assertiveness is an aspect of self-respect and other respect. It is honest recognition that both parties have legitimate needs. Assertiveness is essentially a quality of being clear about what you need while respectfully recognizing the needs of others. Achieving personal goals in life requires assertiveness, going for what you want. Not loosing identity and life purpose in interpersonal relationships requires assertiveness. Assertiveness increases the sense of personal control and self-worth. So get up and say hello. Avoid sitting in the corner talking to the cat (for the whole evening, cats are nice too but not great companions if you want to go bowling, they have small thumbs!). And remember...just have fun (but try to not spill taco sauce on anyone's head).

Change Perspectives

Learning to reach out and say hello, to think of making the other person feel welcome and recognized, is a solid way to build connections and overcome shyness. What is shyness? It is an excess focus on self. Shyness is a self-absorbed phenomena. The focus of attention is the self, not the other person. That is not bad, it is just not a great strategy for making a connection with someone. Many people feel reluctant to take social risks. There is the natural concern about being rejected and embarrassed. If two individuals with that same fear of rejection come together it is obvious how the whole thing becomes a rather diabolical negative feedback loop. Both parties are self-absorbed, thinking about their own potential failure, rather than thinking about helping the other person feel comfortable, welcomed, worthy. Someone has to jump in. If you experience some social self-doubt you are not alone. Remember that many others experience it as well. Generosity of spirit is a medicine that helps in that situation. It counters the root of shyness, which can include self-focused thinking and a sense of low expectancy for success or high expectancy for rejection. Generosity is about giving to others.

So one strategy for social self-doubt it to focus on the other. That immediately takes focus of self. Think of how to make the other, who might be self-conscious, feel recognized and valued. This similarly pulls focus off self and onto other and gives one a job. It is also infused with the quality of generosity, and the root of that is to generate, to have capacity, to be capable. That is enhancing of self-worth and positive expectancy. Also, remember that everyone needs friends, but not everyone wants to be our friend. No problemo! We still act graciously, even if surrounded by social snobs and slobs (is that a judgment, oops). It is what it is. We are only responsible for our own thoughts, feelings and behaviors, not others. Use positive self-talk, "How can I make these people feel welcome. What will I give to the world today?" Practice state management, take deep breaths, stand tall and smile (which will give a good impression anyway). Introduce yourself, say hello. Remember, if someone is immediately closed down and rejecting there is a very good chance that he or she is a shy person. It is not a personal rejection. We offer and we know we have done our part. The world keeps on turning. Tomorrow is another day. We keep learning, walking down the path until we reach our destination.

Manage Your State

As mentioned above, manage your state. Heart rate goes up, voice starts to crackle a bit. Take some deep breaths. Call on your inner ally. See and become your accomplished self. Apply any strategies you have in your tool kit to self-organize and stay on task, meet new people, reach your goal. Start small, take small steps. Set actionable, achievable goals: say hello to 3 strangers this week; have a short conversation with the cashier; smile when you pay your bus ticket. Accept the fact that you may be more physiologically activated in social situations, no problem, it is what it is. Reframe that arousal as readiness to act, prepared to meet any situation (which is what nature intended after all). Be mindful of thoughts, feelings, behaviors, and work on being okay with not being okay at times. Practice staying. Practice talking, just keep talking (and listening, really important). If you run out of things to say try, "Blah, blah, blah…" Breath and relax. Do not run away, and if you do, be mindful, not harsh or self-critical, remember "I don't know how to do that yet, but…" If your head is filled with negative self-talk remember "That is a thought/feeling. I am not my thoughts. I no longer support that thought. I no longer need that thought." Replace negative internal narrative with positive self-talk, "I am having fun. My conversation will help someone feel better about his or her life." Focus on the other, not on yourself.

SUMMARY

Humans are social organisms. We need each other. Social isolation has actually been found to be associated with stress and serious illness and death. Durkheim was one of the pioneers in this field, looking at the relationship between social isolation and suicide rates in Europe. Contemporary research shows that some of the biggest sources of stress for humans are rooted in social separation, such as going to jail, getting divorced, or the passing of a loved one. Indeed social support is an essential resource for a successful life. That can come in the form of instrumental support, informational support, appraisal and emotional support. Developing connections with a good friend or two can take some work, but worth the effort. One strategy is to find people with similar values and interests by going to places and events that interest you, like joining a book club or a softball team. Birds of a feather flock together they say. At times it can be a bit more challenging to build friendships if someone is quite shy. Shyness can be a self-focused state based on fear of rejection. The reality is that no one likes everyone. Some people will like us. Some will be neutral. Some will run away. No problem. The answer, be yourself. It is what it is. Recognize that many other people are self-conscious as well. Work on helping others to be relaxed, to be seen as good, valued, and interesting. Recognize that you are learning and developing important new skills, that takes practice and some time.

MIND-BODY PRACTICE

Sitting Meditation

This week practice mindfulness of breath, body, thoughts/feelings, sensations. Or practice Hum Sah concentration meditation. Cultivate relaxation and equanimity. If working with shyness then pay attention to body sensations, positive and negative, and internal dialogue.

Mindful Awareness

Be aware of social patterns this week. Notice old patterns that may no longer be of great value, and acknowledge your social strengths. Notice communication skills and any areas of social self-consciousness. Bring awareness to these patterns and work on small steps related to some aspect of those patterns, such as smiling or saying hello. Begin to be more aware of how Environment, Person (thoughts, feelings, sensations), and Behaviors (such as avoidance) work together to support each other.

Priming

Think of your goals for the week. Use priming mental imagery to see the most incredible week/semester of your life so far. If you are working on social skills see the desired state as clearly as possible. Pick some small step goal to work on this week and see that outcome clearly. Think of why a positive change would be useful, your motive, and begin to think of some strategies to begin to make small steps in the right direction.

REFERENCES

Ainsworth M, Blehar M, Waters E, Wall S. *Patterns of Attachment*. Hillsdale, NJ: Erlbaum; 1978.

Bowlby J. *Attachment and Loss, Vol. 1: Attachment*. New York: Basic Books; 1969/1982.

Brunner EJ, Marmot MG. Social organisation, stress and health. In: Marmot MG, Wilkinson R, Wilkinson G, editors. *Social Determinants of Health*. Oxford: Oxford University Press; 2005:17-43.

Burns R. 2012 Military Suicides Hit Record High of 349. *Associated Press*. January 14, 2013. Available at: http://www.military.com/daily-news/2013/01/14/2012-military-suicides-hit-record-high-of-349.html716. Accessed July 22, 2014.

Cacioppo JT, Hawkley LC. Social isolation and health, with an emphasis on underlying mechanisms. *Perspectives in Biology and Medicine*. 2003;46(3):S39-S52.

Cassel J. The contribution of the social environment to host resistance. *American Journal of Epidemiology*. 1976;104:107-123.

Cozolino L. *The Neuroscience of Human Relationships: attachment and the developing social brain*. New York: WW Norton; 2006.

Durkheim E. *Suicide: a study in sociology*. Glencoe, Ill: The Free Press; 1897 (1951, English translation).

Grant N, Hamer M, Steptoe A. Social isolation and stress-related cardiovascular, lipid, and cortisol responses. *Annals of Behavioral Medicine*. 2009;37(1):29-37.

Hari M, Kujala V. Brain basis of human social interaction: from concepts to brain imaging. *Physiological Reviews*. 2009;89:453-479.

Harris AHS, Thoresen CE. Forgiveness, unforgiveness, health, and disease. In: Worthington EL, editor. *Handbook of Forgiveness*. New York: Routledge; 2005

Harvard Men's Health Watch. Marriage and men's health. *Harvard Men's Health Watch*. July 2010. Available at:www.health.harvard.edu/newsletters/Harvard_Mens_Health_Watch/2010/July/marriage-and-mens-health?utm_source=mens&utm_medium=pressrelease&utm_campaign=mens0710, Accessed June 5, 2014.

Holt-Lunstad J, Smith TB, Layton JB. Social relationships and mortality risk: a meta-analytic review. *PLoS Medicine*. 2010;7(7):e1000316.

McLuhan S, Staines D. *Understanding Me: Lectures and Interviews: Herbert Marshall McLuhan*. Toronto: McClelland & Stewart; 2005.

Molloy GJ, Stamatakis E, Randall G, Hamer G. Marital status, gender and cardiovascular mortality: behavioural, psychological distress and metabolic explanations. *Social Science and Medicine*. 2009;69(2):223-228.

Rosenthal R, Jacobsen L. *Pygmalion in the Classroom: teacher expectation and pupils' intellectual development*. New York: Holt, Rinehart and Winston; 1968.

Sherwood CC, Subiaul F, Zawidzki TW. A natural history of the human mind: tracing evolutionary changes in brain and cognition. *Journal of Anatomy*. 2008;212:426-454.

Sheridan M, Fox N, Zeanahe CH, McLaughlin KA, Nelson CA. Variation in neural development as a result of exposure to institutionalization early in childhood. *PNAS*. 2012;109(32):12927-12932.

Office of Public and Intergovernmental Affairs. VA issues new report on suicide data. U.S Department of Veterans Affairs. February 1, 2013. Available at: http://www.va.gov/opa/pressrel/pressrelease.cfm?id=2427. Accessed May 18, 2014.

Witvliet CVO, McCullough ME. Forgiveness and health: A review and theoretical exploration of emotion pathways. In: Post SG, editor. *Altruism and Health: perspectives from empirical research*. New York: Oxford University Press; 2007:259-276.

Life Purpose & Career Clarity 16

I bring quality to the work that I do. I embrace my life.

CHAPTER THEMES
- Finding a Career Path
  - Values, Aptitudes, Interests, Skills, Personality
- Lacking Career Vision
- Selecting a Major
- Marketing to Employers
- Life Meaning

In this chapter we are going to consider life purpose and career clarity. These are big issues that merit serious attention. It is fine to just go through life, following the currents, sailing from shore to shore whichever way the winds take you. In that scenario life gives you your purpose. That is certainly one way to do it. Another approach is to chart your own course, with a clear destination in mind. Both methods work, but it can be very satisfying to find one's calling and following that path.

Life's Work

Perhaps there are parallel universes in which there is a parallel you having cornflakes for breakfast right now. That other you might be sitting there thinking that there is too much work to do today, looking outside to see if it is going to rain. But let us say for the sake of argument that there is no parallel universe and no parallel you. If that is the case then we can truly say that there is nothing and no one exactly like you in the universe. You are it, the only you that ever was, the only you that ever will be. If that is the case, then it is reasonable to suggest that the most important thing we have to offer to the world is who we are, our unique, authentic self. Joseph Campbell, a pre-eminent scholar of world mythology, once said that, "The privilege of a lifetime is being who you are." There is a great deal of suffering and ignorance out there. We all have something unique to give to the world, a gift no one else can give. You are the gift, and the world needs what you have. So if you get stuck, wondering about what difference you could make in the world, the simple answer is right there in the mirror. You are the difference.

Finding a Career Path

One of the reasons to think seriously about career is that it is such a big part of our adult life experience. We spend about a third of our waking adult hours in some form of employment. People commonly work from ages 20 to 65, and probably longer in the future with the changes coming in Social Security and Medicare. That is about 50 years, a big slice of a person's life. So the idea of finding a career that is a good fit, that is financially and emotionally rewarding, and that leaves behind a better world, makes good sense.

Like all things in life, career vision comes to different people in different ways. Some people seem to know from the earliest age what their life work is, while others can spend years trying to find their best fit. If you already know what you want to do in life that is great, but please continue reading anyway for the sake of some fine-tuning. If you do not know, particularly true for college students, getting more career clarity needs to become a primary goal. It does not have to be a crystal clear vision, in the ballpark is fine. Getting some general sense of career direction, however, is a very important step as it helps to illuminate the choice of major, which courses to take, internships worth considering, and all related activities.

This next section will focus on building a picture of your unique values and skills. That clarity can help in fine-tuning your selection process. For those lacking clarity, spending time exploring values, aptitudes and skills is essential. For those who do have a clear sense of career direction this information is still quite useful. It is one thing to know you are going to be a plumbing contractor, accountant, lawyer, or nurse. It is another to know exactly what variation of those specific careers will suit you best – corporate tax accountant or district attorney, med surg or obstetrics nurse. So now we will look at some of the core elements related to finding your career – life values, interests, aptitudes, and skills.

Life Values

One of the reasons that people do not make progress with their life passions is that they lack awareness of their core values. Having inspiring work and a meaningful life is like a good marriage. The more a couple shares core values, such as shared views around finances, child rearing, politics, or religion, the higher the probability they will get along in the long term. Couples with divergent spending patterns are more likely to be in conflict about money, for example. If on the other hand a couple shares values, talks about similar things, finds similar truths to be self-evident, there is a quality of ease and mutual reinforcement in that connection. A couple like that would naturally find each others company rewarding. Research in social psychology supports this idea – we like people who are like us, birds of a feather flock together. Knowing core values can play a similar role in finding a satisfying career path. If we know our values we will be more able to recognize if a particular career or job environment reflects those values. It can help us get a sense of rightness, of fit, a quality of flow. Spending some time reflecting on personal values and considering careers in which those values are encouraged and rewarded is a useful exercise.

> **REFLECTION**
>
> ### My Values
>
> What is the most important thing in your life, what do you value, what would you fight for? The purpose of this exercise is to reflect on what you really value, what you see as important, what makes you feel like you are living your true life, following your true path.
>
> This exercise includes three related values lists. It may be helpful to write them down on one sheet of paper with three columns, for sake of comparison. At the top of the page give one column the heading *Personal Values*, the second *Career Values*, and the third *Core Values*. Spend about 10 minutes on this. Start with the first column listing things that are important in your personal life. The simple way to start is just to write down, "I value...," then fill in the blank, "nature, money, family, my country, peace..." Do not think too much about it, just let the ideas flow, just let them come to you. Set a timer and keep writing for 5 minutes, let the ideas just flow. Then repeat the process for career values. "What I value in my future career is... being outdoors, intellectual stimulation, teamwork, making a good income..." You can include words related to the type of work, the impact of the work, the work environment (social and physical), anything relevant to you. Work on this for 5 minutes. When you are done with the first two items look for common themes and prioritize and enter them in the third column.
>
> _____
>
> _____
>
> _____

Aptitudes

You may remember in Chapter 1 there was an idea proposed by the Chinese sage Confucius. He said that some are born with natural ability, some obtained success through study, and others acquired it only after significant trial and effort. In the end, however, the gift achieved by all of them was the same. The point is that if there is something you really want, and if you put your mind to it, apply some sweat, you can get it, you can accomplish great things. That is an important truth. There is another aspect to that story, however, that is an equally important consideration when it comes to careers and it has to do with that issue of natural ability of which Confucius wrote. A nature ability can be called an aptitude. Some people have an aptitude for music, a gift for music, while others naturally excel at math. Mozart and Newton are good examples of individuals who respectively had clear aptitudes for music and math.

Why is aptitude an important consideration? Because most rational people would agree that it makes less sense for people to pursue specific careers if they have limited abilities in those domains.

For one thing, on a very practical level, it will be harder to compete with people who do have natural abilities in those areas. May individuals who become elite professional athletes most assuredly have gifts in the area of their sport, a natural ability. They run faster than other people, have greater endurance, are able to jump higher. It would not be impossible to develop those abilities and compete, it is just a bigger commitment than for someone with a natural ability. Another benefit of working with one's natural ability or aptitude is self-efficacy. If someone has an aptitude for something they are going to be more competent at it and get more positive feedback from others. Both of those will enhance self-efficacy, which can increase positive feelings about the activity and the willingness to work on improving it.

So being in a career that matches an aptitude, a natural ability, can contribute to a sense of fit, work-related self-efficacy, and recognition by others (since we all have egos that is probably a good thing, it is a reward and that is motivating). There are individuals in China who are considered national treasures. These people have developed great capacity in their given fields, such as an elderly traditional medicine doctor who has a particular talent for pulse diagnosis. These individuals are quite renowned in their fields. Although there is little doubt that they worked diligently to develop their skills, it is also quite likely that they possessed innate abilities that served as the foundation for their accomplishments. The traditional doctor who got remarkable results with patients was also probably very good at developing rapport with his patients, had a keen ability to notice subtle detail, a strong intuitive sense, a very good memory, and effective analytical thinking skills.

Does aptitude predict a good fit? Not necessarily. You can have an aptitude, but lack an interest in applying it. For example, I had a student once who was quite good at math, possessed a natural aptitude, but who lacked any serious interest in math related careers. He was more interested in writing, for which he also had an aptitude. He was in conflict with his parents around this issue, not sure who won. If he did end up pursuing a career in writing it is quite possible that the math aptitude would still emerge, such as becoming a science or technical writer. Aptitude is just one piece of the equation.

Assessing Aptitudes

There are a variety of ways to assess aptitudes. One simple strategy is to look at the areas of your life where you have naturally excelled in the past, or places where others have commented about one of your abilities. In addition, there are a number of psychological tests that are used to assess aptitudes. These tests can measure aptitude for specific vocations, or more general work aptitudes, or intelligence. One example is the Inventory of Work-Relevant Abilities (IWRA). This test measures aptitudes in sales, management, artistic ability, reading and language, social abilities and other areas. The Differential Aptitude Test (DAT), and the OASIS-3 Aptitude Survey, tend to measure more general aptitudes, similar to an intelligence test. The DAT measures various types of reasoning, verbal, mathematical, abstract and mechanical, and space relations. OASIS-3 is similar but includes manual dexterity.

> **REFLECTION**
>
> **My Aptitudes**
>
> There are a variety of ways to assess aptitudes. One simple strategy is to look at the areas of your life where you have naturally excelled in the past, or places where others have commented about an ability of yours. Take a piece of paper and for the next five minutes write down things you are good at, across the board. Does not matter if big or small, work or hobby, silly or serious. Jot it down. "Can eat more pizza than anyone else in my dorm." Awesome. Put that on the list. Even if it seems irrelevant or silly it can be informative. It could provide insight into more general abilities, interests or personality qualities that could be directed into career relevant activities.
>
> _____
>
> _____
>
> _____

Interests

Another useful career filter is personal interest. As the name suggests, interests have to do with things you are interested in. (Duh! Great definition huh.) An interest does not imply that you have a natural aptitude, or any level of skill, but that you have an interest, a curiosity, a desire to know more. A person can have an interest in reading, drawing, collecting insects, sports statistics, puzzles, building robots, amateur astronomy, learning languages, travel, dance, computer programming, understanding how the body works. The interest could have been there from a very young age. Who knows where it came from, but it is real, a natural curiosity for certain things. It is great to do work that relates to a natural interest, because then you are getting paid to do something that you would do on your own anyway. That is indeed awesome. To reiterate an important point, it is important to remember that just as aptitude does not imply interest, interest does not imply aptitude or skill.

Assessing Interests

As with aptitude, there are a number of instruments that are available to help you learn more about personal interests, and how those interests relate to specific careers. Two well-validated measures are the *Strong Interest Inventory* and the *Campbell Interest and Skill Survey* (Campbell, 1995; Donnay, 1997). The *Strong Interest Inventory* is used to measure interest related to work, leisure activities, and academic subjects. This one is commonly used in college career centers. The *Campbell Interest and Skill Survey* is another instrument used by college career centers and career counselors. It is based on the work of Dr. David Campbell, an expert in the field of career counseling. It measures interest in 29 areas, such as public speaking, counseling, writing, mathematics and animal care. These 29 areas are organized into 7 key themes: influencing, organizing, helping, creating, analyzing, producing, and adventuring. It provides information on interest in specific aspects of work, specific careers, and career related skills. Various interest assessment tests can be found online. Some are free and some charge. Make sure you know if there is a fee (and how much the final total will be) before you submit an online survey for processing. I had one student who was quite surprised when he got a credit card charge for almost $100 that he was not expecting. Read the fine print, or give them a call to clarify. Scams and legitimate but expensive services abound.

> **REFLECTION**
>
> **My Interests**
>
> Take out a piece of paper, and for five to ten minutes just jot down ideas about things that you like to do, where you like to spend your time, what attracts you, who you like to talk to and about what. Again, it might seem irrelevant, silly, no matter, just write it down. All of this information provides insight into who you are and where you want to go. Have fun.
>
> _____
>
> _____
>
> _____
>
> _____

Skills

Skill is the ability to do a particular activity. A skill may be based on an innate aptitude or something that has been learned. Skills can range from more general capacities, such as being an effective listener, to very specific skills, such as computer programming in Java or doing high-end welding. Employers will always look at general aptitudes and personality characteristics when considering the fit of a job candidate. Beyond that, if a job requires a specific skill set, such as sales, drawing, math, or carpentry, they will be looking to evaluate that skill as well.

Assessing Skills

Skill assessment can be very general. It can also be very specific if the assessment is for a particular task. General skill assessments will typically include basic academic skills (writing, reading, math), people skills (listening, teaching, negotiating), management skills (managing money or people), technical skills (operating and maintaining equipment), and systems skills (making decision or evaluating organizations). It is a good idea to inventory your marketable general and specific skills. Doing that can be as simple as putting some headings down on paper and listing skills under each. Headings can include communication – written, verbal, nonverbal; critical thinking; math and science; creativity/arts; research; planning; organizational skills; management; interpersonal skills; teaching, including coaching; administration; helping, counseling; mechanical skills; construction; financial skills. Hmm, where to put taxidermy? There are many skill inventories available online and in books. Many are free of charge to the user. Doing a quick web search for "skills inventory" or "career planning" will take you to a number of sites. Look for sites with the dot *edu* or dot *org* endings. Those will be the best fit if you are a college student. Sites ending in dot *com* are commercial and more likely to charge a fee for service. As mentioned above, the *Strong Interest Inventory* and the *Campbell Interest and Skill Inventory* are two assessments that also provide insight into skills. You can typically take those assessments through your college career center. Your campus career center will also help with the interpretation of results and guide you toward other resources and next steps, including knowing about specific majors on campus, advising opportunities, and much more.

> **REFLECTION**
>
> **My Skills**
>
> Take out a sheet of paper, ten to twenty minutes, reflect on your skills. Make a note of strengths or weakness in each area, perhaps number -1, 0 and +1 for each. Include the following: communication skills (writing, reading, verbal/nonverbal); people skills (listening, teaching, negotiating, coaching, counseling); management/organizational skills (managing money or people, organizing, planning); research/science skills, critical thinking; creativity/arts; technical/mechanical skills (operating and maintaining equipment); systems skills (making decision or evaluating organizations); physical skills (manual dexterity, hand-eye coordination, endurance); building/construction/design. Note the skills, related classes, and related job experience. Do a review and inventory of work related skills after that. Keep this list close by your resume. You can strengthen your resume with some integration of these specific skills. Consider classes to fill in gaps.

Personality

The final area of exploration for career assessment is the match between personality and life work. Personality is not about aptitude, interest, or skill. It is more about how we experience life and the world in general, how we approach and operate in the world, how we feel comfortable in it. Introvert and extrovert are examples of personality characteristics, obviously different from each other. If you have twins, one an introvert and the other an extrovert, they would probably be more comfortable and productive in different careers, or different specialties within the same career. Both could be lawyers, but one might be defending clients in court and the other doing international tax research for a corporation. Individuals who enjoy creating and maintaining order may do well as accountants or landscape architects. For those individuals it is gratifying when things line up at the end of the year or when the garden is in full bloom. Risk taking is another example. Individuals who enjoy high risk and adventure may do well as journalists with international assignments. Most of us with egos may think of ourselves as risk takers, but when push comes to shove we would actually not want to be pushed or shoved into the shark tank. So assessing personality, being honest about who we are, and looking at the match between personality and career is another helpful element in effective career planning.

Personality Assessment

MBTI

One of the more widely used measures of personality type is the *Meyers-Briggs Type Indicator* (MBTI) (Myers & Peter, 1980). This instrument consists of 93 questions that measure four broad categories of personality. The four categories provide information on how a person: (1) gets information; (2) engages with the world; (3) makes decisions; and (4) manages interactions. Answers to these questions are used to sort respondents into one of sixteen possible personality types. These personality types, based on data from a large population sample, is used to match personality with career satisfaction. The assumption is that people with similar personalities will have related career interests.

Answers to the MBTI questions provide information on where the person lies along a continuum within each of the four personality categories, leaning left or right of center. Depending on which side of the fence they fall on the person gets one of two letters to indicate personality type for that category. So for example, the assessment of how one engages in the world provides information on an introvert/extrovert personality orientation. Depending on where test takers lands on the scale they get an I (introvert) or an E (extrovert) for that characteristic. Completion of the entire test results in a four-letter indicator of personality type, with each letter corresponding to one of the four personality categories, such as INTJ (Introvert, iNtuitive, Thinking, Judging).

The Extravert and Introvert category relates to how we engage the world and how we get our energy. Extraverts are energized by engagement with the outside world. They need to be with people, involved in things, going places, active. Introverts prefer inner reflection. They have a greater need for private time, away from the crowd and the hustle. In terms of Sensing and iNtuiting (getting information), a Sensing person is interested in tangible information, data, something that can be measured and known directly. The iNtuitive type is interested in information that is more abstract, ideas, possibilities rather than realities. Thinking and Feeling relate to how people make decisions, the basis of their judgments. Thinking people rely on logic and analysis for their decisions. The emphasis is on the task at hand. Feeling types make decisions more on the basis of feeling versus logic. They also consider the impact of their decisions on others as part of their process. Finally, Judging and Perceiving describes how we relate to the outer world. Judging types seek to create order in the world or to have order in their experience of the world. Perceiving people have less of a need for order and closure in their experience with life. They have more flexibility in relating with things and people.

The possible combinations of letters (I/E, S/N, T/F, J/P) result in 16 different personality types based on the various combinations of indicators from each of these four categories, one letter from each category. So if Lucy took the test and found out that she was an ENTJ she could use that score to see what kinds of careers other ENTJ's have enjoyed. There are free versions or equivalents of this test in books and online. There are also versions of the MBTI that are fee-based. The fee-based versions should provide a detailed report of findings. This test is also probably available through most college career centers.

Holland Hexagon

Another very popular personality oriented assessment is based on the work of Dr. John L Holland. He is well known for creating the Holland Hexagon (Holland, 1996; Hutchinson, 2000). The hexagon, a six-sided figure, is used to represent major categories of life interest and seeks to match personality type with suitable work environments. Holland's model begins with two pairs of opposing qualities based one's preference for working with *people* or with *things*, and the preference for working with *data* or *ideas*. Within these attributes at each corner of the hexagon are the six personality types. They are Realistic, Investigative, Artistic, Social, Enterprising, and Conventional. According to Holland's theory people with similar personality traits would naturally be drawn to interact with each other, investigative types would be attracted to investigative types, artistic to artistic. The model proposes that individuals who work in environments that match their type will be more satisfied with their chosen career and more successful at it.

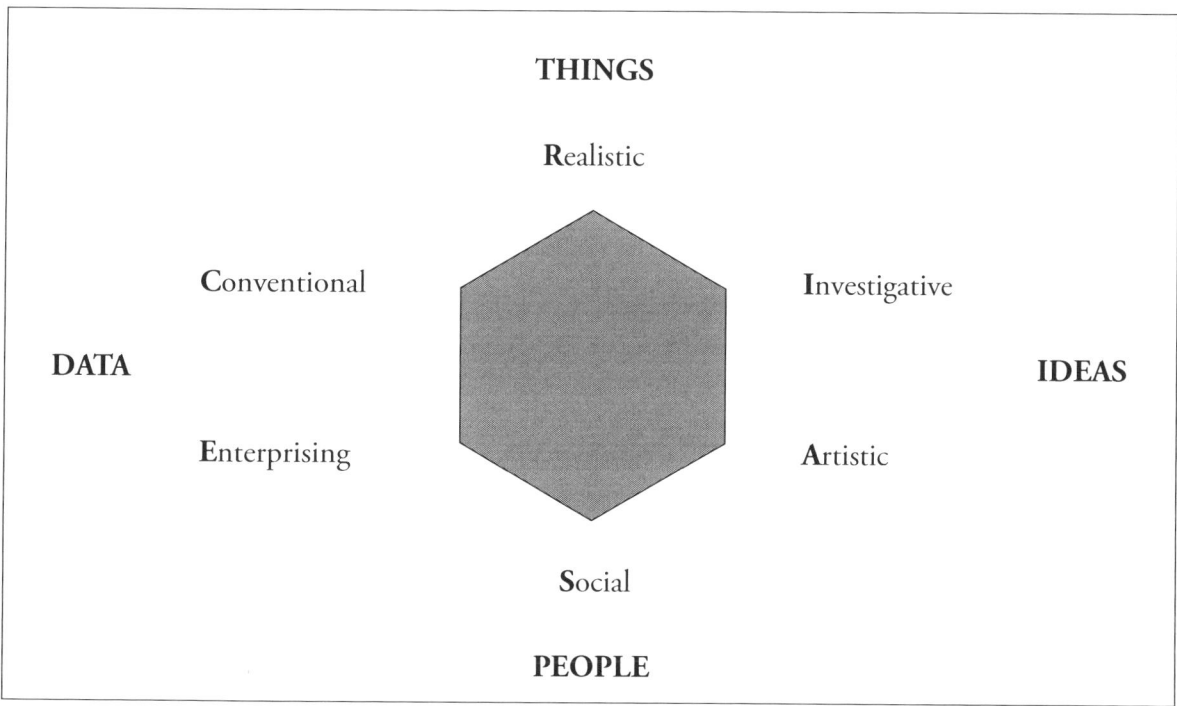

One simple way to do the assessment is to imagine that you are attending a party with strangers. The party is in a very large house with many rooms. At this party (it must be in LA, I hope there's a pool) people have congregated in different rooms based on their personality type. One room is filled with Enterprising types, another room has the Artistic folks (maybe a soap opera star or two?), and so on. To get a sense of your career-personality orientation imagine yourself at this party (use the diagram above) and decide which room you would spend the most time in. (Note, because the party is in LA (Santa Monica specifically) they only have a juice bar upstairs, no alcohol in the house!?? That might take some of the pressure off the decision. Also, please avoid the room with the orange door. I'm just asking. It's your choice of course.) So do this for each room in the house. Create a rank order. List which room you would spend the most time in all the way down to the least time. To help get a sense of who is in each room here is some more information about the guests:

Realistic people enjoy working with machines, tools, outdoor work.

Investigative people are interested in solving problems, doing research, learning how things work.

Artistic people are involved in fine arts, languages, writing, jobs involving creativity and self-expression.

Social people love to work with others, helping them with their problems, teaching, training, being good listeners and communicators.

Enterprising people are interested in leadership, persuasion, motivating others, risk taking and decision making. They have good verbal skills and love being the center of attention.

Conventional people are organized, efficient, and enjoy working with numbers, data, financial information, and processes. They tend to be more structured and methodical.

Once you have picked your rooms look at your top three ranked choices. These are the types of people and places and careers that would suit you best. It should be noted that Holland did not believe that most people were one specific type. He felt that individuals were more typically a combination of two or more. According to Holland the types that are most likely to be compatible with each other are the ones that are closest to each other on the hexagon.

Personality Type	Most Compatible	Compatible
Realistic	Realistic	Investigative & Conventional
Investigative	Investigative	Realistic & Artistic
Artistic	Artistic	Investigative & Social
Social	Social	Artistic & Enterprising
Enterprising	Enterprising	Social & Conventional
Conventional	Conventional	Enterprising & Realistic

REFLECTION

My Personality

Which characteristics best describe you? Which rooms in the house party do you want to spend time in? What other types are you drawn to? Write these down and think of a few careers where those kinds of aptitudes, skills, and personalities might be found.

Putting It All Together

After some research and contemplation the career searcher has a good sense of values, aptitudes, interests, skills and personality. Let us say a person is a bit more of a research type, with some math aptitude (not great, but pretty good), an interest in how things work, a bit more of an introvert, and very good writing skills. Perhaps the person decides to become an engineer, slogs through the math courses, continues to work on writing, and graduates with an engineering degree. That person could be very well suited to work on an engineering or design team developing grants and contracts, writing technical support documents, or working with sales and marketing teams. There are ways to put all of our abilities, interests and personality characteristics together for an excellent career fit. It can take some serious thinking and exploration, but the investment of time (probably at least months, not days or weeks) can result in many, many years (50?) of career satisfaction. That is a good return on an investment.

Like all important decision making processes, or problem solving tasks, it is useful to apply an effective strategy, recognize it will take time and commitment, and that initial solutions may not fit and will require a rerun or a refinement. It is what it is. Dealing with the ever-changing nature of life is part of life.

Lacking Career Vision

If after a serious exploration of values, interests, aptitudes and personality there is still a lack of career vision then there may be some other things to consider.

Repeat the Process

First it may be useful to go back over the same territory, to spend more time over a winter or summer break and really immerse yourself in the project of finding a major and a career path. A few months of deep exploration can make a lifetime of difference, a 50 years of getting paid to do something that fits who you are difference.

Develop General Skills

The second thing is to not get hung up on having to know exactly what you are supposed to do. Some folks have strong interests at a very young age, like biologist E.O. Wilson. From a very young age he had an interest in insects. Deep, natural interests like that can lead to a career, as it did in his case. But having an interest does not usually equal a very specific career. Interest in insects, easy, only a few possible outcomes. You can work for a frog, be an exterminator, or do biology research (kidding, lots more). Interest in writing, there are lots of things a person can do with good writing skills.

The point is that if you follow your interests and aptitudes, and always work on developing general skills that employers look for, then over time you will build a foundation for a variety of jobs as well as for specific jobs. Student often get hung up thinking they need to know exactly what they are supposed to do. Not the case. At the undergraduate level the majority of students are getting a general education. Yes, there are a few majors that require very career specific training, like nursing or accounting. Even there, however, you are getting a more general introduction to the profession, with more specialized training coming later in the workplace or in graduate school. If you choose a major based on your aptitudes, interests and personality, and develop general and specific work related skills, you will be well prepared for the broader job market. You will have solid transferable skills useful in a variety of settings. Do not let the perfect get in the way of the good, as they say. These days many people will have multiple careers over a lifetime. That is a consequence of jobs evolving due to new technologies, population migration, and global workforce trends. Having good core skills, a problem-solving orientation, a solid dose of optimism, AND THE ABILITY TO LEARN NEW THINGS (A GOOD LEARNING STRATEGY), will serve most people well in their career futures.

Remember that every class you take provides an opportunity to develop general skills. Use class assignments to help you improve your writing, your speaking ability, interpersonal and teamwork capacity, math skills, foreign and computer language skills, all of these are transferable resources. No matter what, use every class as a chance to develop and grow. Be passionate about each class, recognize what a precious opportunity education provides. Also, when you take classes think about what you like or dislike about the subject. Think about the class in terms of your interests, aptitudes, personality (but remember also that the dislike can be related to low self-efficacy in an area, not related to aptitude or underlying interest, remember "I don't know how to do that yet, but..."). Periodically reflect on who you are and what you love to do. You might not like the class but you love the writing assignments or the group work. Invest time in your education to learn and develop core skills. This is very important. Use the resource of education wisely.

This Too Shall Pass

The third thing is to acknowledge less visible causes. Perhaps it is not just a lack of information about values and interests, but something that is obstructing the ability to get clarity, one of those collars that need to be removed. For example, a person may not be able to see her dream career because she was never empowered to think big, or she was told girls cannot be engineers or helicopter pilots. If she dared to think big it would upset the balance in her family, the unwritten understanding of who is supposed to be successful and who is not, of what this child should become. If personal career vision is truly difficult then get creative. Pray for vision, meditate on it, pull Tarot cards, ask for information in dreams, start using Priming and see yourself as being completely clear about what you want to do in your life. Set a specific day and time in the not distant future where you will be clear, at least 3 to 6 months from this point, July 29th at 4:30pm, clear vision. Work on self-worth and self-love. Talk to faculty and advisors, undergraduate advisors, major advisors. GO TO THE CAREER CENTER.

In terms of classes, take the ones that you have an interest in and pay attention to where your strengths seem to be (and remember the impact of low self-efficacy on expectancy; do not let old beliefs hold you back). See where you like to invest your study energy, what kinds of students you like to talk to (the six room house party in LA), what you like to think about. Look at career descriptions in books, online. Talk to people who do what you think you might be interested in. Get an internship and try out working in that field for the semester. You can often earn credits for internships and you will learn something about a career path and about your current career strengths and weaknesses. If you are depressed, lonely, dealing with drug and alcohol or other life challenges, then *go talk to someone*. If you are a student you are paying tuition and that tuition pays the salary of the counseling folks. They are there to help. Work diligently on getting more clarity. Never give up. You will know.

When I was a freshman in college I had a clear vision. I wanted to be a philosopher, someone who contemplated about the meaning of things, especially what it meant to be human. "Oh great," I thought. "I will be a philosopher, living under a bridge, like Socrates running around in a shabby tunic." Eventually I stopped stressing about it and focused on doing whatever I did as well as I could. I took courses that fit my areas of interest – understanding human nature and how to help people move into more productive patterns in their lives. I had thought about a psychology degree, but that was not exactly what I wanted. I also had interests in healthcare, education, and broader social systems and their influence on individual behavior. I followed my heart, "followed my bliss," as Joseph Campbell would say. I dropped out of school twice for short periods to pursue related interests. I eventually declared a social sciences major with three cognates - sociology, psychology and philosophy (with a focus on Eastern philosophy). By my senior year I was taking graduate classes in sociology and doing an internship in healthcare policy at the State Capitol. That became the foundation for a degree in public health at UCLA, a PhD in social psychology at UC Santa Cruz with an emphasis in health behavior, and formal study in both meditation and traditional Chinese medicine. I have had a number of related careers including running my own businesses and being a college professor, and I have always focused on getting paid to do what I love and work that is of value.

Use any period of uncertainty as an opportunity for continued exploration of values, skills, interests and personality. It is a precious opportunity. Certainly not knowing can make people anxious, but it is actually a very rich phase, full of potential. Remember, "If there is a problem I will work diligently to manage it and resolve it." Work on your general education and other general university requirements. Take courses that let you explore possible interests and career paths, classes that will inform your ultimate decisions. Whatever classes you choose, take them seriously, do the best you can. If you find out during the semester it is not your thing, use the class as a platform for developing general skills, use it, do not lose it. It is what it is. Let it be a more general learning opportunity. Get involved in extracurricular activities and internships that can help fill in the picture of self-understanding. Do something to give back to your community. Doing now, versus waiting to figure it all out later, is self-empowering. This is especially useful if the lack of clarity is a result on being unplugged, disempowered. Working on clarity is living your life, getting plugged in, having power. Contribute and you will see what you are made of. You will see what speaks to you. Meditate on it, image it, research it, do it. Do not be afraid of the not knowing. Go into it. It is a rich field of possibilities, the essence of creativity and discovery.

Selecting a Major

Selecting a major is a very important task in the undergraduate educational journey. Your general undergraduate education helps you to become a more capable global citizen, a more productive, informed and conscious individual. Your specific major channels that energy into a career focus. Let us take a moment to consider the process of selecting a major.

Why Select a Major

One major benefit of selecting a major sooner than later is that it gives you a focus, especially if your major is clearly related to your career objectives. Having a major/career focus gives you a clear goal to work on, a motivating goal, not just passing a class, but doing well and getting a fulfilling job in this area of study. Selecting a major narrows the list of possible courses to take. The path to completion becomes clear. That focus streamlines the degree completion process, increasing your efficient use of time in school and saving you money. It also gives you access to specific advisors sooner, people familiar with future career paths. In addition, for very popular majors, being declared as a major is often the only way you can get into certain classes. So selecting a major sooner than later is a key to greater motivation and to effective use of time in school.

In my Academic Achievement class I have the seniors in the room share their thoughts with the class about the value of having a major. This is done for the benefit of the first and second year students, especially those who still do not understand its importance. The older students all tend to agree that declaring a major made a clear difference in their school performance. It gave them direction and focus. I also ask them to answer that question because they are on the other end of the pipeline. They are close to graduating, preparing to enter the job market. They get it. It is real for them. They clearly understand the value of finding a major sooner and focusing time and energy on building capacity in a career-related domain, so they will be more competitive in the job market.

Final note in this regard, I will occasionally have a student in my class, sitting in the cosmic ejector seat about to be catapulted out into the job market, who has done very little in the way of preparation, no clue what they want to do. Not a good strategy. Are they freaking? Yes, often they are. Sooner than later is the best plan. Get a clue on who you are, what your skills and aptitudes are, where you would like to land (ballpark good, no need to pinpoint third base), make a decision (best fit for now), and go to town on it.

How To Pick One

Think of Future Careers

Your general education is just that, your general education. Very important. Your major is preparation for the world of work ahead (both actually contribute to that outcome, but major is a specification of that process). So idea number one, *your major prepares you for a career*. It is therefore important to *consider what career you might like* to do and *pick your major based on that*. Key idea – you do not pick a major for the sake of the major, you pick a major for the sake of a career. Think about where you want to be in five or ten years and pick your major based on that. The major will end in a few years, your career will go on for decades. Pick you major based on possible career interests.

So getting clear(er) on career interests should help inform your selection a major. If you do not have a very specific career in mind, but know you want to use one of your key aptitudes, like math, then a degree in Math, Physics, or Computer Studies could be an excellent foundation for many careers. Indeed, most people have majors that prepare them for a variety of careers. The goal is to get a general sense of where you want to land on the job map, where you will be able to put your aptitudes, interests, personality and skills to best use, feel a sense of accomplishment and contribution. You want to find the general region, the room in the house (art, research, social service), and then pick a major that is more likely to get you into that room. Employers hire the package that is you – abilities, motivation, skills, personality. They do not necessarily hire the specific college degree. *Once again for emphasis, do not select a major for the sake of having a major. Select a major for where the major takes you.* Your major is not the end point. Your career, or life work, is the end point. The ideal is to start with a sense of career and work backwards from there.

Do the Hard Work
Second, please, please, please, please, please do not choose one major because it is easier than another major. Seriously. That is not an appropriate criterion for making an informed decision. Pick the major you need for your future career, so you end up with a greater chance of getting paid for doing what you love to do. If you want to be an engineer you need to take the math classes. If math is a hard subject for you then you should consider taking fewer classes each semester, take a single math class in the summer, use tutors and other campus resources, and be realistic about how much time it will take to get the work done and to complete the major. Learning is a process that requires time, commitment, patience and persistence. Period. Do not avoid a particular major just because you lack certain abilities. If you really want that major, but lack certain skills, then consider remedial classes. Spend an extra year in school if you need to. Do whatever it takes. It is better to build progressively and be well trained than to try to jump steps and have significant missing pieces. Everyone can get better at everything. You may never be the best, but you can be better. *You just have to want it and then you just have to do it*.

Consider a Minor
If you have competing interests then one idea is to declare a major and a minor. Rather than taking random courses the minor gives you a secondary focus. It also often shows up on your diploma or certainly on your resume. It shows a potential employer that you are not a one trick pony, you have a curiosity about life and diverse interests. You bring more to the table. That is added value. Same salary, more ability, that is good. Employers like that. Studying politics, but also have an interest and aptitude for writing? Consider combining a political science degree with a minor in English or journalism. Interested in math? That could become a minor in math paired with a degree in business, teaching, computer programming, or graphic arts. Those types of packages make you more interesting to an employer. It also makes your life richer, growing in multiple domains of interest and skill.

*Also, p*eople change, interests change. You start down a track and eventually you realize that you do not really have the aptitude or interest for a particular major or career. Not a problem. If you already invested a lot of time in that major it might make more sense to just complete it and add a minor related to your new found interest. If not too far down the road, consider changing course and getting the degree that you think will serve you best in the long run.

Do Not Chase Money and Be Practical – Make Money
Do not choose a career simply because you think it will make you a lot of money. Careers change as the world changes and the career you chased for money may not be as lucrative in the long run. Work gets outsourced to other countries, technologies replace workers, too many people get trained and the field is saturated. Many things can affect a career path. Do something that will bring you joy and make the world a better place (in addition to paying the bills, money is good).

Although it is not a good idea to chase money, it is a good idea to make money, and more is often better than less for a number of reasons. When picking a career and a major it is useful to consider longer term earning potential. You can do quite well with a simpler job and an average wage is you live within your means and save. That can actually be a nice way to live a life, and works quite well for many people. Some people will even forego a much higher potential salary because what they really want to do is important to them. That is awesome. As long as we are making conscious choices it is good.

There are also jobs that are not glamorous but pay reasonably well. There are, for example, an increasing number of high-end industrial jobs coming back to the United States and too few skilled workers for the positions. People want to follow their bliss and those jobs do not seem to fit the picture. The reality is that any job, done with dignity and a commitment to quality, can be a source of accomplishment and fulfillment. The job may not appear glamorous, but making a good salary provides the basis for doing other things in life in addition to work. Work is a part of life, not the defining core. Those types of jobs can be a very good choice as well, a key to a balanced life. In the traditional Zen monastery everyone works, everyone participates in the daily chores, big and small. It is not necessarily the work, it is the presence one brings to the work that matters. With the right attitude any job becomes a vehicle for practice and the deepening of insight into the nature of self and life.

Final Thoughts

Seek clarity, choose a major, and then get to work on that major. Some people enter the university with a declared major and stick with it, some start with a declared major and then change their minds once they start taking classes, others arrive undeclared. All good. If undeclared the goal should be to have some sense by the end of sophomore year and then to get to work on major requirements starting junior year. Until a major is selected time can be spent on satisfying general requirements and taking courses to explore options. *Continue to spend some of your time each semester working on getting clear about your values and aptitudes until you select your major.* That should be a key task on your To Do List each semester until a major is declared. Also, use the campus career services to take career aptitude tests and talk to the career counselors to help you achieve greater clarity. Follow your bliss. Take courses that appeal to you, try an internship, get involved in extracurricular activities. Do what it takes to get a sense of your best path. If you do not have clarity about a career then let the courses and majors that attract you be your guiding light for the moment. Take those courses as a means to explore. That will increase clarity, and all of the courses, well executed, will prepare you for a career that you cannot see clearly yet. All good if you bring quality and commitment to the process. Let your passion be a guide.

Marketing to Potential Employers

There are some things, regardless of what is changing in the world of work, that are of value to employers. National employer surveys find that the key qualities employers look for are motivation and a good work ethic, communication skills, team/interpersonal skills, analytic and computer skills, organizational skills, fit with the culture, related work experience, problem solving skills, ability to make the organization money, online/social media skills, accuracy, maturity, reading, writing and computing skills, willingness to follow company policies, and versatility (can do diverse tasks). As mentioned already, every class you take provides an opportunity to work on one or more of these core skills. Even if you think you hate a class, you can change your attitude toward it by turning it into an opportunity to develop these core skills. Boring teaching – that is a great opportunity to develop motivation and a good work ethic, and finding ways to get the information as painlessly as possible. Team project bogged down by the problem child. That is a great opportunity to develop problem solving skills, social skills, and management skills. "I don't know how to do that yet, but I will learn."

Your Resume

Before you graduate you will definitely want to fine-tune your resume. Creating a good working resume when you are in sophomore year will help you reflect on strengths and weaknesses, and it can be a tool to help guide your course selection. Use your working resume like an ongoing Accomplishments List. It is empowering to see that you have completed an internship, been on the Dean's list three semesters in a row, received the highest grade in your biology class. Put it into your working resume for your sake, and then yank it out when creating your public version. It will probably inspire you to accomplish more as you see your list of achievements growing.

The key elements of an effective resume include your name and address, education, and job experience. It should be 1-2 pages in length, neat, clear, organized and well written, with zero typos or grammatical errors. As a career visioning exercise you could also make a hypothetical future resume with your ideal career at the top and the jobs or skills underneath. That can be a way to meditate on the future and to get a sense of your dream job. It becomes something of a roadmap. Start at the goal and work backwards from there. That strategy can help you think about what the best route might be to get to the desired state, making it a useful career planning exercise. I want to do medical engineering. What would be the best major, courses, internships, summer jobs? You can search online to find information from people who are doing what you are interested in. Read about their journey, their evolution, to see what steps they took to reach their destination. You want to be a Supreme Court Justice. Look at the career trajectory of a few of the Supreme Court members to get a sense of what it takes to get a seat. Start with the goal and work backwards to determine a path.

Mock Interviews

Another good idea is to take advantage of mock interviews if they are available at your campus career center. A mock interview can give you a sense of what to expect in a live job interview, provide information on the types of questions you will be asked, and help you develop your responses. It is a way to prime the interview event. Your mind and body have been through it. You are not going in cold, and that can be quite helpful in managing expectations and emotions.

Internships and Job Fairs

Internships, job fairs and other networking opportunities are helpful ways to develop skills and make connections. Internships provide exposure to work settings and insight into the day-to-day tasks within a career. That can give you additional information on whether a particular career is the right fit for you. It is also a great way to learn specific job and career skills. Possibly most valuable, internships provide you with direct employer contact, and that can lead to a job right out of school. The employer knows you. You have learned the skills needed for the job. You are ready to work on the first day. When you get an internship, act like an employee, from day one.

Job fairs are chances to meet potential employers, find out what employers are looking for, what kinds of questions they are asking, what kinds of experiences and training they prefer. There is no need to wait until you are graduating. Early exposure will increase your familiarity and comfort. A job fair can also provide an opportunity to find an internship or to ask about what other classes might be useful to increase your marketability or ideas on what major to take. Most people staffing booths at jobs fairs are helpful individuals who are happy to support your success. There are no dumb questions. Just drop in and explore.

Finding Life Meaning

Ultimately, perhaps the most important reflection in this whole process is on the journey of life itself, living a meaningful life. What are the consequences of not choosing? What are the results of not acting? What does it mean to live a meaningful life? A meaningful life may just come to us, but it is probably more likely to be the result of a sense of direction and of the conscious choices we make to follow that path. I remember once meeting a woman who wanted to get married and have a child. Her friends were all trying to find partners, not having luck, things not working out. This woman had such a clear vision that within a year she was married and then in short order after that she was pregnant. Her husband had been married before and in the beginning of their relationship he was clear that he did not want more children. Then, there you have it, some time later, they had a family. Love is like that. He was willing to start over again in order to have that relationship, but I digress. The point is that she got clear, very clear, very committed to her vision. She found what she wanted, and it made three humans happier.

Ecological/Holistic/Sustainable

One thing that will become increasingly important in the years, decades, and centuries ahead (if we can change our ways in time) is that we will be required to live our lives and make our decisions more consciously in light of the greater good. The space for self-serving, narrow-minded, self-centered thought and action is shrinking by the day. We will need to evolve a vision that is more inclusive, more holistic, one that contributes to a world that is sustainable, balanced, and which recognizes the worth of others and the necessity to preserve nature. What was meaningful in the recent past may no longer be meritorious in the near future. The planet and all of its children will need us, increasingly, to live lives based on shared values, mutual respect, and continual improvement.

That's it for now. Go get em tiger!

SUMMARY

In this chapter we looked at the process of getting clear about life work and selecting an appropriate major to take you to that career destination. Career clarity was explored in terms of personal values, aptitudes, interests, skills and personality. All of these play a role in finding a rewarding career. There is often not one perfect fit, but a variety of roles in which we can use and satisfy these interests and abilities. The goal is to find a place where we can use our gifts, make a rewarding living, and contribute in a meaningful way to the greater common good. We also looked at the qualities that employers are looking for in employees, and how any class can be an opportunity to develop general and specific employable skills. Ultimately, finding a place to make a meaningful contribution will result in a more fulfilling life journey for most people.

MIND-BODY PRACTICE

Sitting Meditation

This week practice mindfulness of breath, body, thoughts/feelings, sensations. Or practice Hum Sah concentration meditation. Cultivate relaxation and equanimity.

Mindful Awareness

Be mindfully aware of your approaches to school activities this week.

Priming

Think of your goals for the week. Use priming mental imagery to see the most incredible week/semester of your life so far. If working on career clarity or a major, then imagine that you have complete clarity about what you are going to do and that you are stoked about it. See yourself as clear and enthused.

REFERENCES

Campbell DP. The Campbell Interest and Skill Survey (CISS): A product of ninety years of psychometric evolution. *Journal of Career Assessment*. 1995;3(4)391-410.

Donnay D. E.K. Strong's legacy and beyond: 70 years of the Strong Interest Inventory. *Career Development Quarterly*. 1997;46(1):2-22.

Holland JL. Exploring careers with a typology: what we have learned and some new directions. *American Psychologist*. 1996;51(4):397-406.

Hutchinson T. Measuring the success of the Holland Hexagon. *Quality & Quantity*. 2000;34(1):103-110.

Myers IB, Peter BM. *Gifts Differing: understanding personality type*. Mountain View, CA: Davies-Black Publishing; 1980.

Personal Finances & Abundance

17

I wisely acquire, manage, use and preserve life's resources.

CHAPTER THEMES
- Financial Literacy
- Funding Education
- Making Money, Saving & Investing
- True abundance

In this chapter we will look at the topics of financial success and abundance. What is the difference? Financial success relates to the acquisition of money and material resources. We need money and material resources to live. We need food, water, clothing, shelter, goods and services. Even the Buddha, a monk with few possessions, said that poverty impeded spiritual practice. Money, or its equivalent, is an essential element of human societies. Equally or probably more important, however, is our inner sense of abundance.

Money is a psychological phenomena, a shared symbolic energy system. You can see that clearly when you watch the volatility of stock markets. There is always the potential for dramatic losses in the monetary value of stocks when fear sets in and people start to sell. That happened in the United States in the 1990's when the dot com bubble produced radically overvalued stock prices in companies that were making zero profits. "Irrational exuberance" was how then Federal Reserve Chairman Alan Greenspan described the growing price bubble (Greenspan, 1996). That fragile bubble did indeed pop, with dramatic consequences to the US stock market. Many of those high-flying companies lost one-hundred percent of their market value within the course of a year. Just like that, poof, gone. Every dollar invested in those companies was also gone.

Money is important. Given the inherent quality of change in the time-space matrix, however, it is essential to build inner security as well, a sense of abundance that comes from our own happiness, confidence, and optimism. It also comes from knowing that we possess core skills to deal effectively with life's challenges. It may sound cliché, but wait until there are lean times and see who is miserable and who is coping. The individuals who have developed inner resources, in addition to outer assets, will most likely do the best. In this chapter we will explore both of these concepts, inner resiliency and outer sufficiency, abundance and wealth.

The Meaning of Money

There was a wonderful book, *Your Money or Your Life,* written by Vicki Robin and Joe Dominguez in 1992. In their book they described how money was equivalent to your life force. You work in exchange for something, typically money. You give someone your time and they give you money. An essential point of the book is that we are selling someone a portion of our life, the energy in our battery. They take the time/energy we sell to them so that they can use it to achieve ***their goals***. That time/energy is no longer ours, we sold it. It is now theirs. In exchange for our time/life energy we get some money or its equivalent.

Your battery only has so much juice. Most people have about 79 years of life, a few more or less depending on genetics and on how life is lived. In exchange for giving away this most precious gift, our time and our energy, we get money. The key point. Our life force, our life time (hours, days, weeks, years), is the most precious thing we have. If a person is given money for their life force and then spends that money foolishly, they have tossed the most important thing they own out the window, like yesterdays garbage. It is like leaving the flashlight on all day, when it adds little value. That person is using up the battery and getting little in return. If we use money carelessly, thoughtlessly, then both our money and our life energy are gone, forever. The light is now a bit dimmer because the battery is running down. If a person spends wisely, however, they have something of equal value to what they have given away, maybe even something better, like more wisdom.

Dominguez and Robin advised that if we equated money to our life force we would use it more wisely, spend more consciously, less habitually, less addictively, and invest more prudently for the greatest good of self and others. Investment done skillfully could even create the possibility to retire sooner than later, more freedom to do whatever work or activity is most important, while there is still some energy left in the battery, some light left to shine.

Financial Goals and Financial Literacy

People with clear financial goals, even basic ones, do better in the long run financially. They are much more likely to achieve financial independence, and to do so sooner than later, compared to those who fail to plan. Effective planning, however, requires a sense of what the goal should be and an understanding of what it will take to get there. For that it is important to start learning some key financial concepts, to start developing some financial literacy.

In this section we will introduce some core concepts of financial literacy. These will include ideas about making money, funding education, creating and using a budget, identifying expenses, calculating income, setting priorities, making more informed financial decisions, debt management, understanding credit and using credit cards, saving and investing, record keeping, taxes, and home ownership. Each of these topics could be its own book, like lots of things presented in this book. This is an introduction, pointing the way. Financial needs and goals change during different phases of life. Financial literacy is consequently a lifelong learning process. So let us explore some core concepts to get things rolling.

Making Money

People can do fine financially without higher education, but for most people, more school will lead to more pay. It does not have to be a conventional college degree. It could be a technical school where you learn up a good paying trade like welding or computer network installation. Whatever the educational path, for most, it is probably a good investment. Why? The world is changing. We live in a global environment that is increasingly information and technology oriented. Even if you have no interest in technology, you will probably be working with technology in most careers in years ahead, including most factory jobs. Higher education exposes you to some of the technologies present in today's work environments and gives you the ability to learn those still to come. In addition, *time used wisely in college*, from community college on up, provides an opportunity to improve skills in writing, math, interpersonal communication, problem solving and critical thinking. All of these are important transferable skills used in any career making a person more employable.

Although there are many jobs that do not require a BA, if an employer has a stack of 200 resumes they will probably be more inclined to favor the BA versus AA versus high school (unless it is a lower level job, which generally equals low pay). When I see students who are in their first year at the university, then two years later, then four years later, there is a world of difference, and it is not just the difference of being four years older. There is usually a significant change in maturity, confidence, and ability. In terms of the financial consequences of more education, it is estimated that the lifetime earning difference between a high school diploma and a BA degree is about a million dollars. That is huge, the difference in home ownership, better education for your children, more opportunities for travel and life enrichment, a greater ability to help others in need, better health outcomes, living in safer neighborhoods, a more relaxed retirement (or even the possibility of retiring at all). So getting a good education is a useful step for most people in terms of greater financial potential and life success. Plus, more education improves the odds for job advancement, and that brings opportunities for developing natural talents and even higher income.

Funding Education

The cost of higher education is moving in one direction, higher, higher cost education. Finding ways to help pay for college is important. The rising costs also underscore the importance of making decisions sooner than later, in terms of choosing a major, considering career path, selecting appropriate classes, being motivated and maintaining a high GPA, getting internships and placements, and engaging in an effective job search. There are numerous ways to fund college including loans, work-study, and scholarships. We will consider a few of them here.

Key Terms

Loan — Money borrowed from a lender. That money can be used to purchase a house, buy a car, pay for school. The total cost of the loan includes the principal, the interest, and fees.

Principal — The amount borrowed from the lender. Tuition and books run $5000. You borrow $5000, and use it to pay for tuition and books.

Interest — Lenders are in business to make money by providing loans. They do that by charging interest, typically a percent of the amount borrowed. If you borrowed $5000 for one year and the bank charged 10% interest per year, you would owe the bank $5500 at the end of the year, principal plus interest.

Fees — The lender may charge various fees for originating the loan (processing your application) or administering the loan. It would be like ordering a package online and the seller tacking on shipping fees.

Strategies

Loan — Only borrow if needed
Principal — Only borrow as much as needed
Interest — Find the lowest interest rates
Fees — Find the lowest fees

Loans

Government Loans

There are three main options for school loans – government loans, private loans, and loans or gifts from family. Government loans are an excellent choice. A well-educated population is the foundation for global competitiveness and leadership in national and international affairs. It serves a government well to make sure its citizens are properly educated. A political party or government that does not encourage quality education is shortsighted indeed, clearly not living in the global 21st century. The government is actually the largest provider of financial aid to students in the United States, through the Federal Student Aid (FSA) program. This program provides two types of loans – the Federal Perkins Loan and Stafford Loans. The Federal Perkins Loan is a 5% fixed interest loan of up to $4,000 a year with a cap of $20,000 for undergraduate education. It is based on exceptional financial need. Application and repayment are through the school you are attending.

Stafford Loans are variable rate loans. Unlike fixed rate loans, such as the Perkins loan, the interest rates on the Stafford can vary, moving higher and lower, hence the name variable rate loans. Those rates, however, cannot exceed 8.25%. They are adjusted annually on July 1 with notification to borrowers if a rate is changing. Both Stafford and Perkins loans come from and are repaid to the Federal government directly. There are several repayment plans ranging from 10 to 30 years. The Stafford loan comes in two versions, subsidized and unsubsidized. If you can verify financial need you can qualify for a subsidized loan in which the government pays the interest on the loan while you are in school. That is great. The other option is an unsubsidized loan. Students can obtain those regardless of financial need, but they require that the student pay the loan interest once the loan is granted. Less ideal. Since you need the money you will probably not be able to pay that interest during school. That unpaid interest is added to the principal (the base amount of the loan). When you add that unpaid interest to the original loan you can end up with a significantly higher amount due.

To qualify for federal aid you need to complete the Free Application Federal Student Aid (FAFSA) form. It is also important to either explore the website or talk with the financial aid advisors at the school you are or will be attending. Various factors affect the amount you will be able to borrow such as whether your parents claim you as a dependent on their Federal income taxes.

Private Loans
Private Loans are another option. Credit unions and banks are sources of private loans to students. When seeking private loans there are several important questions to ask: who has the lowest interest rates and fees, best repayment plan, and most helpful customer service. Compare Federal and private options before making a decision. Also, see if your school is associated with a specific credit union. Check their rates before considering a commercial bank, as credit union rates may be lower.

Family Loans
A final loan option is to borrow money from family members. Even better, if you have grandparents who believe in you and who have some financial flexibility, see if they can provide a gift of financial assistance. In either case, money from a family member often comes with more flexible repayment terms and lower or no interest. Remind them that if you get a good education and a higher paying job you will not have to come back home to live with them.

Scholarships
Scholarships are another excellent source of money to help with books, tuition, and living expenses. A scholarship is a gift that does not need to be repaid. There are many scholarship opportunities available to students; you just need to find them. Many universities also provide their own scholarship opportunities, sometimes university-wide, sometimes within specific colleges or departments. Universities that are part of a larger system, like the University of California campuses, may have system-wide scholarships as well.

Sources of scholarships include private family foundations, non-profit organizations, government programs, and businesses. Scholarships have diverse goals including supporting students based on academic achievement or athletic ability, or on specific characteristic, such as race, gender, religious affiliation, career path, being from a particular region of the country, and other criteria. The application process for smaller scholarships can be fairly simple. A few hours of work can get you $500 or $1000. That is not a bad use of time. Other scholarships provide considerably larger amounts of support, such as full tuition for four years. Those are naturally going to be much more competitive.

In addition to providing financial support, getting a scholarships looks good on your resume, showing you to be thoughtful and proactive in your education and wise in managing your school finances. It also shows potential employers that you are unique in some regard that made you stand out compared to others in the same selection pool. When looking for scholarships it is best to start with university financial aid sites. Look at their recommendations and suggestions. You can also ask your campus librarian for ideas. There are less scrupulous companies out there claiming to offer genuine help for a fee, but their services may be quite limited and of little real value. So be on guard for deception and fraud as well (there are no free lunches). When you find a possible scholarship to apply for make sure you give yourself sufficient time to write a solid application, to get feedback and revise, and to gather any required letters of support from faculty or community members.

Grants
Grants are another form of financial support that do not have to be repaid. Grants are based on need and ability. The largest of these is the Federal Pell Grant. Pell Grants are given for undergraduate education and teacher credential preparation. They range from $400 to $5,500 per academic year and are based on the course load the student is taking. Other grants include the federally funded Academic Competitiveness Grant (ACG), which only provides support for two years, and for smaller amounts. A third source is the National SMART grant that is for high achieving third and fourth year students in the sciences. There may be state and university grants available, and other sources as well. Your campus financial aid office and website will have more ideas.

Work-Study & Other Employment
The Federally funded Work Study program is another useful way to help cover college costs while potentially acquiring some career skills. Eligibility for Work-Study is based on financial need, and is available to undergraduate and graduate students, as well as those in professional degree programs. The hourly pay rate will be minimum wage or higher. Earnings do not affect your financial aid eligibility, but they do become part of your total financial aid package. Once accepted for work-study you will typically still have to find an available position and interview for it. Most of the jobs are on campus with convenient or flexible hours. In addition to providing financial support, work-study can be a way to get experience related to a future career. For example, you might find work in a campus lab or work with children in the campus day care. Information on work-study is available at your campus financial aid office.

Another option is to get a job. The advantages of a paid job are better finances, a chance to work on career skills, and an opportunity to build your network of future jobs contacts. Working is also a way to build maturity and responsibility. Students who work are often more organized and productive, because they have to be. The disadvantage, work can get in the way of school. Students who take on too much work have a higher risk of not performing well in school or not finishing school at all. It has been observed that beyond 20 hours a week (and that is quite a bit) graduation rates drops significantly. Some outside employment may be necessary, but too much can be quite counterproductive. If working, it is important to plan classes and study time wisely. Build your schedule around school, not around work. Remember to also reduce expenses where possible and look for other sources of funding, such as scholarships and loans, and consider taking fewer classes.

University Support

Many universities, especially private universities, offer tuition waivers based on financial need. The waivers can be quite substantial. Top tier colleges and universities make a commitment to enroll low-income students. If you think you might be eligible check into tuition waivers.

Employer Support

Employee development programs may also provide support for an employee's continuing education. This can be part of the benefits package offered by a company. Support is generally for specific majors and degrees that benefit the employer. The support typically requires a commitment to the company for a number of years of work beyond the completion of the degree. This can be an excellent way to earn an MBA, for example, a degree that can be quite expensive if paid for out of pocket. The Human Resources department would be the best place to obtain information on availability, eligibility and requirements.

Other Considerations

Other ideas to consider include the Parent PLUS loan. These are loans to the parents of students and not the student directly. They can be given to families who claim the student as a dependent. These loans are not income-based, but do require a review of credit history. The parent is responsible for repayment of these loans, and the student must be enrolled at least part-time.

Also, in terms of planning ahead for college, there is the 529 Plan, which is a college savings plan similar to a 401k plan. The 529 Plan allows anyone to contribute to a college savings fund. Earnings are free of federal income tax and the money can be used for any college expense. Other options include prepaid tuition plans through a specific university. These are custodial accounts to be used by the child to fund education at that university when he or she reaches the age of 18 (or 21). Information on these programs can be found in the Uniform Gifts to Minors Act (UGMA), and Uniform Transfers to Minors Act (UTMA). Some other options include a Coverdell Education Savings Account, which is essentially an education individual retirement account (IRA), and Series EE bonds and savings bonds.

Managing Student Loans and Debt

Managing student loans and debt is a very important step in developing financial literacy and independence. Borrowing money wisely and thoughtfully managing loan repayment is an essential life skill to learn. One strategy is to not borrow money. Instead of loans fund your education via grants, scholarships, and work-study support. Those are direct gifts that do not require future repayment. Finishing school with no or few loans reduces stress and increases immediate job income. In that scenario, once you start working the money you earn each month is all yours. You will not have to send part of it to repay a creditor.

If you do need to take out a student loan, however, then make sure you have considered all of your options. Federal loans will probably provide the best interest rates and repayment plans. Family loans might be even better if available. Consider how much you need to borrow. That factor might influence or even determine which school you decide to attend, but, do not let the sticker price of a university unnecessarily deter you if that is your preferred school. As mentioned above, many universities are willing to reduce tuition costs on the basis of financial need, and attending the right school might increase your long term earning potential.

Finally, think about any loan in terms of post graduation impact. Six months after completing school your student loans come due. The standard repayment plan is ten years, but other options are available. Make sure you understand the interest and repayment requirements of the loan you select. Different loans, such as the Federal Perkins Loan and the Health Professions Student Loan have different repayment terms. Also, recognize that after you graduate you will have additional costs of living that you might not have now, such as car payments and higher rent. Once your loan comes due make sure you pay on time. Delinquent payments result in late charges, potential negative reports to credit bureaus, and other undesirable effects. Paying on time will improve your credit rating, a good thing for the next time you need to get a loan, such as when you want to purchase a car or house. If for some reason repayment becomes a problem do not delay in contacting the loan agency and seeing what options are available, such as a loan deferment or a possible change in the payment plan. If you end up with a number of loans you can also consider consolidating them, putting them all together into one loan, possibly with a lower interest rate. That makes for easier management and less money spent in the long term.

Final thought. Students today are racking up larger and larger school debts. Folks are graduating owing tens of thousands of dollars. That is money that will be taken from every future paycheck for years to come. This is money that could have been used for rent, food, car payments, fun and travel, saving and investing for the future, buying a house, funding your child's future education, and many other important opportunities. Keeping tabs on educational expenses while in school and trying to maintain less versus more debt is a good strategy for longer term financial success. Keep it all in balance – school, work, family, health and fun. It is better to borrow some money if needed rather than overloading classes or working 40 hours a week in order to graduate a semester sooner. That said, borrow less if possible, and none is less than less. Develop a strategic plan that allows you to get good grades, avoid excess debt, and have a sense of well-being and accomplishment. As we say, it is what it is, and having good problem solving and decisions making skills makes the ride that much smoother.

Creating a Budget
Another key to financial literacy is spending and saving wisely. One way to develop that habit involves using a budget. Money we do not spend is money we save. Money we save is money that can be used for growing our net worth, contributing to our financial independence. It is fun to spend. It is necessary to spend. There is also needless spending (money out the window, lost life energy), and that equals less money available for the future. Needless spending is exacerbated by credit cards. It is easy to buy something with a credit card because there is a sense that it does not cost anything. We are just sliding a piece of plastic, no money is exchanged. It can be amazingly seductive, deceptive, easy to do. The shock comes at the end of the month when the credit card statement arrives. Really $2,078, how did I spend that much money???

Whether it is cash, check or credit card, it is very easy to spend money, especially when it is not clear how much money is coming in and how much is going out, and for what. That is where a budget becomes enlightening. It provides that information. It helps you to live within your means. Living within your means equals not spending more than you are making, not increasing debt, and ideally spending less and saving. Here are the steps for a basic budget:

First – list all of your monthly sources of income, to get a sense of what is coming in. That might be money from a job, work-study, some support from your folks, a student loan check for the semester.

Second – list all of your monthly expenses. Create major expense categories to help make the process simple and organized – rent, groceries, gas, phone, entertainment and so one. In those categories enter the weekly amounts for those expenses.

Third – review. After a few months you will see what your typical expenses are. Some will be fixed expenses, those are predictable and not as readily modifiable, like rent and car or alimony payments. Some will be variable expenses that may change from month to month. These can include meals and entertainment, clothing, and gas for the vehicle.

Fourth – once you have all of that information, total the income and expenses. It is then possible to see if there is a surplus or deficit. If there is money left over then you are in luck. Save that for a rainy day, or if you are able you can invest it. Stash it into the bank for saving, or an Individual Retirement Account (IRA) for your future.

Fifth – the final step, whether you are spending less than you are taking in (good), or spending more (living outside of your means), you now want to consider where you can make some cuts. This is especially true if you are spending more than you are making. That is not sustainable and inevitably leads to trouble. Can you spend less on groceries and eat as well. Can you spend less on gas and ride your bike more. Do you need to buy clothes all the time? If you drank less you would clearly save money, be healthier, and get more work done in school. If you ate out less you could reduce expenses, learn to cook better, and with a little imagination be eating healthier meals. Look at ways to trim your budget and use that as a creative path to success and happiness. It can be a game to see how much fun you can have while spending little money. There are even websites devoted to the topic. If you live in larger urban centers they will list the fun and inexpensive or free things to do. Just search for tags like "free things to do in Name of City." Once you are happy with your budget and have a version you are comfortable with it is still important to check it periodically to make sure you are on track and staying within your means.

Managing Debt
Debt can be a very real drag on one's success in school and life. It can also be an essential tool for leveraging resources. It depends on how it is managed. Managing debt wisely is another essential financial literacy skill. If you have budgeted your income and expenses, and you have less money than you need, then it is important to first review your variable expenses to see what can be cut.

Can you buy a less expensive shampoo, or eat more grains instead of meat, take the bus to work a few times a week, bring food from home instead of eating out for lunch. Simple things like that can really begin to make a difference over time. Investing in a stovetop espresso maker for $40 and $10 for a pound of coffee will provide years of very nice coffee (refilling your coffee container every now and then of course). A pound of coffee produces about 40 cups. If you paid $10 a pound that is twenty-five cents a cup. If you go out and buy a coffee or latte you easily spend between two and five dollars. The math is easy. At home, $10, with milk and sugar, maybe $20, for 40 cups. At a cafe from $80 to $200, depending on how crazy your grind is. Convenience you say. Time how long it takes to make a cup at home and how long it takes to go to the cafe, park your car or lock your bike, wait in line, get a cup and find a table. The math is still easy. Is it fun to go to the cafe and get a coffee, yes, do that. Also, consider the life force you are giving a merchant for that cup of coffee, and consider making a few more cups at home. I suspect with some experimenting you will come up with a better brew than you get from the typical non-barista barista.

If reducing expenses here and there does not solve the problem of outflow surpassing inflow then you need to look at fixed costs. Reducing fixed costs might require downsizing your dwelling, moving into something a bit less expensive, or getting a housemate. Maybe it will mean parking the car in the garage for a while and using the bike more often, or ride sharing. If reducing variable and fixed costs does not solve the problem then it is time to bring in more money through work, loans, scholarships or other means.

Credit Cards

If you have credit card debt, or want to manage credit card expenses, there are a few simple things you can do. Credit cards are certainly handy. If you do want to use a credit card then the key is to find the card with the lowest interest rate and fees. Low rate cards may be easier to obtain through your local credit union. Many universities have affiliated credit unions, so that can be a good place to look. Searching online can be another way to do comparative shopping, checking for reviews of provider quality, customer service, and costs related to interest and fees.

If credit cards become a problem, an easy way to spend too much money, then just keep a credit card in the drawer for emergency use only. Use cash or checks instead. If credit cards become a serious problem then just cut them up and replace them with a debit card, which is a plastic version of cash. If you do not have cash in the debit card account it will not let you make the purchase. Simple. You cannot overspend. Another option is to just use cash. Carry a specific amount in your wallet as your allowance for the week. Once that is gone you are out of money. Simple. That is the way life works for many people in the world. It is a very good discipline. Once you have created a reasonably detailed budget you will know how much money you spend on average each week and for what. You can then give yourself that much to spend, in cash. That is all. That strategy leads to greater momentary fiscal awareness. "This is what I left to spend this week. Do I really need to buy another red snookow? Will it make me happier, healthier, closer to my goals?"

If you have multiple cards, with outstanding debt on more than one of them, see if they can be consolidated into one card, ideally the one with the lowest interest rate and fees. Many companies will allow a one time, no cost transfer of debt from one card to another. They want your business (they actually want your interest payment), so they will take your transfer of credit card debt with no initial cost. If not consolidated, then *pay down the cards as quickly as possible,* especially the card with the highest interest rate. If consolidated, then pay down the card as quickly as possible. Always pay the monthly minimum, on time. The late fees are where banks really make money. Those fees are often very high. Pay more than the minimum whenever possible. That pays down the principal sooner, which lowers the interest, and gets you out of debt sooner (just make sure there is no penalty for early payment – tricky dogs). Finally, considering taking money out of savings, which is often making next to nothing in interest, and use that money to pay off credit cards, where you will definitely be losing money on interest.

Saving and Investing Money

Understand Money as a Resource

It is important to become more financially literate and to develop a plan for your saving and investing. Once you have a plan, implement it, stay informed and committed, and reach your goal. Research shows that people who plan and who have clear financial goals do better in the long run. If you want to retire with some money in the bank and the ability to live in a style you prefer, then you will need to plan, and the sooner you develop and implement the plan the better off you will be. Studies show that people who have greater financial literacy and who plan for their financial futures tend to have higher wealth levels at retirement. Lusardi & Mitchell (2007) analyzed data from the Health and Retirement Study. They compared two groups of individuals, ages 51-56 at the time of the study, in terms of wealth and financial position based on financial literacy and planning. The results of the study provided solid evidence of the importance of both. Individuals who were more financially literate and who planned effectively did significantly better in the long run. Even planning a little compared to not planning at all made a marked difference in long-term wealth accumulation. What was of interest in the article was that individuals at the lowest percentiles of wealth were actually worse off in 2004 than their counterparts in 1992, due to inflation and shrinking wages. There was also a significant difference in terms of race with Blacks and Hispanics being financially less well off than Whites. A similar difference was found for those who were less well educated. Education, including learning about managing one's financial resources, is a key to future security. Become financially literate. It is your future.

Spend Less

One of the keys to saving and investing is based on the old adage of paying yourself first. This means to take part of your income, if possible, and to give it to yourself instead of someone else (not spending). That money, which has not been spent, can be applied to savings, or put into an investment (even better), or a tax protected retirement account, like an Individual Retirement Account (the best). If there is outstanding debt that money can also be applied to pay down credit card or other types of debt. Shop smarter, buy cheaper, buy less, buy nothing, pay with cash instead of credit cards, save and invest the rest.

Invest Sooner than Later

An important financial literacy goal is to save and invest early. Why? Compounded interest. Consider three options. The first is putting $1,000 in the bank with 0% interest per year (no interest). In 40 years what will it be worth? Turn over the card – $1000! Due to inflation over those 40 years it will actually be worth much less than that. Tell grandma how much a gallon of milk costs. She will be shocked. A gallon is still a gallon, right? That is inflation at work. Fifty cents does not go as far as it used to! Over time the cost of things generally inflate, they go up. Of looking at it another way, the value of money goes down. That carton of eggs cost sixty cents in 1970. It is two dollars today. That same dollar bill buys a lot less in 2010. So that $1000 put in the bank 40 years ago buys a whole lot less milk and eggs today.

So why not just spend it all immediately? That is one solution for those who want to end their life impoverished. Here are two alternatives. The first is to invest the money in an account with non-compounding interest, say a steady 10% at the end of each year. Every December 31st your $1,000 gets a 10% interest payment, or $100 added to the account each year. In 40 years it will be worth the original $1000 plus interest ($100 per year interest, times 40 years = $4000). The total in 40 years would be $1000 principal + $4000 interest = $5000.

The second alternative is to put the money into an account with compounding interest. So you start with the same $1000 but you are earning 10% compounded interest each year. Every December 31st interest is calculated. The difference with compounding interest is that the annual interest is not based on the original $1000. It is calculated based on the total current investment, which includes interest from year to year. So the base upon which the interest is calculated is growing annually. With compounding interest the longer something is compounding the more money it can make for you over time (the reason to start sooner).

It can be quite inspiring to see how your money is earning you money, and the difference can be staggering. Comparing the three approaches, with no interest, $1000 in 40 years equals $1000. In 40 years non-compounding interest of 10% equals $5000. Compounding interest at 10% a year for 40 years results in $45,259. In the table below you can see a comparison of an initial investment of $1000 over 40 years comparing simple interest and compounding interest. Again, the differences at the end of 40 years are substantial. This speaks to the important point of getting money into an account as soon as possible, adding as regularly as possible, and keeping money in the investments as long as possible, so it can grow for you. If you want to play with numbers yourself you can find online calculators which let you see how the relationship between initial investment, length of investment, and interest rates over time. Just search for "compound interest calculator."

Years	Investment Not Compounded	Investment Compounded
Investment	$1000 at 10% annual interest	$1000 at 10% annual compounded interest
1 year	$1100	$1100
10 year	$2000	$2594
20 year	$3000	$6725
40 year	**$5000**	**$45259** = a difference of **$41259**

Basic Rule – Diversify
When you do start investing one of the gold standards is to have a *diversity of asset classes*, some stocks, some bonds, depending on your age and risk tolerance. I was having dinner once with a cousin who is an investment counselor. He was talking about an elderly customer who had all of her life savings in one stock, one stock! Fortunately it had worked out for her, but what if that stock had been Enron or Worldcom, both of which tanked and lost all their value. She would be in the poor house, or her kid's house, if they were kind enough to take her in. One of the simplest ways to have a diverse investment portfolio is to invest in a number of mutual funds or ETFs, such as a large cap fund, mid cap fund, international fund and bond fund. Again, the more financially literate one becomes the better one will be at knowing how to get the most out of their investments.

Also, when investing, it is generally advised that you think in terms of the long run. Many people do not think much at all, herd mentality. When things start going south they run for the door, and so do lots of other rabbits. The result, a rabbit stampede, and what a mess that is. Very few get out alive as the place burns down around them. Warren Buffet, philanthropist and one of the worlds great investors, once said that successful in investing was not related to intelligence, but rather to the ability to control urges that get other investors in trouble. Markets are volatile, but have shown consistent growth in the long run. It is very hard to time the market. Get rich quick schemes are generally better at making the scheme originator rich, not the participants. Practice mindful awareness, be informed, manage emotions, make good decision, deal with challenges, focus on quality and long term goals, and keep learning.

In addition to investments, you will need some cash reserves in case of emergencies or other short term needs beyond the expected. One of my colleagues here in San Francisco keeps $500 in his earthquake kit. He says that a roll of cash is as important as storing some food and water. It is a key to getting things handled when there are no banks open and the ATMs are down.

Opening a Retirement Account
There is a great old Japanese movie called *The Taxing Woman*. In the movie a gangster is hiding his wealth, and thus paying no taxes. The woman, a tax agent, is trying to ascertain his worth. At one point he talks about not drinking from the glass until drop by drop the liquid fills to the top. Then, he said, as it overflows you can drink. The point for our purposes is not extreme deprivation, but rather that small additions over time lead to abundance in the future. People often postpone investing, as they postpone other important life decision, because the first step looks too big, or they have no plan, or they still believe that the collar is on. The simple solution – take a small step.

These days there are a number of retirement savings vehicles with very low initial entry requirements. You just have to search the web to find them. A very good vehicle for starting an investment habit is opening a ROTH IRA. Do a search for, "low initial investment individual retirement account." You can open an IRA through your credit union, bank, and all the major brokerage firms. The key to building wealth is early and steady contribution, drip by drip into the glass. There are a many millionaires in this country who did not win the lottery or get hired early into some mega-success technology startup. Maybe they worked as a plumber, or a police officer, or grade school teachers, or they had a mid-level management position. The thing that made them millionaires was that they paid themselves first, they put money into their retirement accounts on a regular basis, often through an automatic contribution that came right out of their pay check each month. They also lived within their means, did not spend money needlessly, and they enjoyed what they had. Did they forfeit the good life? If you asked them they would probably say no. They travelled, entertained, sent their kids to college, gave to important charities, but they did all of that with an eye on fiscal prudence. They were financially literate and applied that knowledge for their long term benefit and for the good of others. I suspect many of them also clearly understand that money cannot buy happiness, happiness starts within.

On a similar note, if you do happen to be employed and your employer provides some form of defined-contribution retirement account, like a 401k or 457 retirement account, then you should if at all possible max out those options. Those plans take money out of your paycheck, before it gets taxed, and puts that money into the retirement account. That money is not taxed until you take it out at retirement, at which point most people are making less income, so they have lower tax rates. Plus, since it has been sitting there, hopefully for many years, it has been invested and the interest has been compounding. That takes some financial literacy and planning, but come retirement time you will be very, very, very, very happy you did your homework.

Finally, no matter what kind of investments you have, understand what you own, learn more about investing and invest wisely. Do not plan on outsmarting the professionals who have a team of trading professional and 24/7 data centers crunching the numbers every millisecond of every day. Timing the market is hard if not impossible for the experts (look at the collapse of Lehman Brothers in 2008). If the people running the markets did not see that coming how can the average consumer investor do much better. Get rich schemes are probably a good way to lose money, and lose it fast. Keep it simple, learn as much as you can, keep it invested, do not use it prematurely unless there is a very serious need, and enjoy it when you are ready to stop working.

Start Thinking About Retirement Now
No matter how old you are it is useful to think about retirement. Employ the strategy of starting at the end, the desired state. If you think about where you would like to end up in your life, it gets you thinking about how you will get there, what the best solution path will be. It is a good exercise to think about what the later part of your life will look like. Will you have grand children. Where will you live. What will your health status be. How much money will you have. Will you be able to retire, by when? In terms of money, decide on how much and by when. Once you have done that then come back to the present and begin to explore the best ways to get there. There are plenty of online tools to help you actually consider options and calculate annual savings and investments needed to attain that target. Just search for "retirement planning, and retirement calculators." That is a good exercise to spend some time on, a critical piece of financial literacy and solid planning. Is this important? Yes, when Social Security was created the average life expectancy was about 60 years of age and retirement was 65. People retired and in a few years a high percentage passed away. Also, a much larger percentage of the population was working, contributing to the social security system. Today people are living much longer, maybe a third of their lives in retirement. That is a

lot of years to pay for. If you do not want to eat dog food and live in a box under the bridge then planning now is not a bad idea (and a box under the bridge can be a very affordable alternative to a condo).

Buying a House
One of the bigger purchases most people will ever make is a house. It has the potential to be an investment, but not necessarily. The best perspective is to think of it as a place to stay. There are advantages and disadvantages to owning and renting, depending on the job market, cost of housing stock, your income, how long you will be in a location, and other factors. Learn more about it. Think about it sooner than later. If you are going to be in one place for a while, generally at least five years, then buying may be a good idea. It can be a practical thing to do for the right person at the right time. Do the homework and make the best informed choice.

Some Simple Principles
Remember that what you need is not always the same as what you want. Money management begins with taking care of what you *need* first, then what you want if you are able.

Make a budget for yourself and keep it.

Be conscious of how much are spending, on what and why. Make it count. Follow your goals and values.

Determine the amount you need for fixed costs like rent, car payments, and other items. Reserve a percentage for comforts and special events.

Live within your means.

Be patient in acquiring things. Buy based on actual need. Save up and pay in cash.

Buy durable, quality items. Buy used. Re-use. Recycle. Enjoy what you have.

Increase your savings, reduce your spending.

Learn how to invest the money you are saving wisely.

Use cash for purchases when possible, or debit cards, reduce use of credit cards if they are an issue. If you use a credit card consider one that provides points that you can use for air travel or other purposes.

Pay off your debt. Pay off your credit card debt as soon as possible. Stay out of unnecessary debt once you have gotten clear. Use debt wisely.

Remember that making a living is just one part of life. If we work more in order to buy things that we do not really need we will have less time left for the other areas of our development and happiness. Our money comes from the precious moments of our life that we have given to someone (an employer/customer). How much money do you really need in order to be happy? Live a healthy lifestyle, reduce stress, celebrate friends and family, enjoy life, stay in love, give back to your community, be useful.

True Abundance

Abundance is not about the money. Money is just one aspect of abundance. Money is an abstraction, a symbol. It is an important resource that contributes to education, health, adventure. Money used wisely is a very good thing, and like all tools, in the wrong hands (heart and mind) it can become a great burden, a dangerous weapon, a means to personal ruin and societal decay.

Abundance, by comparison, is bigger than that. Abundance is about our life. It includes our physical, emotional, intellectual, spiritual, behavioral and environmental well-being and contribution. Abundance is also a discipline, a way of being. The keys to an abundant life include these elements...

Mind & Spirit

Equanimity

Wisdom

Having a sense of inner peace and personal meaning

Mental clarity and awareness

Positive attitudes and beliefs about self, others and the world

Acceptance of life and the challenge to grow.

Contributing to world peace and social justice.

Environmental awareness and contribution.

Connection with inner self, higher power, life force.

Heart

Relationships

Connection with other people in a mutually beneficial way.
Love of self and others, positive attitudes, happiness, friendship and intimacy,
encouragement, tolerance, honesty, honoring feelings, open communication,
positive sexuality, patience, understanding, acceptance, growth, compassion

Work

Honest work, contribution to the greater good, meaningful involvement,
productivity, enjoyment, security, respect, accomplishment, achievement

Financial Freedom

Income for self and family, income for those in need, support to the community

Body

Vitality

Taking care of the physical being

Energy, flexibility, strength, endurance, aerobic fitness,

Relaxation, healthy body image, playfulness, courage

SUMMARY

The chapter begins with a reflection on the meaning of money and why it is important to not waste what we spend our precious life energy to earn. This leads to the main chapter content of financial literacy. Research has found that individual who do even modest financial planning will be much more well prepared financially in the long run compared to those who do not. Financial literacy involves understanding how to make money, work with a budget, borrow prudently and manage debt effectively, and why investing sooner than later is a good idea. The chapter concludes with thoughts on true abundance.

MIND-BODY

Sitting Meditation

This week practice mindfulness of breath, body, thoughts/feelings, sensations. Or practice Hum Sah concentration meditation. Cultivate relaxation and equanimity.

Mindful Awareness

Be mindfully aware of your approaches to school activities this week. Also pay attention to your relationship with money. Recognize money as a symbol for life force. Notice how you are using this life energy.

Priming

Think of your goals for the week. Use priming mental imagery to see the most incredible week/semester of your life so far. See yourself as having a solid foundation in financial literacy and being able to make a good living to support yourself and loved ones and to give back to the community and others less fortunate than yourself.

REFERENCES

Greenspan A. The Challenge of Central Banking in a Democratic Society. Washington: Annual Dinner and Francis Boyer Lecture of The American Enterprise Institute for Public Policy Research. December 5, 1996. Available at: http://www.federalreserve.gov/boarddocs/speeches/1996/19961205.htm. Accessed October 9, 2014.

Lusardi A, Mitchell OS. Baby boomer retirement security: the roles of planning, financial literacy, and housing wealth. *Journal of Monetary Economics*. 2007;54(1):205-224.

Robin V, Dominguez J, Tilford M. *Your Money or Your Life: 9 steps to transforming your relationship with money and achieving financial independence*. New York: Penguin; 1992.

You & the World 18

> *I appreciate the interdependence of all things.*
> *I give my gift to the world today.*

CHAPTER THEMES
- The New World
- Giving your Gift to the World
- Cultivate Wisdom and Compassion
- Streaming

As we enter the 21st century the global community faces significant challenges and opportunities. The planet is indeed shrinking as a result of advances in communication and technology, improved transportation infrastructure, population growth and immigration, trade reform, and other historic forces. It has been suggested by many educators that the United States is poorly prepared to deal with these changes. Inadequate preparation in foreign language, a lack of knowledge of history and world affairs, and disinterest in science and math, have all been suggested as significant hazards for economic development, national security, and our continued global success as a nation.

The New World

In 1492 it took Christopher Columbus about a month to sail from Spain to the Bahamas. Today you can get there is about 9 hours by plane. In 1610 Galileo came into serious conflict with the Church for proposing that the sun was the center of our universe. In the early 20th century our Milkyway galaxy was believed to be the extent of the universe. Today we know that there are over 100 billion galaxies in the visible universe, and that 90% of the universe is believed to be invisible dark matter (that is, we are in the dark about what it is, and also, we cannot see it).

It is estimate that invasive species, pollution, global warming, and loss of habitat may result in the extinction of 30-50 percent of all animal and plant species within the next 100 years. Many biologists consider the planet to be facing a level of extinction unequaled since the age of the dinosaurs, some 65 million years ago. A recent 10 year study published in *Nature* reported that 90 percent of the ocean's large fishes have already disappeared as a result of over-fishing and related factors. There are now over 7 billion people living on earth with global population increasing at almost two-percent per year. At that rate the population is expected to double in about 50 years.

According to UNICEF one out of every two children in the world lives in poverty and 30,000 die each day as a result. UNESCO reports that there are approximately one-billion adults in the world unable to read or write. The U.S. government allocates $150 million in aid to help educate the world's poorest 2 billion children, many living in predominantly Muslim countries. The state of Vermont spends 6 times that amount per year on education. Over half-a-million people die from measles each year, mainly children, yet immunization costs approximately thirty-cents per person. Forty-million individuals are infected with HIV, including many women and children. The World Health Organization predicts a global epidemic in type 2 diabetes by 2030. This dramatic increase in type 2 diabetes is clearly associated with major changes in dietary and exercise habits. US advertising expenditures for breakfast cereals, soft drinks, candy, gum, and snack foods totaled $2.4 billion in 1997.

Use of networked computers was largely used for military and research purposes during the 1960s and 70s, in part funded by the National Science Foundation and the Department of Defense. During the 1980's and 1990's the internet transitioned from a government sponsored enterprise to a public and commercial communication platform, completed in 1995 when the National Science Foundation Network (NSFNET) was decommissioned. It is now estimated that approximately 10% of the world's population regularly accesses the internet. It is estimated that there are approximately 10 billion searchable pages on the web in 75 languages. In 2005 the total number of searches performed was 55 percent higher than the year before, 5.1 billion searches. Online advertising in the US topped $10 billion in 2005. One in ten Americans has dropped use of traditional telephones and now uses cell phones exclusively. Many are transitioning from desktop or laptop computers to smaller mobile devices such as tablets, smart phones and watches.

We are experiencing unprecedented change on the planet. The problem or challenge is that humans do not tend to think preventatively. We often need a catastrophe to wake up. We engage in procrastination on a global scale. We wait until finals, until the final hour, then we urgently rush around to deal with the mess that has emerged as a result of our inattention. It is like the story of the tortoise and the hare or of the ant and the grasshopper. Not only do we humans procrastinate, react versus prevent, we also tend to act egoistically, what is good for me, and who cares about you. The challenge is that many of the problems in the world today are shared, the actions of others do indeed affect everyone. Air pollution, nuclear proliferation, civil war, population migration, overfishing, increased consumption of meat, driving bigger cars, all social phenomena with social consequences. So solving current and future problems will require the we all participate, the combined efforts of all of us, the intelligent, respectful, interaction of humanity.

Giving Your Gift to the World

A Daily Practice

One place where we have some immediate control over the fate of the planet is by what we bring to our lives each day, what we do consciously to make a difference. There is an old Indian saying,

"Hastasya bushinam danam," which translates as, "Giving is the ornament of the hand." A nice practice in this regard is to ask yourself first thing in the morning, "What will I give the world today?" This simple practice carries a number of benefits. First, it makes you immediately think of what you have to offer. It is self-acknowledging and self-empowering. It says, "I HAVE something to give to the world," *something to give to the world*, not just to family, or community, but to the world. So it is a statement of capacity, and the implication is large capacity. The next thing it does is that it gets you to think about your gifts, what is it that you can give to the world, what unique gift that would be of value. The final and critically important thing that it does is that it provides a focus for that day that is outside of self, it immediately reduces what the Dalai Lama refers to as self-cherishing. By focusing on others there is an equivalent reduction in self-focus, which means a reduction of limiting beliefs, such as self-doubt or unworthiness. The simple practice is actually quite brilliant, healing and empowering self, while benefitting others, a win-win. A related technique to begin building our recognition and capacity to give is provided at the end of this chapter, the Streaming Technique.

Volunteering

Another way to make a difference sooner than later is to look for opportunities to volunteer. Volunteering is an excellent way to give back to your community, develop new skills, learn about careers, network with organizations you might want to work with, or fields you might want to work in, meet new people, and make new friends. Especially in this age of shrinking community resources it is very important for folks to volunteer and help out. If you are thinking of volunteering the first thing you need to consider is what type of work you would like to do or what type of organization you would like to work with. You can start by creating a list of your skills and interests. Then do some research to see if there are any organizations that might need those particular skills or match your particular interests. You can search online, ask friends, or visit your campus community service program to get leads. If you care about the environment, then search for local or national environmental groups. If you care about the poor, then think of local churches or community programs that serve the low-income community. When you find one or more then contact them to see if they could use your help. Some organizations have a well-established volunteer program, others not so much. It is probably a good idea to start with ones that do, at least at first. If they have a track record with volunteers it will probably make for a smoother landing and a better experience. Contact them, set up a meeting if it sounds promising, or attend one of their volunteer trainings or other events. Then get out there and pitch in!

It is also possible to do community volunteer work and receive academic credit for it. In that way you learn, contribute, make friends, have fun, and put in some miles toward graduation. If the volunteer activity is related to a for-credit class then it will show up on your transcript. In no suitable community service classes are available then see if an independent study course is possible. Also make sure it goes on your resume and becomes a piece of your story in graduate school or job applications and interviews. The group you volunteer for can also be a potential source of letters of recommendation. Volunteer work shows that you care about people and the community and that you can work with other people. All of that looks good to potential employers and graduate school application committees. It shows you are more than a book-bound student, you have depth, you care about your community. Depending on your career plans the organization you volunteer with may be a road to a job, especially if they are affiliated with a larger national organization. At the least they can become part of your referral network. If you have three job candidates who all possess the right skills the one who gets the job is often the one with the referral connections, the 'who you know' factor.

Promote Peace, Justice and Democracy

Work for peace, social justice, and democracy. As the world shrinks in size it will become critical for humans to start solving problems in new ways. "Is there a better way to do this?" The costs of war and social unrest are huge in terms of pain and suffering, economic impacts, lost productivity in society, environmental degradation, and much more. Many factors contribute to conflict, including lack of understanding and respect, poor communication, cultural and linguistic barriers, inequity of resources, constrained opportunities, and oppression. Transformation begins with respect for self and others, thinking of the suffering of others and how we can make a difference in the world, supporting institutions that work for justice and non-violence, and fostering non-violence in our own thinking, communication, families and businesses. Develop a righteous sense of fairness. Be righteous. Get politically involved, or at the very least vote. When you vote, think of the impact your candidates can have on local, national and global problems. The politics of fault-finding is petty, self-serving, and inadequate. Promote problem solving and mutual benefit. If a politician cannot solve problems then he or she does not belong in political office. Vote with your wallet every day. When you make a purchase think of the injustice or justice behind that product, the impact on the environment, and your actual need.

Live Sustainably

I knew someone who was distressed at the potential extinction of the polar bear, yet she kept her heat on during the day when she was at work as she did not want to come home to a cold house. Those two things do not compute. There are simple solutions to that problem, such as a timer on the thermostat or putting on a sweater for 20 minutes while the house heats up. We need to begin to think in terms of real solutions to real problems. Small steps can make a big difference. Learning to live within our means is one essential piece.

There are a lot of simple things we can do, fun and healthy things, that make for a more sustainable lifestyle. This can be replacing a few lights with lower energy consumption bulbs. If you do not like the light from certain low energy bulbs then just use them in areas that you do not frequent as much, even that makes a difference. Plant a garden. Urban gardens are becoming increasingly common. My old city of Detroit has been working on bulldozing burned out urban decay and introducing inner city farms. That immediately reduces blight and vandalism, while providing much needed green space and healthy food in a corridor that does not have much of either. There are many vegetables that are actually quite easy to grow, such as tomatoes, carrots, squash, lettuce and basil. Start composting. Change showerheads to conserve water. Get a good water filter and a stainless steel water bottle and stop buying bottled water. Many brands of bottled water are basically tap water, not particularly good anyway, and the amount of plastic waste in landfill is enormous. Start riding your bike more. It is good for you, easier on the environment, and fun. I remember reading about a fellow who started riding a bike as part of an environmental commitment. He lost so much weight and started to feel so much better physically that when the campaign was over he did not give up his bike. Bikes are fuel efficient! Think of ways to spend less money. If you are saving money you are often going lighter on the environment and taking better care of your body. For example, eat less meat. If you reduce your consumption of beef and pork you will be doing your heart a favor as well as the planet. An incredible amount of corn has to be grown to fatten a cow for slaughter. That is grain that humans could eat. Also, if you eat more legumes in place of that meat you can save a bundle of cash. It is amazing how taking care of the planet and taking care of each other is often the best way to take care of ourselves.

Find Balance

All work and no play, not so good. Everyone has a dog nature, the part that wants to run and bark. Life is too short to just work all the time, and equally too short to just loaf around wasting precious moments lost in space. It is a matter of balance. In the ancient Indian Vedic system the qualities of a balanced life included kama, artha, dharma, moksha. Kama relates to pleasure and happiness, the basic human drive for reward. It emphasizes appreciation of the moment, of pleasant experiences as an expression of bliss, but to avoid attachment. This can include enjoying experience as diverse as love making, eating, being physically active, the joy of art, music, the outdoors. Artha relates to cultivation of material prosperity. To be financially stable provides the basis for doing more good in the world. It provides the basis for cultivation of wisdom and greater learning and understanding of life. Dharma is one's responsibility to family, society, the greater good. It is being of service, doing your work, fulfilling your life calling, your destiny. Moksha is the final stage and it relates to liberation. The ultimate liberation is freedom from attachment, delusion, ignorance, fear, all the things that hold us back, the collars that keep us from taking that next step. These four in balance present a ideal mix of enjoying the simple pleasures of human existence, obtaining material resources, being responsible and contributing to society, and pursuing deeper meaning and freedom.

Cultivate Wisdom and Compassion

Those humans! What a funny bunch. If it was not for them the world would be a different place. But hey, they are here, so we have to figure out creative ways to work with them. What is it that makes humans act so oddly at times? Certainly one aspect is that ego of theirs. That interesting sense of "I" that they have. "Because I have the biggest hair, I am obviously the most important, so I need a golden toilet seat." "Uh, ok, if you really think that would make you happy, let's get you that golden toilet seat." Well you know the story, golden toilet seats are notoriously cold in the morning, so then they need a toilet seat warming device, which requires a larger bathroom, and that means a bigger house, and on and on it goes.

Maybe what is even more ironic is that despite that great big 'I' standing in the middle of things is an overwhelming lack of self-awareness by many people in a lot of places a lot of the time. Like many other built-in features that sense of ego is an excellent device for self-preservation. Like our teeth and claws and cleverness, it helps us to stay alive another day, which is just what evolution wants. The 'I' quality, our I-dentity is one of the big cogs in the machine that keeps things rolling in an evolutionary sense. The problem is that if human ego is operating at a lower level, closer to our animal nature of reproduction and basic survival, things can get pretty ugly (and sadly they often do, just watch the news). That would be okay if we were just rats living in burrows, but we are not. We have nuclear weapons that can obliterate entire cities in an instant. We have massive trawlers that can catch and decimate fish populations and turn the oceans into deserts. We have intricately intertwined global economies, where blind greed can topple one or two giant banks and destabilize the whole works. We face an increasingly shrinking planet, with more people, and finite resources. We need to work with ego in new ways, recognizing it, studying it, managing it, employing it constructively.

How to do that? There are two time-tested methods, powerful but not simple – cultivate wisdom and develop compassion. Wisdom is discrimination, discriminating truth from untruth – this will take me higher, this will bring me down. This is in my highest good and the highest good of others, and that is not. Very often the distinction is quite clear if we are willing to open our eyes and look. The truth is right there. Then we make a choice. Making good choices is built on having guiding goals, living those goals, checking in on a regular basis, on what is the most important thing to do right now, and being mindful during the flow of the day. Living in wisdom draws on our frontal cortex, more conscious self-reflection and awareness of goals and the long road, the consequences into the future.

The other half of that package is the cultivation of compassion. What is that? It is essentially implementing the great message of loving your neighbor as your self. The practice of compassion changes our relationship with 'I', with self. In a compassion-oriented practice the self begins to recognize others more consciously, more intentionally. Empathy can emerge and deepen. We can become part of a greater web of humanity and existence. The microcosm and the macrocosm meld together into a single whole. With the growth of these two elements of wisdom and compassion we begin to see through the veils of family dynamic, of culture, of evolution, to a deeper mystery. We begin to see things as they really are, not how conditioned mind and body want them to be, higher human potential becomes more visible.

Keep Learning and Growing

As the Dalai Lama once wrote, "Never Give Up!" Sometimes it is clear that a problem is a problem. It is visible. We can see it, indeed, maybe everyone can see it. Something is broken and needs to be fixed, but that does not mean it will get fixed. The dishes get washed even when the dishwasher is broken. The marriage goes on even though there is no communication and no real intimacy. There is plenty of food in the world and yet people go hungry. Yet, in defense of inaction, sometimes indeed it can be very hard, maybe even impossible, to make the needed change right now, maybe ever. Some things are just like that. It is not practical to leave the marriage because of little children, no money to fix the dishwasher, war prevents food distribution. In those situations we just have to do the best we can. At other times, however, change is possible, and it is just a matter of vision, belief in self and others, and starting to do something, just starting. That is all that is required, *taking that first small step*. Action toward change, toward freedom and happiness, results from our commitment to learn and grow, to move closer to our true work, step by step, day by day, one breath at a time. Until there is an end to suffering I will never give up.

The Streaming Technique

Many of the ideas presented in this chapter suggest giving to the world. Giving can feel threatening at times though, when there is a sense of scarcity. How can we give when we feel like we do not have enough for ourselves? One strategy is to find our inner abundance and give from that place. That is a strategy that lets us practice giving without feeling like we are going to run dry, like learning how to invest in the stock market using Monopoly money. Using play money allows a person to take calculated risks and grow in confidence without feeling the pain of real loss.

Streaming satisfies those criteria. It is a method for expanding our giving capacity in a way that does not feel costly. In this technique we imagine tapping into the vast energy of life and using that energy as a source of gifts for the world. Buy pulling from that profoundly vast source we are able to practice giving and giving and giving, without feeling like we are losing anything. In actuality we will feel like we are gaining in that process, and indeed we are. Streaming is a simple process we can use to build our awareness that we have enough, more than enough, that we have capacity, that we are indeed rich.

Instructions for Streaming

1. Sit Quietly And Relax
Take several slow deep breaths. Allow the mind and body to relax.

2. Select a Recipient
Reflect on the person, or people, or place you will be sending energy to.

3. Inhale Energy In, Affirm, Exhale an d Concentrate
Inhale and draw energy in through the top of the head and bottom of the spine. Imagine that this energy comes from a vast, universal ocean of love, or healing energy, or power, or whatever else feels right to you. Tap into whatever life energy is most appropriate for the recipient you will be streaming to. The key is to understand that you are tapping a virtually endless pool, a phenomenally vast resource (something on the scale of the cosmos here, we are talking mythic). There is no using it up in anyone's lifetime. See that energy as visible light, if possible. Breathe it in. As you exhale concentrate the light and energy in your heart space. As you concentrate the energy in the heart region think to yourself, "I am concentrating love/power/peace/healing energy in my heart." See the light building up in the heart space.

4. Repeat
Repeat this process three times (for three breaths in and out), more breaths if you have more time.

5. Inhale and Concentrate Energy
On the fourth or final inhale focus on the heart. As you inhale take the energy you have stored in the heart and concentrate it even more. Imagine it being compressed, the way coal is compressed to diamond. Make it intensely dense and powerful. Also, think of the recipient you will be sending this energy to. See that person in your mind.

6. Exhale and Send the Energy
With the final exhale send this concentrated energy out from the heart. It is like an arrow released from a bow. It shoots out of the body streaming across the sky toward the chosen person, people or place. The energy is not attached to you. It is an independent flow of energy. It can be a ball of light, a stream of light, an arrow, a shooting star, whatever image seems most fitting. Watch it as it arcs through time and space.

7. Observe the Recipient
Watch the recipient receive the energy. Watch the energy entering their body or their space. See the recipient changing as the wave of energy moves through. See them transform, filled with joy and healing light.

8. Enjoy
Sit with that awareness for a moment and appreciate the ability to share positive energy with another.

Who to Stream To
You can stream to anyone, alive or deceased, loved or loathed, close or half way around the world. The great thing about the process is that the person does not have to be there. They can be very far away, on lots of levels. You can stream to groups of people, like victims of civil war. You can stream to physical locations, like a rainforest or the entire earth, or to animals like polar bears in the arctic. You can a send energy anywhere you think it would be of value. Stream to someone that you care about. Stream to someone who has hurt you in the past, as a way to begin healing that pain. Stream to someone you are having trouble with in the current moment. Stream to yourself.

Final Note on Streaming
This is a true story. I once had a student who had not seen her father for several years, and only very rarely heard from him. She decided to stream to him. That night after class she went home and there was a message on her answering machine from her father, just a few words. He said, "Sending the same back to you."

Summary of Steps

1. Sit quietly and relax
2. Choose a recipient
3. Inhale and draw energy in through the top of head and bottom of spine.
   Exhale and concentrate the energy in the heart region.
4. Repeat this breathing process three times.
5. On the fourth breath concentrate the heart energy completely.
6. On the exhale send a stream of energy to the intended party.
7. Watch the other person receiving this energy.
8. Sit with that awareness for a moment and know you are helping the world.

SUMMARY

In this final chapter we considered a few of the challenges facing us. There are many. The only practical way to work through these issues is for more people of the planet to come together, using common intelligence and commitment to a better world, to break down the barriers to successful resolution. Many of the roots of these and other problems reside within our hearts. We have a choice. We have a great potential. The future is indeed in our hands, minds and hearts. Now is the time. Starting right now, we change the world forever.

MIND-BODY

Sitting Meditation

Cultivate wisdom and compassion, a lifelong practice.

Mindful Awareness

Be mindfully aware of the interplay of Environment, Person and Behavior. Look for opportunities for growth and continual improvement.

Priming

Think of your goals. Use priming mental imagery to see the most incredible life for yourself, loved ones and others.

RESOURCES

Priming Guidelines

1. Determine Your Goal
You may want to use one of your basic life goals for this exercise. Limit yourself to one or two goals to work on. Too many items will diffuse the focus. Goals to work on might include taking care of your health (eating well, getting more exercise), positive connections with people, being productive and getting a lot of work done, being more confident or compassionate.

2. Close Your Eyes & Relax
A good time to prime the day is in the morning right after meditation, or soon after getting up before you begin your day. Whenever you do it, always take a moment to relax before starting the imagery. One simple relaxation method is to count backwards from ten to one. Exhale and count one number down with each breath. [Other tips: tell yourself that your hands they are warm and heavy; let shoulders and jaw relax completely

3. Sense/See Yourself in a Comfortable Space
If you are not yet skilled at imaging you can just pretend that you see the image, even if you see nothing at all, that is fine. See yourself sitting in a chair at home (or some other relaxing place, like at the beach). You look very, very happy. You are happy because you have achieved your dream. It is now a truth.

4. Tell Yourself That You Feel Excellent
Tell yourself that you feel excellent, incredible. Specify that you look and feel happy because you have achieved your goal. Specify that goal. For example, you can say, "I feel wonderful because my energy was incredibly high all day, I exercised, got a tremendous amount of work done, and had wonderful connections with people! I love how I feel." Let yourself feel energized by your own happiness about this. The wording should be personal, positive and present tense.

5. Create a Strong Body Energy
This experience will be more powerful if there is a corresponding positive body feeling. If we give an image a strong positive charge it will be more memorable, as we tend to remember powerful emotional experiences, negative and positive. If the image does not evoke a noticeable positive feeling then just remember something in your life that was a most incredibly positive experience. That memory will reactivate the proper psychophysiology immediately. You will then have the proper body-mind state to empower yourself.

6. Increase the Intensity
Make the entire experience more intense. You can do this with self-talk "I feel amazing. What an incredible day/feeling. I am so happy," or by making the colors or images more vivid, or by intensifying the body state.

7. Do an Integration Breath
Inhale and breathe the image/energy into your lower abdomen, then exhale it even deeper into your being. Inhale it back up to the body surface, then exhale it out to the universe.

8. Conclude with an Anchoring Affirmation
The affirmation is, "I am committed to...." Reconfirm your personal goal. "I am committed to having the most wonderful relationship possible." Then go out and enjoy the day.

Dr. Burke's 18 Principles - A Learning Life

1. I don't know how to do that yet, but I will learn.

2. I know my goals.

3. I can already see that this is going to be one of the best days of my life so far.

4. I am aware of my experience, of where I am right now.

5. I regularly ask myself if there is a better way.

6. I know that learning requires efficient acquisition, persistent integration, and quality display.

7. I practice intelligently in order to remember, understand, and grow.

8. I select the best strategy. I am committed to mastery.

9. Before acting I consider what the most important thing is for me to do next.

10. I maintain balance. If there is a problem I work diligently to manage it and resolve it.

11. I recognize thoughts and feelings. I am not my thoughts and feelings.

12. I have a choice. I make informed decisions and I act on them accordingly.

13. Every day I make progress on my most important life goals.

14. I feel awesome!

15. I respect myself. I treat others with respect.

16. I bring quality to the work that I do. I embrace my life.

17. I wisely acquire, manage, use, and preserve life's resources.

18. I appreciate the interdependence of all things. I give my gift to the world today.

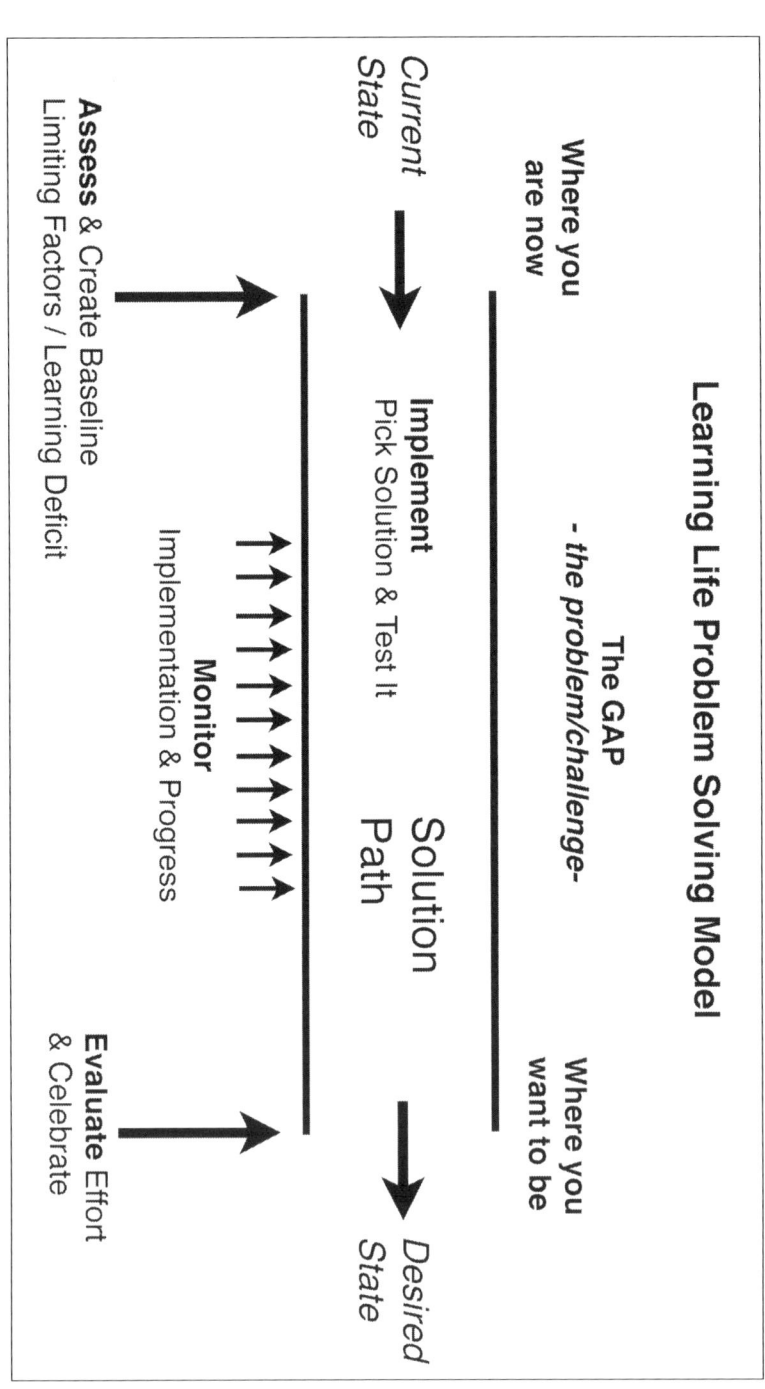

Dr. Burke's 8 Metawareness Questions

Before a Learning Task

1. Task Clarity

What is the task at hand? What exactly am I supposed to do? What is the expected outcome or product (including how much, by when, and with what quality)? If there are options in terms of what you can work on then pick the most important item. Ask yourself, "What is the most important thing for me to do right now?"

2. Motivation

Why am I doing this, what is the purpose/value/goal (external/for others and internal/for me)? How does this activity fit with my personal and academic goals?

3. Strategy

What is my strategy? How am I supposed to do this? What is the best way to do this (including tools)? Where is the best place to do it? If this is a multi-party task, who else is responsible, and for which aspects?

During a Learning Task

4. Task Focus

How am I doing? Am I on task? Am I actually doing it? Really? Am I staying on task and on target (efficient, effective, most skillful)? How can I get more intense with it, really into it?

5. Task Reorientation

If I am not on task, or drifting, what one simple step can I take <u>right now</u> to change that? Consider the Wheel, use Metawareness, what can I change in person, behavior, or environment that will help me stay on task? (See Chapter 13 for ideas.)

After a Learning Task

6. Effect/Effectiveness

How did it work out? What was the grade, response, my sense of accomplishment? How was the quality? How could I improve and do even better next time?

7. Efficiency

How long did it take? How much did I get done? Is there a better way to do this? Could I have done anything differently, what should I repeat in the future, and what should I change in the future?

8. Holistic Reflection

What else? Consider the Wheel, is there something at the level of person, behavior, or environment that could be modified to improve the process? Sit down, close eyes, pause for a few minutes and ask "What else?" Sit in silence, reflect, and allow insights to come.

Checklist for Research Paper

❑ Schedule project (work backwards – start with deadline and schedule from there)
    ❑ Format check
    ❑ Final review
    ❑ Writing / editing
    ❑ Detailed outline
    ❑ Simple outline
    ❑ Brainstorming & topic selection
    ❑ Read assignment and understand goal

❑ Read assignment and understand the goal (metawareness practice)

❑ Preliminary research – exploration of topic(s)
    ❑ Library databases
    ❑ Google Scholar / Google
    ❑ Books, news, magazines
    ❑ Other sources

❑ Topic selection

❑ Working title

❑ Elaboration – research, read, cut-paste/print materials, write

❑ Simple outline (like a book table of contents)

❑ Elaboration – research, read, cut-paste/print materials, write

❑ Detailed outline

❑ Elaboration – research, read, cut-paste/print materials, write

❑ Prepare final copy
    ❑ Read out loud
    ❑ Have another person read / Take to Learning Assistance Center
    ❑ Edit

❑ References – pick style (e.g. APA or MLA), check text and reference list format

❑ Format check
    ❑ Your name, course/date, title, page numbers, headings, binding, print

❑ Turn it in – on time (get an A)

Study Group Contract

Course: _____

Date: _____

Commitments

Before each study group session determine the goal of the meeting, the desired state.
Attend class regularly.
Do not copy homework (i.e. do not skip class and expect the group to cover for you).
    The group can be a resource when you do need to miss class.
    Number of class sessions that can be missed to remain in group _____
Attend group study sessions, on time.
Participate actively in study sessions, cell phones off.
Complete individual assigned tasks before group meetings.
Turn in all group assignments on time.
For group problems everyone shares their answers and their solution process.
Assist other group members with course material as needed.
Seek assistance from other group members for material not understood.
Apply critical thinking and do not assume group answers are always correct.
Apply effective communication skills, listen, do not criticize, encourage each other.
Communicate honestly about group concerns and listen to group concerns
Apply effective team skills, work collaboratively on group assignments.
Distribute work equitably.
Maintain the confidence of the group (not to discuss group events outside the group).
Assign roles, take turns serving as session coordinator/leader.
Accept termination from group if participation is below group requirements.
Evaluate group outcomes and consider process improvements.

Group Members

Name	Signature	Email	Cell Phone

PLANNING – Schedule for Week of _____

	MON	TUE	WED	THU	FRI	SAT	SUN
5							
6							
7							
8							
9							
10							
11							
12							
1							
2							
3							
4							
5							
6							
7							
8							
9							
10							
11-12							
	MON	TUE	WED	THU	FRI	SAT	SUN

PLANNING – Schedule for Month of _____

SUN	MON	TUE	WED	THU	FRI	SAT

PLANNING - Graduation Schedule

	Fall	Winter	Spring	Summer
Year 1				
Year 2				
Year 3				
Year 4				

Healthy Recipes

Adamanand's Famous Kitchari Recipe

This is a recipe based on the ancient principles of traditional Indian medicine (Ayurveda). It builds strength, is easy to digest, and provides a complete protein. Kitchari can be the foundation of a simple, healthy, organic, and inexpensive dinner. If we had a billboard we could easily say – "Over 1 billion served!" This recipe serves 4.

Ingredients (all organic is the best)
- Organic basmatic rice – 1cup (wash well)
- Organic lentils – 1 cup (wash well)
- You can use any kind of lentil. Several that are quite nice in this dish are black beluga lentils, or French green lentils, or masoor dal pink lentils, or yellow mung beans.
- 1/2 onion - chopped
- Several cloves of garlic – sliced thin or chopped
- 1 carrot – chopped in ¼ inch pieces
- 2 potatoes – peeled and cubed
- Other vegetable (some chopped greens is a nice addition) 1 cup
- Spices
- 1 tbsp coriander
- 1 tsp cumin
- ½ tsp tumeric
- ¼ tsp peper
- ½ tsp salt (or to taste +/-) or 1 tbsp of soy sauce

Warm oil in a large pan over medium heat. Add onion and garlic and fry at medium heat until onion starts to become somewhat transluscent. Add salt and spices and mix ingredients over low-medium heat for a minute or two (be careful not to burn, turn down heat, or throw in water if too hot and move to next step). Add 8 cups of water. Add beans and bring to a boil, lower to medium heat and cook for 15 minutes. Add carrots, potatoes, and rice and cook for another 20 minutes low-medium heat (simmer) with lid on. Depending on the type of greens add those toward the end (so not overdone). Add more water as desired during cooking for a more soupy consistency. Serve and garnish with chopped cilantro, some olive oil or ghee, tamari, balsamic vinegar, or tabasco/chipotle/habanero sauce (personal choice, all optional).

Housemade Granola

This recipe makes 4-6 servings.
- 3½ cups organic rolled oats
- ½ cup california almonds
- ½ cup cashews
- ½ cup coconut
- 2 tbsp canola oil
- ½ cup honey
- ¼ cup maple syrup
- 2 tsp vanilla extract
- 2 tsp ground cinnamon
- Pinch of salt

Blend dry ingredients, then toss with wet ingredients. Spread mixture into a large baking sheet. Put into preheated over at 325°F. Bake for about 60 minutes, turning the mixture about every 10 minutes to avoid burning (watch the heat). Remove from oven.

How to Boil an Egg

No kidding. Like many things, having the right strategy can help you get the results you want. Same goes for boiled eggs.

Ingredients: A few eggs and cold water.

Place the eggs in a pot and cover with cold water, about and inch above the eggs. Turn heat to high and bring to a full boil. Once boiling turn off the heat and cover the pot. For softer yolks wait 6 minutes, for firm not hard 10 minutes, for hard boiled eggs 12 minutes. Once the time is up take the eggs out, crack them a bit, and place in cold water for about a minute. This helps to stop the cooking and improves shell removal. If you are not going to eat the eggs immediately then do not crack them and just stick them in the refrigerator in a container. They will last about 5 days, easy protein on the run, great for salads.

Stovetop Quesadilla

Ingredients: Tortilla (large flour tortillas best), cheese, other ingredients as desired

Place about 1/2 teaspoon of olive oil or butter in frying pan, warm. Place tortilla into oiled pan. Warm the tortilla on both sides. Add grated cheese to one half of the tortilla, and other items to the other half. Those items could be crumbled tofu, tomatoes, onions, beans, rice (you may want to pre-warm these items). Do not overfill. Let the tortilla with ingredients heat on a low-medium flame, watching to not burn the bottom. When the cheese is soft enough fold the tortilla in half with a spatula. If you like, you can also add salsa, lettuce, avocado or other favorites before folding it up. Cut into quarters and enjoy.

Lifestyle / Current State Assessment

Date_____

You can use this chart or create your own. Keep information on any of the items included here that are useful for your own insight and understanding. The main objective is to begin to gather information on your CURRENT STATE, related to the behavior/thought/body state you are planning on modifying, such as quitting smoking. Use the chart to help put that issue into perspective. How does it appear in relation to the rest of your life. Record quantity, quality, and other insights for two weeks. Write a summary of insights into the patterns you have noticed (such as when, where, why you smoke cigarettes). BE SPECIFIC AND DETAILED, be aware, learn about your self.

Date	Sleep	Meditation	Priming	School/Work	Study	Exercise	Food	Energy	Mood	

SUBJECT INDEX

A
Abundance, 324, 327, 342
Action Plan, 166, 252
AIR, 67
Alameda study 271
Appraisal, 186, 206, 214, 297
Aptitudes, 310
Attribution, 11

B
Baseline, 35, 89
Budgeting, 334

C
Cannon, Walter, 184
Carbohydrates/sugar, 275
Calendars, 166
Career path, 308
Cause and effect diagram, 93
Change management, 164
Checklist, 94, 124, 360
College major, 319
Continual improvement, 8, 75, 93
Cooking, 285
Compassion, 349
Conditioned mind and body, 9
Coping, 189

D
Decision-making, 225
Dopamine reward circuits, 9
Drugs and alcohol, 287

E
Emotional literacy, person, 207, 221
Emotions–neuroanatomy, 205
Emotions–dysregulation, 207
Employment, 322
Equanimity, 199
Evaluation, 35, 91, 261
Exercise, 286
Expectancy, 10

F
Fats, 278
Fiber, 281
Fight-or-flight, 184
Financial literacy, 328
Food, 285
Friendship, 297
Fun, 135, 215
Funding education, 329

G
General Adaptation Syndrome, 185
Generosity, 346, 351
Goals, 17, 247
Grants, 332
Gratitude, 214

H
Habit modification, 247
Healthy aging, 272
Healthy lifestyle, 275-276
High fructose corn sweetener, 277
Holland Hexagon, 315
Homeostasis, 184

I
Interests, 311
Isolation, 299

J
Journaling, 220

K
KAGI, 149, 178
Kaizen, 8, 75
Kobasa, Susan, 19

L
Lazarus, Richard, 187
Learned helplessness, 9, 39
Learning, 6
Learning strategies, 103
Learning strategies–acquisition, 99
Learning strategies–integration, 119
Learning strategies–display, 139
Loans, 330

M

Managing debt, 333
Mason, John, 187
MBTI, 314
Memory strategies 127-136
Meditation, 202
Mental imagery–Priming, 7, 37, 216
Metawareness, 101, 358
Metacognition, 100
Micronutrients, 281
Mindful awareness, 7, 67, 70
Mindful learning, 55
Mindfulness–historical perspective, 56
Mindfulness–philosophical foundations, 57
Mindfulness meditation, 58
Mindfulness of breath, 62
Mind Maps, 133
Monitor, 35, 89, 122
Motivation, 141, 176, 179

O

Observational learning, 115
Note taking 104
Open inquiry, 116
Optimism, 214

P

Performance oriented display, 147
Personality 313
Prefrontal cortex, 19, 205, 233, 246
Priming, 42
Pro-inflammatory diets 282
Problem focused coping, 190
Problem-solving model 7, 32, 80
Process flowchart, 94
Procrastination, 178
Professionalism, 141
Protein, 280

Q

Quality, 77

R

Reading strategies, 111
Resources, 11
Resourcefulness, 11
Reviewing, 127

Role models, 256
Root cause, 77

S

Saving and investing, 337
Scheduling, 121, 128, 166, 175, 252
Scholarships, 331
Self-acceptance, 11
Self-efficacy, 10, 119
Self-talk, 11, 218
Selye, Hans, 185
Sex, 288
Senescence, 272
Skills, 312
Sleep hygiene, 288
Social justice, 348
Social support, 255, 296
Stages change, 264
State focused coping, 190
Streaming, 351
Stress–disease, 189
Stress response, 9
Stress, theories, 184
Student loans, 330, 333
Study groups, 125
Study skills, 119
Study time, 120-125
Supplements, 281, 283
Sustainability 348

T

Test taking, 142
Task, 32, 120, 122, 175
Time management, 164
To Do list, 124, 167
Triggers, 191, 253

V

Vicarious learning, 41
Volunteering, 347

W

Water, 282
Wheel model, 8
Wisdom, 349
Writing papers, 146

"Everything that has a beginning has an end."
--The Oracle, *The Matrix Revolutions*

"No matter what is going on. Never give up."
--The 14th Dalai Lama, *Never Give Up*

"...With us move millions of others, our companions in awakening from fear.
At the bottom we discover water, the healing water of compassion.
Right down there in the thick of things, we discover the love that will not die."
--Pema Chodron, *When Things Fall Apart: Heart Advice for Difficult Times*

Thank you for participating in this journey with others on the path of a learning life. I sincerely hope that some of the ideas in this book have been of benefit to you and that your life continues to be enriched. Best of wishes on your adventure. May you find the success that brings you happiness and the happiness that brings you success. And never forget – never give up.

--AB

Made in the USA
San Bernardino, CA
24 January 2015